PERSONALITY
IN THE
SOCIAL PROCESS

PERSONALITY IN THE SOCIAL PROCESS

Joel Aronoff
Michigan State University

John P. Wilson
Cleveland State University

LEA LAWRENCE ERLBAUM ASSOCIATES, PUBLISHERS
1985   Hillsdale, New Jersey   London

Lawrence Erlbaum Associates, Inc., Publishers
365 Broadway
Hillsdale, New Jersey 07642

Library of Congress Cataloging in Publication Data

Aronoff, Joel.
   Personality in the social process.

   Bibliography: p.
   Includes indexes.
   1. Personality and situation.   2. Social interaction.
3. Small groups.   I. Wilson, John Preston.   II. Title.
BF698.9S55A76   1985   302.3   84-24680
ISBN 0-89859-526-6

Printed in the United States of America
10 9 8 7 6 5 4 3 2 1

For

Gideon　　　　*Matthew*

Eve　　　　*Michael*

and in memory of Alex

Contents

Preface   **xi**

**PART I   A THEORETICAL APPROACH TO PERSONALITY
          IN THE SOCIAL PROCESS**

Chapter 1   Personality in the Social Process   3
              A Potential Framework   6
              The Relationship Between Primary Needs
                and Acquired Motives and Traits   11

**Chapter 2   The Personological Bases of Social
              Responsiveness**   18
              Maslow   19
              Freud   23
              Fromm   24
              Murray   26
              Jung   28
              Erikson   32
              Conclusion   37

Chapter 3   Dimensions of the Person   38
              Peripheral Motives Derived From
                the Need for Safety   39
              The Need for Love and
                Belongingness   43
              Peripheral Motives Derived From
                the Need For Esteem   46
              Peripheral Traits Developed From Primary
                Needs   48
              Conceptions of Psychosocial Maturity   55
              Personological Elements for a
                Theory of Interactions   62

Chapter 4   **Dimensions of the Situation**   65
Situational Variables   66
Task Variables   68
Group Structure   72
A Model of the Mechanisms Underlying Social
    Psychological Events   74
Group Process, Structure, and Outcome   79

Chapter 5   **Interactional Patterns: A Model of the**
             Person in the Situation   89
The Interaction of Personality
    and Situational Variables   90
The Interaction of Personality
    and Task Variables   92
The Interaction of Personality
    and Stages of Task Demands   94
The Nature of Group Process Activated by
    Personality Variables   99
The Nature of Group Structure Activated by
    Personality Variables   111
The Outcome of Social Activity   123

PART II   THE INITIAL SOCIAL RESPONSE

Chapter 6   **Social Perception**   127
Approaches to Person Perception   130
The Construction of the Social Image   132
The Empirical Study of Person Perception   134
Interactional Studies of Person Perception   142

Chapter 7   **Information Processing**   150
Stage I: The Acquisition of Information   154
The Empirical Studies   157
Stage II: The Processing of Information   163
The Empirical Studies   165
Stage III: Goal Setting   172
The Empirical Studies   174

Chapter 8   **Interpersonal Attraction**   178
Stages of Interpersonal Attraction   182
Personality Moderators of Attraction   187
The Empirical Studies   190

PART III   COMPLEX FORMS OF SOCIAL INTERACTION

Chapter 9   **The Initiation-Concurrence Dimension of Group Process**   209
Initiation: The Attempt at Social Influence   210
Concurrence: The Response to Social Influence   223
Summary   241

Chapter 10   **The Affiliative-Disaffiliative Dimension of Group Process**   243
The Pattern of Interaction   245
The Empirical Studies   248
Motivational Determinants of Affiliative-Disaffiliative Behavior   258
Interactional Studies of Prosocial Behavior   263

Chapter 11   **Negotiation Processes**   269
Four Modes of Interpersonal Negotiation   274

Chapter 12   **Group Structure**   293
Role Differentiation   294
The Bases of Rank   300
Power and Reward   302

PART IV   THE OUTCOME OF GROUP PROCESS: TESTING THE MODEL OF THE PERSON IN THE SITUATION

Chapter 13   **The Performance of Individuals in Groups**   307
The Principle of Congruence   307
The Situation   313
The Task   317
Group Structure   327
Summary   337

Chapter 14   **Epilogue**   338

References   343

Author Index   377

Subject Index   389

Preface

This book presents a new way to ask an old question. Many fields have considered the nature of the influence that members of a group exert on the course of social events. Social science provides another way to examine this issue. Moreover, social science has a particular strength: It helps us to phrase questions more precisely than before, it encourages us to follow a line of reasoning systematically, and it requires us to evaluate our ideas in light of a particular kind of evidence. We want to use these strengths to explore systematically the ways that factors in the person and in the environment together may shape the emergence of social behavior.

When we began to outline this type of model, we did not envision how complex, demanding, or rewarding the project was to be. One of our pleasant surprises was to learn that, despite the use of widely varying ways to conceptualize personality processes, a massive body of empirical evidence is available which, when considered collectively, provides strong support for a core set of hypotheses about the ways that personality variables become part of the process of social interaction. It was even more exciting to discern a clear pattern in the types of social events that result from the influence of personality processes across widely varying situations.

At present, this kind of discussion is usually stated in the form of interactional theories, which attempt to specify how personality and environmental variables jointly determine adaptive behavior. We want to use the available empirical work to generate a model that is more systematic and specific than has been attempted to now. We also want to outline a set of deductions from a fairly well-shared set of initial premises about the elements of personality and social psychology that, at least, have the merit of being clear. If the reasoning used is faulty or the predictions inaccurate, then it should be easy to determine the ways in which this model is wrong. In each of the major areas that we address, we propose a set of hypotheses that can be evaluated in terms of the existing fund of empirical information.

The theory presented in this book builds upon the major theoretical perspectives in personality and social psychology. Stated simply, it is an initial effort to construct a systematic analysis of the interaction of personality variables with the major features of the social world. This approach begins with an attempt to determine the set of dispositional variables that seem involved in most of the broad features of adaptive social behavior. If we can identify the central elements of such an inclusive set of variables, despite the different labels attached to them by different researchers, then it will be much easier to follow the effects of personality across the many different types of adaptive social behavior.

This approach leads us to use a different form of organization than is usually found in books on personality and social behavior. We follow our effort to determine the common core of dispositional elements with a series of chapters that tracks their effects through the course of social behavior. We look first at the initial steps through which the individual perceives and encodes the information that constitutes the stimulus field. We follow the consequences of social cognition into the more complex forms of interaction that comprise group process and result in the different levels of productivity reached by individuals working within groups. This organizational strategy also represents what we believe to be a desirable form for the next stage of research in personality and social behavior. Rather than continue to expand the correlational network associated with single personality variables, we need to investigate how our personological resources can help to explain those features of human activity that constitute the primary units of social psychology.

We want to express our appreciation for the strong support we received from the Department of Psychology at Michigan State University, now chaired by Gordon Wood. It has offered the most hospitable environment possible in which to work over the years. We want to thank our colleagues Marilyn Aronoff, Avi Assor, Victor Battistich, William Crano, Lester Hyman, Linda Jackson, Norbert Kerr, Richard Petruska, Albert Rabin, Tish Ward, Laura Wilson, Glenn Wright, and Robert Zucker for the continuing stimulation and assistance that they provide. We want to express our special sense of gratitude to Lawrence Messé, our partner in most of this research. His generosity and skill have enriched all our work. Much of the stimulation and guidance for this work came from Abraham Maslow, David McClelland, and Dick Neisser. Their advice and criticism have been deeply appreciated.

Joel Aronoff
John P. Wilson

A THEORETICAL APPROACH TO PERSONALITY IN THE SOCIAL PROCESS

1 Personality in the Social Process

The history of personality and social psychology describes an increasing process of discovery. As social scientists explored the social world, phenomena that once appeared to be the product of a few variables were understood, instead, to result from the action of many. Faced with a much more complex work agenda, specialized research programs emerged to examine the many factors that seemed to compose a social event. Nearly a century of work on personality and social psychology has clarified major portions of the social process, providing us with the series of social processes that we understand quite well. However, as our theories developed out of the study of these apparently separate phenomena, it has been difficult to bring them together into a broader statement that might be applied more generally. With a substantial empirical foundation now in hand, the time seems right to take the generalist's point of view and use this information to develop a more comprehensive approach to the study of people in social situations.

These aspirations are not new. There have been highly influential formulations suggesting that social behavior is the result of the interaction of variables in the person and in the environment. This "interactionist perspective," as phrased dramatically in Lewin's equation, $B = f(P,E)$, is a widely accepted framework within which to cast research and interpret results. However, as Endler (1981) points out, the interactionist approaches have not yet become a theory because they have not yet specified the elements involved or the mechanisms through which the interaction occurs.

Part of the problem may lie in the fatal word "and." Social scientists typically discuss personality with phrases such as "personality and culture," "personality and social psychology," or "personality and the situation." These phrases make it appear that two entirely different classes of variables are brought together for the purposes of an unusual study. A simpler assumption is possible. We can assume that a social event occurs when a person responds to the features of an environment with a set of behaviors designed to accomplish some goal. This assumption allows us to develop a parsimonious approach in which we can identify the ways in which features of the environment influence the ways in which personal goals are sought. This simple proposal focuses on the fact that all social activity is addressed to some goal. More important, this proposal permits us to ask additional simple questions: What are the goals that people seek? What are the characteristics of the person that make the environment such a powerful source of determinants of human behavior?

These questions direct us to a highly controversial principle that can help us advance toward a compact theory of social processes. Clearly, the situational, task, and group variables are involved in the social process through the impact they have on the human beings who perform that social event. We suggest that in order to understand the effects that these environmental variables have on social interaction, we need to consider the nature of the people involved as the mediator of those effects. This principle proposes that an identification of the characteristics of the people involved in an activity can improve our ability to predict, and to understand, their selection, processing, evaluation, and response to the powerful set of features that constitutes the social world.

This principle places a great deal of responsibility on an area of psychology not noted for its ability to reach a dispassionate consensus. However, major developments since World War II may allow us now to move ahead as rapidly as other areas of psychology. As Hogan (1982) has pointed out, in the past our most important theories of personality have come from work in psychiatry and clinical psychology. As such, our systematic ideas emerged from the narrow world of psychopathology; our concepts have been shaped to handle the diagnosis and treatment of symptoms. For the most part, our concepts have not been designed to explore the full range of complex social behavior that is the subject matter of social psychology. Even more important, the clinician had to treat human beings in great pain. This pressure upon clinicians to respond to their patients authoritatively made it difficult for them to tolerate uncertainty about the accuracy of their ideas. With so much at stake, it is not surprising that clinically based ideas fostered the highest forms of intellectual partisanship.

Our present situation has changed dramatically. The ideological choices that were so important in the past, with very few exceptions, no longer burden progress in the field. We have many new ideas derived from the study of a wide range of human activity, we enjoy work on many topics that were formerly taboo, and most investigators feel quite comfortable crossing theoretical frameworks in the course of their work. At this point, we are also able to take advantage of the significant progress that has been made in more than 3 decades of empirical work. Active research programs studying the social consequences of significant personality variables have taught us a great deal about the ways in which these variables influence human behavior. Similarly, there have been significant methodological advances in operationalizing variables, designing experiments, and analyzing data. This is an exciting period in which to study personality. With these advances in hand, this seems to be the appropriate moment to develop a more unified approach to the study of the person in the social situation.

We assume that these efforts will prove as useful to traditional work in social psychology. Just as broadening the scope of the human activity that must be considered by researchers has greatly stimulated the development of basic concepts in the field of personality, so too should a more inclusive point of view improve the ability of social psychologists to explain the nature of some of their most important results. Virtually all purely "social" explanations include significant implicit assumptions about the properties of the social actors. We expect that more serious attention to the characteristics of the people engaged in social activity will greatly improve the power of social psychologists to explain the effects of social experience.

For these reasons, it is likely that a theory of social behavior that can bring to Lewin's generalization the degree of detail necessary to make specific predictions rests in part upon a view of social experience that includes factors within the individual. Thus, if we assume that social variables produce their behavioral consequences through the impact they make on the person, then it is important for social psychology to identify the variables within the person that allow the social variables to make such an impact. Therefore, the purpose of this book is to identify which personality variables are most significant for the social process and to explore how they contribute to the shaping of human social behavior. We attempt to develop, and substantiate as much as the existing literature permits, an approach to the study of the interaction of personality and social variables that will meet these goals.

The literature on personality structure is vast, raising the danger that a systematic review of important work might consume an entire book before our task even began. Fortunately, we can find our most important line of reasoning in a key proposition shared by many of the extensive treatments of personality. Most systematic proposals in personality and social psychology assume that key aspects of the environment are pleasant or painful, rewarding or punishing, reinforcing or aversive. Because most of what we know about personality comes from an examination of the characteristics of the social environment that maintain goal-seeking behavior, a major part of our solution is provided by the answer to a simple question that originates in both the fields of personality and social psychology. Our attempt to identify the goals that are sought by the individual, as well as our effort to understand the nature of the experience provided by a social event, together hinge upon a common question: What are the reinforcers provided by the social experience? In this and the following two chapters, we attempt to demonstrate the agreement that exists for a set of propositions about the nature of reinforcement.

A POTENTIAL FRAMEWORK

Let us first consider how the major classes of variables might be related. We can then consider which approach to personality will be most useful for the broad analysis of the social process. As we work toward a more unified framework, we must accept the likelihood that the resulting model will be complex. Given the quality of work that has been done in social psychology, it is likely that the variables have been identified correctly and that few can be reduced to another. Indeed, it is possible that a more comprehensive orientation will uncover additional variables. Our approach in taking the generalist's point of view is to assume that all the major variables need to be included, that these variables are linked in some way, and that our task is to discover the likely pattern of their relationship and a terminology that will help us to move comfortably from a discussion of one variable to another.

Table 1.1 presents an outline of the major types of variables that we believe form the social process. This table also indicates the nature of the linkage that we believe to exist among these classes of variables. Because even a simple social event is too complex to represent accurately on a single page, Table 1.1 simply outlines a point of view for us to explore more specifically in the body of this book. Our strategy is to follow this outline in later chapters with a series of more detailed proposals that deal with individual parts of this larger model. Through such a "levels of magnification" approach, we hope to reach the level of specificity that is needed to provide a testable theory of social psychology.

Table 1.1 follows many other approaches to interactionist theory (e.g., Carter, 1951; Cartwright & Zander, 1968; Endler & Magnusson, 1976; Hackman & Morris, 1975; McGrath, 1964) by attempting to isolate the major classes of variables that constitute the person and the environment. In developing an interactionist theory, our concern in the analysis of the person is with the motives, traits, cognitive structures, beliefs, values, and emotional states that influence the person's response to the social world. In the analysis of the environment, we are concerned with the three major features of the social world within which individual behavior occurs: (a) situational variables, such as the physical and the human characteristics of the setting; (b) task variables, such as the difficulty, complexity, ambiguity, and importance of the activity, as well as the different types of information-processing operations inherent in any task; and (c) group structural variables, such as the nature of the status, role, power, and reward systems.

Beyond simply listing significant variables, Table 1.1 presents our suggestion that social behavior emerges through the following process: (a) The individual, concerned with obtaining certain goals, and functioning within a specific range of intellectual and emotional skills, engages in behavior that (b) takes place within an environment that has a specific situational, task, and group structural nature. (c) These environmental features interact with the properties of the person to evoke a subjective emotional, cognitive, and motivational response in the person that (d) leads the person to produce specific behavioral acts that fall along the coordinates of a two-dimensional interpersonal space (the performance styles). As each of the members of an interaction is engaged in the common task within that environmental setting, (e) their joint behavior produces those characteristics of group process, group structure, and group outcome that are of interest to social psychology.

However, there is a serious problem in the use of such models. As Bem (1972) and Mischel (1973) have argued, if we need to specify a long list of personal and situational variables to account for the appearance of a single instance of social behavior, then we do not have a theory of interactions. Instead, such a list would be simply a notational device without either predictive or explanatory power. In fact, as Bem and Mischel maintain, if we need to know as much about a social act in order to predict it as we will learn after we measure it, we have a tautological rather than an interactionist theory. The requirements of an interactionist theory are the same as those that are expected from any other: We need a relatively compact set of theoretical propositions from which we can generate a wide range of social phenomena.

We have already outlined a possible direction that might help us solve some of these challenges to a theory of interactions. We have suggested that social variables obtain much of their power to influence social behavior through the impact they have on the person involved in that activity. If this assertion is correct, then closer attention to the systematic properties of the person may yield a significant gain. If we can clarify some of the apparent confusions concerning human goals and establish some principle for reducing the vast number of personal characteristics, then it may be possible to explain which environmental variables have a significant impact on the person and how they, together, are able to affect social behavior.

Therefore, the major task of this chapter is to indicate a way of thinking about personality structure that will advance research on social behavior. We need to develop a working model of human functioning that is comprehensive enough to fit the complexities of most aspects of social life and, yet, is not so detailed that it interferes with productive experimental work. Is there a comprehensive way of thinking about personality so that a relatively limited

TABLE 1.1
Elements of the Social Process

Inputs to the Social Process — The Person	The Environment	Individual Subjective Response	Complex Social Processes
Personality Variables	*Situational Variables*	*Types of Subjective Response*	*Group Processes*

1. Motives
2. Traits
3. Beliefs
4. Values
5. Abilities
6. Cognitive structure
7. Moods
	1. Physical
	2. Personal
	
	Task Variables
	1. Task characteristics
	  a. Difficulty
	  b. Complexity
	  c. Ambiguity
	  d. Importance
	2. Sequential information processing requirements
	  a. Orientation
	  b. Selective attention
	  c. Aspiration level
		1. Emotional
		  a. Mood
		  b. Attraction
		2. Cognitive, perceptual, and attributional
		  a. Distortion
		  b. Denial
		  c. Accuracy
		3. Motivational
		  a. Aroused
		  b. Nonaroused
			1. Performance styles
			  a. Initiation–concurrence
			  b. Affiliation–disaffiliation
			2. Negotiation processes
			  a. Bargaining stance: firm–yielding
			  b. Problem-solving technique: flexible–rigid
			  c. Modes of interdependence
			    Adversarial
			    Exploitative
			    Ingratiating
			    Integrative

d. Search persistence
e. Organization of work
f. Generation of solutions
g. Evaluation of solutions
h. Implementation

Group Structure

1. Absent
2. Present
   a. member congruent
   b. member incongruent

Group Structure

1. Differentiation
2. Rank
3. Power
4. Reward

Outcome

1. Individual: satisfaction
2. Group: cohesion
3. Task: performance

number of variables can be identified and studied across the spectrum of situations that are the province of social psychology?

This sounds like a simple task, for after nearly a century of research, at least the outlines of a comprehensive model of personality should be clear. Unfortunately, a consensus does not exist because the disputes between schools of personality did not resolve their differences. Similarly, experimental personality psychologists did not agree on a common set of variables on which to work. For this reason, our first task is to see how far we can close the distance between the very many valuable ideas that seem quite different from each other. We believe that there is a strong convergence among many of the most important ideas and an impressive array of research findings to support these theoretical convergences. In this and the next two chapters, we attempt to demonstrate that our existing theories can lead to a compact model of personality that will greatly help to understand the role of the individual in the larger social process.

In an unusually thoughtful comparative analysis, Maddi (1976) noted that every theory offers proposals about the genetic "core" characteristics of the person as well as sets of acquired "peripheral" characteristics that result from the course of experience. Maddi's distinction between core and periphery of personality helps us to identify and compare those sets of variables that have parallel status in each theory. This distinction greatly facilitates our search for convergences among the theories, and it helps to introduce our general approach to personality.

In the next two chapters, we attempt to demonstrate that personality structure can be understood best as deriving from sets of "primary" needs (the core tendencies) around which "acquired" motivational, cognitive, affective, and behavioral structures develop that enable the person to satisfy the requirements of a primary need. Because we base our approach to social behavior on a detailed proposal about the relationships between specific core and peripheral variables, we need to discuss briefly the nature of these variables and the types of links that may exist among them. We follow this brief overview of our approach in this chapter with a more substantial review in chapter 2 of the core motivational constructs of several of the most influential personality theories. In chapter 2, we hope to show the great similarity in the way that human goals are viewed by apparently highly dissimilar theorists. We then present in chapter 3 a discussion of selected peripheral variables in order to explain their possible relationship to the small set of primary needs. We hope that this discussion of an illustrative set of motives and traits provides a principle to reduce what appear to be hundreds of discrete peripheral variables into a much smaller set. In addition, we hope that this discussion provides the compact theory of personality moderators that Bem and Mischel argue is needed to create a meaningful theory of person-by-situation interactions. A final discussion attempts to show how the many descriptions of psychological health follow from, and can be incorporated into, this point of view and can help us to understand some important results in the experimental social psychology literature (e.g., McGuire, 1968; Staub, 1978).

THE RELATIONSHIP BETWEEN PRIMARY NEEDS AND ACQUIRED MOTIVES AND TRAITS

Primary Needs

There is great disagreement about the content of the human core. Existing proposals (see Maddi, 1976) range from that of force that must be discharged (energy), to the organism's requirement for certain types of reinforcement from interpersonal events (needs), to tendencies to maintain a state of equilibrium among cognitive contents (cognitive consistency). Although this list only begins to present the available alternatives, the definition that is selected strongly influences the kind of predictions that can be made about the effect of personality on social behavior. Because each position is plausible, especially for limited sets of social phenomena, we suspect that it is premature at this point to settle on a comprehensive theory. In the absence of a general theory, it seems most useful to take a middle-level position that incorporates many of the strengths of most theories, yet is able to tolerate their contradictions.

The most satisfying position that we can presently formulate recognizes that social behavior seems designed to attain specific classes of reinforcement from social experience. Although psychologists vary in the way they phrase this observation, the underlying idea has always seemed a necessary starting point when defining motivational constructs. In general, terms such as "primary needs" are used when it is not possible to reduce a class of environmental reinforcers to what would appear to be a more basic set. Therefore, although it may be premature to speculate about other attributes of this construct, it is possible to discover a limited set of reinforcers in the empirical and theoretical literature. From these descriptions, we can posit several sets of primary needs that activate the individual to seek certain types of responses from the environment. All other questions, such as physiological location, periodicity, and tension increase or reduction, are less important than the recognition that some internal source leads the organism to seek highly specific sets of events from the environment. We attempt to show that it is possible to identify sets of primary needs, around which peripheral characteristics develop, and that such constructs contain significant power to explain social behavior.

Acquired Motives

A variety of research programs have identified a large number of important human characteristics that develop in the course of the individual's life. Some of these programs grew out of the clinical tradition and were concerned with broad clinical variables such as anxiety, the oral personality, or self-esteem. Other approaches were more experimentally oriented, like Murray's (1938) brilliant taxonomic work that isolated personality factors such as the needs for achievement, affiliation, or approval. Still other approaches came out of the political psychology tradition and were concerned with factors such as the authoritarian or Machiavellian personality, which seemed necessary to explain important political events. At this time in social psychology, we feel comfortable describing people as being more or less anxious, sociable, mistrustful, or cognitively complex or as more or less concerned with the needs for dependency, dominance, order, or self-abasement. These terms are only a few examples of the many different ways that seem necessary to characterize the people who create those parts of the social process with which social psychology is concerned. Not only do these terms seem to be a useful way to speak about human beings, but substantial bodies of research have shown the importance of these variables for all sorts of social events.

The theory of personality that we bring to social psychology must recognize the many ways that people differ from one another. It must also be able to account for the ways in which these characteristics emerge from the course of experience. Finally, its explanatory power will be greatly increased if a way can be found to relate these acquired characteristics to one another. We believe that there are several important characteristics of the primary needs (as suggested by many personality theories) that permit us to relate many of the acquired characteristics to the primary needs, as well as to explain the pattern of interrelationship among many of the acquired variables.

In this chapter, we suggest a way to think about the socialization experience that seems helpful in relating the acquired peripheral characteristics to the primary needs. From our vantage point in social psychology, rather than developmental psychology, a fact that has struck us as being extremely important in devising a model of the socialization experience is that a pattern of clusters of these peripheral variables has emerged from studies on normal adult populations (see Wilson & Aronoff, 1984, for a review of this evidence). We can illustrate this pattern by giving a few examples from what seem to be the two main clusters. For example, anxiety, dependency, mistrust, and authoritarianism usually are all positively correlated with each other. Similarly, self-esteem, dominance, the need for achievement, and Machiavellianism usually are also positively correlated with each other. Even more interesting, the variables within a cluster generally are negatively correlated with the variables in the other cluster. In chapter 4, we list the variables that seem to be empirically (as well as conceptually) related to each other. At this point, we wish to use this fact to generate a set of hypotheses about the nature of acquired motives. We then expand this discussion by considering what we learn from the analysis of acquired traits.

Clearly, the variables that are called acquired motives result from the course of experience. Yet, we need to ask what there is about experience that should so regularly yield a specific pattern of interrelationship among quite different types of variables. This commonly demonstrated pattern of relationship raises the question of how best to account for the different clusters of variables, and how best to account for the specific variables that appear within each cluster. In addressing these questions we believe that an assumption in many personality theories can be expanded into a parsimonious, but far-reaching, solution. To put this assumption into its most general form, it is possible that this regular pattern among the peripheral variables appears because the primary needs possess two features that structure the way social events are experienced by the individual during the developmentally important period. Let us consider each of these potentially powerful features in turn.

First, we have noted that the characteristics of the individual frequently determine which aspects of the environment provide a reinforcing effect. In parts II, III, and IV, we review extensive experimental evidence demonstrating that, although social situations frequently offer a full array of rewards, the dominant characteristic of the individual selects out from among this array just those that are "needed." The individual's selection of the type of reinforcement in adulthood may also occur during the developmental process. We assume that, to the extent the major concerns of a person during the formative years are organized around a primary need, then that primary need determines which environmental experiences have the greatest developmental effect on the individual. In other words, the primary needs may direct the individual into a reinforcement selection process during this period of life as well. If this is true, then the other rewards that may be available in the interpersonal environment will not exert much influence upon the developing personality during the socialization experience. We hope to show that this factor greatly helps to explain the pattern of positive correlations that are found among peripheral variables that seem to be related to a particular primary need.

Second, personality theories usually assert that there is a fixed sequential order in which the several primary needs phase in to affect the behavior of individuals. This "prepotency" principle provides a second reason why only certain classes of environmental reinforcements have an impact on the developing personality. This principle states that when a primary need appears, it has the ability to "motivate" the individual and control the effects of the experience. Many theories argue that when a primary need has been optimally satisfied, it loses this ability to control the effects of experience, which is then taken over by the subsequent primary need. For the same reasons, the effects of still later developing primary needs are not apparent because they have not yet begun to organize the experience of the individual. If the appearance of the peripheral variables is affected by the underlying primary needs, then we hope to show that this second principle greatly helps us understand the consistent pattern of negative correlations among peripheral variables that seem to be associated with different primary needs.

These two factors allows us to view the process of learning in childhood in a much more powerful way. The usual theoretical generalization is that behavioral patterns, and the individual characteristics that support them, are established through the reinforcement history of the individual. However, we begin with the idea that the most prepotent primary need stimulates the individual to behave and, through the ensuing interpersonal transactions, to perceive, evaluate, and be affected by those environmental events that can reinforce that need. Following most personality theories, we assume that if sufficient rewards are found, the behavior associated with that primary need should end and the next primary need should phase in without additional environmental intervention.

How should we understand the consequences to the person when the primary needs, in some or in large measure, are not satisfied? Obviously, many interpersonal environments provide only partial satisfaction for a primary need. Most important, different depriving environments present considerable variety in the type of partial reward they offer. It may be the differences in the kinds of deprivation experiences that lead to the different peripheral states within each cluster. We suggest that these alternative interpersonal environments offer the individual different types of coping strategies, in which the deprived need is offered different paths toward partial reward. These alternative interpersonal environments are similar in that they all provide some form of partial reward of the primary need, but they differ in the modalities of the relationships that provide the reward. It is possible that acquired motives develop through social experiences such as these and that acquired motives can be defined as a deprived state of a primary need together with a set of cognitive devices learned to cope with the conditions of partial reinforcement.

An example may clarify this theoretical description. To illustrate this process, let us assume, with Seligman (1975), that the organism has a need for prediction and control and that it uses the environment to provide these types of reinforcements. In human terms, this generalization means that a family that deals with a child in rejecting, confusing, or unstable ways deprives that child of experiences that satisfy this primary need. Further, we can easily imagine that such families may still differ in the specific ways they offer the child partial reinforcements for the need of prediction and control. For example, such families may offer the child protection, but only in return for differing types of behavior, such as obedience or neatness. Minimal degrees of protection from the family may result in an individual who is highly anxious or withdrawn, whereas more contingent granting of care may result in an individual who is highly dependent, orderly, or approval-seeking. Personality characteristics such as anxiety, dependency, or approval-seeking have a long history in empirical research as separate entities, and yet, somehow, they seem related to each other. It seems useful to see them as resulting from a socialization history composed of common deprivation experiences as well as alternative paths through which some form of the primary need has been satisfied.

We can now summarize our hypothesis. We propose that primary needs lead the individual to search for certain types of rewards from interpersonal events. When such rewards are not received, a state of anxiety appears. Depending on the types of partial rewards that people (e.g., parents) are capable of providing, the individual develops alternative behaviors toward those people or objects that provide the partial reward. Through the events that create the deprived state, an acquired set of cognitive elements becomes associated with the deprived need, including such factors as the contents of the person's self-image, the person's expectancies from the world, and the means-ends connections between the self and the objects of the world. Additionally, from the same deprivation experiences, certain types of emotions or beliefs may become associated with the complex of elements forming around the deprived need. In chapter 3, we attempt to show that the great majority of the peripheral motive and trait variables can be defined in this way.

Acquired Traits

Most approaches to personality also use more complex dispositional factors, often called traits, to account for the regularities observed in behavior. Yet, as Borgatta (1968) noted, "What is to be included in a definition of 'traits' is not self-evident," (p. 510). Guilford (1959) defined traits as "any distinguishable, relatively enduring way in which one individual varies from others" (p. 6). Allport (1961) and Cattell (1950) also offered broad definitions with approximately the same lack of specificity. The problem with such imprecise definitions, which do not use the detailed constructs that are available to psychologists, is that they are unable to support a differentiated model of social behavior. Let us see if we can include these factors in our overall proposal.

In defining both the primary and the acquired needs, we focused on the attribute of striving for a specific set of rewards from the environment. The dispositional factors called traits, however, seem to include additional elements beyond the requirement for specific types of rewards. Conceptually, traits such as assertiveness, sociability, suspiciousness, authoritarianism, or Machiavellianism seem to have important features in addition to acquired motives, as we have defined them. From the phenomenological and behavioral descriptions used to define such traits, it seems that they are complex factors composed of different types of psychological elements: (a) several acquired motives; (b) broad cognitive schemata; (c) emotional and temperamental features. For example, a complex trait such as authoritarianism, as portrayed by Adorno, Frenkel-Brunswik, Levinson, and Sanford (1950), is composed of motives (e.g., dependency), beliefs (e.g., rigid moralizing), and emotional states (e.g., anxiety). Distinguishing among motivational, cognitive, and emotional components of traits increases our ability to explain different aspects of social behavior. If these different constructs have any special meaning, it is because they make possible different predictions about behavior. It may be that the motive component affects one aspect of behavior, whereas the belief or emotional components affect others. We use this type of distinction when we explore the different areas of social behavior that a personality construct is supposed to predict.

A final point to consider is the relationship among the various traits. It is noteworthy that traits fall into the same set of clusters as do acquired motives (Wilson & Aronoff, 1984). Further, to the extent that evidence is available from developmental studies, traits seem to have the same types of socialization antecedents as do the other variables in the cluster. This pattern may be based on the possibility that a childhood experience has a similar effect across the different areas of personality. For example, the general experience of rejection in childhood is associated with the acquired motive of dependency, the emotional state of depression, simplicity of cognitive schema, and the conventional stage of moral development. Although this line of speculation opens the door to many more questions (e.g., when does a childhood experience lead to an acquired motive and when to a similar-sounding trait?), it does allow us to return to our basic hypothesis. The regular pattern that we find for traits may appear because they, too, are organized around a deprived primary need and serve as highly developed psychological structures designed to pursue those kinds of rewards. Traits may be acquired in the same way as peripheral motives: It is possible that these cognitive and affective elements develop around a deprived primary need in order to provide the defensive structure that serves as the specific pathway of adaptation.

Before completing this overview, we should emphasize the similarities between parts of our proposal and contemporary cognitive approaches to personality. Recently, Mischel (1973, 1979, 1984) has integrated a variety of cognitive approaches into an alternative view of personality. Mischel's position, which combines a variety of "learned" cognitive elements such as schemata, encoding strategies, subjective stimulus values, and self-regulation systems, is offered as a substitute for the many dynamic approaches to personality, with the expectation that it will account more accurately for the full array of social behavior usually studied in social psychology (see Cantor & Kihlstrom, 1981). Comparing the different types of constructs used by Mischel with the elements that we have included in the definition of a trait, we find the major difference between them is that Mischel does not consider the issue of reinforcement.

Most dynamic and social learning theories postulate that new motives are acquired in the course of social experience, but there is little understanding of just how this is achieved. In Walters and Parke's (1964) critical phrase, "By some alchemystical process the base metal of habits is transmuted into the glittering gold of drives or, to change the metaphor, into elusive motivating forces whose name is legion" (p. 233). It is certainly true that both dynamic and social learning theories have postulated a legion of variables to account for the different types of goal-seeking behavior, without an explanation of either the process of development or the basis of their interrelation. An additional strength of our proposal is that it permits us to incorporate the strengths of the dynamic approaches with the strengths of Mischel's cognitive social learning position. From dynamic psychology, we obtain constructs that help us account for the direction and the intensity of reward-seeking behavior, as well as a basis for explaining the organization among the variables. From cognitive social learning theory, we obtain a much clearer conception of exactly which psychological elements are learned through the course of social experience. Our proposal suggests that these two approaches complement each other very well. Each approach contributes elements that are missing in the other, and together, they seem to offer a powerful, wide-ranging, and yet compact model of personality.

2 The Personological Bases of Social Responsiveness

Personality theories are a significant resource that may help us to identify the major reinforcers of social behavior. Although the study of personality theories often appears to be merely an exercise in the history of psychology, we need to remember that it has been these psychologists who have most closely examined the social devices through which people pursue their goals. As we explore these theories for our special purpose, we do not feel the need to be either complete or evenhanded in reviewing these alternative proposals. In this chapter, we wish only to see if we can use these theories to extend our understanding of the biologically based motivational elements within the individual, clarify the changes produced by their developmental history, and thus be in a better position to investigate their effects on social behavior.

Although these theories seem to present a set of irreconcilable positions, it is still possible that these original proposals correctly identified many aspects of the individual that play a significant role in those social processes of concern to social psychology. We have noted that if we concentrate on the psychological phenomena that each of the theories describe, rather than on their provocative terminology, we are much better able to perceive the convergences in the theories. We can illustrate the possible value of this approach with an example from Jung, as he is probably the extreme case of a theorist whose acceptance has been hindered by the language in which his theory has been cast.

For Jung, as well as for his critics, the terms *collective unconscious* and *archetype* seem to be as important for the existential stance they offer as for their delineation of significant psychological processes. Yet, if we examine the psychological phenomena underneath the burden of emotional associations that the language is expected to provoke in the reader, the psychological constructs that Jung employed appear to be quite congruent with those described by other theorists. For example, although burdened by an extensive review of anthropological symbolism, Jung's (1953) discussion of the "Mana" archetype clearly presents psychological phenomena that are very close to those identified as the "need for dominance" by Murray (1938) and the "need for power" by McClelland and his associates (e.g., McClelland, 1975; Veroff, 1957; Winter, 1973). Similarly, although the "Mandala" archetype is presented in such a way as to provoke the reader to deal with his or her own religious stance, the psychological phenomena that Jung (1959) delineated so early under this rubric are really only an interesting instance of the need for consistency among one's psychological attributes, as discussed by Lecky (1945), Kelly (1955), Festinger (1957), or White (1963). Therefore, we suggest that it is useful to concentrate on the phenomena with which the original thinkers were concerned and take some liberties with their definitions so that their very great strengths can be collected together.

Following this approach, we hope to show that the major propositions of many personality theories converge upon a common set of statements about the primary needs. Although the theories cover a wider range of topics, because of our special interest in identifying different types of reinforcement, in this chapter we concentrate only on the variables that are claimed to be "core" motivational elements in the theories of six psychologists. We have chosen theories that have been developed in depth, have had a wide influence of some kind, and most important, are greatly dissimilar from each other. We discuss: (a) Freud, because he is both the founder of modern personality theory and the originator of a great many of its most important ideas; (b) Murray, because he attempted to write a non-Freudian theory on which to base empirical research; (c) Fromm, because of his lifelong concern with demonstrating the power of social variables to determine the nature of personality; (d) Jung, because of his attempt to chart the range of biologically based elements in personality; (e) Erikson, because his theory came after the originators and their critics and so was in position to synthesize the many subsequent additional proposals; and (f) Maslow, because we believe that his theory contains the common core of the other theories and is phrased in such a way as to provide the most useful theoretical base for social psychological research at this time. Therefore, we begin by presenting the motivational part of Maslow's theory in order to facilitate the later comparisons we wish to make between his theory and the others. We present Maslow's theory in somewhat greater detail than the others because we wish to rely on it as common vocabulary for the later parts of the book.

MASLOW

In his statements on motivation, Maslow attempted to blend his belief in the validity of dynamic psychology with the many proposals suggested by other theorists. His hope was to develop a more inclusive theory that would find commonalities in seemingly dissimilar motives through the discovery of their common core. Such clusters of variables, Maslow felt, were based on five core elements that were related to each other in the form of an ascending hierarchy of prepotency. These five sets of needs, each of whose functional appearance was contingent on the relative prior satisfaction of those needs believed to be more basic, were termed the physiological, safety, love and belongingness, esteem, and self-actualization needs.

1. The Physiological Needs.   On the first level, Maslow included a range of simple biological needs recognized by all physiologists. On this most basic level are the needs for food, sex, water, optimum levels of salt, oxygen, and temperature, as well as the need for sleep, relaxation, and bodily integrity. Maslow began with these organismic demands both in order to be complete in his accounting of the body's requirements and to point out the obvious fact that no further psychological development is possible if they have not been attained. Many fields, ranging from physiology to anthropology, describe the organism's behavior during the state of physiological deprivation. These needs are so basic, in fact, that little variation in complex social behavior can be accounted for in terms of the search for these rewards.

Unfortunately, Maslow's use of the term "physiological needs" hindered the recognition of his most basic proposition: All of the needs described in his theory have their origin in the human organism. This term was an unfortunate choice, because it is in the consequences of the reward history of the later stages that the more interesting types of social behavior can best be understood.

2. The Safety Needs.   The safety needs center around the requirement for an understandable, secure, and orderly world. Maslow (1970) categorized the various manifestations of the safety needs as the needs for: "security; stability; dependency; protection; freedom from fear, from anxiety and chaos; need for structure, order, law, limits; [and] strength in the protector" (p. 39). Underlying these apparently different states is the common factor of the "need for prediction and control," as described so well by Seligman (1975). When these needs are not satisfied, a large variety of cognitive, emotional, and motivational conditions are created. Individuals may see other people and themselves, as well as the world in general, as unsafe, unjust, inconsistent, or unreliable. Hence, they seek for, or attempt to create, areas of life that offer the most stability and protection. Therefore, deprived safety needs appear in personality as *beliefs* about the world, *states* of discomfort, and *desires* to create a situation that solves these discomforts.

At its most extreme, the deprived state for an individual is one of inability to handle social relationships, situational events, or personal feelings, leading to a personal subjective state of confusion, disorientation, inadequacy, helplessness, or anxiety. The person may feel that the world is unreal, experience a constant sense of dread, feel confused, or on the verge of a breakdown. In a less extreme form, the individual believes that other people or the world in general are threatening in some way or else unpleasantly undependable. There is a general belief that other people or institutions cannot be relied upon, which leads to a pervasive orientation of mistrust. This may appear as a general conviction that matters are out of control or as a specific personal belief that someone is dangerous.

As social psychologists, our interest lies in the steps the individual will take to relieve these discomforts. These individuals may move beyond simply experiencing feelings of insecurity or inadequacy by demanding a relationship in which someone else provides care or solutions to problems. These needs may be a straightforward desire for assistance or a desire for a relationship, such as marriage, which will provide care. More generally, the anxiety may lead the individual to seek out major economic, political, or religious institutions that appear to possess the strength that is lacking personally. Alternatively, it may seem best to withdraw from the social situation and find order in a narrowed range of activity. Finally, when faced with the impossibility of finding safety in these maneuvers, the anxiety may lead to either fantasy or real attacks on those perceived to have put the individual in the difficult position.

3. Love and Belongingness Needs.   The love and belongingness needs center around the desire to experience intimate relationships with other people. Individuals motivated on this level desire contact, intimacy, warm and friendly relationships, and they function well in interpersonal situations. The central expression of this need is a clear desire for a warm companionate relationship, which encourages congenial activities on the basis of approximate equality among peers. It is important to recognize that, in Erikson's terms, mutuality of involvement and concern is the central characteristic, rather than the behavioral criterion of two people spending time in close physical proximity to one another (e.g., Schachter, 1959). However, the expression of affection for those who take care of the person, or for those who are cared for, should be understood as a resultant of the satisfaction of *other* types of psychological needs.

Together with the affective bond that may exist between two people is the broader need to belong to a wider group. This phenomenon, not yet well studied in social psychology, is understood as a special need for belonging, being one of a group, and having identification with group goals or a place in a group. In terms of the dynamics of group process, it is seen as something other than the sum of libidinal ties among group members. Rather, it is the need to be concerned with the characteristics of a psychologically significant unit.

When the anxiety associated with a deprivation state of the need is removed, the individual is able to give and receive affection without a pressing sense of needing to feel fulfilled. Similarly, when individuals have successfully satisfied this need for intimacy, they feel a stronger subjective sense of rootedness and membership in psychologically meaningful groups. To use Maslow's ideas, these people begin to have a wider identification with the species and a greater understanding of their place in the significant community. Through these developments, these wider social referents become an integral part of their personality. These strengths, together with those achieved at prior stages, increase these individuals' sense of well-being by permitting them to enjoy social relations in a more complex and integrated way.

4. Esteem Needs.   The esteem needs center around the issue of firmly establishing a high sense of self-worth, which is achieved both through the appraisal of actual competence in one's own activities and through receiving the esteem of others because of one's actions. Maslow (1970) classified the manifestations of this need into two subsidiary sets. First, there is "the desire for strength, for achievement, for adequacy, for mastery and competence, for confidence in the face of the world, and for independence and freedom. Second, . . . the desire for reputation or prestige (defining it as respect or esteem from other people), status, fame and glory, dominance, recognition, attention, importance, dignity or appreciation" (p. 45). Other manifestations of these needs are indications or expressed desires for self-reliance, self-acceptance, power, confidence, competition, trust in one's own abilities or self, leadership, and autonomy.

One of Maslow's strengths as a theorist was the ability to see commonalities in apparently disparate phenomena. The weakness of this list, however, is that this collection of characteristics combines core needs with those peripheral states that have emerged from a process of adaptation to the experiences of one's own life. The common element that underlies this variety of states, we believe, is the need for competence, as described by White (1963).

When the esteem needs have been reasonably well satisfied, there is a sense that challenges can be met with confidence, that required skills exist or can be attained, and that one's abilities can be relied upon. The need for competence should cause people to welcome responsibility for their effects upon the world, because it is through these acts that this particular type of reward is obtained. Similarly, the world, no matter how complex, should appear to be one that provides desirable opportunities to exhibit one's skill. Because there is such identification with the results of one's activities, these activities take on great importance and thus provide a clear sense of purpose. From such events emerge the positive quality of cognitive self-evaluations. People compare themselves to what they ideally want to be, like and approve of themselves, and see others as liking and approving of them, too.

When experiences fail to provide these rewards, the deprived state develops. The different levels of gratification possible and the different types of adaptation offered underlie the many types of peripheral variables that seem to be related to the deprived state of the need for competence. The general characteristic of the deprived state, which underlies these multiple peripheral states, is the sense that the individual has not been fully effective, cannot confidently rely on his or her abilities, and thus is *searching* for experiences that will develop a strong sense of self-worth. For the deprived individual, interpersonal relationships and group tasks are important primarily as vehicles through which this as yet unobtained sense of efficacy can be developed.

5. The Need for Self-Actualization.   The stage of self-actualization is the part of Maslow's theory for which he is most widely known. It refers to one's wish for self-fulfillment, after one's earlier needs have been satisfied, and is expressed in those idiosyncratic ways most desired by the individual. Because the descriptions of this state focus primarily on the cognitive and emotional side of personality, with a very sparse discussion of motivation, we defer a discussion of what the underlying process might be until chapter 3.

FREUD

Freud's complex delineation of personality structure maintained that the motivational core is rooted in the somatic processes of the body. These organismically based sexual, aggressive, and ego drives provide the energy that motivates behavior, and experience creates a structure that channels these forces in socially appropriate ways. Thus, although the core processes are a constantly regenerating source of energy, the final structure of personality is the set of learned defensive reactions to the impulses developed in psychosexual maturation.

Motivational Constructs

1. *Ego Instincts.* These are physiological and cognitive needs, ranging from a tendency to preserve life, to the need for food, water, and other such physiological requirements, to the desire for interesting stimulation (curiosity).
2 *Sexual Instincts.* This is the sexual drive, the aim of which is the release of tension. It originates in the body and is expressed through a series of bodily zones, which mature in a fixed order.
3. *Aggression.* In early stages of the theory's development, a drive of aggression was seen as a component of the sexual drive being expressed at the anal stage. In later formulations, an aggressive drive was raised to the status of an independent major drive.

Comment. It is curious that a self-conscious theory of motivation provides such a reduced set of core motivational constructs. The ego instincts, for example, are found basically as parenthetical remarks in Freud's writings. At times, discussions of these instincts are the recognition of the obvious (e.g., the need for food) whereas in other discussions they serve as unexamined "other" factors when a theoretical argument needs completing (e.g., as in the early presentations of the topographical theory, when some agency was needed to institute the repression). Last, as in his scattered discussions of curiosity, they appear briefly as a puzzled note acknowledging the presence of an important phenomenon that does not fit neatly into his theoretical scheme. Aggression, too, is a phenomenon that never aroused Freud's usual level of conceptual lucidity. Aggression could not be reduced easily to other terms, provoked major disputes within his early group of co-workers, and was seen variously as an instrumental response to frustration, as a component of the sexual drives, as a component of the ego instincts, and finally, raised to the level of a separate major organismic trend (see Bibring, 1941).

The sexual drive, of course, underlies the bulk of Freud's theorizing and needs little elaboration here. What is of interest for the tasks of this book is to recognize, as Klein (1970) points out, that Freud's great contribution was to develop a clinical theory of elaborated defenses, developed through experience, in order to reach an accommodation between the sexual drive and the external world. It is ironic that a theorist who was so criticized for giving excessive weight to biological drives should have made his great contribution to understanding the effects of experience. Freud clung tenaciously to the major theoretical emphasis that he placed on sexual drives for fear that introducing other considerations would trivialize the importance of this drive. However, at this stage in the development of personality theory, we can bring additional drives into our models without in any way reducing the importance of sexuality.

FROMM

Fromm, in contrast to Freud, is often unclear in his thinking about core personality attributes. However, in various places in his prolific writings on the influences of economic and cultural forces on personality, he (1955) does discuss at least five basic needs that correspond closely to the needs proposed by Maslow.

Motivational Constructs

1. *The Need for Relatedness.* The need to become involved with other people in dependent, dominating, or loving ways and to become part of a social group.

2. *The Need for Transcendence.* The need to be an initiating actor in the world; to make things happen; to create.
3. *The Need for Rootedness.* The need for membership in a social group.
4. *The Need for Identity.* The need to be an autonomous actor with a clear sense of self.
5. *The Need for a Frame of Orientation and Devotion.* The need for meaning.

Comment.   The constant tension in Fromm's writings on personality lies in the difficulty of reconciling his main concern with the social bases of human experience with the usual concerns of motivational analysis: accounting for the intensity and direction of behavior. Thus, although Fromm's (1955) main theme is the position "that the basic passions of man are not rooted in his instinctive needs, but in the specific conditions of human existence . . . ," (p. vii), his critique of society eventually forces him to consider "universal criteria for mental health which are valid for the human race as such, and according to which the state of health of each society can be judged" (p. 12). In other words, in a career of sociological analyses, the logic of his position eventually forced him to devote at least one chapter to the consideration of the human core. This reluctance to consider the core elements likely explains why his account is, at the same time, redundant and unclear. With Fromm, we must examine even more carefully than usual the phenomena that he presents and rewrite his definitions.

Although not included as part of his formal list of core elements, Fromm precedes that discussion by noting the "imperative" requirement that the needs of food, water, and sex be satisfied. We can assume these needs are so self-evident that Fromm is implying that this group of bodily requirements would overlap with the broader set outlined by Maslow on his first level of need.

Of more interest is the psychological basis for his postulating the need for relatedness. Fromm begins his discussion by noting the separation of the human being from a secure integration within nature. The condition of separation is described as one of great insecurity and anxiety, and the potential ways of achieving relatedness that he outlines appear to be devices to reinstitute this fundamental security. It is most reasonable, then, to assume that the need for safety is the core element of this need and to see the bulk of the discussion about dependency, domination, and love as referring to peripheral characteristics. However, the emphasis that Fromm places on love (e.g., "primary potential for love . . . " p. 37) seems to indicate that love holds a special place for him. Although the discussion is not clear on this point (see Fromm, 1956), we might tentatively conclude that love is an independent motivational system.

Similarly, the need for rootedness seems based on the reinstitution of a sense of security in much the same way as Fromm's discussion of the need for relatedness. The point of difference appears to be that with the term related-ness Fromm is focusing on the individual's sense of personal safety. In the discussion on rootedness, however, he speaks of a broader sense of security found in the need for a place and a group. Thus, from our point of view, the major motivational component is the security need, because the group need appears to be an instrumental technique for instituting a sense of safety. Al-though Fromm does not explore the potential for loving mutuality (in Erikson's terms) in his discussion of the social relationships that provide this sense of safety, the strong positive value that he does place on environmental, familial, and group membership begins to stand by itself. As with his first need level, we wonder how much of an injustice we do to his perceptions of personality if we see in his discussion of such instrumental behavior an addi-tional core element as well, which Maslow and Erikson term "belong-ingness."

The need for transcendence, translated into Erikson's language, is a state-ment about the need for competence and accomplishment in the events of the world. The focus is on a strong need to take purposeful actions as opposed to experiencing the control of others passively. His fourth need, the need for identity, is very similar to the requirements discussed by Erikson and, simi-larly, includes the need to know who one is as an actor. In other words, this need incorporates many of the phenomena that Fromm presents under the need for transcendence. From our point of view, we can easily see these two need levels as one: the phenomena included in Maslow's postulation of a need for esteem.

The need for a frame of orientation and devotion is similar to the require-ments discussed by a wide variety of theorists under the name of exploratory behavior or curiosity (see Cofer & Appley, 1964; Fiske & Maddi, 1961) or the need for understanding or meaning (Frankl, 1962; Jung, 1960; Maslow, 1963; White, 1963). Thus, from an examination of the phenomena presented as core requirements by Fromm, we derive the following types of core ele-ments: (a) physiological needs; (b) safety needs; (c) esteem needs; (d) cogni-tive needs; and most tentatively (e) love and belongingness needs.

MURRAY

In Murray's view, the core of personality resides in the viscerogenic needs (e.g., the need for food) as well as in a sphere of ego energies associated with the pleasures of activity, achievement, and effectance. For Murray, the dep-rivation of the viscerogenic needs creates the tension that motivates behavior. The psychogenic needs, such as the need for achievement or approval (the pe-ripheral characteristics, in his terminology), are assumed to be created in the course of development through the usual processes of learning. Although these psychogenic needs are based on the core viscerogenic needs, Murray introduced a modest prepotency principle, which proposed that the viscerogenic needs took priority in utilizing environmental resources as reinforcements.

Motivational Constructs

1. *Viscerogenic Needs.* These are the primary requirements of the internal body processes. These physiological needs refer to the positive incorporation of objects, such as food, air, water, and stimulation; responses to distentions in the body, such as sex, lactation, and excretion; and the body's avoidance of painful substances or events.
2. *Pleasures*
   a. *Activity pleasure.* The rise and discharge of energy through uninhibited movement or thought.
   b. *Achievement pleasure.* The elation of overcoming or mastering difficult obstacles.
   c. *Effect pleasure.* The relative gain in pleasure achieved through the removal of dissatisfying or unpleasant states.

Comment.   The viscerogenic needs play little role in the uses Murray, or contemporary psychology, has made of his theory. For the most part, they are seen as the organismic givens and serve as a useful explanatory force only in that the more complex taxonomy of personality is derived from them. The psychogenic needs, defined as both reaction systems and wishes, were seen developing through the social experiences that satisfied the primary needs. The viscerogenic needs, then, are similar to the usual list of simple physiological requirements. A very helpful use that Murray made of the standard viscerogenic needs was to combine several to account for those psychological properties described by Freud under the rubric "libido." Murray defined libido as a construct composed of the elements of sex and tactile stimulation seeking.

The pleasures outlined by Murray were presented by him as a weak first approximation to a theory of emotion. From our point of view, activity pleasure has motivational properties in that the individual seeks uninhibited body movement. It is similar to the pleasures of muscular movement described by Erikson in his second stage but without the important component of autonomy concerns. Therefore, it is outside the major dimensions of Erikson's theory. It is also somewhat similar to some of Maslow's description of the state of self-actualization ("the free use of abilities . . . "). We return to this issue at a later point in chapter 3. The description of achievement pleasure seems very much like the resultant of esteem gratification. Effect pleasure, on the other hand, does not seem to incorporate specific motivational characteristics but is, rather, an aspect of the reward-seeking characteristics of any gratification process.

Murray's great achievement, of course, was in the creation of a taxonomy of peripheral motives. His distinctions among variables, as well as his definitions, provided a conceptual basis for much of the experimental work in personality that followed. The weakness of his approach was that he did not indicate the nature of the relationship among those variables nor upon what principle it might be based. This we hope to provide in chapter 3.

JUNG

Of all the personality theories, Jung's proposals are the most difficult to integrate with the rest of the field. Yet, because his ideas are so different, if we can show that they refer to the same set of psychological phenomena, then our presumed identification of a common set of reinforcers is made more plausible.

A central problem in integrating Jung's ideas with those of other theorists lies in the complex way he accounts for motivation. Jung begins with a nonspecific energy as his primary motivational construct, which is expressed concretely through biologically rooted archetypes. Unfortunately, even the general definitions of the archetype are blurry in the extreme. At times they are defined as genetically based cognitive structures (Jung, 1953, 1960), whereas at other times they are more ambiguously defined as "potentialities" for developing these cognitive structures in an individual's lifetime (Jung, 1959). To make our reading even more difficult, in a theory that gives primary explanatory weight to the concept of the archetype, there is not even a listing of all the archetypes proposed by Jung. To compound the problem further, Jung felt it essential to insist on a Lamarckian origin for these archetypes in some prehistoric period of the human race. Curiously, other than in the discussion of the hypothesized archetypes, Jung's theory is not too dissimilar from a contemporary psychoanalytic model such as Erikson's.

Jung understood the archetype to be an image through which a general form of energy is expressed. Therefore, by his definition, an archetype is *not* a motive. Jung draws the distinction between image and motive still more sharply when, in several obscure essays (Jung, 1960), he speculates that each individual archetype might have its own specific energy and then posits a remarkably McDougallian list of instincts in addition to the archetypes. However, several considerations lead us to question this definition of an archetype. The most important of these is Jung's argument, and impressive clinical demonstration, that all archetypes have the power to press for some channel through which they might appear.

Thus, when all of the problematic elements of the theory of archetypes are set aside, what remains in the psychological descriptions are delineations of separate categories of force that meet the usual criteria used to define a human drive (Cofer & Appley, 1964). These drives: (a) are unlearned; (b) impel the individual to behave; (c) select certain stimulus configurations of the environment as differentially relevant; and (d) cannot be extinguished. Rather, nonexpression of the archetype causes the individual to be more narrowly focused on attaining these specific rewards through a wide range of instrumental behaviors (from dreaming, to symptom formation, to cultural ritual) as compensations for that which had been deprived. In this section, we list the major archetypes that emerge from our reading of the corpus of Jung's work and ask, in the language of contemporary psychology, what motivational forces appear to underlie these phenomena.

Motivational Constructs

1. Libido. This term is used to denote a nonspecific life energy that is created by a field of tension between opposing archetypes. Individual behavior results from the association of this general energy with the specific form provided by an archetype. In Jung's theoretical writings, this concept is used loosely and on what appears to be an ad hoc basis. Primarily, his discussion of libido seems to be useful merely to emphasize the distinction that Jung wished to draw between his understanding of the wide range of human concerns and the highly specific sexual emphasis on which Freud insisted.

2. Instincts. In two minor addresses to English-speaking audiences, Jung (1960) introduced the concept of instinct as a set of biologically based impulses to action that energized the archetypes. Little additional use was made of these constructs, which are quite similar to those of James and McDougall. Our impression of the theoretical status of these constructs in Jung's work is that through them Jung was acknowledging what seemed obvious to him and his English audience, and so uninteresting in light of the original contribution of the archetype.

a. *Hunger.* Jung presented this "impulse" as a specific example of the "instinct for self-preservation." We can only assume that by this he was acknowledging all the usual biological requirements.
b. *Sexuality.* This term appears without definition. We can assume he is referring to sexuality as defined by Freud.
c. *Drive to activity.* Jung provides examples, rather than definitions, for this term. He states that this "drive" includes "the urge to travel, love of change, restlessness, and the play instinct" (p. 117). Interestingly, Jung states that "this urge starts functioning when the other urges are

satisfied" (p. 117). The common elements, as we read the brief reference, are the *pleasure of physical activity* and *curiosity*.
  d. *Reflective instinct.* Through this term Jung described the ability of the individual to reflect on his behavior. Thus, the term appears to be a way of stating that cognition is a natural function of the human organism.
  e. *Creative instinct.* This is the process of going beyond the repetition of previously experienced thoughts to develop new ideas. Jung stated that he was unsure if this process should have a genuinely instinctive status. His emphasis is that this ability is "compulsive" and natural. Because he makes little theoretical use of this ability, we should probably see it and the "reflective instinct" as properties of the cognitive system. As such, both processes would properly lack motivational status.

3. Archetypes

  a. *The Shadow.* This archetype is "the 'negative side' of the personality, the sum of all those unpleasant qualities we like to hide, together with the insufficiently developed functions and the contents of the personal unconscious" (Jung, 1953, p. 66). This concept plays two very large roles in Jung's writings. In the first, it is used loosely to signify that *any* undeveloped potentiality accumulates great power to disrupt stable functioning. As a shifting residual category, then, the term is perhaps useful from the point of view of psychopathology but does not provide a basic element of a general theory of personality. The second use, however, is more important because, as is clear across the corpus of Jung's writing, he subsumes under this term the impulses for food, sex, and aggression. He writes that all of these phenomena have autonomous power to control personality until they find sufficient levels of expression.
  b. *The Great Mother.* Through this construct and several related ideas, Jung described a combined image of the need to give and to receive protection, nurturance, and love. He used the same term for the entire constellation of relationships between caregiver and care receiver. Within his description of the human life cycle, for the child, the images of the Great Mother were seen as expressing the need for a protector who cared only for the child and who would help the child develop all of its early abilities. For the adult, male as well as female, the term was used to represent a need of creation through careful attention and love of a weaker individual. In contemporary language, the terms that express this phenomenon for the child are the need for dependency and, for the adult, the need for affiliation and nurturance.
  c. *X* [*The Need for Belonging?*]. Across the range of his writings, Jung presented casually what we read to be a need that is not given the sepa-

rate status of a named variable. Jung frequently emphasized that individual social identity is significantly affected by membership in a racial, ethnic, or cultural group. Because living with others was seen as an inescapable necessity, there is, at the minimum, an experiential pressure to develop the self partially through the characteristics of the group. But beyond this requirement, Jung stressed that the individual *needs* to become a member of such a group. If this reading of Jung is correct, then implicitly at least, he assumed there is a need for belonging that should be included on the list of the motivational factors he described. However, because this conclusion is inferential rather than based on a clear term from Jung's theory, its ascription to Jung must be made in the most tentative way.

d. *Mana.* In the discussion of the psychology of archetypes such as Spirit, Fire, Trickster, Father, or Grace, a major emphasis on a human need for potency across a wide range of social domains is evident. Jung stressed that the individual expression of this need may take the form of concern with intellectual attainment, social control, subjective strength over one's inner processes, or images of the gods. The common element of a need to express power runs through all these discussions. In this area, the descriptions are so extensive that there is no difficulty in determining the nature of the process that he had isolated, nor is there difficulty in substituting a contemporary term to bring the phenomena into our general discussion. Through all of these separate terms, Jung was speaking of the need for power in the same way as did McClelland and his associates (McClelland, 1975; Veroff, 1957; Winter, 1973).

e. *Unity.* The goal of personality development was seen by Jung to be the balanced expression and clear coordination of all psychological elements. The central construct that synthesizes all of these elements is the Self, which Jung (1953), in his descriptive way, called the "unknowable essence which he cannot grasp as such" (p. 236). This unhelpful definition is very similar to that of Erikson's and holds the same conceptual status in his theory. What is important in Jung's use of this construct, presented under such archetype names as the Self, Mandala, or God, is a motivational principle that plays a major role in his theory. This central motive is the force that causes the individual to resolve any inconsistencies that may exist among the disparate elements of personality. With this integrating principle, Jung presented in more powerful form a construct given major emphasis in a wide variety of psychological theories (Festinger, 1957; Kelly, 1955; Lecky, 1945; White, 1963).

There are three archetypes receiving major treatment by Jung that do not seem to possess real motivational characteristics: the Persona, the Anima, and the Animus. Although Jung does claim that each are potentialities that must find expression and can cause pathology if undeveloped, examination of their characteristics seems to require that the phenomena they represent be seen as the expression of other, more basic psychological processes. The Persona, for example, is a cognitive system composed of those characteristics needed to meet the expectations and demands of the society. Thus, the Persona is not a motivational construct as much as it is the resultant of the cognitive process that forms sets of identifications with the social role to be assumed by the individual. The process of identification, under the constraints of the society, more properly should be seen as a function of the Ego in a way similar to our conclusion regarding the conceptual status of the last two 'instincts." Similarly, the Anima is defined in the traditional way as the set of "feminine" characteristics of personality (emotional, nurturant, and alogical) and the Animus as the set of traditionally "masculine" characteristics (judgmental, productive, and logical). Only the affiliation and the achievement aspects of these ideas have motivational properties, and these can be subsumed under other constructs discussed earlier. The other characteristics are bipolar dimensions of emotional or cognitive responsiveness.

In conclusion, we suggest that the best way to understand Jung's focus on the *power* of the archetype is to postulate a set of biologically based motives as the source of the power. Thus, in our opinion, the change that appears necessary for this theory is to replace the concept of a general energy source with a set of forces that correspond to the major outlines of the *characteristics* of the archetypes.

ERIKSON

Of all the modern personality theorists, Erikson has provoked the widest interest among students, clinicians, and recently, researchers. His theory, founded securely in psychoanalytic thought, addressed itself to all the major criticisms of the classic Freudian position and has so broadened that framework that it can accept the major contributions of the alternative theories. Erikson hoped to write a theory that was somatic, psychological, interpersonal, and social and to develop a way of thinking about personality that would fit comfortably with what had been learned from cognitive, learning, developmental, and social scientists since the path-breaking books of Freud.

Our purposes, though, do not require a full examination of the entire theory, and so we review only the motivational components that seem to underlie the eight stages of human development presented by Erikson. In delineating these "universal" periods, Erikson used as his criteria certain specific psychological "issues" that appear and must be dealt with *in sequential order*. Our major problem in using this part of his theory is pinning down precisely the organismically based issues that follow the epigenetic blueprint. Although a strength of Erikson's proposals lies in the rich description of each stage, he, too, is unclear just where we need specificity. As a psychoanalyst, Erikson (1963) is comfortable with libido theory and explicitly utilizes it in selected theoretical interludes as *the* force that brings about the individual's interaction with others. Yet, the special contribution of his theory is the presentation of the different developmental tasks required in each succeeding stage. Our problem lies in how to view the causes of the defining characteristics of each period. Maddi (1976), by presenting the psychosocial crisis under the heading of the "peripheral states" (p. 292), seems to say that the defining causes may lie in the developmental tasks set by society. Yet Maddi does not discuss what makes the stages appear in a fixed sequence across differing cultures.

Maddi's (1976) clearest comment on this issue, that "Erikson's position is a peculiar, though intriguing, conglomerate of Freud and something like a fulfillment position" (p. 292), provides helpful guidance. To Maddi (1976), a fulfillment position is nothing less than a statement that "forces" exist in the human being to develop their potentialities in a "course determined by something like a genetic blueprint" (p. 102). Thus, our task is to examine the characteristics of each stage and delineate the common psychological elements. From this review, we hope to discover the core components and compare them to those proposed by other theorists.

1. Trust Versus Mistrust.   Erikson begins his account of human development with a rich description of the helplessness of the child and the urgency of its bodily needs. In the social relationship that is the consequence of the parents' responding to these needs, Erikson sees the basic issue to be one of trust in the "consistency, continuity and sameness" of the world. In other words, there is a major pressure to establish *a sense of regularity* in one's object relationships with oneself and others. "The general state of trust . . . implied not only that one had learned to rely on the sameness and continuity of the outer providers, but also that one may trust oneself and the capacity of one's own organs to cope with urges. . . ." (Erikson, 1963, p. 248). The danger in these social events is that the response will not be regular, and so it will lead to a sense of mistrust of self and others. To examine these events more closely, we must ask what would explain the ability of these social events to have the effect of a specific reward or deprivation. Following the logic used earlier in the discussion of Jung, it would appear that some version of a primary need is required. In the case of this first stage, then, the concern for continuity and regularity is an alternative way of broadly phrasing the need for prediction and control, as Maslow does in his presentation of the safety needs.

2. Autonomy Versus Shame and Doubt.   In the second year, the increased muscular and cognitive abilities bring the individual into a greatly expanded range of interactions with the world. This biological maturation of abilities makes possible a much more active set of involvements with the world across a wide range of locomotor, manipulative, and communicative behaviors. The child's concern is with making events occur, or not occur, which leads Erikson to use the term "autonomy," in the sense that the individual is capable of being in command of some major events. From the descriptions of the subjective meaning of these activities, however, the psychological issue appears to be the same as the first stage: a concern with prediction and control. The new development during this stage appears to lie in the cognitive sector of personality in that the increased ego capacity allows the child to realize that *it* is the cause of the action. Although the issue of choice introduces elements of self-esteem, this appears to be only a rudimentary form of what will later become a major concern. Specifically, what is only beginning to be introduced here is the issue of measuring one's own *worth* or the *quality* of one's accomplishments. The lack of successful activity in this stage has its major effect on the emotional and cognitive level. The description of negative consequences makes us feel more certain that Erikson's intent is to describe issues of control at this stage. Shame is defined as an emotion in which one fears the withdrawal of approval from others; doubt is the cognitive precipitate of unsuccessful activity, the conclusion that one cannot control events or oneself in appropriate ways.

3. Initiative Versus Guilt.   Events during this stage continue those of the earlier developments. The new element is that there is a clearer, conscious understanding that the individual is the cause of important life events and has a clear sense of the *goals* of the activity. A simple example of the way children use bikes can serve to highlight the distinction between the second and third stage. In the second stage, the child is involved with the manipulation of the pedals or handlebars and is simply pleased to make them move. In the third stage, the child plans ahead of time to have the adventure of going all around the block. Psychologically, these activities are predicated on the firm sense of being in control without major issues to resolve: "He is in free possession of a surplus of a energy which permits him to forget failures quickly and to approach what seems desirable . . . with undiminished and more accurate direction" (Erikson, 1963, p. 255). What appears to be new at this stage, although presented by Erikson mainly in terms of Oedipal activities is the broad sense of determining just *how* good you are. This new issue of personal worth, together with the description of the dangers of such experience leading to self-imposed overcontrol and feelings of worthlessness (guilt), introduces the concern with self-esteem as a major new element.

4. Industry Versus Inferiority.   The fourth stage coincides with the child's involvement in the major social institution of the elementary school. This experience greatly broadens the range of tasks that are set before the child and introduces opportunities and responsibilities that are inevitable for a member of that society. It is a time when the child "becomes ready to apply himself to given skills and tasks, which go far beyond the mere playful expression of his organ modes or the pleasure in the function of limbs. . . . He can become an eager and absorbed unit of a productive situation" (Erikson, 1963, p. 259). This constant theme of productivity—the focus on what the child can accomplish—runs throughout Erikson's description of these activities. Children, through observation of the effects of their behavior in the world, are establishing a clear sense of their "worthwhileness." The danger of learning their inadequacy is that it completes the social foundation of the individual as someone who is inferior and thus not likely to be a worthy member of his or her society. As in the third stage, the range of behavior in which the child is engaged is determined by both the maturation of personal abilities as well as the social pressures of the tasks that the society will set. The nature of the effective reinforcement, however, seems to involve the need for self-esteem directly. With the successful completion of this series of activities, which measure one's ability as an actor in the world, the individual then turns, in the next stage, to clarify the specific nature of his or her phenomenological self.

5. *Identity Versus Role Confusion.*   With the biological changes of puberty and movement into the adult world as a comprehending member, the different identifications created through the child's past activities come under great strain. Early understanding of self may no longer serve under these pressures, nor may a sufficient basis have been established that would allow the adolescent to project himself ahead comfortably to what is now seen as his future self. Worse still, as Erikson describes so vividly, the adolescent may not be able to project ahead at all.

Two types of psychological processes appear to underlie the dramatic, and melodramatic, experiences that take place. A continuing theme runs throughout the discussion of this stage: the search for a "sense of continuity and sameness." Erikson's works are rich in description of the areas of life that become involved: the commitment to large goals and ideologies, the outgroup scapegoating, the trying on of costume in hopes of evoking a self, the creation of a negative identity. Although much more inclusive than his predecessors, Erikson's discussion of ego identity delineates the power of the principle of self-consistency to mobilize all forms of human behavior in its behalf. The power of this "force" can best be seen in the discussions of the negative identity where Erikson makes the point that simply "receiving" a socially nonintegrated identity is not satisfactory. The cognitive elements must have some internal ability to recognize and reject inconsistency and inadequacy, as Jung describes for the Self, which makes a clearly asocial identity more satisfactory than none at all.

The second principle that underlies the passion with which goals are chosen remains the concern with personal worth. In choosing an ideology, Erikson (1963) notes that not only must it be clear and predestined, but it also must imply that "the best people will come to rule . . . In order not to become cynically or apathetically lost, young people must somehow be able to convince themselves that those who succeed in their anticipated adult world thereby shoulder the obligation of being the best" (p. 263). The comparative statement of concern for being the best is the demand of those whose sense of self-esteem is intense but not yet firmly established.

6. Intimacy Versus Isolation.   It is the mark of adulthood that the clarity of personal identity permits another concern to emerge. The discussion of intimacy in friendship and love is presented in terms of the psychological factors that stand in the way of the full genital expression of sexuality. But, as Erikson (1963) goes on to note, it is "a process which we really do not understand" (p. 265). His description, then, from one point of view, states that this need is something other than a concern for safety, esteem, cognitive consistency, or sexuality. He also writes of an eagerness to fuse with another and mutuality of devotion which only partially defines the nature of this concern. Perhaps the definition of love as a desire to become part of another is as clear as we can be at this time.

7. Generativity Versus Stagnation.   This stage is described as a period of actively guiding the next generation. What seems clear in the discussion is that the concern is with more than providing care to one's own children and those parts of society for which responsibility has been assumed. The emphasis here is on a special kind of productivity: the need to become responsible for the "quality" of succeeding generations, the results of one's career, and one's institutional organization and its output. Although in many ways the phrasing is in terms of nurturance, the emphasis on quality and meaningfulness indicates that relationships are being described in which the psychological elements have to do with a mature form of self-esteem as much as with intimacy. It appears that Erikson is pointing out that by this time the individual can have achieved a firm sense of self-worth so that the earlier comparisons of being "better than" no longer have any importance. Rather, at this stage there can be a growth of involvements and the assumption of greater depths of responsibility for the successful development of others and a concern for the quality of their achievement. One may wonder at this point if the free use of "energy," which Erikson describes at this time, is not the mobilization of one's potentialities — of skill, ability, and concern that Maslow had in mind when he spoke of self-actualization.

8. Ego Integrity Versus Despair.   Perhaps before we present the major issue of this last stage, it should be noted that in Erikson's theory of the life cycle the goal of successful experience, or the conception of mental health, is not successful progression through earlier stages to a final utopia. Where hierarchical theories, such as Maslow's, view optimal development as stages toward the full expression of potentialities, it is the special contribution of Erikson to have pictured optimal function at each stage in life. With that said, we can understand this last stage not as the complete flowering of personality, but rather as a need to find meaning and achieve self-acceptance after the "triumphs and disappointments" of life. From our point of view, what makes it a special stage is that this type of experience has accrued, and the saliency of the end of life sharpens the need to find meaning and worth in what has been experienced. Thus, it is within these special circumstances that these needs, which have developed earlier, appear to have a different phenomenology, although the motives themselves are not new.

CONCLUSION

Of all the personality theories, Erikson's appears to us as the most inclusive and most detailed. Indeed, its scope is presently stimulating even further theoretical work to make its propositions clearer, to expand the range of behavior that these can help explain, and to distinguish still additional stages. As the theory that tried to deal most inclusively with the phenomena described by other theories, Erikson's proposals provide the most useful way of understanding the complexity of the human personality within one systematic theoretical framework.

As we reviewed Erikson's major proposals, we tried to identify the basic psychological elements that he believed contributed to the events at each stage. We recognize that our analysis is an oversimplification of Erikson's ideas, which reduces much of our ability to understand the nuances of human behavior. We risk simplifying these ideas because our purpose is to identify a set of dispositional constructs that permit us to use experimental techniques to study the role of personality in the social process. Unfortunately, given the present conceptual and methodological skill in social psychology, Erikson's theory is too detailed to be put to broad research use. It simply contains too many variables for our present research skills to handle adequately. Maslow's ideas, however, appear to encompass a major part of the motivational core of Erikson's theory, as well as to approximate the core of other theories. Although Maslow's theory of the hierarchy of needs is sufficiently detailed so that it can account for wide ranges of complex behavior, it is still economical enough to permit careful experimentation. Therefore, although Erikson's theory appears to be the best available for idiographic research, Maslow's theory seems to offer a convenient heuristic with which we can carry out the type of nomothetic research that we rely on in this book. In the next chapter, we argue that this set of common elements provides a way to understand the commonalities among the large number of peripheral motives and traits that have been the subject of so much research.

3 Dimensions of the Person

Research in social psychology deals primarily with the functioning of adults in a complex world of other adults. This focus directs our attention to the wide range of characteristics, acquired in the course of an individual's experience, that seem to have a significant impact on social events. However, as we attempt to coordinate the vast bodies of research on the social effects of the many acquired variables, our immediate problem is to devise an approach that allows us to move beyond the intuitive sense that many variables are similar and, therefore, should be expected to yield parallel social effects. In this chapter, we discuss a way to understand the empirical relationship among acquired motives and traits through an analysis of their possible connection to the primary needs. Our expectation is that if we can discover at least some of the commonalities among some of the most important acquired variables, as well as the features that distinguish them, more of this vast body of research may become much more accessible to many investigators.

As we described earlier, it may be useful to think of acquired motives as different types of adaptational mechanisms that provide some form of satisfaction for a deprived core need. For this purpose, Maslow's ideas about core needs seem to be a convenient heuristic with which we can approximate and summarize the ideas of a wide range of our most keen observers of human behavior. Therefore, we use Maslow's suggestions as a way to make a first-level organization among the many acquired characteristics that have played such an important role in social psychology. In addition, in the more descriptive sections of this and other chapters, we are able to augment our explanations of the psychological contributions to social events with the more detailed set of ideas provided by Erikson's theory.

THE PHYSIOLOGICAL NEEDS

As most theories maintain, the initial requirements of the organism include a set of biological demands that seem essential for survival. It appears that the objects that satisfy this set of needs must be provided or else the process of disease begins. It is not clear if there are acquired characteristics based on the physiological needs, because it appears that the person either gets the necessary food, water, oxygen, and salt or else begins to suffer physical deterioration. For our purposes, in social psychology we gain two simple benefits from a consideration of the biological necessities. First, it seems clear that personality functioning focuses upon these variables whenever these needs are seriously deprived. Second, optimal experience in this area seems to result in certain positive emotional consequences. We return to utilize this apparent emotional gain in the final discussion of this chapter.

PERIPHERAL MOTIVES DERIVED FROM THE NEED
FOR SAFETY

Of all the primary needs, the need for prediction and control has received the most attention in clinical studies and in experimental research. The study of variables such as dependency, anxiety, insecurity, neuroticism, hopelessness, mistrust, or incompetence has made available a rich fund of information on the psychological states that result from the deprivation of this need. In this section, we wish to describe some of the most important mechanisms through which the individual may come to feel some sense of control over his or her actions. As we argued earlier, we believe that the peripheral motives develop as integrated response patterns that serve to reduce the feeling of anxiety by structuring experience in controllable and predictable ways.

Kagan (1972) suggests that negative affective states such as anxiety, fear, shame, and guilt are the consequence of cognitive uncertainty due to the person's inability to predict future events. Such a person feels insecure, anxious, and uncertain and believes that he or she cannot master a situation in a satisfying way. Thus, cognitive misconceptions can lead to the syndrome of withdrawal, passivity, anxiety, and other behavioral correlates of this state. In the behavioral area, Seligman (1975) describes the same form of response with respect to the phenomenon of learned helplessness:

> Laboratory evidence shows that when an organism has experienced trauma it cannot control, its motivation to respond in the face of trauma wanes. Moreover, even if it does respond and the response succeeds in producing relief, it has trouble learning, perceiving, and believing that the response worked. Finally, its emotional balance is disturbed; depression and anxiety, measured in various

ways, predominate. The motivational deficits produced by helplessness are in many ways the most striking. (p. 22)

Seligman found that passivity, withdrawal, lack of competition, and a general lack of response initiation were characteristic consequences of uncontrollability:

> We have seen that a major consequence of experience with uncontrollable events is *motivational:* uncontrollable events undermine the motivation to initiate voluntary responses that control other events. A second major consequence is *cognitive:* once a man or animal has had experience with uncontrollability, he has difficulty *learning* that his response has succeeded, even when it is actually successful. Uncontrollability distorts the perception of control. (p. 37)

Thus, uncontrollability is a major component of the safety-oriented motivational syndrome. Through such experiences, the safety-oriented individual has learned to feel anxious, helpless, inadequate, incompetent, mistrustful, and insecure because his or her response repertoire has not produced effective control of situations. The safety-deprived person stays in a relatively high state of emotional arousal with negative cognitions about the self as agent-in-the-world and negative emotional arousal of anxiety, fear, depression, anger, and hostility.

If the failure to predict events causes anxiety, then this uncertainty gives rise to the search for information (Kagan, 1972) to indicate when a more reliable outcome may occur. In the *safety-signal* hypothesis, Seligman proposes that this anxiety can be moderated by specific stimuli that indicate when danger is present or absent. Seligman provides a great deal of evidence to show that as long as an outcome is predictable, even if the experience is thoroughly unpleasant, the organism can prepare to cope with it and so feel safe.

Kagan's and Seligman's ideas help explain the value to the individual of apparently self-defeating peripheral motives such as self-abasement. Safety-oriented persons have had childhood experiences in which their attempts at dealing with the world are characterized by confusion and uncertainty. In other words, their childhood was characterized by uncontrollability and unpredictability. The development of peripheral motives provides a means to control the anxiety that such experiences produce. Each of the very different motives to be outlined provides both an explanation for events and a set of behaviors for coping with the results of their past traumatic experiences. As long as the coping mechanisms (e.g., the peripheral motives) are working, they will reduce the level of anxiety that is felt. Yet, although the subjectively felt anxiety is controlled at a reduced level, these stable motives do not permanently extinguish the anxiety response because they do not eliminate the past threat upon which the anxiety is based. Thus, the peripheral motives are coping devices that control the anxiety and persist as stable characteristics of personality because they are based on a continually regenerating anxiety-producing mechanism.

There are a variety of ways in which an individual can adapt to the need for safety. Table 3.1 presents four of the most important peripheral motives developed from the need for safety: abasement, dependency, approval, and order. Although it is likely that a person employs more than one of the safety-based motives in social encounters, there may be a predominant motive and behavioral modality that brings a sense of control and predictability while reducing the level of anxiety. A more detailed analysis of these motives could be made, but our goal here is to outline broad differences in the types of coping strategies that can develop.

Abasement

Abasement is the tendency to establish control and prediction of others' actions by self-deprecating maneuvers. Feeling inadequate, inferior, incompetent, unlovable, unworthy, and "sinful," such people appear to atone for their weakness through self-punishment, compliance, and passive surrender, as well as confessions of inadequacy and helplessness. By acting in such a seemingly self-defeating style, the self-abasing person actually attempts to control the degree of pain that he or she experiences, while simultaneously

TABLE 3.1
Peripheral Motives Derived from Safety Needs
(adapted from Murray, 1938)

Peripheral Motive	*Behavioral Definition*
1. Abasement	To blame oneself; to surrender, apologize, confess, atone, comply, and accept punishment.
2. Dependence (succorance)	To seek aid, protection, sympathy, or help.
3. Approval (deference)	To admire, emulate, cooperate with, yield eagerly to, and willingly serve a leader.
4. Order	To structure events through controlling the arrangement of persons and objects, such as:
Rejection	to exclude or ignore others;
Contrarience	to assume a negative or oppositional stance in relation to others;
Acquisition	to work for possessions;
Conservance	to collect, repair, or preserve objects;
Retention	to be miserly in retaining possession of objects.

invoking the sympathy and pity of others. The function of such behavior is to set limits on unpredictability and retain some degree of control over events by forcing a reliable pattern of responding from others.

Dependency

Dependency is another solution to feeling mistrustful, anxious, and insecure. This motive has as its goal the formation of a dependent bond with another person. Dependency is a psychosocial mode in which one passively or actively structures a stable subordinate relationship in order to feel secure, trusting, and calm. Extremely dependent people depend on others to help them "get" and "take" from the world in a predictable and controllable way, and they fear the loss of a powerful protector. Individuals with a strong motive for dependency fear being stranded to simply "get by" on their own. Thus, the safety motive of dependency will manifest itself in fantasy, emotion, and action as the need for union to restore or maintain some form of the basic sense of trust, which makes the world seem manageable.

Approval

Unlike that of dependency, *approval* is characterized by a more active attempt to win the approval of others. Individuals with a strong motive of approval are deferential towards others and are often overly eager to serve, cooperate, and model the actions of those who are admired. Lacking a strong sense of competence, approval-seeking people are doubtful as to their ability to regulate transactions with others adequately. Thus, they are ready to conform, to cooperate with, or to model others as necessary to increase the sense of control and predictability. In large measure, such people believe that by emulating others they will experience the positive consequences of efficacious action. Furthermore, the approval, sanction, or assurance of others informs them that they are properly controlling themselves. Approval from others becomes that external structure that provides the predictable social milieu.

Order

The peripheral safety motive of *order* is characterized as the careful structuring of events by directly imposing order on interpersonal relationships, the self, or the world. Within the different forms of controlling behavior, it is useful to distinguish the special concerns of order from others that we call dominance (self-assertion, mastery, and ascendancy) and discuss later as an esteem need. Order, as a peripheral motive for safety, is typically a rigid, controlling, retentive, and manipulative interpersonal orientation. The individual with a strong safety motive for order perceives that a well-arranged environment and highly structured social situation are necessary to a sense of well-being. Without control over events or the actions of others, they experience anxiety and helplessness. In Eriksonian terms, these individuals tend to "hold on" rather than freely "let go" of thoughts, emotions, and actions. Holding on to well-learned defense and instrumental coping strategies is necessary to feel safe and not anxious. These various strategies, which Murray (1938) labeled the needs for acquisition, conservance, order, retention, rejection, and contrarience, enable the individual to predict the probable outcome of a given situation. In this sense, then, these mechanisms are safety-signals because through them the person has a way to comprehend most social interactions. Thus, there is a special sense of security in having a well-defined social order, which can minimize the degree of unpredictability and uncontrollability.

THE NEED FOR LOVE AND BELONGINGNESS

It is curious that there are very few studies, other than those in the need for affiliation program, that are concerned with issues related to human love and intimacy. This is especially surprising because so much literature, drama, and art have made this problem a central theme. The absence of empirical work not only limits the range of research findings that can be reported later, but also makes it difficult to visualize how such a need is developed into peripheral states. Although our task in distinguishing among peripheral states was relatively easy for the safety and esteem needs, we do not have a wide range of accepted technical terms that may be used for the phenomena of this stage. As a consequence, it is even more important to examine these phenomena carefully and keep our terms in an even more tentative status.

We face many difficult problems in conceptualizing love as a motive. There are phenomena that seem to have all the characteristics of a purposeful pursuit of a distinct class of rewards. There is ample evidence, particularly from the clinical and developmental literature, that when these rewards are denied, behaviors result that have all the characteristics associated with the definition of a neurosis (Maslow, 1965). Conceptually, however, love as a subjective experience appears to be quite different from this goal-oriented phenomenon. This subjective state is associated with people of very different personality structures and is experienced in almost all types of situations. This wide appearance makes it extremely difficult to argue that this is an independent core motive, unless we want to take the position, as others have done with other motives (e.g., Seligman, 1975; White, 1963), that this is *the* single orienting motive. A further complication comes from the fact that there are a wide variety of milder states, such as "interpersonal attraction" or "liking," whose nature seems quite close to love. These milder forms appear in such a wide variety of contexts and intensities that it is very difficult to formulate a satisfactory common definition.

Centers offers several definitions that help to clarify these different types of human response and allow us to sort this experience into different places in our theory. First, Centers (1975) defines love in the following way: "Love on the part of one individual for another is the response or responses evoked in the first individual through his experiencing of rewards, pleasures, or need gratifications as products of his interactions with the other" (p. 45). It is important to recognize that, in this definition, the satisfaction of *any* motive produces a common pleasurable subjective response that is associated with the object that has produced it. Thus, this definition focuses on the pleasurable subjective feeling toward the many people (or objects) who satisfy any of a variety of our needs and thereby separates this response from the specific purposeful seeking of a specific form of a need, which we can also identify as love.

The more limited form of this response, which we may call "interpersonal attraction," is included by Centers under the term "initial attraction." He defines this as the "resultant of the perceived, subceived, imagined or unconsciously anticipated gratifyingness of interaction with the other" (p. 49). The anticipation of the pleasurable response is based on direct experiences of a similar kind that had occurred in the past. In Centers' thinking, the anticipatory pleasure is an unconditioned response associated with people or objects who are the conditioned stimuli. We may set aside the precise type of learning that occurred and simply note that Centers is proposing that, based on one's past history, the expectation of reward evokes an intervening emotional pleasurable response toward that person. This subjective state is felt as attraction.

These emotional responses cover much of what has been isolated in love. If the production of these common pleasurable responses were all that occurred, then there would be no independent status to love as an independent motive. What is missing in Centers' analysis is the part of the phenomena that involves purposeful goal seeking and the behaviors that have been shown to be a consequent of its deprivation. The need for intimate involvements does seem to meet the criteria that we have been using for a separate primary need.

From our reading of the phenomena selected by Maslow and Erikson to illustrate these concerns, we propose that the common issue appears to be a need for *intimacy,* in the sense of fusion of Ego boundaries. The interpersonal referents of the need for intimacy seem to fit the phenomenon called love, and the wider social referents seem to fit the phenomenon called belongingness. To the extent that an individual experienced difficulty in loving relationships, a deprivation state in the area of intimacy is created. This state produces anxiety, as with the safety needs, which leads to the development of coping mechanisms to reduce the anxiety. The specific content of the anxiety states associated with the deprivation of this need centers on difficulties with intimacy. The individual feels lonely, without friends, family, or lovers, or alienated, without roots in a community that has importance to him or her.

There seem to be a variety of ways for individuals to cope with these states. In general, we notice strategies of interpersonal relationship that permit the individual to be included, or to participate, in the lives of others without risking the vulnerability of fusion of identity. For this general desire, we are temporarily using the term "inclusion." Table 3.2 summarizes the types of behaviors that seem associated with this general motive.

We have identified six major modes of achieving some measure of intimacy which appear to be at the level of the other peripheral motives. The first mode refers to the person who finds participation through passively joining the activities of the group. Such a person wants to be included, achieves it by compliance with the requests made upon him or her, makes no direct emotional demands, and gives no intimacy to others. In the second mode, the person earns the right of participation by overestimating the worth of other members and relates to them through admiration and flattery. This behavior creates distance between people, which protects him or her from the demands of true intimacy. A third form allows the person to participate actively in interpersonal relationships by entertaining others. By providing a means to relieve group tensions through clowning, a nondemanding form of acceptance is achieved. In the fourth type of activity, the person earns membership by offering him- or herself to be the butt of the group's activities. In other

TABLE 3.2
Peripheral Motive Derived from Love and Belongingness Needs

Peripheral Motive	*Behavioral Definition*
Inclusion	To participate in the lives of others through:
	a. passive compliance;
	b. overestimation and flattery of others' virtues;
	c. being entertaining;
	d. being a scapegoat;
	e. provoking others to test the limits of their tolerance;
	f. pledging fidelity to an abstract concept of the group.

words, such a person relieves tensions by becoming the scapegoat of the group. This concern is different from the peripheral characteristic of self-abasement in that, although a desire to be hurt is held in common, in this case it operates to yield a sense of membership, not to provide a reduction of uncertainty. The fifth concern for affection from others manifests itself by testing the limits of other people's tolerance of aversive behavior. This peripheral motive is the desire to annoy so that others will have to give demonstrations of their level of concern. The last peripheral motive is the investment of self in an abstract concept of the group. Through pledging fidelity to the nonpersonal aspect of a group, this individual is able to avoid the personal aspect of intimacy and still achieve membership in a wider entity. Whatever the variant, inclusion is most fundamentally an attempt to find some guarded form of involvement with others so that some degree of intimacy can be achieved.

PERIPHERAL MOTIVES DERIVED FROM THE NEED FOR ESTEEM

With sufficient gratification of the needs for safety and intimacy, the esteem motive then emerges more fully. When this striving toward greater competence is frustrated, a state of anxiety develops because a sufficient degree of self-worth has not been attained. The peripheral motives that develop around this primary need are also different types of coping strategies through which an individual seeks partial gratification. As with the earlier levels of core needs, the peripheral motives, although successful in reducing the level of perceived anxiety, never prove successful in removing the deprivation. In this way, these coping strategies can provide some degree of gratification and yet remain stable elements of personality because the source of anxiety is not removed.

As with the need for safety and intimacy, there is great variability in the ways individuals strive for partial satisfaction of esteem needs. Table 3.3 presents the definitions of four of the major peripheral motives developed from the need for esteem: recognition, dominance, nurturance, and achievement. Although each of these peripheral motives varies somewhat in form, interpersonal manifestation, and expressiveness, they are all concerned with establishing or maintaining a strong degree of positive self-evaluation.

Recognition

This is an attempt to achieve respect by focusing the attention of others on those deeds which the individual believes to be meritorious, important, and significant. The striving for *recognition* can include exhibitionistic acts of self-dramatization and the seeking of honors, fame, or glory, as well as at-

TABLE 3.3
Peripheral Motives Derived from Esteem Needs
(adapted from Murray, 1938)

Peripheral Motive	Behavioral Definition
1. Recognition	To attempt to command respect by drawing the attention of others to one's actions, through the seeking of honors, or by succeeding at extremely difficult feats.
2. Dominance	To establish one's worth by controlling, persuading, dictating, and directing others.
3. Nurturance (generativity)	To establish and maintain one's sense of worth by responsibly caring for the development of persons, generations, and institutions, as well as the quality and significance of achievements and products.
4. Achievement	To be competitive in meeting standards of excellence across a wide range of transactions with the world.

tempts to succeed at monumental projects. The individual displays this activity in order to receive recognition for competence as the maker of thoughts, products, emotions, or actions worthy of respect. Initially, the individual achieves these judgments through the recognition that others give to the value of his or her efforts. Such confirmation of attempts at being efficacious, whether by boasting, fantasy, or hard work, yield some subjective sense of competence. Only later, when there is realistic self-appreciation and congruence between aspirations and ability, will the individual be able to make personal self-evaluations.

Dominance

The esteem motive of *dominance,* as distinct from the safety motive of order, is primarily an attempt to establish one's sense of worth by being a persuasive, effective leader who directs the actions of others. Such individuals are assertive in interpersonal transactions because they want their actions to have an impact on the other members of their group. The dominance motive often centers around the goal of creating a hierarchy in social relations so that the individual gains respect as the person who makes particular events occur. Stated simply, dominance is a concern for a skillful display of interpersonal activity through which the individual controls and directs others in order to verify his or her own sense of worth. Much of what Winter (1973) describes as the need for power can be included under this definition.

Nurturance

Dominance and recognition hold in common the establishment of self-respect through interpersonal influence either directly by initiating structure and leading others or by winning accolades through individualistic actions of various kinds. *Nurturance,* on the other hand, is an esteem motive concerned with establishing or maintaining a sense of self-worth by responsibly caring for the development and well-being of persons, institutions, and generations, as well as the quality and significance of one's products. This definition includes all that Erikson subsumes under the term "generativity."

However, it is important to distinguish nurturance as a motive from nurturance as a behavior. For example, although most parents nurture their children, the motivation for such activity may vary greatly from parent to parent: One can nurture to feel secure sexually, to satisfy dependency needs, or to develop a clear identity. Nurturance, as an esteem motive, means that one wishes that the object of caring will mature in the fullest possible way. Nurturance is therefore mutual in nature; being generative enhances the self-esteem of the object and the agent, and it incorporates a more inclusive social perspective that recognizes the complexity of persons, roles, situations, and emotions.

Achievement

The striving for esteem gratification may also occur outside the realm of interpersonal activity. *Achievement,* as an esteem need, refers to the desire to be broadly efficacious in meeting standards of excellence across a wide range of transactions with the world (McClelland, Atkinson, Clark, & Lowell, 1953). One may gain a sense of self-respect by being better than another at a task, as well as by undertaking difficult feats in mastering the environment or constructing objects to make life easier. This motive includes achievement motivation of various types in which the individual attempts to meet personal goals. In large measure, it is the competition with a standard of excellence that differentiates this esteem motive from the others, with a sense of satisfaction gained when the standard has been reached.

PERIPHERAL TRAITS DEVELOPED FROM PRIMARY NEEDS

A trait can be understood to be a compound of internal elements, such as motives, cognitive structures, beliefs, values, and emotions. To this point we have concentrated on the transformation of the core motivational factors, through experience, into peripheral motives. Although we might speculate that traits are organized structurally around dominant motivational factors or that their cognitive and emotional elements are simply associated with the motivational factors because of a shared set of childhood experiences, the empirical fact is that traits fall into the same set of clusters as motives do (see Wilson & Aronoff, 1984). Earlier we argued that different components of a complex trait might make the individual responsive to different aspects of a situation. Therefore, before reviewing the clustering of traits, we need to outline briefly the type of cognitive and emotional variables that appear to be involved.

Each type of variable is of such significance that it deserves major treatment in itself. Such presentations do exist, and we cite some of the works that have been most helpful to us. Here, we wish only to indicate, in a general way, how we have found it useful to think about these variables.

Cognitive Structure.   One aspect of the cognitive system has had a good deal of influence in the study of individual functioning in social contexts. The dimension of simplicity–complexity of the cognitive structure has been studied intensively (e.g., Harvey, Hunt, & Schroder, 1961) and has found many direct applications in social psychology in the areas of group structure, process, and behavior (see Tuckman, 1964, 1967, as good examples of this theory's use). Basically, this dimension is seen as increasingly integrated information-processing structures, ranging from concrete structures that process incoming information in a simple way to highly differentiated abstract structures that are able to perform multiple operations. From the point of view of traits, it is likely that this structural dimension underlies Rokeach's (1960) dogmatism variable, Cattell's (1957) Conservative versus Experimenting factor, or Gough's (1964) Suggestible–Original dimension.

Strength of Cognitive Control.   In the psychoanalytic tradition, the Ego is presented not only as a set of manipulable means–ends connections, but also as a set of internal control structures that regulate and evaluate incoming stimuli, direct motor behavior, and control the perception and the expression of emotion. Although the description of this structure emerged from the clinical literature under the term "ego strength," an examination of these functions shows how easily direct connections can be made to those processes studied by experimental psychologists. These structures, then, possibly created through the same experiences that shape the peripheral motives, are likely the control structures underlying a wide variety of traits such as impulsive, inhibited, obsessive, foresightful, flexible, or calm.

Schemata, Beliefs, Expectancies, and Values.   The aspects of the cognitive system just discussed focus mainly on the strength and organizational arrangements between the cognitive elements. The specific content of these elements is a third aspect of the cognitive system that appears to be related to traits. Most generally, these can be thought of as cognitive schemata that organize perception, cognition, and behavior (Cantor & Kihlstrom, 1981). These schemata provide the categories that are available for perception and are beliefs about the likelihood of success of a behavioral response or the appropriateness of a response in a particular situation. For example, a trait such as mistrust contains cognitive categories of types of people that may be encountered, estimates of confidence in the pursuit of goals, and specific sets of actions that may be least unfavorable.

Rotter's (1966) description of the dimension of internal–external locus of control is a useful example of the possible involvement of all three of these types of cognitive elements in a complex trait. Rotter defines this variable as the extent to which individuals *believe* that events in their lives are either under their personal control or determined by external forces. If we were to follow Rotter's definition, this dimension would be thought of as a specific type of cognitive schema. Although beliefs do seem to be present, given the impressive array of social variables that the dimension of internality–externality controls (Lefcourt, 1976a), it is likely that the degree of abstractness as well as the strength of schemata (or control structure) are involved as well. One of the psychosocial "strengths" achieved with the successful resolution of early stages, as seen by theorists such as Erikson and Maslow, is precisely the formation of these kinds of field-independent control structures. If the level of control structure develops through the same experiences that affect core needs and create specific beliefs, then we can easily integrate what is meant by such diverse constructs as autonomy, origin-pawn (de Charms, 1968), and internal–external locus of control, and we can understand why they all follow the same correlational pattern that underlies peripheral motives.

For our purposes, much of what is studied under the heading of *values* can be understood from the same cognitive point of view as Rotter's work on the locus of control. Rokeach (1968) in an intensive study of values, sees them as comprised of beliefs about the desirable or preferable. He writes, "To say a person has a value is to say that he has an enduring belief that a specific mode of conduct or end-state of existence is personally or socially preferable to alternative modes of conduct or end-states of existence" (p. 100). This relatively clear definition, which sees values as cognitive representations of criteria for evaluating behavior, as internal commands that certain classes of behavior must or must not be taken, is fairly widely shared (e.g., Williams, 1968). Because the set of values studied by Rokeach also falls into the same correlational pattern as the peripheral motives, it is easy to see them as the cognitive representations of the experiences that affect the core needs in the course of development. For example, the difficult childhood experiences that lead to the creation of a dependency motive correlate positively with values such as "salvation" or "national security" and inversely with values such as "ambitious" or "courageous" (Rokeach, 1973).

A more wide-ranging point of view, such as Kohlberg's (1969) theory of moral development, focusing on the organization among cognitive elements, fits easily into a theory of schemata. But unlike Rotter's constructs, it is not yet clear if this much more complex theory is equally isomorphic with our proposals (see Green & Haymes, 1977; Ward & Wilson, 1980, for different opinions on this problem). Empirically, however, safety-oriented people often show lower levels of moral development than do esteem-oriented people. Therefore, we limit our consideration of values to the level of analysis as represented in Rokeach's work.

Tables 3.4, 3.5, and 3.6 present a conceptual sorting of many of the traits and behavioral styles that we found in the research literature. This typology is organized around the dominant motivational level that we believe determines their appearance in social behavior. As there are far too many traits mentioned in the literature, with much overlap between them, we are not able to discuss each one individually. Although the basic factor structure underlying them is presently being studied quite actively (see Hogan, 1982; Wiggins, 1973, 1980), the conclusive empirical work has not yet been completed. Moreover, not all of these traits have been used in social psychological research. Therefore, these tables present a best guess, based on the simple dictionary definition of the terms, as to how the clustering among the traits should fall.

It is unclear if we can distinguish between traits associated with physiological and safety needs. For the physiological needs, the trait correlates *might* include characteristics such as low affect, lethargy, and despondency or character traits such as unenergetic, listless, tired, weak, inability to concentrate, and poor ego functioning. Conceptually, however, these appear to be part of the helplessness syndrome as described by Seligman, and so might as easily be thought of as part of the safety-need complex.

For the safety-oriented individual, the typical affective state is often characterized by high degrees of anxiety, shyness, tension, worriedness, and depression. The personal attributes include a large number of traits such as: sobriety, silence, detachment, dependency, reserve, conformity, externality, approval-seeking, abasement, deference, group dependency, retentive hoarding, obedience, acquiescence, overcontrol, insecurity, inefficaciousness, incompetence, clinging, suspicion, mistrust, and so forth. In terms of the typical modality of cognitive functioning, such individuals tend to be rigid, constricted, anti-intraceptive, and inconsistent, with the political matrix of the belief system generally appearing to be authoritarian, dogmatic, ethnocentric, and conservative.

Associated with the core tendency of intimacy, we find that the typical affective state is one of emotional sensitivity and lability, with the personal

TABLE 3.4
Traits Derived from Safety Needs

Theorist/Author, Reference, Test, Trait Characteristics

Adler (1956)
Inferiority, insecurity

Adorno, Frenkel-Brunswik, Levinson, & Stanford (1950), F-Scale
Obedient, status-oriented, hostile, anxious, rigid, suspicious, intolerant of ambiguity, anti-intraceptive, submissive to authority

Bales (1979), SYMLOG
Authoritarian, abasing, hostile, order, isolated, anti-authority, approval seeking, submissive, conforming, anxious, tense

Cattell (1970), 16PF
Reserved, detached, emotional lability, submissive, dependent, introspective, indolent, withdrawn, anxious, dogmatic, approval seeking, anxious, conservative, concurrent, joiner, tense

Erikson (1982)
Mistrust, passive, dependent, guilt, anxious, shame, overcontrol, withdrawn, inferiority, conforming, isolation, despair, stagnation

Freud (see Fenichel, 1945)
Passive, envy, pessimism, self-belittlement, rigid, overcontrol, punctual, precise, meticulous, self-hatred, isolated, timid, plainness, suspicious

Fromm (1947)
Passive, submissive, servile, cowardly, gullible, sentimental, egocentric, rash, arrogant, seducing, exploitative, hoarding, indolent, inert, pedantic, obsessive, cold, childish, conforming

Gough (1964), CPI
Inhibited, avoidance, shy, apathetic, restricted, passive, suggestible, uncertain, self-abasing, cautious, awkward, lazy, impulsive, stubborn, wary, aloof, mistrust, inhibited, disorderly, insecure, submissive, shallow, conforming, methodical, dependent, passive

Rokeach (1960) D-Scale
Dogmatism, anxiety

Rokeach (1968) Value Survey
National security, salvation, clean obedient, polite, family security, forgiving, self-control

Rotter (1966), I-E Scale
External locus of control

Schutz (1967) FIRO-B
Need for control

Shostrom (1963) POI
Time incompetence, other-directed, low self-regard, low spontaneity

TABLE 3.5
Traits Derived from Love and Belongingness Needs

Theorist/Author, Reference, Test, Trait Characteristics

Bales (1979), SYMLOG
Warm, positive, friendly, expressive,
cooperative, loyal, affiliative

Cattell (1970), 16PF
Outgoing, warm hearted, participative,
conscientious, adventurous

Erikson (1982)
Intrusive and inclusive modes of interpersonal
behavior, jealousy, group membership, and identification

Fromm (1947)
Need for rootedness, love

Gough (1964), CPI
Sociable, amiable

Hogan (1975), Empathy Scale
Empathic

Rokeach (1968), Value Survey
Helpful, mature love, true friendship, loving

Schutz (1967), FIRO-B
Love, intimate, emotional closeness, hate, cool,
reject, associate, interact, mingle, belong,
member, join, lonely, outcast

characteristics including conformity, loyalty, amiability, other directedness, gregariousness, and jealousy. As we pointed out in our discussion of peripheral motives associated with this level, it is noteworthy that the list of traits potentially involved is significantly shorter than those at other levels.

The esteem-oriented person, in contrast to the safety-oriented individual, is generally characterized with sets of what are usually seen as positive affective attributes. These people tend to be calm, relaxed, happy, serene, and emotionally stable, as well as more exuberant and spontaneous, with demonstrable expressions of pleasure, optimism, and excitement. The esteem-oriented person may be described as autonomous, competent, forthright, placid, confident, brash, self-reliant, boastful, independent, self-supportive, responsible, assertive, dominant, achieving, constructive, tolerant, accepting, having internal locus of control, inner-directed, mature, bold, self-

TABLE 3.6
Traits Derived from Esteem Needs

Theorist/Author, Reference, Test, Trait Characteristics

Adler (1956)
Superiority

Adorno, Frenkel-Brunswik, Levinson, & Stanford (1950), F-Scale
Independent, democratic, flexible, tolerant of ambiguity, open-minded

Allport (1961)
Self-esteem

Bales (1979), SYMLOG
Dominant, achievement-oriented, nurturant, recognition

Cattell (1970), 16PF
Participative, outgoing, calm, stable, assertive, expressive, alert, conscientious, adventurous, self-reliant, flexible, insightful, self-confident, self-willed, relaxed

Christie and Geis (1970), Mach V
Machiavellianism

Erikson (1982)
Trust, active, autonomy, integrity, self-reliance, initiative, assertive, competence, self-confident, generative, intimacy, integrity, identity

Freud (see Fenichel, 1945)
Optimistic, brash, vanity, pride, courage, genitality

Fromm (1947)
Active, assertive, accepting, adaptable, trusting, idealistic, self-confident, practical, patient, tenacious, purposeful, efficient

Gough (1964), CPI
Confident, persistent, assertive, initiative, ambition, active, resourceful, outgoing, enterprising, original, enthusiastic, ebullient, sharpwitted, self-accepting, versatile, productive, capable, dependable, serious, industrious, honest, patient, tolerant, diligent, cooperative, dependable, organized, dominant, progressive, alert, psychological minded, adventurous, appreciative, gentle

Rokeach (1960), D-Scale
Open-minded

Rokeach (1968), Value Survey
Sense of accomplishment, independent, capable, self-respect, courageous, exciting life, responsible, inner harmony, equality, broadminded, ambitious, freedom, cheerful, imagination, wisdom, world beauty

Rotter (1966), I-E Scale
Internal locus of control

Shostrom (1963), POI
Time competence, inner-directed, self-actualization, acceptance of self and others, spontaneity

dramatizing, adventuresome, warm, outgoing, competitive, realistic, self-reliant, experimenting, spontaneous, consistent, flexible, democratic, imaginative, liberal, intraceptive, or psychologically minded.

Reviewing this large set of "positive" qualities in the light of the psychosocial strengths achieved by the successful resolution of the esteem-need stage, it is useful to distinguish between these and other traits that are associated with a *need* for esteem concern. Thus, traits from this list such as brashness, boastfulness, competitiveness, or self-dramatization seem to have the quality of seeking esteem reinforcements, whereas the balance seem to be cognitive and emotional characteristics of those whose esteem needs have been satisfied.

CONCEPTIONS OF PSYCHOSOCIAL MATURITY

Every personality theorist, as well as every psychologically minded person, at some point wonders what we would be like if all had gone well in our lifetime. Although most work in psychology deals with coping devices of some sort, there are many conceptions of psychological health available that allow us to complete our model of the influence of personality on the social process. This ideal conception of health is valuable for theoretical reasons, and it is even more helpful in understanding the social effects produced by those real individuals who do seem to share in *many* of these characteristics.

Interestingly, although the background of those writing about psychological health is widely different, the psychological portraits of the healthy person share many features. Offer & Sabshin (1974) and Maddi (1976), summarizing this extensive literature, present a series of parallel descriptions of this psychological state. For example, Freud thought of the psychologically healthy individual as possessing the ability to "love and work productively." By this seemingly simple definition, Freud meant that an individual could maintain mutually satisfying intimate relations and could work productively in a career unhampered by neurotic conflicts or unresolved past emotional problems. Other psychoanalytically oriented theorists would characterize psychological health in similar ways. Fromm conceived of psychological health as the productive orientation formed by the attributes of trust, flexibility, open-mindedness, respect for others, and a humanistic value orientation. Jung characterized the achievement of selfhood as the unity and balance of all the dimensions of the personality structure. Adler and White both characterized psychological health as active mastery, competence, and the striving toward effective self-esteem. Neo-Freudians, such as Horney, characterized mental well-being as the congruence between the ideal and real self, with rational thinking produced by the absence of debilitating ego defenses. In the idiographic tradition, Allport, in an unusually clear presentation, characterized the healthy individual as having extension of ego boundaries, good interpersonal relations, emotional stability, accurate self-perception and self-acceptance, problem centering, humor, and objectivity, as well as a uniform philosophy of life. In her comprehensive review of the mental health literature, Jahoda included such characteristics as positive self-concept, continued growth of basic organismic processes, integration of personality, autonomy, accurate perception of reality, and environmental mastery. The correspondence among the characteristics of the psychologically mature person, as seen by the early personality theorists, is remarkably close.

A more contemporary developmental perspective on psychological maturity is found in the work of Kohlberg (1973). Although he did not write a theory of personality per se, Kohlberg's (1969; 1971) conceptualization of moral stages as a developmental sequence of greater cognitive complexity is useful because his description of the postconventional stages centers around the concern for universal moral principles. This final cognitive stage includes the value orientations of respect for individual dignity and integrity, equality and universal justice, acceptance of individual differences, and the struggle to be consistently moral.

Of all the portraits of the psychologically healthy person, perhaps none is as comprehensive as Maslow's (1970). This should not be surprising, because much of his career was spent trying to understand mental health and its relation to the need hierarchy. As we saw earlier, his views incorporate most of the attributes that appear in more limited form in other theorists' writings. Table 3.7 presents the 15 major characteristics that Maslow (1968, 1970) thought to characterize the self-actualizing person and indicates their correspondence to other theorists' views of psychological maturity.

Maslow's description of self-actualization has often been criticized as merely reflecting his own value system or as being an artifact of the way his subjects were selected (e.g., Smith, 1969). From a developmental perspective, however, it is not difficult to determine that these characteristics *necessarily* follow a successful childhood: Some of these characteristics reflect the absence of defensive attempts at lower need gratification, whereas others are the psychological outcome of successful experience at each stage of life.

We noted earlier that Maslow's view of self-actualization as the final stage in the need hierarchy seemed to call for an unnecessary additional motivational level. A more parsimonious way of conceptualizing self-actualization is provided by Erikson's (1964, 1968) idea that optimum experiences at a stage produce sets of characteristics that are the basis of health for that and later stages. Thus, an alternative way of accounting for the characteristics that Maslow describes as "suddenly" emerging in the state of self-actualization is achieved by noting the results of successful experiences at each of the earlier stages within his hierarchy. From this point of view, these characteristics accumulate to provide virtually all the psychological attributes that define the hypothesized state of self-actualization.

In Tabel 3.8, we once again list the psychosocial crises that, to Erikson, are the psychological issues to be resolved at each stage. In a subsequent essay, Erikson (1964) speculated about an additional set of psychological strengths that are achieved with the successful resolution of each stage. To Erikson, these ideas were phrased tentatively as a preliminary survey of a new dimension of the Ego. Although the exact conceptual status of these variables is unclear in his writing, we can use them simply as additional aspects of the achievements of successful experience at each of the stages of life. Table 3.8 presents the definitions that Erikson gives for each of these additional characteristics.

As we argued in chapter 2, Maslow's theory can be seen as a simplification of the major core need propositions outlined by Erikson. This allows us to simplify our presentation of the psychological gains achieved at each stage of organizing our analysis in terms of Maslow's stages. We assume that greater attention to the richness of Erikson's discussion of the events at each stage will amplify our presentation of how these characteristics are achieved. Here we only wish to outline a way to think about the sequences of psychological development. Although the following discussion is phrased on the theoretical level, it is based on the widespread study of the origins of psychological competence. Works such as Coopersmith (1967), Stollak (1978), White and Watts (1973), Block (1971), Murphy and Moriarity (1976), Ainsworth and Bell (1974), and Yarrow, Rubenstein, and Pedersen (1975) present or summarize much of the research that has accumulated to date. Although the focus of most present studies has been on the early years of life, their success has stimulated much of the research needed to complete the empirical picture throughout the life span.

Physiological Needs

When the basic forms of physiological gratification are provided, a bodily sense of well-being results. The comfort, satiation, quiescience, and sense of fullness at having met these needs are cognitively perceived as a state of pleasantness and well-being. The most basic sense of trust in one's own body is derived from these experiences. Illness, injury, chronic or acute deprivation trigger an awareness that something is awry. In the phenomenon of "self-actualization," the individual is acutely aware of internal states and actively seeks to maintain good health and optimal physiological well-being. This can only come about when there is the sense that one is a well-functioning organism.

Safety Needs

For the majority of the psychological functions that characterize self-actualization, such as a nondistorting perception or an ability to see new

TABLE 3.7

Parallels Between Maslow's Description of the Characteristics of Self-Actualization and Conceptions of Psychological Maturity in Selected Theoretical Works

Characteristics of Self-Actualization	Selected Personality Theorists										
	Adler	Allport	Angyal	Erikson	Freud	Fromm	Jahoda	Jung	Kohlberg	Rogers	White
1. More efficient perception of reality	X	X	X	X	X	X	X	X	X	X	X
2. Acceptance of self, others, and nature	X	X	X	X	X	X	X	X	?	X	X
3. Spontaneity, simplicity, naturalness		X		X	X	X			X	X	
4. Problem-centering		X		X					X	X	
5. The quality of detachment; the need for privacy							X				
6. Autonomy from culture; will, active agency	X	X	X	X	X	X	X	X	X	X	X
7. Continued freshness of appreciation										X	
8. The mystical experience; the peak experience				X				X		X	
9. Gemeinschaftgefuhl (social interest)	X	X							X	X	

10. Close interpersonal relations	X		X		X			X
11. Democratic character structure	X		X			X		X
12. Discrimination between means and ends; between good and evil	X					X		X
13. Philosophical, nonhostile sense of humor				X				
14. Creativeness	X		X	?	X	X		X
15. Resistance to enculturation; transcendence of culture				X	X		?	X

TABLE 3.8
Erikson's Conceptualization of the Development of Ego Strength

Psychosocial Crisis	Ego Strength	Definition of Stage-Specific Ego Strength
Trust vs. Mistrust	Hope	The enduring belief in the attainability of fervent wishes, in spite of the dark urges and rages that mark the beginning of existence.
Autonomy vs. Shame and Doubt	Will	The unbroken determination to exercise free choice as well as self-restraint, in spite of the inevitable experience of shame and doubt in infancy.
Initiative vs. Guilt	Purpose	The courage to envisage and pursue valued goals uninhibited by the defeat of infantile fantasies, by guilt, and by the foiling fear of punishment.
Industry vs. Inferiority	Competence	The free exercise of dexterity and intelligence in the completion of tasks, unimpaired by infantile inferiority.
Identity vs. Role Confusion	Fidelity	The ability to sustain loyalties freely pledged in spite of the inevitable contradictions of value systems.
Intimacy vs. Isolation	Love	The mutuality of devotion forever subduing the antagonisms inherent in divided function.
Generativity vs. Stagnation	Care	The widening concern for what has been generated by love, necessity, or accident; it overcomes the ambivalence adhering to irreversible obligation.
Integrity vs. Despair	Wisdom	The detached concern with life itself, in the face of death itself.

forms in old configurations, it is essential to attain the attributes described by Erikson's first three stages. A basic sense of trust, an ability to be apart from the flux of impressions (autonomy), or the capacity to understand that the person can control events is a prerequisite for not defending oneself against that which is not already known. Possessing these strengths permits the free perceptual, cognitive, and emotional exploration that is the core of what was called self-actualized functioning. Erikson's description of the ego strengths of hope, will, and purpose is an enriched elaboration of the meaning of prediction and control, as defined by Seligman. These ego strengths are not merely phenomenological descriptions, but rather the postulation of increasingly strong internal control structures to protect and direct the individual's experience with social stimuli.

Love and Belongingness Needs

Another major element in the description of self-actualization centers around the quality of interpersonal relations. A characteristic such as democratic character structure is a good example of an element of the self-actualizing syndrome that has been criticized for being based on Maslow's own value system (e.g., Smith, 1969). However, from a developmental perspective, if individuals are able to commit themselves to close relations with others, to become understanding and accepting of those with whom they are involved, then the psychological outcome is to believe that others have similar and equal value. Thus, a democratic character structure is hardly a reflection of the cultural values of the period in which Maslow was writing; rather, it is probably one of necessary social psychological consequences of successful intimacy relationships.

Self-Esteem Needs

When people are actively concerned with demonstrating their competence, they may be able to understand others and society as Kohlberg describes for the later stages of moral development, or instead they may use this ability behaviorally to dominate, manipulate, or misuse others to achieve a stronger sense of self-worth. However, when people have been efficacious in their transactions with the world, they reach the point where there is the realistic determination of their abilities, limitations, and potentialities. From these should come a broadly based sense of competence that will allow them to cope successfully with, and be able to enjoy, interpersonal relationships, personal emotional states, and social events. With a firm sense of self-worth, there is no need to control, manipulate, or belittle others. The last features of Erikson's stages—the psychosocial strengths of generativity, care, integrity, and wisdom—are based on this self-assurance and support the final range of abilities that describe self-actualized functioning. Capacities such as problem-centering, detachment from social influences, nonhostile humor, and a greater concern for justice are based on not only an absence of defensive attempts at gratification but the free-ranging cognitive abilities that are the logical outcomes of a strong sense of personal growth.

It is interesting that although the definition of psychological health was debated rather unproductively, nevertheless, experimental psychologists actively explored the social consequences of many of the attributes that are used consistently to define this state. Throughout the book, we examine serious programs of research by experimental psychologists that bear directly on the point of view we have just outlined. This permits us to move directly from the hypotheses outlined in Table 3.7 to review extensive programs of empirical work. For example, there has been intense experimental effort to understand such phenomena as the psychological bases for distortions in person perception, inefficiencies in information processing, misuses of leadership, inability to cooperate, difficulties in negotiation, or nonproductivity of groups. In each case, the social psychologist is usually interested in discovering the bases for more accurate social cognition, more capable leadership or membership, more harmonious forms of conflict resolution, or greater productivity of groups. The theoretical exploration that we have just reviewed forms part of an implicit system of explanation that has been widely shared. We hope to show how much these research programs may benefit from a more explicit personological point of view to permit apparently separate programs of work to be used to evaluate or support each other, as well as to generate a wider range of hypotheses about the ways people function in social contexts.

PERSONOLOGICAL ELEMENTS FOR A THEORY OF INTERACTIONS

The material reviewed in this chapter permits us to conclude our discussion of the first of the major elements needed for a theory of interactions. In the next chapter, we provide a similar analysis of the social situation, and we are then in a position to propose a model of person-by-situation interactions. Inasmuch as it would be totally unwieldy to discuss the interaction of all the personality variables in combination with all the social variables, we have identified 11 variables that appear to have interesting, contrasting, and important social consequences. In our theoretical and empirical discussions, we use these 11 variables to develop and evaluate a model of interactions. Brief definitions of these variables, shaped to help explore specific hypotheses about their social consequences, are offered in Table 3.9.

These 11 variables are taken almost entirely from the taxonomy of personality variables published in Murray's *Explorations in Personality* (1938). We

TABLE 3.9
Definitions of Selected Peripheral Variables that Affect the Social Process
(adapted primarily from Murray, 1938)

Dependency	The need to defend against anxiety by establishing predictable social transactions through constructing a care-receiving relationship with another person.
Abasement	The need to defend against anxiety by constructing self-deprecating and self-defeating modes of interaction with other people.
Approval	The need to defend against anxiety by constructing a deferential, participative, and admiring relationship with a protective superior.
Authoritarianism	The complex trait that defends against anxiety through the characteristics of conventional values, hostility, stereotyping, antidemocratic attitudes, strong defenses against intraception, and a submissive, uncritical attitude toward authority.
Order	The need to defend against anxiety by actively organizing tasks and social transactions in precise and detailed ways.
Affiliation	The need to establish intimate egalitarian involvements with another person in mutually satisfying social transactions.
Machiavellianism	A complex trait that achieves a sense of self-worth through constructing amoral, manipulative, opportunistic, and exploitative modes of interpersonal transactions.
Dominance	The need to establish self-worth through demonstrations of directing, influencing, and persuading others.
Nurturance	The need to establish self-worth by responsibly caring for the successful development of persons, generations, and institutions.
Achievement	The need to establish self-worth through successful competition with standards of excellence in the pursuit of task-oriented activity.
Recognition	The need to establish self-worth through personal displays that gain admiration, respect, praise, and prestige from others.

selected illustrative variables from this work primarily to ground this aspect of our presentation in the strength of the seminal contributions of the remarkable team headed by Murray. In several cases we felt that, based on the empirical work stimulated by Murray's book, we could add a bit more to their definitions. In the case of the need for nurturance, we felt that it would be helpful to orient the definition more toward Erikson's (1963) concept of generativity in place of the more behavioral description provided by Murray. This allowed us to sharpen the motivational underpinnings of the construct. Finally, we included two broad traits, one from each cluster, that have been identified since Murray's book was published. Each of these traits— *authoritarianism* (Adorno et al., 1950) and *Machiavellianism* (Christie & Geis, 1970)—has stimulated major research efforts that have resulted in substantial bodies of important empirical findings.

In general, these variables are similar to those discussed earlier in the chapter. The need for affiliation presents problems because the empirical literature does not provide a set of peripheral states, with well-understood social effects, for this hypothesized primary need. Until that is accomplished, we use a global affiliation construct. In the later substantitive chapters, when appropriate research is available, we discuss the social effects of the broader set of personality variables associated with each cluster, such as anxiety, dogmatism, the need for power, or internal–external locus of control. However, we expect the set of theoretical propositions that we present for the 11 illustrative variables to allow us to integrate the interactional patterns of other variables without too much difficulty.

The measurement of these variables presents a separate problem. In the case of dependency, authoritarianism, Machiavellianism, dominance, and achievement, the available instruments are sufficiently robust to give confidence in the results of studies using them. In the case of abasement, order, affiliation, nurturance, and recognition, the existing instruments are either less validated or multidimensional. Results from studies using such instruments must be evaluated cautiously in light of the total context of any particular experiment. However, the importance of the constructs is clear, and theoretical efforts can proceed with the hope that they will stimulate the needed psychometric work. The need for approval presents a special case. The correlational pattern associated with this variable, since it was introduced by Crowne and Marlowe (1964), occasionally is not congruent with the definition of the construct. Because Murray's description of the related construct of deference is both clear and meaningful, we use it as the basis for the definition of the need for approval; we also rely, as well, on a variety of less well-established instruments to explore its social effects.

4 Dimensions of the Situation

The wide divergence among the classifications of the social environment has severely hindered efforts to develop a model of interactional processes (Endler & Magnusson, 1976; Magnusson & Endler, 1977). Category schemes range from those that lump social phenomena on the basis of the most inclusive principles to those that divide them on the basis of the narrowest difference. Category schemes also originate from the most diverse methods such as free-response descriptions, checklist observational judgments, and factor analytic examinations of many types of responses. Our approach is simpler. We derive the elements of our classification system from the major features of the situation that have been shown to be important in decades of intense experimental work in social psychology. For example, social psychologists have often found it necessary to isolate a similar variable, such as task complexity or social status, to explain the nature of their results in areas as diverse as information processing, persuasion, prosocial behavior, conflict resolution, or group productivity. This approach to deriving a category system for the social situation has the added advantage of allowing us to know in advance that the elements included indeed have serious social consequences.

In this chapter, we present the situational, task, and group structural characteristics of the environment (as identified by research programs in social psychology). When it seems necessary, we organize the discussion into subcategories to make distinctions among environmental factors that lead to important differences in the resulting pattern of behavior.

SITUATIONAL VARIABLES

Situational variables refer to all those characteristics of the objects and people with whom we interact. To help tease out important separate effects, it is useful to distinguish between physical and personal characteristics of the situation. The major forms of each of the physical and personal variables are listed in Table 4.1. Let us consider each in turn.

Physical Attributes

Physical attributes refer to the state of the nonhuman material elements of the situation, such as the temperature, hour, locality, noise level, density of population, and the resources (money, equipment, food, etc.) needed to complete the task. These variables often seem to have their greatest impact on people as stressors that make working in that situation more frightening, painful, or difficult. Nonstressful levels of these factors should not disturb any participant of a social situation who is within the normal range of personality functioning; intermediate levels should affect some kinds of people but not other kinds; and intense levels should affect everyone. Although this aspect of the situation is not varied in most experiments in social psychology, it is important to realize that a low level of these variables has usually been set. In most of our experiments, for example, we set a nonstressing level (i.e., people are not too hot; the noise level is not too high; people are not fright-

TABLE 4.1
Types of Situational Variables

I. *Physical Attributes*	
1. temperature	5. resources
2. hour	6. number of people
3. locality	7. size of space
4. noise level	8. configuration of space: control of gaze barriers distance from focal point

II. *Personal Attributes*	
1. sex	5. weight
2. race	6. status
3. age	7. physical attractiveness
4. height	8. distribution of personality and ability characteristics

ened because the event takes place in a safe environment), so we are often not aware of its effects. Real life, unfortunately, is more varied — and stressing — than are our experiments and provides the more interesting case in which specific characteristics of people make some of them more susceptible to stress.

An important additional feature of the physical environment is the way that the material objects are arranged to form the spatial characteristics of the situation. The spatial organization of an environment is so obvious that few people have studied how it affects individual behavior. An obvious characteristic of space is its size: Is there enough space for group members to work comfortably at the task? If not enough space is available to manipulate the task materials actively, we assume that this feature of the situation will be stressing to the participants. Of greater interest is that the configuration of objects creates a special dimension to that situation. Rooms have backs and fronts, doors and windows, tables and chairs. Some positions in space are closer to a "focal point" than others are; some positions control the direction of gaze or discussion from other positions; some positions are closer to exits, and others are hidden by barriers. A few studies, such as those of Sommer (1969), have begun to explore how different configurations of space promote cooperative or competitive interactions. Others, such as that of Strodtbeck and Hook (1961), have shown how certain configurations (i.e., the head position at a rectangular table) foster the emergence of the person occupying that position as the leader of the group. In the next chapter, we explore whether certain personality characteristics make some people more sensitive than others to the configuration of space within which the social event occurs.

Personal Attributes

A situation is often composed of other people. The effect of the characteristics of the people with whom the interaction is to occur has been studied quite vigorously in social psychology. Table 4.1 lists some of the member attributes that have been most actively investigated and whose effects are fairly well understood. Because there are so many types of member attributes, it is highly unlikely that a single mediating principle is sufficient to account for all of their effects. Two important characteristics of the "other" group members require special attention. First, many of the member attributes (e.g., sex, race, status, age, height, and weight) provide a basis for a social ranking system in which those individuals possessing more highly valued characteristics more easily assume the more important positions within the group (e.g., Strodtbeck & Hook, 1961). As we note throughout this chapter, there appears to be a differential degree of responsiveness to more highly valued external social characteristics for certain personality types.

Second, in regard to the effect produced by the distribution of personality or ability characteristics within the group, differential interactional patterns are expected for specific combinations of personality (e.g., groups composed of dominant and submissive members, more and less sociable members, more and less cognitively complex members). The general mechanism that seems to underlie the many possible combinations of group members that can be devised appears to be whether the members satisfy or frustrate each other's needs or preferred cognitive or behavioral styles. To the extent that the combination of members' characteristics affects the level of their subsequent mood, we can expect it to lead to a process loss (i.e., Steiner, 1972) that interferes with optimal levels of group functioning.

TASK VARIABLES

In chapter 1, we argued that in order to develop a compact theory of social behavior we must find a way to understand human activity as varied as the first few minutes of a social encounter, problem solving in our laboratories, or work at a real job. Each of these activities is quite different from the others, but in each case, the people involved must solve a problem set by that activity. It is useful, we believe, to think of these activities as "tasks" that the environment sets before these people. By the term task variables, then, we refer to a set of characteristics inherent in the activity at which the group members are engaged. In this section, we try to amalgamate the most important properties of the task studied in social psychology into as concise a group of categories as seems reasonable. The first set of these categories includes the dimensions of task difficulty, complexity, ambiguity, and importance. Table 4.2 summarizes the way these dimensions of the task appear in real social events. In the following section, we discuss briefly each one of these dimensions in order to indicate how these dimensions can underlie the many different kinds of human social activity.

Task difficulty refers to the fact that some problems are harder to solve than others or that higher levels of intelligence seem required to find a solution to some problems. Briefly, tasks vary in the degree to which they require greater degrees of abstraction, rigor in definition, organization and capacity in memory, and fluency in manipulation of the information. A task also may be more difficult because there may not be enough information provided to select a particular solution confidently; there may not be sufficient time available within which to work at the most effective pace; or excessive physical or psychological costs may be incurred.

Task complexity refers to the number of different types of tasks inherent in the problem. This type of complexity arises because the task must be broken down into subtasks, because different kinds of information are needed to reach a solution, or because there are a number of competing tasks or alternative solutions that must be examined and evaluated.

TABLE 4.2
Dimensions of the Task

I. *Difficulty*

1. Requirements for greater abstraction, rigor, organization, and manipulation of information

2. Provision of insufficient time or information and demands for excessive physical or psychological input

II. *Complexity*

1. Number of subtasks

2. Variety of information required

3. Number of competing tasks

III. *Ambiguity*

1. Clarity as to which task needs to be done

2. Clarity of operations required to reach goal

IV. *Importance*

1. Need for solution

2. Social value of task

Task ambiguity refers to the degree of clarity that exists both in defining the nature of the task that must be done as well as in deciding on the nature of the operations required to reach the goal. In other words, tasks can vary in the degree to which they allow the people involved to believe that they understand the nature of the task as well as understand the type of activities required to complete that task successfully.

Task importance refers to the extent to which other events are contingent upon the successful solution of that task. We can think of this dimension as a characteristic of the work process as well as events in a person's life. Some parts of a job are more important than others because they make a greater contribution to the solution of the overall work. For example, to a discussion group working to solve a problem, outlining the solution is a more important part of the task than is clarifying a minor technical point. In the same way, the importance of tasks *as a whole* may vary because of the different impact that they have on other groups (e.g., a discussion group will see their work as more important if their solution contributes to the work of other groups). Similarly, events in a person's life vary in the degree to which they are important to that person. This dimension can be illustrated by an instance both from real life and from our experiments. Consider the contrast between a bystander observing, at one time, a person fainting and, at another time, the person bumping into a pole. From the point of view of potential danger to the person, observers should conclude that fainting is a more important event in that person's life than bumping into a pole.

In addition to these dimensions of the task, it seems that most of the events we study in social psychology follow a fairly uniform sequence of stages. These stages, or the subtasks that people confront, are a series of separate information-seeking and information-processing requirements that must be completed in order to solve the problem set by that task (Kelley & Thibaut, 1969). In order to make this relatively abstract way of looking at human activity clearer, consider again the range of phenomena with which we are concerned in experimental social psychology. On one hand, we want to understand brief events performed by one individual in a fairly reduced social context, such as bystander intervention in an emergency situation. On the other hand, we also want to understand extended events performed by large numbers of people in complex social contexts, such as large task-oriented groups working within natural organizations over periods of weeks. Most of the phenomena with which experimental social psychology is concerned (e.g., the study of social influence, negotiation, and group problem-solving processes) falls at some intermediate level of time, number, and social complexity. Yet, however different each of these activities may be, each requires that the people involved in that task explore the situation, select certain parts of the problem to perform, and then find ways to reach their goals.

This point of view extends Kelley and Thibaut's (1969) conception of social events as information-processing tasks by noting that there are different kinds of information-processing tasks underlying any activity. What makes these activities different are the ways these subtasks are utilized. Although it is always possible to expand or reduce a category system, we hope to show in the chapters to follow that a sequential eight-stage system is a useful way to record the demands that most tasks make. From this point of view, an important factor that makes the activities just listed different from each other includes the requirements for (a) different types of information processing, with (b) different degrees of concentration in each type, and (c) different degrees and patterns of recycling through the sequential stages. Seeing each of these activities as representing different degrees of emphasis of a common system allows us to make real progress toward a unified model of social psychology.

In large part, this specification of sequential task stages is based on the common core of ideas that emerges from the work of those social psychologists interested in the sequence of decision-making activities in emergency situations (Latané & Darley, 1970; Schwartz, 1977) as well as those interested in more formal definitions of stages of group development (e.g., Bales, 1950; Tuckman, 1965). In later chapters, we hope to show the utility of their ideas to the more general analysis of social events.

Thus, thinking of social events as information-processing tasks that must be managed by the participants leads us to propose the following sequence of information-seeking and decision-making stages:

1. *Orientation.* A task requires that the individuals engaged in that social event must recognize the meaning of certain social stimuli, including becoming aware that they are "connected" in some way with the ongoing event. They must have some degree of awareness of the acts that will constitute that event and the connection of these social events with a larger social context.

2. *Selective attention.* Most social situations are composed of complex sets of stimuli. As a task is carried out, the participants choose the sets of stimuli from among the many to which they will respond. We use the phrase "sets of stimuli" broadly to indicate that the whole range of contextual, personal, task, and structural features of that social event must be screened, evaluated, and reduced.

3. *Aspiration level.* Following the recognition that a specific set of acts is to be performed, individuals set the level of accomplishment that they will seek. Few social acts are dichotomous (e.g., to help or not to help). Most have fairly wide ranges of accomplishment that can be established (e.g., how much effort one is willing to expend helping another; how accurately a page should be proofread; how ambitious an initial negotiating position should be). Therefore, the set of initial acts that is performed within a specific task is strongly influenced by the level of performance that has been established for that task.

4. *Search persistence.* Information must be collected in order to solve most tasks. Thus, a simple feature of the initial stages of social events is the time and energy committed to the seeking of the needed information. Search persistence is involved from the very beginning of a social transaction, but we list it as a fourth stage to indicate that after it becomes clear *what* sort of information the participants decide must be gathered, it is important to note the *amount* of information that is gathered before decision-making processes are undertaken. Of course, some tasks (e.g., arithmetic problems) require virtually no information gathering for our usual experiment subject. Other problems (e.g., moral dilemmas) require greater amounts, and many production tasks in natural groups require extended periods of information seeking.

5. *Organization of work.* Once the task is defined, work must begin. Even when fairly brief acts, such as initial contacts in the acquaintance process, are considered to be tasks, a *plan* for handling the activity of the participants must be developed. This stage, however, is easiest to consider in terms of a several-person production group. Members must be aware that the activity of several people needs to be coordinated and that the solution depends on joint efforts. If there is an awareness that subtasks or qualitatively different tasks are involved, a procedure has to be developed to assign, evaluate, regulate,

and integrate these separate activities. Many of the social structures of a complexly differentiated group emerge at this point in order to perform these different functions.

6. *Generation of solutions.* An essential ingredient of a task is the discovery of its solution. Even simple tasks, such as bystander intervention, require the consideration of the range of options that is available. Thus, most tasks require a stage when the range of possible solutions is generated. Indeed, in many kinds of task-oriented groups, this is the longest stage and is considered by members to be the "work" of the group. The number of solutions discovered, of course, is set by the characteristics of the specific task as well as by the level of aspiration and ability of the participants.

7. *Evaluation.* Following the generation of a range of possible solutions, an evaluation process is necessary to examine the adequacy of the potential solutions before a decision can be reached. Although not a necessary part of the task, participants may use other criteria that appear to be derived from other social events during this stage, such as considering the merits (i.e., the status or expressed competence) of those participants who formulated proposed solutions.

8. *Implementation.* Finally, after the decision is made, the task remains to be completed: a "hello" must be emitted, a person rescued from distress, a scale point checked on a group moral dilemma questionnaire, or a city built. This stage may be seconds, hours, or decades long, and it puts into operation the solution realized by the work of the earlier stages.

As we indicated earlier, this eight-stage scheme is an attempt to identify and order the different types of demands required by most tasks. As such, this linear scheme is an oversimplification of the way interaction proceeds in a real group. These different demands can vary in intensity and appear simultaneously (e.g., information search during generation of solutions activity), as well as cycle through many iterations of each form of activity. In the next chapter, we outline our expectations of how different personality characteristics lead people to perform at different levels of activity in each of the stages, and in the substantive chapters, we discuss how the nature of different tasks (e.g., emergencies as compared to group problem-solving tasks) requires different levels of activity in each of these stages by different kinds of people.

GROUP STRUCTURE

The last essential element that enters into the formation of a human event is the nature of the social group that the person may confront. In most social events, people enter an existing group that has a fairly clear set of structures and norms regulating their social experiences. This is certainly true for most occupational, political, or religious experiences and is a strong, if not dominant, element in what are perceived to be simple social events. Even our fairly unstructured laboratory experiments usually provide major features of a complete social structure within which people are asked to work. In the laboratory, individuals are often asked to provide leadership functions of a specified nature in order to expedite the work of a problem-solving group. More usually, experiments are designed to examine directly the effects of major aspects of group structures on group process and outcome. It is only in the less common case (e.g., the acquaintance process, early stages of social movements, or leaderless experimental groups) that an unstructured experience is provided for individuals within which a group structure emerges over the course of those individuals' interactions. Even in carefully contrived, unstructured experimental groups, for certain kinds of people the experimenter or the instruction sheet provides many of the leadership functions.

There are as many different approaches to social structure as there are to personality, and all are subject to some significant type of criticism. In order to avoid a definitional debate, we follow the approach taken by Cartwright and Zander (1968) as closely as possible. Their approach has not only shaped much of the work on groups, but it also provides the benefit of emerging from the types of social events that we discuss in the empirical chapters of this book.

Because important elements of group structure can *emerge from* an extended group process as well as *enter into* its initial stages, it is convenient to postpone a detailed discussion until the end of this chapter (readers may wish to turn ahead to Table 4.4 to review the list of variables that need to be examined). However, there are two considerations about group structure that should be raised before we begin to examine how all of these variables enter into the social process. First, a group structure may be present or absent when individuals begin their social activity. As we indicated earlier, this question more usually appears as the extent to which clear, structured elements are provided to participants rather than as the total absence of structure. The second consideration is more complex. Groups provide members with a means to satisfy their needs, and yet individuals differ in widely varying ways. There is abundant empirical evidence demonstrating the different types of structures that are better suited for the optimal performance of different kinds of people. The conclusion that can be drawn from this literature is that certain types of structures are more congruent with specific characteristics of the group members than are others. Therefore, if we visualize individuals being introduced into an existing structure, our expectations of the nature of their performance depends on whether that structure is congruent or incongruent with the characteristics of that specific set of people. In the model of group process that we present later, we assume that an incongruent structure contributes to the "process losses" that Steiner (1972) describes and, in this way, reduces the level of that group's performance.

A MODEL OF THE MECHANISMS
UNDERLYING SOCIAL PSYCHOLOGICAL EVENTS

With the primary components of the social process outlined, we are ready to propose a model that specifies the mechanisms of their interaction. We do this in two stages. In this section, we present a general model that specifies how these components are linked to create the social phenomena with which we are concerned. However, from an interactionist's point of view, any actual social event must be understood as an instance of the interaction of this general process with specific personal variables. The discussion in this section, therefore, is followed in the next chapter by a more extended presentation that details how the personal variables interact with this general process to form the phenomena of interest to social psychology.

We visualize social behavior as emerging in the following way. The individual, concerned with achieving certain goals and functioning within the limits set by specific abilities, engages in work that occurs within a specific environment. The types of personal concerns — their origins, interrelationships, and other properties — are those outlined in chapter 3, and the environment is formed by the properties of the situation, task, and group. We propose that each attribute of the situation, task, and group defines the social context and that as social behavior occurs a person's concerns must interact with *each* of these environmental attributes.

Environments, of course, vary considerably from each other. The major way in which they vary is through the level that exists for each of these attributes. Thus, behavior is based on the interaction of the specific personal variables with the specific level of each of the environmental variables that is provided, either naturally or experimentally. The variation in type and intensity of personal goals and the variation in level of environmental attributes determine the shape of the interaction. Therefore, the level that exists for each of the environmental attributes is of critical significance for the resulting behavior. To consider an extreme instance, when a social attribute is entirely absent, the individual's behavior may be heavily affected by the strength of personal goals. For example, we may bring individuals of a particular personality type together in the laboratory and ask them to work on a problem without specifying how they should organize their group. In this case, the absence of a social structure permits the *personal* goals of the individuals to determine the nature of their interaction much more heavily than if group members were presented with an existing social structure. At the opposite extreme, individuals may be presented with a set of environmental conditions, such as experimental instructions, whose strength is such as to override the strength of personal goals. For example, if we present an obviously better and worse alternative in a coalition experiment, we should expect such task attributes to determine the behavior of our experimental subjects. Often in our experiments, we can confirm our theoretical predictions simply by the level we set implicitly on this wide range of additional variables. In this last example, given a satisfactory level of involvement on the part of most participants, which can be provided by a reasonable reward that most people want, such as additional credit toward their grade in introductory psychology (i.e., a shared personal goal), we need only moderately tax their power of rationality (another personal attribute) in asking them to discriminate between a better or worse alternative. By these and other implicit levels set on additional environmental variables, we can generate what appears to be a purely *social* social psychology.

Individual Subjective Response

We are suggesting that the interaction of personal and environmental variables should be considered in the broadest and most inclusive way. Although it is possible to outline an extremely detailed set of possible subjective events that might occur as the individual's personal goals are engaged by a particular social environment (e.g., Schwartz, 1977), it is preferable at this point to be more general and defer such a discussion until later. It seems useful to note simply that three broad classes of subjective events can occur as personal and environmental variables are engaged. Given the specific properties of a personal variable:

1. A specific environmental variable may have little subjective impact on the individual. For example, a task that provides achievement rewards may not affect an affiliation-oriented person. Similarly, a person strongly concerned with the need for achievement may not be affected strongly by the configuration of the space in which the task is to occur (whereas a person concerned with dominance may be affected).

2. The environmental variable apparently may be rewarding to the person. In this case, we would expect a positive emotional response followed by a fairly direct set of behavior in pursuit of that particular goal. For example, the task that provides achievement rewards would furnish a real incentive to a person strongly concerned with the need for achievement and thus evoke a fairly strong set of achievement behaviors. Similarly, a configuration of space offering a focal point that controls the direction of gaze and discussion should provide an incentive to a dominance-oriented person.

3. The environmental variable apparently may be unpleasant to the person. In this case, we would expect a negative emotional response followed by

one of several possible defensive sets of behaviors. These defensive behaviors may range from some form of disengagement from the task, to defensive distortions in social cognition, to active aggressive behavior against that social task. It is likely that the choice among the possible alternative defenses is a function of additional characterological variables (e.g., the hostility component of the trait of authoritarianism) or environmental variables (e.g., group structures that diminish the person's degrees of freedom in response to the task). For example, an affiliation-oriented person may find competitive instructions disturbing and defend against unpleasant feelings by attempting to delay participating in the competition. In the same way, a dominance-oriented person may find the high status cues characterizing a person with whom he or she is expected to interact disturbing and thus distort the initial set of attributions in order to make that person less threatening.

These relatively few, broad types of subjective responses give us a convenient tool to find our way among the interactions of the great many personal and environmental variables. The prediction of the resulting behaviors is based on the specific properties of the variables producing one of the three types of subjective responses.

Behavioral Response

Thus, the person must deal with a specific social context that is characterized by levels set on each of the environmental attributes. Following the initial subjective responses, which could be seen as part of the *orientation* phase of the task, the person continues to explore the problem set by the task through all of the following task stages. At this point, we must decide on the most useful way to characterize the behavior produced by individuals working at the task. Unfortunately, typologies of behavior are almost as numerous as typologies of personality variables. Much of the difference among the typologies is produced by differences in the level of abstraction used (e.g., a frequency count of commands as compared to overall ratings on the social role of leadership). Typologies also vary on the level of inclusiveness chosen in each category (e.g., using a general socioemotional category as compared to breaking socioemotional behavior down into acts of friendly recognition, humor, hostility, solidarity, etc.). Because we need to consider the specific types of acts through which the different phases of the task are carried out, we need a fairly detailed category scheme that permits us to remain close to the actual behavior.

These requirements are amply met by the category system devised by Bales (1950) and his colleagues, who have provided much of the most interesting work on small groups. Although the system expands and contracts to suit special purposes, its appearance in the Borgatta modification (Borgatta &

Crowther, 1965) provides great flexibility in capturing the behavior of individuals working within most small groups. In addition, early in his work with small groups, Bales divided member behavior into task and socioemotional dimensions, a distinction that was to be of great value in both narrow and broad analyses of group activity. The distinction between these two dimensions was formalized more sharply into the circumplex model of Leary and his associates (Freedman, Leary, Ossorio, & Coffey, 1951). In the circumplex model, these types of activity were seen as orthogonal bipolar dimensions whose relative joint weights established the different social roles that appeared in groups. The Leary and Borgatta modifications of the Bales system seem ideally suited to represent social behavior. They provide a systematic way to capture the variety of human activity within a relatively manageable category system (see Benjamin, 1984; Wiggins, 1980).

When we sought a system to represent the behavior of individuals working at the different stages of the task sequence, it seemed that they could be represented quite accurately as a set of specific acts that fell along the coordinates of the Leary grid. For example, as the person begins to deal with the first set of demands of the task, it will usually be in terms of specific acts, such as opinions on how the group might best proceed or requests for direction. These two examples illustrate the initiation and the concurrence poles of the task dimension. Also, individuals will often act in terms of friendliness and concern for the other people present or in terms of criticism or hostility toward other people, which define the affiliation and the disaffiliation poles (Battistich, 1979) of the socioemotional dimension. Similarly, the demands of each of the remaining task stages require, to greater or lesser degrees, behavior that can be placed along these same coordinates. Table 4.3 presents Borgatta's specific Interaction Process Scores (IPS) categories (with a few additions of our own) that characterize the behavior expressed at each of the poles of the Leary grid. We choose to work with this system rather than Bales' (1970) subsequent scheme for two reasons. First, the utility of the newer system has not yet been demonstrated by a significant body of research, as have his earlier approaches. Second, two of the three factors in Bales' new system are unipolar, and we sought a system that represented active and contrasting modes of behaviors. In a two-dimensional model, nonactivity can be represented efficiently at the common zero point.

The Social Field

To summarize our model up to this point, we visualize the individual, guided by a set of personal goals, beliefs, and abilities, engaging in work that takes place in an environment characterized by a set of specific situational, task, and group attributes. The initial response to the overall social situation is a subjective one, in response to the interaction between the specific levels of

TABLE 4.3
Social Behavior Expressed at Each Pole of the
Task and Socioemotional Dimensions

I. *Task Dimension*

1. *Initiation pole*

   a. Procedural suggestion (6)
   b. Suggests solution (7)
   c. Gives opinion, information (8, 11)
   d. Gives analysis, evaluation (8)
   e. Draws attention, clarifies (12)
   f. Asks for opinion, analysis, evaluation (13)
   g. Disagrees (14)
   h. Acknowledges communication (4)
   i. Coordinates member effort toward goal

2. *Concurrence pole*

   a. Concurrence, compliance (5)
   b. Personal inadequacy (9, 15)
   c. Asks for help due to incompetence (15)

II. *Socioemotional Dimension*

1. *Affiliation pole*

   a. Friendly, social recognition (1)
   b. Considerate, empathic
   c. Raises status (2)
   d. Social sensitivity
   e. Concern to ameliorate group differences

2. *Disaffiliation pole*

   a. Aggression externalized beyond group (10)
   b. Aggression toward group members (17)
   c. Withdrawal

Note: Adapted from Borgatta and Crowther (1965).
The identifying numbers indicate Borgatta's Interaction
Process Scores (IPS) categories.

the personal and social variables. The subjective response leads to a set of behaviors that can be represented as falling along the coordinates of the Leary grid, as indicated in Table 4.3. As work progresses, the individual responds in a similar interactive way to the new factor of the changing demands of the different task stages. We can expect the demands of each task stage to change the importance of specific personal and situational variables as work progresses through the task sequence to the final implementation stage.

When more than one person is engaged in the activity, a way must be found to represent their joint behavior. Individually, each person can be understood to be represented by the features of the model just presented, including the behavior of the other person as one of the social attributes of the situation. However, joint behavior leads to another level of abstraction. Social events are behavioral, but they may also be supraindividual. From the point of view of the *emerging* group, there comes a time when the behavior of group members is recognized and formalized into a set of expectations and norms. These expectations and norms are, to a greater or lesser degree, shared by group members as the basis for regulating their joint activity.

We complete the preliminary phase of introducing our model by describing the kinds of interpersonal and social elements that develop through extended interaction among group members. Although each of the behaviors reviewed in Table 4.3 can be thought of as an act of a single individual, it is an old insight in social analysis that events in groups are based on the reciprocal influences of members upon each other as they work jointly toward some goal. Therefore, the elements of group process must be described as the resultants of the interaction of group members. Cooperation, for example, is a widely used descriptor of group events and, by definition, indicates the joint efforts of members in working toward a common goal. Although we might speak of the "cooperative" or "prosocial" *orientation* that individuals bring to the interaction, cooperation is a particular mode of *inter*dependence that can be determined by a particular set of behaviors produced by more than one member of the group. Similarly, the term leadership is an elementary part of any analysis of group process. Although we can examine the personal characteristics of those who are appointed or rated as leaders as well as examine the type of behaviors such a person might produce, it is commonly recognized (e.g., Cartwright & Zander, 1968) that leadership behaviors as a mode of influencing other group members are strongly affected by the characteristics of those being influenced. Thus, an analysis of leadership functions (or followership functions) is best understood through the analysis of the influence process between members. These elements of group process, structure, and outcome are outlined in Table 4.4.

GROUP PROCESS, STRUCTURE, AND OUTCOME

I. Group Process

1. *Performance Styles.*   The Borgatta category system gives us a means to operationally define the different patterns of behavior that produce the group's work. Leadership, followership, and other group roles emerge out of the combination of these different types of behaviors. The Leary grid itself speculatively names a set of group roles emerging from varying combinations of strength of the two interpersonal (task and socioemotional) dimensions. The specificity of Borgatta's scheme not only allows us to move directly to-

TABLE 4.4
Elements of Group Process, Structure, and Outcome

I. *Group Process*

1. Performance styles. The array of emergent behavioral styles (see Table 5.4).

2. Negotiation processes.

   a. bargaining stance: firm–yielding
   b. techniques of information use: rigid–flexible
   c. modes of interdependence: adversarial, exploitative, ingratiating, integrative

II. *Group Structure*

1. Differentiation.

   a. differentiation of function between positions
   b. complexity of function within each position

2. Rank.

   a. bases of ranking: internal–external
   b. distribution of rank across positions

3. Power.

   a. bases of power: reward, coercive, legitimate, expert
   b. distribution of power across positions

4. Reward.

   a. bases of reward allocation: time, effort, ability, group maintenance
   b. norms of reward distribution
   c. array of intrinsic rewards in group activity

III. *Outcome*

1. Individual: satisfaction with self, group, task
2. Group: cohesiveness (solidarity, attraction)
3. Task: productivity (quantity and quality of task work)

ward the empirical investigation of their processes, but also allows us to develop a more fine-grained analysis of different styles of each role. A few possible combinations of behaviors should serve as an illustration of the potential power of this system to capture the events of group process. The set of acts called "procedural suggestion" (i.e., when an individual suggests the type of event that the group should undertake) is, of course, the preeminent leadership act. We can see the power of this system to define group roles by considering just three possible combinations of other behaviors joined with procedural suggestion: (a) it might appear combined simply with giving opinion, disagreement, and aggression toward group members; (b) it might appear combined with many assertive task behaviors; (c) it might appear combined with many other assertive task behaviors, such as giving opinion, analysis, and coordination of member effort, and also include many affiliative types of behavior. In the first case, we have the operational definition of the narrow and impersonal autocratic leader; in the second case, the strong task leader who can respond well to the full range of task demands with a flexible repertoire of task-related activity; and in the third case, what Borgatta, Couch, and Bales (1954) described as the "Great man," who can combine a wide range of positive task and socioemotional activity to respond most fully to the needs of the group. These three behavioral clusters (and others) have supported a substantial body of experimental work. Many other types of leadership, followership, technician, and scapegoat group roles can be defined operationally in this same way.

The variety of possible combinations of these behavioral clusters is too vast to enumerate here. In chapter 5, we present the behavioral clusters that we expect to be associated with the 11 personal characteristics that we track through the social process. The logic used in that discussion should indicate how to derive the performance styles associated with other personality variables as well as those evoked by situational variables. In any case, these behavioral clusters are not the "atoms" of social interaction to be tabled in a future *Handbook of Social Psychology*. Rather, the clusters are the behaviors expected from the interaction of the independent variables described earlier, appearing along the bipolar dimensions that form the elementary space along which behavior occurs. Performance styles, then, are determined by the properties of the social context, including the personality characteristics of the other people in the process, and represent the types of behaviors that individuals use in order to meet the demands of the task. As the other members of the group respond to the initial patterns of individual social behavior, these patterns are strengthened or modified until an established pattern of individual behavior for each member is confirmed. If the group stays together for a substantial period of time, these established patterns become recognized more formally as sets of expectations or norms that regulate group behavior into future generations of membership.

2. *Negotiation Processes.*   Once members of a group become involved with the demands of the task, they must find a basis for meshing their individual aspirations for what the group will accomplish, their desires for recognition from other members, their expectations of impact on the outcome of the group's work, their preference for group roles and tasks, and the nature of the rewards they hope to attain. In other words, they must develop group processes that permit their initial positions to be integrated into a common

social vehicle for meeting the formal task requirements. Several of the interpersonal dimensions commonly discussed in the negotiation literature are
helpful in understanding the nature of this broader set of interpersonal transactions. We wish to retain some of this terminology because the types of
group processes examined in the bargaining literature on the allocation of reward seem to be of comparable value in explaining the broader set of negotiations upon which the group's work must rest. For example, deciding who will
assume the more onerous tasks (e.g., recording secretary) or determining
how many of a specific person's ideas will be accepted seems to require no less
negotiation than the allocation of reward.

There are three elements of the negotiation process that we wish to identify
at this point because they are central to a wide range of topics that we discuss
later in the empirical chapters. Basically, these are the modes of behavior that
group members use to jointly implement the task and socioemotional behaviors outlined in Table 4.3. First individually and then jointly, members develop a *bargaining stance* toward each other. Given a reasonable level of involvement, it is important to determine how firmly group members maintain
their initial position. As members coordinate their efforts, they vary on the
degree to which they insist that their position be accepted by other group
members. The processes that describe how firmly individuals maintain an initial bid in a bargaining paradigm seem just as useful to explain the process of
obtaining acceptance of member's individual solutions in a problem-solving
task.

Second, as members attempt to influence each other, they also vary markedly in their *techniques of information use.* There is a wide range of ways to
develop arguments designed to convince other members, survey potential
forms of solution to the group's problem, and adapt initial positions in the
face of unexpected events. These forms of information use are cognitive
problem-solving techniques, which can broadly be seen as interpersonal steps
that members take in order to reach their goals. In general, we can evaluate
group process to determine how flexibly members handle the wide array of
information and solutions that is usually available to most groups.

Finally, group members develop *modes of interdependence* to coordinate
their efforts at reaching a solution. A central area of concern in the literature
on interpersonal bargaining is to identify the types of interpersonal problem-
solving strategies that negotiators prefer to use. Individuals may choose to
maximize their own or joint outcomes (i.e., to stress competition or
cooperation), and they may choose to be frank or guarded (i.e., to reveal or
conceal information) in the influence process. By combining these two dimensions of interpersonal problem-solving strategies, we can generate four
commonly studied modes of interdependence: *adversarial* (competitive-
information revealing); *exploitative* (competitive–information concealing);
ingratiating (cooperative–information concealing); and *integrative*

(cooperative–information revealing). Each of these major forms of interdependence is useful to describe a much wider range of group processes than is studied through experimental games. However, because of its precise nature, the bargaining literature does generate clearer information that can be applied to the more fluid and complex events of group process in general.

II. Group Structure

As we noted earlier, there are many approaches to group structure, and a full discussion would take us far from the purposes of this book. It will expedite our discussion considerably to rely on the approach taken by Cartwright and Zander (1968), whose book *Group Dynamics* has done so much to shape the study of small groups. Cartwright and Zander note the common observation that it is "almost impossible to describe what happens in groups without using terms that indicate the 'place' of members with respect to one another [and that] individual members of a group can be located in relation to other members according to some criterion of placement" (p. 486). The characteristics of these interrelated positions form the internal structure of the group. The behavior of the people who assume these different group positions is regulated by the rules associated with the position as long as they occupy these positions.

The helpful example that Cartwright and Zander use to illustrate this aspect of a group is similar to that given in many other introductions to group structure and is worth repeating. They ask readers to visualize the different behaviors of an established vice-president and a junior executive at a staff meeting. They note how authoritatively the vice-president behaves in contrast to the accommodating style of the junior executive. They then describe the behavior of the junior executive when interacting with members of his own staff and note how similar his behavior has become to that of the vice-president. This example, of course, illustrates a basic feature of group structure: There may be different positions within the group, and different sets of behavior are associated with each position.

In this chapter, we are concerned with four features of the positions within group structure: the differentiation of function, the ranking among positions, the nature of power, and the system of reward. We outline each of these four elements in this section and present our expectations of how they interact with personality variables in the next chapter.

1. *Differentiation.* In the illustration taken from Cartwright and Zander, the vice-president and junior executive functions show a staff with two clearly different positions. Division of labor of this kind is an option that allows groups to cope with the many demands placed upon it as the group begins to work on a task. All the information-processing tasks outlined earlier

and all the behavioral categories listed in Table 4.3 to meet these task demands are ways in which the group achieves its purposes. The structural characteristic of differentiation is a group property that indicates the degree to which these functions are divided into different positions within the group. In an extreme form of differentiation, there may be only the one position of "member" within the group. Each person within such a group assumes responsibility for the common set of activities which define that one position. In the contrasting extreme form, activities may be sharply divided into different spheres of responsibility, which generates a group with many different positions. In the first extreme, we have a totally integrated set of functions amalgamated entirely within one position; in the other, we have a set of functions sharply separated into many positions. From the point of view of the group, we can examine the degree of differentiation among the number of positions that have developed. From the point of view of each position, we can examine the number of different functions that define that position. Finally, the fact that these positions are related to each other allows us to examine the number and the control of the connections established among the different positions.

Thus, there are clearly demarcated positions in the two groups in which the junior executive works, and his behavior changes as a consequence of the position he occupies. We can just as easily imagine a group where this differentiation is not made. Most of our experimental groups, for example, consist of undergraduate students occupying the position of "subject," with identical sets of instructions defining their functions in equivalent ways. Of course, we can create differentiated groups in the laboratory easily by distributing separate instructions to each participant.

2. *Rank.* Frequently, the different positions within the group are ranked on the basis of some characteristic. In the example of the formal structure of the organization, the position of vice-president is considered superior to that of junior executive. This differential in rank leads the occupant of the superior position to be more highly valued than those in lower ranks and, in many ways, determines their pattern of interaction. The characteristics on which this discrimination is based can vary markedly across different groups. Although there are many characteristics that can serve to rank positions, it seems useful to group these characteristics into two sets of *internal* and *external* attributes. We hope to show later that attributes within a set are used in the same way in the course of group process. The internal attributes are the many personal characteristics such as competence, intelligence, knowledge, poise, creativity, courage, integrity, cunning, and sociability. The external attributes are those derived from the properties of the larger social system, such as occupation, occupational level, social class, religion, or ethnic group. Physical attributes such as age, sex, race, height, weight, and

perhaps, physical attractiveness (for reasons that we discuss later) also function as external attributes.

   3. *Power.*   As members of a group work together at a task, their separate activities must be coordinated through all the stages of the task sequence. The study of the means by which members attempt to influence each other's opinions and behavior raises the difficult topic of power. We again follow Cartwright and Zander (1968) and assume that power is the capacity of one person to influence another person with respect to a particular state (p. 216). Thus, Cartwright and Zander point out that power has two components: (a) the set of activities that the first person can institute and (b) the characteristics of the second person that make these acts effective. Both aspects of this influence relationship have been greatly affected by French and Raven's (1959) classic analysis of the bases of power. Here, we briefly outline four of the five bases of power that French and Raven identified as underlying the social influence process: reward, coercive, legitimate, and expert power. The fifth form, referent power, is less helpful for our purposes, as it is a type of power that occurs without deliberate acts being taken by the person exerting influence.

   Reward power is the ability of the person making the attempt at influence to provide the rewards that the target person desires. The nature of the reward can vary and, in French and Raven's scheme, is defined in terms of those states desired by the target person. *Coercive power* is the negative form of reward power and is defined in terms of those sanctions that are considered painful by the target person. *Legitimate power* is based on the target person accepting the right of the influencer to prescribe a set of behavior that must be produced by the target. This more complex form of power assumes an existing social relationship between the two participants with norms obligating the occupant of one position to follow the directions provided by the occupant of another position. In terms of our earlier example, the junior executive would assume that the vice-president has the right to direct his working behavior because of the difference in the definition of their two positions. *Expert power* is based on the target person perceiving that the influencer has special knowledge or ability in regard to the behaviors being demanded of the target. In our example, the junior executive would believe that the greater experience of the vice-president in business affairs indicates greater knowledge about the matter under discussion and thus provides a more reliable basis for decision making.

   Each of these four forms of power may be present or absent in a particular group. Obviously, it is fruitless to expect the appearance of expert or legitimate power in a group specifically composed so that all participants are completely ignorant of the task and given the same instructions. However, in the right circumstances (i.e., when the bases of reward or distinction are provided), it is important to examine the influence process to determine what types of power will be utilized, what types of power will be most effective, and how power will be distributed across the positions within a group as a function of the types of people that constitute that group.

4. *Reward.* Members must have a reason to stay in their group. Whether we take a single act as our social unit (e.g., providing help in an emergency), or consider the course of behavior of individuals within emergent or formally structured groups, the gains and losses that people experience is a major dimension of their social experience. Thus, the reward structure of an individual's social experience is a major consideration in any analysis of social phenomena. Major theoretical and empirical efforts have been made in many fields to grapple satisfactorily with this aspect of human performance. We cannot concisely summarize all the major variables, the theoretical positions, and the empirical evidence that have been shown to be of importance. Rather, we have isolated several key aspects of the reward structure of most groups for our discussion in order to complete our analysis of the major elements of the social process. In selecting these features, we have been concerned with identifying those elements that may be equally present in the single act, the emergent group, and the organized group. In this section we attempt to isolate the nature of the inputs that individuals may use when evaluating their own contribution to the group's performance, some major rules governing the distribution of reward in many groups, and the nature of the intrinsic rewards provided by the group process itself.

Bases of Reward Allocation. People make many kinds of contributions to the work of the group, each of which can serve as the basis of evaluating their value to the group's overall success. It is useful to distinguish between the following categories of inputs: *time:* the amount of time that an individual expends at that task; *effort:* the amount of effort that an individual expends at the task; *ability:* the level of competence that an individual demonstrates in work on the task; *group maintenance:* the degree of contribution to the work of other members and the group as a whole.

Distribution of Reward. The second aspect of a reward system is the principle for allocating rewards across group members. Cartwright and Zander (1968) are once again helpful in providing a typology that is complex enough to encompass the basic features of a wide range of distribution rules and yet compact enough to be incorporated into the many other variables of our model.

"Rule 1. Each member's pay is independent of group output and his own score" (p. 412). This rule states that a person agrees to accept a fixed amount of money for working a fixed amount of time. Although we can assume that there is some estimate of the amount of effort and ability that will be demonstrated, the major features of this rule are the predetermined precision of the amount of reward, the lack of incentive for better performance, and the irrelevance of the levels of other people's performance.

"Rule 2. Each member's pay is independent of group output but contingent on his score" (p. 412). This rule emphasizes the level of success that an individual has reached in his own work. It may or may not depend on the level reached by other group members. (a) If the total amount of reward provided to the group is fixed, then the performance of others may increase or diminish the individual person's share (zero sum rule). (b) If the total amount for the group is not fixed, then a strong incentive is provided to each individual to maximize his own level of performance. Thus, the first condition provides a strongly competitive framework within which to work, whereas the second condition provides a strongly individualistic framework.

"Rule 3. Each member's pay is contingent upon group output but independent of his score" (p. 413). This rule fosters cooperation because each member benefits to the degree that all members reach higher levels of performance. This rule reduces the narrow value of individual achievement but makes very salient the issue of the responsibility that other group members take for the total accomplishment of the group.

"Rule 4. Each member's pay is contingent upon both output and his score" (p. 413). This rule combines features of both the cooperative incentives of Rule 3 with the competitive ones of Rule 2(a). Members are given an incentive to jointly raise the group's total output but, at the same time, are made sharply aware of the relative level of performance of each person compared to their own.

Each of these distribution rules offers clear sets of incentives and disincentives to the people they serve. Although the concept of incentives is discussed frequently in the research literature, it is often unclear in defining the economic or social conditions that are supposed to produce incentives. In the next chapter, we argue that the nature of the goals sought by different kinds of people determines the ultimate incentive value of each type of rule.

Intrinsic Reward.   All the different aspects of the task, the situation, and the group process provide a wide array of rewards, ranging from the interest of the task to the sociability provided by the group membership. However, when we examine the social events that provide these rewards, it is difficult to characterize them in ways that are not identical with our list of personality variables. Much that is written about the nature of intrinsic reward overlooks the fact that it cannot be defined in isolation from the specific needs of the individual. To the extent that people are concerned with different motives, few aspects of the social situation provide the same intrinsic rewards to all individuals. What is an intrinsically interesting task to an achievement-oriented person is a frustratingly unstructured task to a dependent person. What is a pleasingly sociable group process to an affiliation-oriented person is a painful one to an authoritarian individual. Therefore, the rewards that an emergent or organized group has to offer a member have already been provided in our definitions of personality variables listed in Table 3.9.

The most common type of nonintrinsic reward is money, and we have little that is new to add to an already vast amount of literature. From our point of view, we work from the obvious observation that all kinds of people find money rewarding and the only somewhat less obvious observation that money both buys and represents many different types of intrinsic rewards: What represents a princely salary to one person is, to another, the representation that the person is the prince.

III. Outcome

The last set of events with which we are concerned is the outcome of the social activity. This aspect of the social process is fairly clear, and so the end points of an individual's or group's work need only a brief introduction. From the individual's point of view, the outcome is the degree to which there is *satisfaction* with the self and the events that constituted the social activity. On the group level, the outcome can be thought of as the strength that developed in the group, which is often thought of as group *cohesiveness*. The most common level of analysis refers to the individual's or group's goals; most tasks are defined by some end state. This can be thought of most inclusively as *productivity*. In some dichotomous instances, productivity can be thought of as success or failure: Did the person help? Did the group win? Did the revolution occur? But more usually, productivity is thought of as a continuous variable: How many problems were answered? How quickly were they answered? How well? In other words, the quantity, efficiency, or quality of the objects or events that define the task are the relatively easily measured dimensions of the outcome of the group's work.

5 Interactional Patterns: A Model of the Person in the Situation

In the previous chapters, we identified what we believe to be the most important elements in the person and the situation. We are now able to offer a theory-based model of social events that incorporates specific personality and situational variables into a pattern of interaction at different stages of developing social phenomena. We proceed sequentially across the model presented in the first chapter (Table 1.1) and discuss each major type of event in turn, while recognizing that no real human event proceeds in such a simple way. Real events, of course, compact or expand the stages and cycle through them many times. Given our conceptual and methodological limitations, if we are to begin, we must impose a clear — if arbitrary — scheme.

The predictions derived from our theory are presented as a discussion organized around a series of tables. We expect readers to wonder immediately whether there is any evidence to support the range of assertions that we make. The answer is simple. If one asks whether there is a satisfactory base of evidence to support all of these assertions, the answer is clearly "no." If one asks whether there is any evidence at all, the answer is "yes, a surprising amount." Yet, although there is a great deal of evidence to report, the facts discovered by social psychology in over 3 decades of work are not distributed neatly across all the important social processes. There are massive amounts of data in a few areas, substantial amounts in others, and many fragmentary facts scattered widely across the processes presented in these tables. Our approach in developing the theory is like the one used by the paleontologist who, from an ankle, elbow and tooth, can reconstruct the whole dinosaur. From the substantial and the fragmentary bases of fact, we have tried to derive an overall pattern of the social process. However, those skeptical of this approach

89

can be encouraged in that our position is much more favorable than the one confronting the paleontologist. Our subject matter is all around us. We have only to undertake a new experiment in order to examine the validity of any part of the model.

THE INTERACTION OF PERSONALITY AND SITUATIONAL VARIABLES

We begin to explore the model by recognizing that the individual brings a set of personal characteristics to a specific situation. As the individual enters the social process by scanning that situation, the specific attributes of the situation begin to register on the person. The early forms of the interaction of the person in the situation come about because the degree to which these attributes have an impact on the person frequently is a function of the properties of that person. Table 5.1 outlines a set of predictions about the degree of impact that certain situational variables have on the individual. Because of the nature of the different personality variables, we expect that some lead to more concern with the specific properties of the situation than others do. Thus, we visualize a complex set of results produced by the specific joint properties of the person and the situation. In presenting the pattern of relationships that is abstracted into Table 5.1, we discuss a few key mechanisms and leave additional exploration for the later empirical chapters.

Personality and Physical Attributes.   For most people, high levels of physical stimulation (e.g., heat, noise, danger, etc.) are generally felt as unpleasant, whereas low levels are barely noticed. However, the world in which most people live is usually characterized by moderate levels of these variables. For this reason, we are most interested in understanding the degree to which different kinds of people feel stressed by moderate levels of stimulation produced by the physical attributes of the environment. Table 5.1 summarizes the degree of impact that we believe moderate levels of these variables have on the different types of people. We expect that the cluster of peripheral variables based on esteem needs will be little affected by moderate levels of stress produced by uncomfortable or unusual situations because of their general psychological base of confidence and trust in self and others. We expect a modest increase in response for recognition and affiliation. However, we expect the response produced by the cluster of peripheral characteristics based on safety needs to vary greatly. We expect that dependency, approval, and order will be strongly affected by new or uncomfortable situations because of the general base of mistrust and lack of confidence in self and others. We expect that abasement and authoritarian persons will also be aroused negatively by such situations but have a defensive structure that per-

TABLE 5.1
The Degree of Impact of Situational Attributes on
Selected Personality Variables

| Personality Variables | *Physical Attributes* | | |
	Stress Evoking	Spatial Configuration	Personal Attributes
Dependency	H	H	H
Abasement	M	L	H
Approval	H	L	H
Authoritarianism	M	H	H
Order	H	H	L
Affiliation	M	H	L
Machiavellianism	L	H	L
Dominance	L	H	L
Nurturance	L	L	L
Achievement	L	L	L
Recognition	M	M	H

Note: H = high
M = medium
L = low

mits them to cope with the stress in more protective ways than persons with needs for dependency, approval, and order.

The physical world is also composed of objects that have some form of spatial relationship to each other. As part of this discussion, we should note the possible effects that might be produced by such arrangements of the objects that constitute physical space. This phenomenon is one of the least studied processes in social psychology, but it seems to be a new, vigorous, and promising area of research. For this reason, it is interesting to speculate on how the spatial attributes of a situation might affect individuals with different personality characteristics (or how they are related to individual goals). Because persons who are dependent, authoritarian, order-seeking, Machiavellian, dominant, and recognition-seeking are all strongly concerned with the interpersonal control of events, we would expect them to be sensitive to, and take advantage of, those features of physical space that either provide protection or foster control over others. Abasement, approval, and recognition-oriented individuals seem somewhat oblivious to the spatial dimension. Achievement-oriented and nurturing persons do not seem primarily concerned with spatial attributes because they are more focused on task-related cues. Thus, spatial arrangements for them become relevant only when associated with task performance. Similarly, we expect that individuals with strong affiliative needs will be quite sensitive to spatial attributes of the situation because of the degree to which they foster interpersonal contact.

Personality and Personal Attributes.   As we noted earlier, there are so many types of personal attributes (race, sex, age, social class, etc.) that it is difficult to outline all the possible forms of interaction. In the predictions presented in Table 5.1, we concentrate on one type of attribute that is easily recognized in the early stages of social interaction: stimuli conveying the varying degrees of *social status* possessed by the other members of the social event. Table 5.1 outlines the degree of impact that we believe this variable exerts on different types of people. For individuals possessing high degrees of concern with dependency, authoritarianism, approval, and abasement, we expect great sensitivity to this social attribute because it indicates that the other person can provide the type of direction on which the person can rely. For Machiavellianism, dominance, and recognition, we expect great sensitivity as well, when this attribute indicates that the other person is a potential source of competition or a provider of praise and recognition. The other personal variables are unaffected by variations in the external status of the other for a variety of reasons inherent in their definition: order, because such persons are especially focused on the task; affiliation, because such persons are more concerned with interpersonal contact than the social rank of the individual providing the contact; nurturance and achievement, because such persons are more concerned with personal success at the task.

THE INTERACTION OF PERSONALITY
AND TASK VARIABLES

Any object or event has a structure that is more or less difficult, complex, ambiguous, or important. As an individual is engaged with any task, each of these dimensions becomes part of that social experience. Our concern, at this point, is to determine the way in which these particular features affect the level of performance of those engaged in the task. Before we present our expectations of the ways in which personality moderates the impact of these characteristics, we want to emphasize the point that this discussion encompasses the entire social context as well as the narrowly defined problem on which the group is to work. The social situation itself possesses all of these features. We can illustrate this point by comparing two standard ways for studying the response of people to emergencies. In the first case, a "student" drops a stack of books and papers in front of the subject; in the second, the subject is in a room and suddenly hears cries of distress coming from the experimenter who is in another room. In both instances, the task set before the subject is whether or not to help. However, although the content of the task is the same in both cases, the structure of the two events is very different. In this illustration, the second case is clearly more difficult, complex, ambiguous, and important than the first.

These structural properties highlight the issue of personal competence to the people engaged in that task. As such, these task properties act as incentives or disincentives to the participants in that social situation. Many studies (e.g., Deci, 1975; Steers & Porter, 1979) address the question of the incentive value of the task, noting that some tasks evoke more enthusiastic work and lead to a greater sense of accomplishment and reward, whereas others lead to boredom and fatigue. Commonly used descriptions of work, such as "challenging," "stimulating," or "interesting," are probably based on some combination of these four dimensions.

As with most of the social phenomena with which we deal, we believe that even though these structural properties are inherent in the task (and thus a fairly easily measured independent variable) this *alone* does not define their level of incentive value. Our expectations of the effect of these task variables on social behavior propose that it is the interaction of the specific properties of the individual and the task that defines the level of incentive provided by the task. These expectations for each of the personality variables are presented in Table 5.2.

For dependency, abasement, approval, and authoritarianism, we expect that more difficult, complex, ambiguous, or important elements in the group task are threatening and arouse feelings of helplessness. Just as threatening features in the situation make people reluctant to engage in that situation, so too should threatening properties of the task lead to a reduction of involvement with that task. Thus, a lower level of involvement should lead to a lower level of performance. In this way, more difficult, complex, ambiguous, and important properties should serve as a disincentive for these personality variables. The concern for order leads to somewhat different predictions. Because the need for order is focused on task success, we expect that difficulty and complexity will have an incentive value, whereas ambiguity will be confusing and so provide a disincentive. The level of importance appears unrelated to the specific properties of this personality variable.

As affiliation-oriented people are capable of handling most aspects of the task, but are also uninvolved with proving their own competence at the task, we expect to find the first three structural dimensions unrelated to their level of performance. Only when importance raises the question of another individual's personal needs should it provide incentive value for affiliation-oriented people.

For Machiavellianism, only ambiguity should offer an incentive, as it provides a wider set of options within which to maneuver. The other dimensions seem unrelated to the characteristic of Machiavellianism. Most of these dimensions allow people concerned with dominance, nurturance, and achieve-

TABLE 5.2
The Incentive Value of Task Dimensions for Selected Personality Variables

Personality Variables	Task Dimensions			
	Difficulty	Complexity	Ambiguity	Importance
Dependency	D	D	D	D
Abasement	D	D	D	D
Approval	D	D	D	D
Authoritarianism	D	D	D	D
Order	I	I	D	U
Affiliation	U	U	U	I
Machiavellianism	U	U	I	U
Dominance	I	I	I	I
Nurturance	I	I	U	I
Achievement	I	I	U	I
Recognition	I	D	D	I

Note: D = disincentive
U = unrelated
I = incentive

ment greater opportunities to display their competence and so offer incentives for improved task performance. Only the task dimension of ambiguity is unrelated to nurturance and achievement needs, though it provides dominance needs with the same incentive value that it does for Machiavellianism. The need for recognition is a more mixed case because it intensely seeks interpersonal validation, but with fewer cognitive resources than the other esteem variables. Thus, the task dimensions of difficulty and importance provide incentive opportunities for confirmation of personal value from others, whereas complexity and ambiguity are disincentives because they tax the cognitive resources of the recognition-oriented person without providing apparent opportunities for personal display.

THE INTERACTION OF PERSONALITY
AND STAGES OF TASK DEMANDS

In chapter 4, we discussed how a task imposes a series of information-processing requirements on group members. Because each stage makes different demands on the people dealing with the task, each stage necessitates different types of concern, requires the engagement of different abilities, and provides different types of rewards to group members. As people respond to these demands, they may be more active and use special patterns of behavior in meeting one kind of task requirement than they are in dealing with another. Close inspection of the behavior required by this sequence of demands shows that a complex series of interactions is likely between different personality variables and different requirements of the task sequences. The overall pattern of interaction that affects the *level of activity* group members are ready to display within each stage is presented in Table 5.3. The actual *type of activity* produced in each stage is presented later in Table 5.4.

Personality and Orientation.   The first information-processing stage requires the person to learn about the task at hand. We expect that the two subjective requirements this might have for the group members are: (a) defining the nature of the task and (b) defining who is responsible for the completion of the task. The first requirement should lead people with order, dominance, and achievement concerns to behave at high levels of activity in this stage, with nurturance concerns at moderate levels. The second requirement should lead people with dependency, authoritarianism, and Machiavellianism concerns to behave at high levels; persons with approval and recognition concerns should behave at moderate levels. People with abasement concerns should feel apathetic to this (as well as to most other task stages), and people wih affiliative concerns should be fairly unconcerned with task completion but rather engage in simply establishing interpersonal contact with the other people present.

Personality and Selective Attention.   Defensive processes help the person cope with social stimuli that lead to feelings of discomfort. As the task is carried out, aspects of the social situation (either parts of the work or other people) can affect the level of attention or cognitive distortion produced in the person. Most personality states lead a person to heightened perceptual sensitivity when that motive is aroused or to defensive responses when the social stimuli threaten *that* state. We expect, therefore, that most peripheral personality states will produce reasonably high levels of selective attention in those situations in which the person is directly involved. In other words, we expect highly specific content of social stimulus by specific personality-variable interactions to appear in the course of social interaction for most personality variables. We would expect more moderate levels of perceptual defense to be produced by abasement, affiliation, dominance, and recognition because of their somewhat stronger defensive system; Machiavellianism, because its defense is opportunism, and order, because its defense is task accomplishment, should be more accurate perceptually. The lower levels of distortion for nurturance and achievement result from their lower need for defensive structures.

TABLE 5.3
The Level of Activity in Each Stage of Group Process for Selected Personality Variables

| | Stages of Group Process | | | | | | | |
| | Information Search | | | | | Decision Making | | |
Personality Variables	Orientation	Selective Attention	Aspiration Level	Search Persistence	Organization of Work	Generation of Solutions	Evaluation of Solutions	Implementation
Dependency	H	H	L	L	L	L	L	L
Abasement	L	M	L	M	L	L	L	L
Approval	M	H	M	L	L	L	L	L
Authoritarianism	H	H	L	L	H	M	M	H
Order	H	L	M	H	H	H	H	H
Affiliation	L	M	M	M	L	M	L	L
Machiavellianism	H	L	H	H	H	H	H	H
Dominance	H	M	H	H	H	H	H	H
Nurturance	M	L	H	H	M	H	M	H
Achievement	H	L	H	H	H	H	H	H
Recognition	M	M	H	H	H	H	M	H

Note: H = high
M = medium
L = low

Personality and Aspiration Level.   Once the person has determined the nature of the task, setting, and group, engagement with the task begins. Because almost all tasks can be performed within a wide range of possible success, social psychologists felt quite early that it was important to understand the mechanisms underlying the level of accomplishment that the individual or group hopes to achieve. In thinking about how a personality variable affects the setting of the level of aspiration, we focus on the level that a person sets in pursuit of personal goals, rather than on the level set by others that the person agrees to pursue. We expect that as dependency, abasement, and authoritarianism do not rely on the quality of work, they should lead people to be content to work at an externally determined level of accomplishment. Dominance and recognition concerns, however, are very much involved with the quality of work as a device to validate personal worth, and so should lead to the setting of high levels of aspiration. Achievement concerns are similar to dominance and recognition, but as they are more limited by considerations of what is reasonable to expect in that situation, they should lead to moderate levels of risk taking and realistically high levels of aspiration. Nurturance, which is also a more realistic concern, should follow achievement concerns. Because approval and affiliation needs lead the person to be more concerned with self-selecting the behaviors designed to please others, we expect them to produce a moderate level of aspiration. Machiavellianism, which is even more manipulatively other-directed than the need for approval, should set moderately high levels as a means to secure a high-status position and therefore the opportunity to influence others.

Personality and Search Persistence.   The amount of time and energy that group members put into gathering the information needed to make a decision seems to be a function of the concern individuals have for the completion of the task. Thus, as dependency, authoritarianism, and approval needs are not task related, we expect low levels of performance at this stage of the sequence. As affiliation-oriented people can become moderately task involved, as a way of being with other group members, we expect moderate levels of this kind of activity. For all the other variables, we expect that they should lead people to be quite active in their basic task work, although for the different reasons that are the bases of their definitions. For example, order concerns should lead people to mistrust the level of effort produced by other people, and so they should work with a narrow and determined focus. Achievement concerns, based on a desire to do high-quality work, should lead people to work with a wide-ranging, flexible, and determined focus. Later on, Table 5.4 presents a detailed means to distinguish between these different styles of search persistence.

Personality and the Organization of Work.   As work progresses, certain people within most groups become quite active in assigning, evaluating, and regulating the activity of the other members. Our simplest way of thinking about this kind of behavior is with the imprecise word "leadership." In the next main section, we attempt a more detailed and more modern specification of that role. At this time, we wish to note that this activity becomes very important at an intermediate point in the group's work and that personality characteristics vary widely in the degree to which they lead people to assume this role. Our definitions lead to fairly direct predictions. We would not expect dependency, abasement, approval, or affiliation concerns to activate this type of behavior. Nurturance, because of its greater concern for the personal feelings of other group members, should show only moderate levels of leadership in spite of its concern with task accomplishment. The other variables, for different reasons, should lead people to display significant levels of leadership activity.

Personality and the Generation of a Solution.   With a work organization decided upon, group members begin to produce the kinds of solutions that might possibly meet the group goal. The peripheral traits based upon the esteem needs are quite actively engaged in this stage. It is difficult to think of a competing element in one of them that would reduce their level of activity in searching for the range of possible options to present to the group. Affiliation, as has been noted, is a concern that is only moderately (and only instrumentally) task oriented. As such, this concern should lead to only moderate levels of activity at this stage. Authoritarianism should lead to a performance at only moderate levels because of its balancing between the competing tendencies to rely on external supports, on the one hand, and to become identified with the goals of higher status and to take responsibility for the task, on the other. By contrast, order is a concern that does take responsibility for the task work. The remainder of the safety cluster, however, leads people to rely on other group members to care about the way in which the task is completed. Thus, we would expect these characteristics to produce only reduced levels of activity at this stage.

Personality and the Evaluation Process.   As work progresses, sets of alternative solutions are produced for parts of the work, as well as for the work as a whole. This range of options has to be reviewed and evaluated if a decision is to be made. In this stage, we are concerned with the question of which personality characteristics lead people to become active in *providing* evaluations of the group's work. At this point of the group's existence, we expect the pattern of activity to be somewhat more varied than at the earlier phases. Within the safety cluster, we do not expect a significant effort to be activated by dependency, abasement, or approval concerns because, in general, these people have transferred responsibility for the task performance to other members. Authoritarianism and order concerns, however, should activate higher levels of involvement in evaluation because of their components that take responsibility for the completion of the work. Affiliation concerns generally lead to lower levels of task involvement, and we could expect a special reluctance to provide evaluation of the work of others. Because of their commitment to task success and lower degrees of concern for the sensitivities of other group members, we expect that dominance, Machiavellianism, and achievement concerns would activate vigorous levels of evaluative activity. Nurturance concerns share the task commitment of the other esteem variables, but the more interpersonally oriented components should moderate their level of activity. The expected level for recognition concerns should be moderate because, although there is real task involvement, there is also the added component that the expressions of positive regard needed from others should serve as a moderating influence on the degree to which critical evaluations of others are produced.

Personality and Implementation.   Although the content of the implementation phase differs widely across the phenomena of social psychology, activity during this phase is fairly easy to predict. The underlying factor that controls the level of activity to be expected in this phase is the degree to which people are committed to completing the task at hand. Thus, for all the reasons already outlined, we expect that dependency, abasement, approval, and affiliation concerns should lead to relatively low levels of implementation activity, whereas all the rest of the peripheral variables should activate relatively high levels.

THE NATURE OF GROUP PROCESS
ACTIVATED BY PERSONALITY VARIABLES

Faced with a social field, the individual must behave. In each of the preceding discussions, we wanted to identify the personal variables that interact with environmental variables to affect the level and type of responsiveness to a social event. These interactions are, by and large, the intervening subjective events that precede social behavior; they are not yet the behavior with which social psychology is most interested. In our last discussion of personality and stages of the task, we began an analysis of the amount of activity that should be expected from different kinds of people faced with different types of information-processing demands. In that analysis as well, we have not yet specified the actual behavior that people produce. Although we present predictions of the readiness to respond, in terms of activity level, for different kinds of people along with the task sequence, we have not yet focused on concrete behavior. All of the preceding sections outline our understanding of the interactional pattern that creates the subjective events leading to behavioral responses. We can now turn our attention to examining what people actually do.

Virtually every construct system that is used to provide an analysis of this type recognizes that actual behavior is concrete and specific: People command, suggest, agree, flatter, criticize, and so on. These concrete acts deal with specific parts of the world in narrowly focused ways. The fact that these acts may be elements of a larger unit (e.g., an overall plan for social behavior) should not obscure the fact that these concrete acts are the material out of which the social event is constructed. These acts are the outcomes of the interactional patterns that have been outlined to this point.

Performance Styles

As people work together in a group, patterns of behavior appear that are commonly thought to indicate the global features of group process (e.g., the leadership or followership roles). In addition, each of these roles may appear in a variety of ways (e.g., in the form of the autocratic or democratic leader). It has been a continuing problem to decide how best to represent these elements of the group process. In chapter 4, we outlined a two-dimensional category system, derived from Bales, that stays quite close to the actual behavior that people produce in groups. This system also yields a fine-grained record of the means through which different kinds of people achieve their varied purposes. In this section, we outline the detailed behavioral pattern that may be expected from people with the psychological concerns that we have been tracking. Table 5.4 presents our expectations of the level of activity that each personal concern will produce in each behavioral category. We believe that the cluster of activity across these behavioral categories is a useful way to specify the nature of social performance that appears within groups.

We hope Table 5.4 makes immediately apparent the many active clusters of behavior that are expected from the personality variables. We hope also that the varied pattern expected from a detailed analysis of only 11 variables shows how necessary it is to use a comprehensive model of personality/ behavior and also that our usual experimental approach of contrasting global behavior expected from two personality variables (e.g., dominance vs. dependency) or two levels of a single variable (e.g., high vs. low authoritarianism) loses important features of social events. The complexity of Table 5.4, with 224 separate predictions, makes a detailed discussion of our reasoning quite forbidding. However, by this time, the personal bases of social responsiveness should be fairly clear, and so we limit ourselves here to an overview of the levels of social activity to be expected from each of these variables.

Dependency concerns should lead people to avoid the kinds of behavior that give direction to the task activity of a group. Instead, there should be concern primarily with following the direction given by those who are providing the initiative in the instrumental work of the group. In other words, based on their feelings of inadequacy, we expect high levels of behavior in those categories that indicate compliance (which includes the carrying out of directives as well as expressing agreement). Additionally, with a primary concern with predictability in the work of the group, we expect little activity in either the positive or negative poles of the socioemotional dimension.

Abasement concerns are not focused on the task dimensions of the group. Rather, they express the person's anxiety through negative behavior both within and beyond the group. Therefore, for this variable, we expect fairly high levels of disaffiliative behavior and activity in the other areas limited to those categories that express inadequacy. Because this mode of adaptation does not lead to a desire for secure protective relationships, we do not expect high levels of compliance, even though high levels of anxiety are present.

Approval concerns lead to fairly high levels of task activity, which are set within narrowly prescribed categories. These concerns lead to participative relationships with an admired superior, and although we expect little initiative to be shown by such people, we do expect enthusiastic instrumental activity within those guidelines that are set by other members of the group. We also expect such people to show great social sensitivity and interest, both in the forms of compliance and friendliness as the way to achieve the secure cooperative relationship with a superior.

Authoritarianism leads to a blunt, narrowly focused, and socially insensitive assumption of responsibility for the task work of the group. We expect high levels of activity in a few instrumental categories that narrowly move the task toward completion. For example, we expect that this concern, which is based on a defensive and fairly inflexible cognitive structure, will lead people to give direction and to disagree. But they will not be able to use broader instrumental strategies such as giving analysis or integrating the work of other group members. Similarly, we expect low levels of positive socioemotional activity and high levels of interpersonal hostility when anxious or frustrated during the group process.

Order concerns are similar to authoritarianism, but even more narrowly focused on the completion of the task. Order differs from authoritarianism by a lack of concern for the relative status of other group members, leading to low levels of compliance and an intense concern with details of the work. We would expect such people to focus on categories such as procedural suggestion, giving opinion, and evaluation, with less concern for the creative aspects of problem solving, self-dramatizing displays, or coordinated work with others. Order concerns also seem to organize social transactions more tightly and successfully than authoritarianism, so we would expect a less intense hostility component, which would lead to lower levels of disaffiliative social behavior.

TABLE 5.4
The Level of Task and Socioemotional Activity for Selected Personality Variables

Personality Variables	Task Activity								
	Initiation								
	Procedural suggestion (6)	Suggests solution (7)	Gives opinion, information (8, 11)	Gives analysis, evaluation (8)	Draws attention, clarifies (12)	Asks for opinion, analysis, evaluation (13)	Disagrees (14)	Acknowledges communication (4)	Coordinates member effort toward goal
Dependency	L	L	L	L	L	L	L	M	L
Abasement	L	L	M	L	L	L	M	L	L
Approval	L	H	M	L	M	H	L	H	L
Authoritarianism	M	M	H	L	L	L	H	M	L
Order	H	H	H	H	L	L	H	L	M
Affiliation	L	M	H	L	H	H	L	H	M
Machiavellianism	M	H	H	H	M	M	M	H	H
Dominance	H	H	H	H	H	H	H	L	H
Nurturance	M	M	H	H	H	H	M	H	H
Achievement	H	H	H	H	H	H	M	H	H
Recognition	M	H	H	M	M	H	M	H	L

Note: H = high
M = medium
L = low

TABLE 5.4 (Continued)

Concurrence			Affiliation					Disaffiliation		
Concurrence, compliance (5)	Self-question, personal inadequacy, nervous laughter (9, 15)	Asks for help due to incompetence (15)	Friendly, social recognition (1)	Considerate, empathy	Increases group solidarity, raises status (2)	Shows understanding, social sensitivity	Shows concern to ameliorate differences in group	Aggression externalized beyond group (10)	Aggression toward group members (17)	Withdraws
H	H	H	L	L	L	L	L	L	L	H
L	H	H	L	L	L	L	L	H	H	H
H	L	M	H	H	H	H	L	M	L	L
H	L	L	L	L	L	L	L	H	H	M
L	M	L	L	L	L	L	L	L	L	H
H	L	L	H	H	H	H	H	L	L	L
H	L	M	H	H	H	H	H	H	L	L
L	L	L	L	L	M	L	L	L	L	L
M	L	L	H	H	H	H	H	L	L	L
M	L	L	M	M	M	M	M	L	L	L
M	L	L	H	M	M	M	L	H	M	L

Affiliation concerns are based on a desire for intimacy in social relations. Although we do not expect a direct task involvement, we do expect that affiliative concerns within a task-oriented group will lead people to work in cooperative ways along the lines set by others. Thus, we expect such people to be quite busy at task work (to give opinions, ask for opinions, and coordinate other people's work), but not to provide the initiative toward task completion. Not surprisingly, we expect these concerns to lead to high levels of positive socioemotional activity and to low levels of activity that might hurt other group members (gives evaluation, disagrees, shows hostility toward group members).

Machiavellianism, because it is such an opportunistic trait, is less simple to present. In evaluating our expectations of a Machiavellian's social responses, we had to distinguish between the likely subjective and likely behavioral responses more sharply than was needed with the other variables. For example, we suspect there is a strong component of hostility in this complex trait, but because exhibiting hostility is usually unproductive, we expect it to appear rarely in social events. Similarly, if it serves their purposes, we expect Machiavellians to be much more accommodating than they really feel. Thus, our predictions in Table 5.4 are based on the behavioral, rather than the subjective, responses expected. To put it simply, we expect Machiavellians to do what is necessary to control the group. In the usual laboratory group, we expect them to be quite vigorous participants who disguise their controlling behavior with a great deal of "apparent" social concern for other members. Behaviors that lead to individual prominence (e.g., procedural suggestion) are used cautiously, and others that show agreeableness (e.g., compliance, considerateness) are used to reduce reactance to their attempts at control.

Dominance concerns lead to behavior that demonstrates the person's competence by controlling the course of events in a social group. We expect vigorous engagement in both giving direction to and participating in the work of the group. Although these people are interpersonally pleasant in a matter-of-fact way (e.g., they can compliment a subordinate) and are not hostile in the usual course of events, the social sensitivities that constitute the socioemotional dimension are outside their area of skill. Thus, we expect substantial activity in all the initiating task-activity categories and little activity in the concurring, affiliative and disaffiliative (unless thwarted) categories.

Nurturance concerns achieve demonstrations of self-worth more through the success of people and institutions than through the completion of task work. Put another way, the object of this concern (or its task) is the development and success of individuals and groups for which the person takes responsibility. Therefore, this concern should lead people to desire the success of the group by fostering the prominence of others rather than through acts of their own prominence. Thus, although there is a genuine involvement in the task, we would expect lower levels of activity in categories such as procedural suggestion, higher rates of compliance, and high levels of positive socioemotional activity.

Achievement concerns are in many ways similar to those of dominance. They differ in that self-worth is demonstrated by the quality of the task success rather than by control of the behaviors of group members. Thus, we would expect vigorous participation in all categories of initiating task activity, with the only exception being that moderate level of disagreement needed to insure the quality of the task work. Similarly, as individuals are not threatened by the success of others, we would expect moderate levels of compliance in response to the successful achievements of co-workers. As a task-oriented concern, we would expect these people to preserve the social amenities in a group without utilizing all the resources of socioemotional activity to further the group process.

Recognition concerns focus less on task success than on the person being acknowledged for ability by other members of the group. Thus, we expect these concerns to engage people in vigorous participation with the task, particularly in those areas that permit self-dramatizing displays of ability. We would expect these concerns to lead people to avoid areas that challenge or antagonize other group members (e.g., procedural suggestion, disagreement) and to use some task categories (e.g., compliance) and the socioemotional categories to earn the friendship of other group members at a level high enough to allow these other people to acknowledge the person's accomplishments.

Occasionally, it is useful to represent the performance of group members in more compact ways. For example, we might want a simple way to visualize the overall performance style of people with dominance concerns in comparison to people with achievement concerns. Such an analysis is concerned primarily with the overall combination of task and socioemotional activity rather than the detailed ways that such performance may be expressed. As Bales' (1950) original work showed, more general measures can record the overall level of activity across all the subcategories of each behavioral coordinate. In this way, a composite performance-style measure can be developed that indicates the major vectors of behavior in this two-dimensional space for each personality variable.

Table 5.5 presents a hypothetical scheme that allows us to predict the performance style of each personality variable along the task and socioemotional coordinates found in Table 1.1. The level of activity suggested in each IPS subcategory in Table 5.4 allows us to estimate the overall level of activity for initiation, concurrence, affiliation, and disaffiliation behavior. For each personality variable, these levels of activity can be expressed hypothetically as the percentages of that kind of behavior that might be possible in a particular situation. For example, if we expect dominance concerns

TABLE 5.5
Estimated Performance Style on Task and Socioemotional Dimensions
for Selected Personality Variables

Personality Variables	Task			Socioemotional		
	Initiation (I)	Concurrence (C)	(I–C)	Affiliation (A)	Disaffiliation (D)	(A–D)
Dependency	5	100	– 95	0	25	– 25
Abasement	15	20	– 5	0	100	– 100
Approval	25	90	– 65	95	10	85
Authoritarianism	75	55	20	0	50	– 50
Order	75	10	65	0	50	– 50
Affiliation	65	30	35	100	20	80
Machiavellianism	90	50	40	100	20	80
Dominance	100	0	100	20	0	20
Nurturance	85	25	60	100	0	100
Achievement	95	25	70	60	0	60
Recognition	85	25	60	70	20	50

to produce 100% of the initiation behavior that is possible in a specific situation, then we can expect dependency concerns to produce only 5% of that amount of behavior. Following this line of reasoning, for each personality variable in Table 5.5 we present a purely hypothetical estimate of the percentage of the behavior that might be expected in a situation. As the polar categories of initiation (I) and concurrence (C) define the task dimension, and affiliation (A) and disaffiliation (D) define the socioemotional dimension, the difference scores of $I - C$ and $A - D$ can represent the style of performance expected along each coordinate for each personality variable (see Fig. 5.1).

We can use the hypothetical scores that we expect to be produced by approval concerns to illustrate the way that a summary performance score can be derived. On the task dimension, we expect that the need for approval will lead to a production of 25% of the initiation behavior and 90% of the concurrence behavior that is possible for an individual to produce in that situation. The difference between the two scores (25-90) is $- 65$. On the socioemotional dimension, we expect the need for approval to produce 95% of the affiliative and 10% of the disaffiliative behavior that is possible. The difference between the two scores (95-10) is 85. The performance style that we expect from people concerned with the need for approval is represented by the scores of −65 on the task dimension and 85 on the socioemotional dimension.

b. Negotiation Processes

Tables 5.4 and 5.5 present the major behavioral orientations of a single individual. However, as two individuals begin to interact, their relationship develops features that go beyond the behaviors just described. Their relationship can be thought of as an additional set of dimensions through which members implement their separate orientations into a joint structure that meets the requirements of the task. Many of the social phenomena that have been studied under the term "group process" describe the variability of

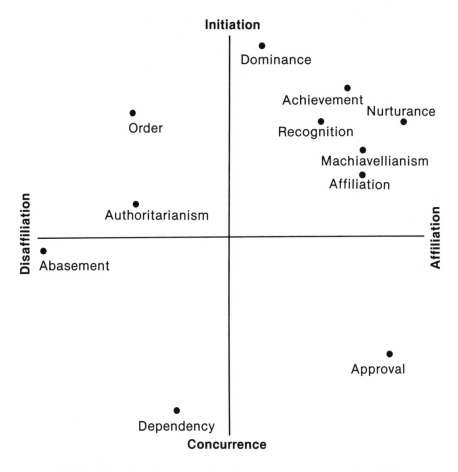

FIG. 5.1   Overall performance style activated by selected personality variables.

groups along these interpersonal dimensions. We expect that personality processes contribute to the nature of this area of group functioning as well.

Table 5.6 outlines the major features of the negotiation process that we expect to be affected by the personality variables we have been following. But before turning to an overview of this aspect of the group process as a whole, it is necessary to review briefly our analysis of the dimension that we called modes of interdependence, which are created from the interaction of two more basic social processes. As we noted earlier, individuals in an interpersonal relationship may choose to maximize their own or joint outcomes (to choose competition vs. cooperation) and to be frank or guarded with the other people they are attempting to influence (to reveal or conceal information as to their purposes). These two dimensions generate four major forms of the problem-solving relationship: adversarial (competitive–information revealing), exploitative (competitive–information concealing), ingratiating (cooperative–information concealing), and integrative (cooperative–information revealing) (see Fig. 5.2). Let us review each mode of interdependence briefly and note our reasons for expecting it to develop from these personality variables.

Adversarial Mode.   Persons with dominance needs use interpersonal transactions to control the activities of the other person. The relationship is competitive because it focuses on the dominance-oriented individuals' own

TABLE 5.6
Relationship Between Selected Personality Variables
and Characteristic Negotiating Orientation

Personality Variables	Bargaining Stance	Techniques of Information Use	Modes of Interdependence
Dependency	yielding	rigid	ingratiating
Abasement	firm	rigid	exploitative
Approval	yielding	rigid	ingratiating
Authoritarianism	yielding	rigid	exploitative
Order	firm	rigid	ingratiating
Affiliation	yielding	flexible	integrative
Machiavellianism	firm	flexible	exploitative
Dominance	firm	rigid	adversarial
Nurturance	firm	flexible	integrative
Achievement	firm	flexible	integrative
Recognition	yielding	rigid	adversarial

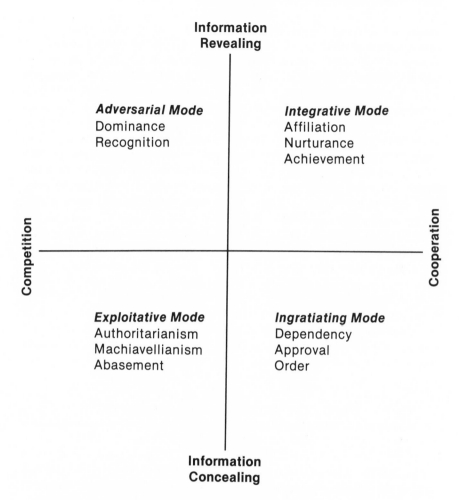

FIG. 5.2   The relationship between selected personality variables and modes of interdependence in interpersonal problem-solving strategies.

personal success, which is defined by their victory over other people in the group. Their strength and self-absorption, on the other hand, leads them to be open and frank about their purposes with the other person. The need for recognition leads to an adversarial relationship for many of the same reasons. It sets up an interpersonal challenge in the social relationship, but the goal is praise coerced from, rather than control obtained over, the other person.

Exploitative Mode.   The hostility and mistrust components of the trait of authoritarianism among peers lead to difficulty in cooperating, and the need to establish a ranking system leads to the assumption of a competitive focus in the relationship. All these characteristics should lead authoritarians to conceal information about their intentions. Machiavellianism, by definition, is the trait that manipulates co-workers in competitive and dishonest ways, whereas abasement manipulates other people by interfering with their work in order to elicit a critical response from them.

Ingratiating Mode.   As both dependency and approval needs focus on the wish to establish stable and subordinate relationships, they should lead people to attempt to work with others in cooperative ways. The lack of confidence that such people have in themselves should lead them to be quite guarded with others in revealing their purposes in order not to increase their vulnerability. The task-oriented focus of order should lead them to cooperate with others if the route to the task is clear. However, if the others do not seem capable, order concerns should lead to an intermediate position. Their level of mistrust should make them cautious in revealing their purposes.

Integrative Mode.   Persons with affiliation, nurturance, and achievement concerns should all find it desirable to work cooperatively with others (affiliation and nurturance) in the common pursuit of success at the task (nurturance and achievement). As the three concerns do not include components of mistrust of self or others, they should be able to reveal their intentions easily.

These modes of interdependence are included in the summary presentation (Table 5.6) of the three dimensions of characteristic negotiating orientations that are often studied in social psychology. Much of the rationale to account for our predictions on the other dimensions has been provided at different points in the chapter, so an extended discussion is not necessary. The strength with which people maintain their initial position, their *bargaining stance,* is fairly easy to summarize. We expect that people will be yielding (or compliant) when they depend on others for support (dependency, approval, authoritarianism), are interpersonally oriented rather than task oriented (affiliation), or need the response from others to confirm their value (recognition). We expect that people will be firm in maintaining their position if they wish to provoke others (abasement), to mistrust others (order), and especially, to control others (Machiavellianism, dominance) or are confident in their ability to solve the task (nurturance, achievement).

The personal bases underlying group members' *techniques of information use* has also been anticipated in earlier discussions. We would expect all the variables in the safety cluster to be quite rigid in their mobilization of information and arguments in the influence process. We expect that the level of anxiety present in each of these variables will lead people to narrow their range of information search, examine few alternative solutions, and respond fairly inflexibly in the face of unexpected events. We expect that both dominance and recognition will handle this dimension of the influence process in rigid ways as well: dominance because of its egocentric desire to establish control over others, and recognition because of its egocentric focus on receiving positive evaluations from others. The other variables should be much more flexible in their techniques of information use. Their component of trait anxiety is much lower than it is for the safety variables, and each of the remaining variables has additional features that encourage people to respond to information, events, and other people in fairly flexible ways: affiliation because of its interpersonal sensitivities, Machiavellianism because of its opportunistic orientation, and nurturance and achievement because their strong commitment to task rather than to personal success leads them to be anxious to make the best use of any useful alternative.

THE NATURE OF GROUP STRUCTURE ACTIVATED BY PERSONALITY VARIABLES

From the point of view of the emergent group, individuals engaged in a task relate to each other through the major behavioral orientations presented in Tables 5.4 and 5.6. As these behaviors continue, additional social procedures develop to further the efforts of group members to reach their goal. In time, these new social processes become the characteristics of the internal structure of the group. As we outlined earlier, the fifth stage of the information-processing sequence requires a procedure to assign, evaluate, regulate, and integrate the many separate activities needed to complete the work of the group. In other words, an organization of positions develops within the group whose main features seem to be the dimensions of *differentiation, rank, power,* and *reward.* In this section, we explore how personality variables may contribute to the specific state of each of these emerging structures within the group.

Differentiation

If the goals of the group are met by the types of behavior outlined in Table 5.4, then groups vary considerably in the way activity is assigned to (or assumed by) group members. At one extreme of the differentiation continuum, all members of the group may assume responsibility for the same set of tasks. This lack of functional division can be thought of as a structure with great functional *integration* in the definition of the social roles. At the other extreme, each task can be performed by a different group member, leading to a structure with great *separation* in the definition of the social roles.

For groups that are homogeneous in terms of the distribution of personality and ability characteristics, we propose that the personality variables will affect the degree of social differentiation through several different mechanisms that are related to the properties of these psychological characteristics (Table 5.7). We expect that the variables in the safety cluster act to restrict the individual's assumption of responsibility. The anxiety and uncertainty components of these variables should lead the individual to desire as little responsibility for as few tasks as the situation permits. Thus, groups composed of members with these characteristics should have sharply demarcated leadership and followership positions, with the several followership positions based as much as possible on a segregated allocation of the task work.

Affiliation concerns, by definition, lead the individual to desire intimate egalitarian involvements with others. For this reason, we expect that groups composed of such individuals will form a structure with fairly equivalent definitions of positions, including a reduced distinction between the leadership and followership positions.

In general, the variables within the esteem cluster lead individuals to engage easily in the task and to wish to assume a wide range of responsibilities. By and large, success at a wide range of activities is the method through which such individuals most easily earn the self-esteem rewards they seek. In

TABLE 5.7
Relationship Between Selected Personality Variables and Activation
of Differentiation and Rank in Group Structure

Personality Variable	Differentiation of Function	Rank	
		Bases of Rank	Ranking of Positions
Dependency	Separation	External	Unequal
Abasement	Separation	External	Unequal
Approval	Separation	External	Unequal
Authoritarianism	Separation	External	Unequal
Order	Separation	Internal	Unequal
Affiliation	Integration	Internal	Equal
Machiavellianism	Separation	Internal	Unequal
Dominance	Separation	Internal	Equal
Nurturance	Integration	Internal	Equal
Achievement	Integration	Internal	Equal
Recognition	Integration	External	Equal

a group composed of individuals pursuing such personal rewards, the resultant structure will be one of fairly integrated positions. It is important to note
that this structure generally emerges, not because it is the one desired by such
individuals, but because when group members each desire to undertake the
full range of activities, they tend to be active in similar ways. This mechanism
underlies the integrated structure we expect to be produced by groups composed of individuals with achievement and recognition concerns. Individuals
with nurturance concerns should function similarly, possibly with the additional feature of a positive desire for an integrated group. However, the final
social product for groups composed of Machiavellian and dominance-
oriented individuals should not be one of integrated positions. Because these
two concerns so egocentrically seek personal control over task activity, we expect that an integrated structure would prove to be unstable. In groups
homogeneously composed of such individuals, we assume the only procedure
that will prove to be stable over time is the one that divides areas of responsibility. Thus, we expect that such groups should have structures with positions
defined as equally responsible and important, but with sharply delimited
ranges of concern. In other words, a stable structure should emerge that is
separated in terms of task responsibility, not in terms of leadership and
followership.

Rank

Our concern with the social property of rank in groups includes determining
the *bases* upon which such distinctions between positions are made as well as
the *degree* to which positions are ranked within groups. In the last chapter,
we presented the specific characteristics that fall into each set of internal and
external attributes. Here, we explore the way that personality variables utilize
these attributes as a basis for ranking and then discuss the degree to which
ranking emerges with the group (Table 5.7).

Because most of the variables within the safety cluster are strongly characterized by anxiety and mistrust, we expect such self-protective individuals to
evaluate others on the basis of the more easily understood superficial external
attributes (e.g., occupational level or sex). Verbal labels, such as we use in experiments to indicate relative standing (e.g., freshman vs. senior), also
should be most effective in generating a perceived ranking with these personality variables. Only individuals with order concerns, because of their focus
on task success, should utilize demonstrated personal attributes, such as
competence or knowledge. In contrast, affiliation and most of the esteem
variables should focus on the more task-relevant personal set of attributes.
Although an external attribute (e.g., differences in occupational level) plau-
sibly can reflect some real differences in degree of merit, the more difficult to
comprehend set of demonstrated personal attributes is a more reliable indica-

tor of success in a particular situation. As the psychological components that might reduce interpersonal contact are not as strong in the affiliation and esteem clusters as they are in the safety cluster, a much stronger search and evaluation procedure can be instituted. Thus, affiliation and esteem-based characteristics should use personal attributes as their base for ranking group members or positions.

The mechanism underlying the degree to which groups establish prestige differences between positions within homogeneous groups is the same as that leading to differentiation of function between positions. In general, groups composed of members with safety concerns seek a member, and then an established position, to assume responsibility for their own work. In its simplest form, this is the division into leadership and followership positions, with the former position ranked more highly than the latter. A subsidiary aspect of the ranking process in homogeneous safety-oriented groups is the question of the determinants that select one individual to occupy that position. In such groups, it is likely that if one member possesses an external attribute that is more highly valued (e.g., higher class standing), this may stimulate a common group decision to allocate that person to the more highly ranked position, regardless of that person's own desires.

Similarly, the same cluster that leads to a lower degree of differentiation in affiliation and esteem groups also leads to an equal ranking of the positions (especially for affiliation, nurturance, and achievement). Machiavellianism does try to make distinctions between group members, and so the positions in such a group should be ranked unequally. Dominance, though ultimately requiring a separated structure, does not focus on small distinctions of merit and so should result in an equally ranked structure, if all members are considered competent.

Power

Cartwright and Zander's discussion of the utilization of and responsiveness to different forms of power rests heavily on the characteristics of each party in the influence process. This general individual-difference approach in the bases of power is helped considerably by the systematic approach to the characteristics of the person we are attempting to provide. The definitions in chapter 3 of the special goals that are sought by, together with other components associated with, each personality variable that we have reviewed greatly simplify this task. Based on these earlier discussions, we can examine each variable briefly to determine the degree of utilization of and responsiveness to the different forms of power. These relationships are summarized in Table 5.8.

Dependency concerns should lead people to rely most heavily on their established position when trying to influence another group member. As they

TABLE 5.8
The Degree of Utilization of and Responsiveness to Different Forms
of Power for Selected Personality Variables

Personality Variable	Utilization of Different Forms of Power			
	Reward	Coercive	Expert	Legitimate
Dependency	L	L	L	H
Abasement	L	M	L	H
Approval	H	L	M	M
Authoritarianism	L	H	L	H
Order	L	H	H	M
Affiliation	H	L	M	M
Machiavellianism	H	H	H	H
Dominance	L	H	H	H
Achievement	H	L	H	M
Nurturance	H	L	H	M
Recognition	M	H	H	H

Personality Variable	Responsiveness to Different Forms of Power			
	Reward	Coercive	Expert	Legitimate
Dependency	H	H	M	H
Abasement	L	H	M	M
Approval	H	M	H	H
Authoritarianism	L	H	M	H
Order	M	L	H	M
Affiliation	H	M	M	M
Machiavellianism	L	H	M	L
Dominance	H	L	H	L
Achievement	H	L	H	M
Nurturance	M	L	H	M
Recognition	H	L	H	H

Note: H = high
M = medium
L = low

feel personally ineffective, they should rely least on providing positive or negative rewards to other people. For the same reason, most forms of power utilized by other people should prove to be effective in causing dependent people to comply with demands made upon them. *Abasement*-oriented people are similarly ineffective in taking strong direct action in an influence attempt, but the hostility component should allow them to use criticism much more easily. By definition, of all the forms of power applied against them, they should be most responsive to a strong and direct act of coercion. *Approval*-oriented people should rely most heavily on providing positive rewards to others, and they find using coercion the most difficult. As they basically have a weak personality structure, which is focused on maintaining a relationship, they should be quite responsive to most forms of influence. *Authoritarianism* is an active orientation that leads these people to put their greatest reliance on their position (legitimate power) when trying to influence another and to fall back on coercion if they are not immediately successful. Because they are interpersonally insensitive, authoritarians will rely least on the reward form of power to control events. Similarly, by definition, they should be most affected by the position of the person making the influence attempt and, as basically a weak orientation, will be influenced by threats and sanctions as well. *Order* defends against anxiety by a strong set of defenses focused on the task. Their lack of interpersonal sensitivity makes providing positive rewards to others least likely, but they should feel comfortable using all the remaining forms of power. The strength of their defenses should make them least responsive to coercion, and their task orientation should make them most affected by expert power.

Affiliation-oriented people should feel fairly uncomfortable in explicit influence situations and try to avoid the leadership role. Within a less explicit task or within social situations, they should rely most on providing positive rewards to other people, and although they can retaliate against an offense, they should rely least on direct negative sanctions. Similarly, they should be most responsive to positive rewards from other people. As a characteristic that desires to maintain pleasant relationships, small coercive attempts should make them yield quickly, whereas strong coercive attempts should be felt as so unpleasant that they will withdraw from the situation.

Machiavellian individuals, by definition, feel comfortable with any form of power and will use whatever form is most effective with the other people. As egocentric manipulators, they should be least influenced by legitimate power influence attempts. It is likely that only direct negative sanctions, forcefully applied, will be successful in influencing their course of action. *Dominance* is much like order in freely using all but reward power. It should be influenced most by expert power, should react strongly against attempts at coercion, and should be susceptible to reward power in the form of recognition of the person's ability or prominence. *Achievement*-oriented people should rely on their ability (expert power) and praise (reward) to influence others. They should use coercive power least, not because it is difficult for them to be critical, but, rather, because of their ease in using expert and reward power. Similarly, they should be most responsive to expert power, especially when they determine that it is based on real competence; they should be somewhat less responsive to reward power and least affected by attempts at coercion. *Nurturance*-oriented people should find using reward and expert power most congenial, and although they can use coercive power, they use it least because of their unusual skill with reward and their ability to effectively engage others in pursuit of a common goal. As with achievement-oriented people, they should be most responsive to genuine competence in influence attempts. *Recognition*-oriented people, because of their own personal need for praise from others, should find expert and then legitimate power to be most congenial and find reward power (because it validates the worth of perceived competitors) the least congenial. If they run into difficulty in the influence attempt, they should fall back on applying coercive power sharply. For these reasons, they should be most susceptible to reward power influence attempts from others. Coercive power should be the least effective with them because it would be felt as too destructive to their hopes for confirmation from others.

Heterogeneous Groups.   These different bases for the utilization of and responsiveness to different forms of power allow us to begin to analyze the social process in groups with heterogeneous personality composition. We have tried to avoid making the model more complex — which would happen if we consistently examined the many possible combinations of personality types at the different stages of the social process. But real groups are seldom homogeneous. The influence process is such a basic dimension of social events that we can achieve substantial insight into the functioning of heterogeneous groups if we examine the ways that power is used and responded to by the different kinds of people. The theoretical material that we have just reviewed should enable us to understand which kind of person is likely to be most influential in heterogeneous situations.

Because group process varies with changes in the environmental variables, in order to explore the influence process in heterogeneous groups we must identify a specific type of event as the social context within which these variables interact. Let us consider, then, the interaction process that occurs when two different kinds of people attempt to move the group decision in the separate directions that they prefer. In other words, let us visualize which aspects of power control the assumption of leadership within the group. Following Cartwright and Zander (1968), in order to explore the likely outcome of this influence event we must consider: (a) which forms of power each type of person is most comfortable using and (b) to which forms of power each type of person is most susceptible.

Two illustrations can show how the patterns of personality and power outlined in Table 5.8 resolve the influence attempt. If a dependent and a dominant person each try to have their suggestion accepted by the other, then Table 5.8 shows that the dependent person commands few forms of power and is susceptible to all forms used by another person. The dominant person, on the other hand, commands many forms of power and is susceptible to fewer than the dependent person. These different patterns of power use and susceptibility are the mechanisms through which this particularly simple influence interaction is resolved in favor of the dominant person.

A more complex interaction is that between a Machiavellian and a dominant person. Given the definition of a Machiavellian, one would assume that such a person should find a way to be successful in any interpersonal encounter. However, the power pattern summarized in Table 5.8 leads to the nonobvious prediction that the dominant person should be more successful. Notice that both kinds of people are fairly similar in the types of power that they can command. The one real difference in power use is that the dominant person does not use much reward power. But as the Machiavellian is not very influenced by that form of power, this lack does not lead to a weakness for the dominant person in this encounter. However, the important difference between them, which predicts the outcome of their struggle for influence, is that the dominant person is less susceptible to coercive power, whereas the Machiavellian is most susceptible to it. As it is easy for the dominant person to apply coercive power, we expect that this imbalance between the two types of people will control the struggle for influence in favor of the dominant person.

Using this reasoning as the mechanism that resolves struggles for influence between different types of people, Table 5.9 summarizes our expectations of the results of all the possible two-person encounters. We cannot discuss each of the 55 types of interactions; however, if we have successfully outlined our reasoning, then it should be possible to derive each of the outcomes listed in Table 5.9 from the power patterns summarized in Table 5.8.

Reward

As the task work progresses, members become concerned with the many forms of gains and losses that they are experiencing. This concern crystallizes into the reward structure of the group, which provides members with the basis to stay at work within that group. Earlier, we outlined three important aspects of the reward structure: the nature of the inputs used in reward decisions, the rules governing the distribution of reward, and the nature of the

TABLE 5.9

The Personality Variable that Determines the Assumption of the Leadership Function in Small Groups

Personality Variable	Dep.	Aba.	App.	Auth.	Order	Aff.	Mach.	Dom.	Nurt.	Ach.	Recog.
Dependency	—										
Abasement	Aba.	—									
Approval	App.	Aba.	—								
Authoritarian	Auth.	Auth.	Auth.	—							
Order	Order	Order	Order	Order	—						
Affiliation	Aff.	Aff.	Aff.	Auth.	Order	—					
Machiavellianism	Mach.	Mach.	Mach.	Mach.	Mach.	Mach.	—				
Dominance	Dom.	Dom.	Dom.	Dom.	Dom.	Dom.	Dom.	—			
Nurturance	Nurt.	Nurt.	Nurt.	Nurt.	Nurt.	Nurt.	Nurt.	Nurt.	—		
Achievement	Ach.	Ach.	Ach.	Ach.	Ach.	Ach.	Ach.	Ach.	Nurt.	—	
Recognition	Recog.	Recog.	Recog.	Recog.	Recog.	Recog.	Mach.	Dom.	Nurt.	Ach.	—

reward itself. Here, we examine the way that personality variables utilize and respond to these features of the group.

In the course of work, group members evaluate the many kinds of contributions that they and other members have made as the inputs upon which reward is to be distributed. It seems useful to classify these contributions into the more inclusive categories of time, effort, ability, and group maintenance. Although no type of input is totally irrelevant as a basis of reward, the different personality variables seem to place a varying degree of importance on each type of input. These degrees of importance used when evaluating the contributions of others and oneself are predicted in Table 5.10.

In general, the mechanism that determines which type of input is seen as most important is the same as that which determines the bases of ranking within the group. Overall, for the variables within the safety cluster, the lower levels of task commitment, aspiration, and responsibility lead them to focus on the more superficial qualities of time and effort. For the variables within the esteem cluster, the high levels of commitment, aspiration, and responsibility lead such people to focus on the ability that members demonstrate in the course of the task work. The recognition of success in the area of group maintenance is of importance to approval (when evaluating self), affiliation, and nurturance, as would be expected from the particular nature of their concerns. The Machiavellian person, by definition, seizes upon any basis for claiming reward and gives most importance to the level of ability displayed when evaluating the contribution made by others.

More specifically, the weakness inherent in dependency and abasement causes such people to focus on the more observable factor of time when evaluating others, whereas the more other-directed nature of approval, authoritarianism, and affiliation concerns will recognize effort as well. For the task-committed order person, ability is the central type of input, with time and group maintenance seen as irrelevant. The esteem variables also follow this general pattern, by and large. Only the need for recognition, because of its concern for self-confirmation, follows Machiavellianism in finding time spent on the task an important input for evaluating the contribution of the self.

In the usual emergent group (e.g., dyads studied in the laboratory), only the reward distribution rules based on time (Rule 1) or ability (Rule 2a) can be used by members to allocate reward. The remaining three rules requires an agency outside the group, which evaluates and rewards the group member's contribution. However, for the sake of an efficient way to summarize the interaction of personality and reward in all types of social contexts, this discussion focuses on the desirability of all five distribution systems in the larger social organization. Table 5.11 summarizes the degree to which the distribution systems are congruent with the characteristics of each personality variable. We assume that the most desirable system is the one that is most

TABLE 5.10
The Degree of Importance of Different Types of Inputs as the Basis of
Reward Allocation for Selected Personality Variables

Personality Variable	Degree of Importance in Evaluating the Contribution of Others			
	Time	Effort	Ability	Group Maintenance
Dependency	H	M	M	L
Abasement	H	M	M	L
Approval	H	H	M	L
Authoritarianism	H	H	H	L
Order	L	M	H	L
Affiliation	M	H	M	H
Machiavellianism	L	L	H	L
Dominance	L	M	H	L
Achievement	L	M	H	M
Nurturance	L	H	H	H
Recognition	L	H	H	L

Personality Variable	Degree of Importance in Evaluating the Contribution of Self			
	Time	Effort	Ability	Group Maintenance
Dependency	H	H	L	L
Abasement	H	H	L	L
Approval	M	H	M	H
Authoritarianism	H	H	H	L
Order	L	H	H	L
Affiliation	M	H	M	H
Machiavellianism	H	H	H	H
Dominance	M	H	H	L
Achievement	L	M	H	M
Nurturance	L	M	H	H
Recognition	H	H	H	L

Note: H = high
M = medium
L = low

TABLE 5.11
The Level of Congruence Between Selected Personality Variables
and Reward Distribution Systems

Personality Variable	Principle Regulating Reward Distribution				
	Independent of Group or Own Output	Contingent on Own Output		Contingent on Group Output	Contingent on Both Group and Own Output
		Zero Sum	Non-Zero Sum		
Dependency	HC	HI	HI	C	I
Abasement	C	I	HI	C	HI
Approval	HC	HI	C	HC	C
Authoritarianism	I	HC	C	HI	C
Order	HI	HC	HC	HI	C
Affiliation	HC	HI	I	HC	C
Machiavellianism	HI	HC	HC	HI	C
Dominance	HI	HC	HC	HI	HC
Achievement	I	C	HC	I	HC
Nurturance	C	C	HC	C	HC
Recognition	I	HC	C	I	C

Note: HC = highly congruent
       C = congruent
       I = incongruent
       HI = highly incongruent

congruent with features of that personality variable (i.e., provides incentive), whereas undesirable systems are defined as those that are incongruent with the characteristics of that personality variable (i.e, provide disincentive).

In general, the same psychological mechanism that we have followed throughout the discussion of the group structure should control the degree of desirability in each of the reward distribution systems. The different systems emphasize reward for individual achievement in varying degrees. Rule 1 stresses that reward is *not* based on individual accomplishment. Rule 3 moderates the pressure for individual achievement through payment based on the accomplishments of the group as a whole. Rule 4 emphasizes individual achievement, although it still uses the larger accomplishments of the group in part. Rules 2a and 2b stress individual achievement in a competitive and a noncompetitive way. Thus, to the degree that the features of a personality variable such as dependency, approval, or affiliation include characteristics that avoid task competence, rules that deemphasize individual achievement provide the greatest incentive. To the degree that the features of a personality variable such as authoritarianism, Machiavellianism, or recognition focus on individual prominence in relation to the other members of the group, rules that emphasize comparative achievement provide the greatest incentive. Similarly, rules that threaten the characteristics of a personality variable, such as Rule 2 for dependency-oriented people or Rule 1 for dominance-oriented people, act as disincentives.

THE OUTCOME OF SOCIAL ACTIVITY

When a group has worked together effectively over a period of time, its members are satisfied, its social structure is cohesive, and its goal is achieved. This desirable state has always been a central topic of interest in social psychology. There is research on every aspect of the social process that examines those characteristics that lead the average expectable set of individuals to perform at their optimum level. There is also a rich, if nonsystematic, literature that investigates specific features of the social process within which specific kinds of people emerge most satisfied and most productive. Our discussion in this chapter offers a way to think systematically about optimal levels of performance.

At each step in the social process, we tried to identify those features of the social context that are most desirable for specific kinds of people. Each aspect of the social process can facilitate or obstruct the attempt of certain kinds of people to reach their goals. It is in this way that the nature of the individuals engaged in the social process defines the degree to which a social attribute is congruent or incongruent with their characteristics. We expect that a social context composed of congruent features will lead to the optimum level of performance possible for those people in that situation. To the extent that these social features are incongruent with the personal characteristics, individuals will become dissatisfied and behave in less efficient ways in that situation. Following Steiner (1972), we can think of the actual productivity of a group as the potential productivity of that group minus the losses it incurs due to faulty group process. The principle of incongruency between the features of the person and the social situation should create the "process losses" that Steiner describes, which lead to a reduction in the level of that group's performance.

Even though we have tried to amalgamate variables as much as possible, the pattern of interaction discussed in this chapter is extensive. Although the theoretical pattern could, and indeed should, be made even more complex, it is now time to turn to the evidence.

II The Initial Social Response

This book is organized so that each successive discussion provides increasingly greater specificity about the complex interactions that underlie social behavior. Through a "levels of magnification" approach, we hope to proceed from the broad theoretical overview of chapter 1 to a more detailed analysis of the ways that personality processes interact with each of the component systems that define the field of social psychology. In part II, the interactive effects of personality, situational, and task variables are examined to determine their influence on individual subjective response tendencies in the very early stages of a social event. At this stage of the social process, the focus is upon the acquisition and comprehension of the major features of the social situation. In other words, the individual is concerned with some of the most important aspects of social cognition: person perception, information acquisition and processing, goal setting, and interpersonal attraction. Each of these psychological activities contributes to the individual's tendency to enter into the more complex interpersonal events. Part II explores the detailed structure of these processes, with our discussion based upon the relationships predicted by a theory of interactions and the empirical results obtained from 3 decades of intense research.

Chapter 6 deals with the content of the early cognitions formed about a social situation. The chapter is mainly concerned with identifying the mechanism by which personality and situational variables interact to increase the person's sensitivity toward certain features of the social field and influence the degree to which accurate cognition is subject to distortion. These early cognitive processes constitute the person's entry point into the stream of social behavior, and so the content of these cognitions should influence the subsequent course of behavior. Chapter 7 describes the processes of acquisition and comprehension of the information that is needed to meet personal goals. The initial orientation to a social situation, as described in chapter 6, stimulates the more complex processes of social cognition, such as the persistence with which additional information is sought, the flexibility with which social stimuli are examined, or the level of accomplishment that is set in the plan to reach the goal. Out of these cognitive mechanisms emerges the larger plan that begins the course of social action. Interpersonal attraction seems to be the final component needed to determine the general response tendency to approach or avoid a social field. Chapter 8 reviews the information that is available to understand how dispositional variables interact with elements of the situation to affect levels of attraction during the early stages of acquaintanceship.

As Table 1.1 shows, at the most global level of analysis, the early subjective events lead the individual to become engaged with (or to avoid) a specific social situation. The outcome of these early stages of social interaction is the more extended social process. The greater level of specificity that is gained when each initial component is examined separately makes possible a theory of interactions at the level of testable hypotheses. We hope to suggest these, and to test them when information is available, in each of the chapters in part II.

6 Social Perception

This chapter begins the exploration of the means through which personality processes influence social behavior. Although the complexity of any human event makes the selection of a starting point somewhat arbitrary, we begin by imposing a much more discrete sequence of steps than actually appears when a real event is structured. This methodical approach has the merit of permitting the systematic examination of many major factors that undoubtedly play a simultaneous role in the early stages of a social encounter. It is useful to assume that the chain of events that underlies social behavior begins when we see another person and respond in some way to the configuration of stimuli that the person presents to us. However, this apparently simple act of perceiving another person is in fact a highly complex one built upon many of the elements discussed earlier. Although we devote a good deal of attention to some of the mechanisms through which personality variables affect our construal of another person, we also expect to identify a set of key principles, together with enough empirical evidence to make them plausible, which can be used productively in later explorations of even more complicated social events.

A social event seems to begin with one person perceiving another person as a physical object in a field of physical objects. Although we may receive the other person as a configuration of stimuli, we quickly construct an image of the other person's attributes and intentions (Warr & Knapper, 1968). This process is usually called person perception, even though the primary psychological acts are those of drawing inferences and making attributions about the other person. Because these initial events are an active constructive process rather than a passive reception of stimuli, even in this early stage of a social encounter we must turn our attention to the internal proceedings in the perceiver that create many of the characteristics of the social objects.

In one of the first substantial research programs to develop in personality and social psychology, a group of psychologists, calling their work the "New Look in Perception," raised the question of how the characteristics of the observer could help to structure the form of the image that was perceived. With great initial excitement, they believed that it was possible to test experimentally some of the major psychodynamic ideas that had come out of the clinical experience. Psychotherapists since the time of Freud have proposed a rich model of internal structures that, they claimed, selected, modified, and distorted the individual's perception of real events. Through standard laboratory procedures, these experimentalists tried to demonstrate that prior knowledge of an individual's characteristics would help them understand the variation in the perceptual process. Examples of this early work are the classic studies by Postman, Bruner, and McGinnies (1948) and by Haigh and Fiske (1952), which attempted to show that the possession of certain values increased the person's sensitivity to those characteristics of the world represented by those values. Operationally, these studies showed that certain personal values were associated with briefer recognition times for words that represented these values. From such tachistoscopic presentations of stimuli, the New Look experimentalists felt that they had brought the real world into the laboratory and had shown the power of personality variables to influence the perceptual process.

Many reviews (e.g., Schneider, 1973; Shrauger & Altrocchi, 1964; Tagiuri, 1969; Warr & Knapper, 1968) have surveyed the massive amount of research that was stimulated by these studies. The debate that followed these experiments pointed out a number of important conceptual, methodological, and statistical problems, which seemed to limit the conclusions that could be drawn from this research tradition. The influence of wishes, values, or beliefs on the impression-formation process seems so obvious that these early experiments were asked to support much more theoretical weight than they could manage. Although these reviews convey the impression that an exciting lead did not reach its potential, there is more than ample evidence to indicate that dispositional factors play an important role in social perception. However, at this point, we need to look beyond such sweeping generalizations in order to identify much more detailed accounts of the interactions of people, objects, and situations.

We can begin to explore the earliest stages of a social event by asking why these experimentalists used brief presentations of words to represent the real world. We can be certain that if there is one thing true of normal perceptual processes, it is that we do not sit intently before a tachistoscope hoping to catch a glimpse of a briefly flashed word! However, the reason for this procedure is clear. These experimentalists were creating ambiguity in the stimulus, either through insufficient time to examine a word or by a lack of clarity in its form. This is exactly the principle that guided the selection of stimulus material for many projective techniques (e.g., Morgan & Murray, 1935). In constructing these projective tests, pictures are chosen in which the shape of the figure is indistinct, the facial expression is unclear, or the context is sufficiently unspecified so that a wide range of actions is possible. It is well known that the clearer the context, the more uniform the interpretation (Tagiuri, 1969).

Where do we find such a reduced social context? This state of social ambiguity can be created in the laboratory, where we can represent a moment of life through a single picture or stimulate an abstract cognitive process by representing a taboo psychological content with a single word. More important, in the real world, such ambiguity also exists in the initial stages of a social interaction. For example, we walk into a room, perhaps under the control of our heightened anticipations or in a state of reverie, sweep a glance across the people and the setting, and absorb a minimum amount of information. In this everyday situation, the context is not clear, the intentions of the people present are unknown, and the outcomes of possible encounters are unforeseeable. At this early stage of a social encounter, personality processes interacting with features of the social context can result in subjective experiences that set up a sequence of psychological steps to cope with apparently threatening events and move the person toward more rewarding ones. In this initial period, the inferences drawn and the behavioral decisions made can begin a chain of events that has significant consequences for the types of actions that will be possible later. Our early set of expectancies, as well as our subjective responses of liking or distaste, helps determine the early set of behaviors that we express, which then becomes part of the social context for the other people to interpret in their own way. The response of other people to us thus starts the genuine encounter that clarifies intention and context and takes us into the beginning stages of forming an interpersonal bond.

In this chapter, we present the major types of available information on the role that personality variables play in social perception. Because the area has been the subject of excellent reviews, we focus our attention on reexamining some of the more consistent findings in light of the model of the social process presented in chapter 5. This model also allows us to coordinate a wide variety of findings on the interaction of apparently disparate personality and situational variables that appear to affect the mechanisms through which the initial inference process takes place.

There are several major approaches that underlie explanations of the effects of dispositional variables on the scanning, recording, and cognitive elaboration of a stimulus. In the early 1950s, the pages of the *Journal of Personality* and the *Journal of Abnormal and Social Psychology* were full of heated debates on the nature of the internal mechanism that could best account for these effects. Sometimes the debates even led to a critical experiment. But in this area, as in so many others, the alternative proposals are all still viable. We begin the discussion of person perception by reviewing some important assumptions made in this research and then outline the major features of our hypotheses on the role of personality variables in the formation of social impressions.

APPROACHES TO PERSON PERCEPTION

Projection. A number of the early studies (cf. Murstein & Pryer, 1959; Tagiuri, 1969) assumed the basic mechanism underlying perceptual distortions to be projection. The term projection has a long and checkered history in the psychological assessment literature, where, in practice, it is often used loosely to identify any psychological process that can be inferred from an individual's description of a set of events. It is unfortunate that this technical term is used so sweepingly because it specifically refers to a defensive cognitive act that permits a repressed wish to be displaced externally so that some form of psychological gratification is possible in fantasy (Fenichel, 1945). The limitation on the explanatory power of this mechanism is that, although projection is a plausible explanation for the consequences of certain types of repressed aggressive or sexual wishes, it does not begin to cover the great variety of perceptual distortions that have been discovered (Cronbach, 1958). More recently, there has been renewed interest in the study of perceptual defensive processes in light of modern advances in the study of information processing (Erdelyi, 1974; Erdelyi & Goldberg, 1979; Klein, 1979; Nielsen & Sarason, 1981). At present, it is not yet clear what conclusions will emerge from this general discussion or how this approach will merge with the broader study of information processing in social settings (e.g., Wyer & Carlson, 1979).

Cognitive Schema. The definition of projection does not seem to fit most of the wide variety of material written in response to projective test stimuli. Although some forms of projection can be inferred from a projective test such as the Thematic Apperception Test (TAT), much of the content that distinguishes between the stories written by different people seems to be the characteristic modes of perception, evaluation, and concern that these people typically express. The expectations, moods, wishes, beliefs, and the structure of relations between people and objects that appear in the stories written in response to the TAT pictures seem to be similar to the person's habitual modes of expression that may be identified by other, more time-consuming methods. For this reason, McClelland, Atkinson, Clark, and Lowell (1953) described the test responses as a "thought sample," in order to indicate their belief that the entire range of the person's psychological structure was being utilized in the mental operation that occurred when the TAT response was constructed.

It is likely that this apperceptive process is one of the major mechanisms that contributes to the phenomena studied in the area of social perception. For example, it seems quite reasonable to assume that mistrusting people will infer that a stranger's actions are threatening, just as they will use that explanation to account for the actions of characters in their TAT story. Similarly, confident people should assume that their limited understanding of a stranger's actions are due simply to the fact that the stranger has not yet acted, just as they will use this reason to explain the course of some apparently fictional event in a TAT story. It is likely that, in some way, we use the state and organization of schemata within our own phenomenal self to define the attributes that we perceive in the external object. In other words, we construct the social image out of a process that includes concrete attributes that are part of the images from our own cognitive system. It is very likely that this apperceptive process varies greatly between people and that many of the differences that appear in the person-perception literature are due to the degree to which this step is taken.

Perception as a Broad Psychological Experience. From the earliest work on social perception, many psychologists focused on the internal experience that is set off by the stimulus and viewed the perceptual act as one that responded actively to these subjective experiences rather than simply to the external stimulus (cf. Eriksen & Eriksen, 1972; Eriksen & Lazarus, 1952; Klein, 1970). All of the early work on perceptual defense is based on the idea that a stimulus can trigger off a state of anxiety in the perceiver that must be dealt with by techniques such as avoidance or attention. The labels of repression and sensitization were given to cognitive strategies that were thought to be major modes of dealing with such subjective states produced by a threat.

It is important to recognize that these apparently minor behavioral approach–avoidance responses have significant interpersonal consequences. Before turning to the main concerns of this section, we should note that the mechanisms for dealing with the subjective states frequently produce behavioral cues to which other people respond. For example, if anxious people respond to ambiguous social stimuli with the experience of anxiety, then their anxiety can be reduced by averting their eyes. However, from the observer's point of view, what is perceived is a person who will not return eye contact. From this cue, the observing person may reach an inference as to the unworthiness of the person observed (e.g., LeCompte & Rosenfeld, 1971; Patterson & Sechrest, 1970). As this belief may lead the second person to avoid the first, it will certainly serve to confirm the anxious person's belief in the nonrewardingness of the world. We review the nonverbal components of the initial stages of social interactions in chapter 8.

The most interesting use of this approach has been in those experiments that deal with the modification of social stimuli by the perceiver. These experiments have varied a great many characteristics of the people to be observed, as well as the characteristics of the perceivers, in the expectation that the interaction of these two classes of variables will reward or threaten the perceiver. It is assumed that the perceiver's attempts to deal with the subjective results of this interaction will result in the wide range of reconstructions of the stimulus that seem to produce many of the most interesting effects in the area of person perception.

Accurate Perception.   Most of the experimental work in the area of person perception tries to show modifications of a "known" stimulus, with the assumption that it is the uninteresting response that accurately records what is "there." To a generalist like Allport (1961) or Maslow (1970), the accurate perceptual response raised an interesting question. Allport, Maslow, and many others argued that accurate perception was not simply to be expected but resulted from a highly specific set of dispositional characteristics in the observer. This proposition raised a great deal of controversy, partly because it seemed to place a value judgment on certain types of people and partly because the practical problems of operationalizing accurate perception in the laboratory led to serious epistemological difficulties (e.g., Cronbach, 1955; Gage & Cronbach, 1955). Yet, however problematic some of this research may be, the questions are still worth pursuing because important proposals on major aspects of the social process, such as McGuire's (1968) elegant model of the relationship of personality variables to the persuasion process, rest on the assumption that certain types of people perceive the stimulus world more accurately.

THE CONSTRUCTION OF THE SOCIAL IMAGE

All perceptual acts are psychological events in which the attributes of the external object impinge upon sets of internal processes in the observer. Our task in this chapter is to consider only one of the fields of perception. We do not consider the neurological, psychophysical, or information-processing approaches to impression formation. Rather, we examine how the characteristics of observers lead them to select, evaluate, and interpret the social stimuli they confront in their environment. In outlining our major hypotheses, we draw upon the major approaches that we have just reviewed to help phrase the central questions of this chapter. Following our interactional model, we need to specify: (a) the types of social events that affect (b) sets of dispositional elements (c) in order to create a psychological experience (d) that leads individuals to construct characteristics of the image with important consequences for the social process.

A Neutral Environment.   If the environment contains neither threats nor rewards, as defined by its likely impact on the specific characteristics of the observer, we expect features of the social field alone to determine the characteristics of the impression (cf. Wyer & Carlson, 1979). For example, the greater "distinctiveness" of some attribute should lead most observers to utilize that attribute more heavily when forming their impressions of a social object (Kelley, 1973; McArthur & Post, 1977). In more specific terms, we would expect that a person characterized by affiliative needs would use the achievement cues provided by the social field to construct an impression only if the cues were quite distinctive.

A Rewarding Environment.   If the environment contains cues that appear rewarding to the observer, as defined by that person's dispositional nature, we expect that those cues will evoke greater degrees of attention and exploration, coupled with a positive emotional response. In terms of the sequence of activity in the different task stages outlined in the last chapter, we expect an interaction of this kind to lead to greater degrees of orientation, selective attention, and information search. For example, we expect that a person characterized by affiliation needs would be much more sensitized to recognize social cues, such as human faces, than would an individual who did not possess these needs. Similarly, a psychological need should lead the observer to perceive ambiguous stimuli as potentially rewarding, and so should lead the observer to construct the image more clearly to provide that type of reward. It is very likely that much of the apperceptive process is based upon this mechanism. These reconstructive processes, of course, are not invulnerable to contextual constraints. If the social environment strongly focuses attention on some aspect of the social field, then we can expect it to override any dispositional effects. For example, if we ask observers to code a videotape of a clearly active and a clearly inactive person working together, we should not expect to find otherwise predictable perceptual biases.

A Threatening Environment.   If the environment contains cues that the individual finds threatening, we expect that an experience in that psychological environment will lead to a substantial negative emotional response. We expect that most individuals who experience this kind of arousal will undertake steps to reduce their level of discomfort. One way to respond to this kind of experience is to use the many types of perceptual defense, most notably denial, that have played such a significant role in explanations drawn from the clinical literature. Of possibly greater importance, a variety of cognitive reconstructions can be used to reduce the level of threat that such an environment appears to convey. For example, the observation of a very competent person may be upsetting to a highly dominant individual. If this is the case, reconstructing the social impression of the person observed in a much less favorable way reduces the discomfort being experienced by the dominant person.

THE EMPIRICAL STUDY OF PERSON PERCEPTION

A brief review of one of the classic early experiments by Postman et al. (1948) can introduce much of the research in this area. The hypothesis tested in this experiment stated that when an individual was strongly concerned with a particular value area, he or she will be especially sensitive to the features of the world that represent those values. They first measured people's value orientations using the Allport–Vernon test, which identifies six major areas of value concern (theoretical, economic, aesthetic, social, political, and religious). Based on the categorization suggested by this theory, they also constructed lists of six words that represented each of the major value areas. Postman et al. used a tachistoscope to present these lists of words rapidly to college students who had taken the values test. They found that the more an individual was concerned with one of these value areas, the more likely the person was to recognize a word from that area at a very brief rate of presentation. These results led Postman et al. (1948) to conclude that "value acts as a sensitizer, lowers the perceptual threshold . . . [and] is an active, selective disposition which in many subtle ways affects the hypotheses and attempts at solution which precede the actual recognition of a stimulus word" (p. 148).

This finding strongly appealed to common sense and proved exciting to psychologists who hoped that a scientific way had been found to study these interesting psychological processes. The finding also found support from a number of other studies, such as Haigh and Fiske (1952), which improved upon many of the procedures, and Vanderplas and Blake (1949), which found essentially similar results by presenting the words aurally (see also Davids, 1956; Lazarus, Eriksen, & Fonda, 1951; Paivio & Steeves, 1963). These studies also provoked a heated controversy about the conceptual, methodological, and statistical aspects of the research, which is summarized in the reviews of the area. Yet, the Postman et al. experiment is significant for having stimulated a major effort to explore the role that dispositions play in perception. In this chapter, we explore the more focused research that has been done following these path-breaking studies. In this discussion, as throughout the book, we organize our examination of the social process in terms of the sequence of peripheral variables that we outlined in part I.

Hunger

Clearly, the place to begin considering the effect of specific needs on perception is the physiological level. Although popular wisdom is certain that physiological deprivation leads to many forms of altered consciousness (i.e., mirages of water fountains in the desert), like most examples of popular wisdom, empirical research has shown this belief to be both right and wrong. For our purposes, this topic is especially interesting because of the simplicity with which the question can be phrased: Will people who are increasingly hungry either be unusually sensitive to food-related stimuli or reconstruct ambiguous stimuli into food-related images?

A number of early studies examined this question (Atkinson & McClelland, 1948; Brozek, Guetzkow, & Baldwin, 1951; Gordon & Spence, 1966; Lazarus, Yousem, & Arenberg, 1953; Levine, Chein, & Murphy, 1942; Sanford, 1936, 1937; Spence & Ehrenberg, 1964; see also Epstein, 1961; Epstein & Smith, 1956; McClelland & Atkinson, 1948; Postman & Crutchfield, 1952; Wispé, 1954, for more complex, but essentially supportive results). We need present only three experiments to make the major conclusion clear.

McClelland and Atkinson projected blank images and smudges on a screen and asked groups of people who had been deprived of food for 1, 4, or 16 hours to identify the object on the screen. They found that as hunger increased, people saw more food images, with the biggest effect coming with 4 hours of deprivation. Similarly, Lazarus et al. (1953), using tachistoscopic techniques, presented groups of people deprived of food for 1, 2, 3–4, or 5–6 hours with pictures of food or nonfood objects. They found that people seemed to have a special sensitivity to recognize food objects after 3–4 hours of deprivation. On the other hand, Brozek et al. (1951), studying truly semistarved volunteers, found no perceptual distortions that related to food imagery — only severe personality changes! Thus, it seems safe to conclude that those people who invented the folk wisdom about ravenous hunger and food mirages were never hungry for more than 4 hours. To summarize, in this area as in so many others that we encounter, the overall weight of the evidence supports the conclusion that moderate levels of motivation contribute a directing force to the stream of behavior, whereas excessive levels of motivation are highly disorganizing (cf. Cofer & Appley, 1964).

Authoritarianism

The broad trait of authoritarianism stimulated the first of the more interesting perceptual bias studies. Provoked by their experience with fascism in World War II, social scientists at the University of California at Berkeley designed a massive study (Adorno, Frenkel-Brunswik, Levinson, & Sanford, 1950) to understand the type of person who would respond to Nazi ideology. From their work, a portrait of the authoritarian personality emerged, which was characterized as rigid, repressed, conforming, stereotyping in thinking, and intolerant of ambiguity. By contrast, the nonauthoritarian personality was described as a liberal person possessing virtually all the characteristics usually attributed to the healthy individual. The test that this group developed to measure the potential for fascism, the F (for fascism) scale, has proven to be as important as the clinical description of authoritarianism and has made it possible to study a wide range of social phenomena that seemed to be related to this trait.

In the area of impression formation, one question that drew a great deal of attention was the likelihood that this trait was associated with the stereotyping style of thinking. Scodel and Mussen (1953) reasoned that, as the authoritarian personality is not very sensitive to the needs of others, cannot tolerate ambiguity well, and needs to identify with the peer group, authoritarians would tend to perceive other people as having values and attitudes that are similar to their own. In other words, because of a fear of becoming close to another person through even such a limited interpersonal act as a visual search, it was expected that the authoritarian person would be forced to use his or her own attributes as an important element in constructing the percept of another person. In contrast, the nonauthoritarian person, with greater interpersonal sensitivity and skill, was expected to be much more capable of engaging in visual search of the other people in his or her social world and, therefore, should be more able to perceive the specific (and varying) individual cues presented by others. For this reason, the nonauthoritarians' social perceptions should be not only more variable, but more important, their perceptions should be more accurate.

To test this line of reasoning, Scodel and Mussen ran a simple experiment that became the model for many experiments to come. They asked students to complete a questionnaire that contained items from the F scale and a number of similar items from the Minnesota Multiphasic Personality Inventory (MMPI). Based on responses to this questionnaire, they formed dyads that paired an authoritarian with a nonauthoritarian student and asked them to discuss radio, television, and movies for 20 minutes. Following this period of conversation, Scodel and Mussen asked each person to fill out the same questionnaire the way that they believed their partner would, in order to test their central hypothesis that authoritarians would be more inaccurate because they would use their own opinions as the basis for forming their impressions of another person. They expected and found that authoritarians would see the other person, even though actually scoring low on the F scale, as basically similar to themselves.

Unfortunately, this experiment could not quite test the accuracy hypotheses because it did not use all combinations of authoritarian and nonauthoritarian dyads; all that it could establish was that both types of people saw the other person as authoritarian (one accurately and one inaccurately). In order to demonstrate these effects, it was necessary to test the remaining combinations of high- and low-authoritarian people. In particular, it is especially important to see if nonauthoritarians would perceive other nonauthoritarians in an accurate way. This flaw in the design was corrected in a follow-up experiment by Scodel and Freedman (1956) and was essentially replicated by Crockett and Meidinger (1956) and Kates (1959). In an excellent discussion of the findings from this set of studies, Kelley and Stahelski (1970) concluded that neither authoritarians nor nonauthoritarians are particularly accurate perceivers — at least in a 20-minute conversation. Instead, the combined results show that authoritarians consistently see others as being similar to themselves, as Scodel and Mussen suggested. However, nonauthoritarians are quite variable in their perceptions and, as a group, tend to see other people as medium in authoritarianism.

Although other research (Burke, 1966; Gabennesch & Hunt, 1971; Granberg, 1972; Jacoby, 1971; Jones, 1954; Lipetz, 1960; Rabinowitz, 1956; Simons, 1966) provides additional support for Scodel and Mussen's complete proposal, it is probably safest to conclude that although nonauthoritarians are not like authoritarians, they are also a much more variable group, which is likely composed of several subsets of people with very different perceptual styles. As some of these subsets of nonauthoritarians may include accurate perceivers and other subsets may not, in order to identify people who perceive accurately, it may be necessary to examine factors beyond those of low scores on the authoritarianism scale.

The early work in this area touched on one other mechanism through which authoritarianism affected social perception. Although the Scodel and Mussen type of research directed attention to the question of inaccuracy in perception due to the egocentric focus of the authoritarian, the formation of a percept can be more highly influenced by other features of the social context. In the research just described, all participants were students of approximately equal status and ability, but few parts of the real world are as homogeneous as the situations that we can contrive in the laboratory. This early observation raised a host of interesting questions, which we follow throughout the book. For example, how is the perceptual process affected when the other person differs in any of the ways discussed in chapters 4 and 5? To which specific attributes in the person to be observed does a perceiver pay most attention? By which attribute is a perceiver most affected? Which characteristics of the percept are most affected by this interaction of the attributes of the perceiver and the other person?

An interesting experiment by Wilkens and deCharms (1962) raised just these questions. Stimulated by an experiment by Jones (1954), which showed that authoritarians were more affected by the power characteristics of their social environment than were nonauthoritarians, Wilkens and deCharms designed a complex experiment to examine how the impressions formed by authoritarian and nonauthoritarian peple would be affected by the nature of the power attributes of the people that they observe. They made four tape recordings that varied the types of power cues used to describe an army officer. In these recordings, Wilkens and deCharms combined strong or weak personal competence cues together with high or low social status cues. The purpose of the experiment was to see which type of cues were most used by authoritarian or nonauthoritarian students in a military studies class in forming their impressions of the army officer. The results of this experiment clearly showed that, in the process that determines the "favorability" of the impression, authoritarians were strongly influenced by social status attributes, whereas nonauthoritarians were more strongly influenced by personal power cues. This finding has been supported by a number of more recent studies (Fry, 1975; Simas & McCarry, 1979; Slotnick & Bleiberg, 1974). Wilkens and deCharms' experiment also gave some indication that authoritarians use external factors in forming the content of their impressions of others, whereas nonauthoritarians use personal factors. The interaction effects that were discovered in this experiment constitute one of the most consistent patterns of findings in the area of personality and social behavior.

External Locus of Control

Perhaps because the locus of control program began after the peak of the personality-based impression-formation research, there are not many studies that have explored the effect of this variable on social cognition. Phares, Ritchie, and Davis (1968) conducted one study which demonstrated that people with an external locus of control recall significantly more negative information from a personally important event than do people with an internal locus of control. In this experiment, subjects received sets of analyses of their personality which combined both highly positive as well as highly negative interpretations from what appeared to be a battery of professional clinical tests. These bogus tests, of course, were the device through which the positive and negative information was conveyed. Phares et al. reasoned that individuals with an external locus of control are less threatened by such negative information than those with an internal locus of control, because they take less personal responsibility for any event.

A second study (Bryant, 1974) yielded a similar negativity effect for the perception of external events. This study examined the degree of favorability of social perceptions that children, classified as internal or external in their locus of control, form of their elementary school teachers. Bryant argued that because people who believe that powerful others are in control of their fate (i.e., externally controlled people) also tend to have much more difficult or ineffective relationships with others, they would tend to attribute many more unfavorable characteristics to their teachers than would be the case for internally controlled people. Bryant studied a sample of white, middle-class, sixth-grade boys chosen from a variety of classrooms in a suburban school district. She found that externally controlled children were much more negative in their perceptions of their teachers than were internally controlled children. Perhaps more important, the unfavorability of the impressions of their teachers was only part of the pervasive negative view of the world possessed by the externally controlled children. This finding is similar to that reported for the associated variable of anxiety by Hammes (1961), Purcell (1952), and many others.

These two studies are helpful to us in several ways. First, they allow us to include the locus of control in the group of important variables whose effects can be followed across the entire range of the social process. Second, they represent a good example of that mechanism of impression formation, which although related to personality structure, is likely not the resultant of a psychological defense process. Rather, it appears to indicate that those cognitive schemata associated with the external locus of control may include a readiness to use a negative overall evaluation to shape the impression formed of another person.

The Need for Affiliation

The definition of the need for affiliation emphasizes that this need is concerned with establishing, maintaining, or restoring a warm and friendly interpersonal relationship. It seems quite reasonable, then, to expect that this variable should direct the perceiver's attention to the human part of the stimulus field. This assumption leads to the simple expectation that people concerned with affiliative needs would be more acute in recognizing the human face.

Atkinson and Walker (1956) performed the basic experiment demonstrating that the need for affiliation sensitizes the individual to the appearance of human faces. They used a simple task in which people were asked to view a screen on which pictures would be projected in ways that made recognition difficult. Each slide was divided into four quadrants, with one containing a picture of a face and the other three containing pictures of neutral stimuli. Across the series of slides there were five different pictures of faces, which were presented in all quadrants.

The results of this experiment showed that people who were very concerned with the need for affiliation had a strong tendency to state that the quadrants of the slides which contained the indistinct pictures of faces were the ones that were the clearest. By contrast, those people who were less concerned with the need for affiliation tended to choose the other quadrants. This clear relationship between need for affiliation scores and orientation to faces is another demonstration, with a different motive, that motivation can increase people's sensitivity to that part of the world that is related to that specific motive. Similar results, demonstrating that people are more sensitive to information related to such high need areas, were reported by Carlson (1961), French and Chadwick (1956), and Taylor and Oberlander (1969). Taylor and Oberlander's study is especially interesting as it provides evidence that a wider range of personal concerns, such as the traits of field dependence and self-disclosure as well as affiliation, is also involved in providing this sensitizing effect to faces.

The results of a study by Solar and Mehrabian (1973) reveal that the need for affiliation not only sensitizes the person-perception process, but also serves as an apperceptive mass to help furnish the content of the impression. Although their experiment raised many issues beyond the topic being considered here, it is important because it demonstrated that the need for affiliation leads the perceiver, in ambiguous situations, to construct impressions of people that conform to his or her special concerns. Solar and Mehrabian presented a series of slides of a person they called Steve to groups of people who were asked to complete a questionnaire as they believed Steve would. Their results showed that people concerned with affiliation formed a much more affiliative impression of Steve than did those less concerned with affiliation.

The Need for Achievement

One final source of information on the sensitizing hypothesis comes from two early experiments in the need for achievement program. Using the technique of presenting stimulus words tachistoscopically, McClelland and Liberman (1949) and Moulton, Raphelson, Kristofferson, and Atkinson (1958) demonstrated that the need for achievement helped to sensitize perceivers to recognize achievement-related words. Unfortunately, there are no studies of which we are aware that demonstrate, in ways parallel to those already discussed, that the cognitive schemata associated with the need for achievement provide an important share of the content of the impression of other people or events. Inferentially, of course, as McClelland et al. (1953) assert, a form of evidence is available to a massive degree. Throughout the enormous research program generated by this seminal book, individuals have been asked to write stories that make sense of ambiguous pictures (i.e., the TAT cards). These stories, of course, are the basic operation through which the need for achievement is measured (which establishes the presence of the motive through descriptions of people drenched in achievement-related imagery). By definition, therefore, people who use achievement-related content to construct their social impressions are identified as high in the need for achievement, an operation that has been validated by the extensive set of behavioral correlates that have emerged from this highly successful research program. However, it would be useful to have a more direct demonstration of this effect.

Dominance and Machiavellianism

There are a series of studies that have explored the effects of the trait of dominance on different aspects of social perception. Together, these studies provide a great deal of information on the type of influence that this disposition brings to the social perception process, the properties of the social situation that affect these personal variables, and the characteristics of the percept that are affected by this person-by-situation interaction. They also provide direct evidence on the mechanism through which the perceptual changes are produced. First, we examine two early studies that framed the question and then we turn to three recent studies that provide a good deal of evidence on the nature of this process.

The major early study that examined the effect of dominance on social perception was unable to find any direct effect at all. Altrocchi (1959), approaching the question of perceptual bias from the broader perspective of social psychology, suggested that impression formation was influenced by the same mechanisms that governed interpersonal behavior in general. Based on Winch's (1955) belief that interpersonal choice rests on the principle of complementary needs, Altrocchi hypothesized that people desire to interact with those individuals whose behavior is reciprocal to their own. In his words, "a dominant person tends to choose to interact with a person likely to satisfy his need to dominate—i.e., a submissive person" (p. 303). In order to construct the phenomenological world in accordance with these preferred interpersonal states, Altrocchi suggested that dominant people should follow a perceptual bias that would lead them to attribute less dominance to the impression they form of others than would be utilized by a more submissive person. Altrocchi selected two dominant and two submissive subjects from a large pool of male students who had been tested with the CPI Dominance scale (Gough, 1957) and made a movie of them demonstrating a model railroad. A larger number of students drawn from the same pool were asked to watch the movie and, among other tasks, to describe each of the four students on the Interpersonal Check Lisk (Leary, 1957).

Unfortunately, the experiment did not show any of the predicted effects. In light of the clear failure of this experiment to support his major hypotheses, Altrocchi suggested that the problem may have been in the method he used. Although there are many possible directions to pursue in rethinking the procedure used in this experiment, one in particular stands out because it introduces a methodological consideration of general importance. A dispositional variable should contribute to forming aspects of the social process only when it is engaged by that social situation. In other words, it seems likely that a person-by-situation interaction yields its effects by producing a subjective experience, which in turn leads to adaptive patterns of social behavior. Therefore, the method used in studying an interaction must insure that the subjective event is produced in just the way that is intended by the hypothesis; the experimental procedure must be strong enough to arouse that disposition, yet not be so arousing as to swamp its potential contribution. It is likely that in the case of this experiment, the difference in the actors' dominance behavior was just not dramatic enough to arouse a significant negative subjective reaction that would lead to an evaluative bias in the dominance-oriented perceivers.

In the same year that Altrocchi's study was published, Jones and Daugherty (1959) presented the results of a complex experiment that was more successful in achieving this goal. The most important difference in Jones and Daugherty's approach to this problem was to assume that a personality variable of the perceiver produces its effects in conjunction with the manifest attributes of the person observed and the social context in which the perceptual act is to take place. Jones and Daugherty tested male students with the political scale from the Allport, Vernon, and Lindzey (1951) test of values and Christie's Machiavellianism IV scale and then had them listen to a conversation between the experimenter and a politically and an aesthetically oriented person. Of great importance, the people listening to these conversations were told that they would meet the people they were listening to in either a cooperative or a competitive interaction. A third group was not told to expect to meet the people on the tapes. In other words, Jones and Daugherty found a way to engage the participants' interest in the experiment and thus, very likely, aroused their dispositions in such a way as to affect the outcomes of the experiment. After listening to these tape recordings, the participants evaluated each of these recorded people on an adjective rating scale. This study reports significant results in those conditions in which these politically oriented dispositions were most engaged (i.e., evaluating the politically oriented person while expecting to meet him under competitive circumstances). The most intriguing piece of evidence provided by this experiment was that the more the perceivers could be characterized by the value of political interest, the more favorable was the impression (cf. Postman et al., 1948). On the other hand, in the most negatively arousing condition (i.e., Machiavellians forming impressions of politically oriented potential competitors), the more Machiavellian the perceiver, the more negative was the impression.

INTERACTIONAL STUDIES OF PERSON PERCEPTION

Following the experience gained in these and other related studies, three recent experiments explored a set of hypotheses that described how individual dispositions help form the impressions that are constructed out of the stimulus properties of the social object in the social context. As just outlined, it was expected that the perceiver's motivational characteristics would affect the reconstructive aspects of impression formation when the person who was observed appeared to possess attributes that engage the perceiver's motives in some way that was appropriate for that particular type of situation. Thus, from this point of view, most dispositional variables should not have a general effect on person perception across a broad range of stimulus persons and social contexts. Rather, dispositions should affect impression formation only when there are factors in the situation that affect that disposition in such a way as to evoke a subjective response that can stimulate adaptive cognitive reconstruction of the social impression.

Each of these three experiments addressed a different aspect of the person-perception process, and each contrasted the impetus that dominance and dependency motives bring to the formation of impressions. Further, each experiment used the same instruments—the CPI Dominance scale (Gough, 1957) and the Edwards Dependency scale (Edwards, 1959)—to measure these motives. Together, for the motives of dominance and dependency at least, they provide a clear set of information on the nature of the impression-formation process.

The First Experiment: The Interactive Effects of the Perceiver's Motives and the Attributes of the Stimulus Person on Impression Formation. This experiment (Assor, Aronoff, & Messé, 1981) used a straightforward procedure, much like that devised by Altrocchi and by Jones and Daugherty, to demonstrate that the attributes of the person who is observed can engage the dispositional tendencies of the perceiver in such a way as to affect the impression formed of that stimulus person. In general, the experiment is based on the assumption that the dominance scale would identify people who would seek high-status social positions as a way to obtain control of and recognition from other people, whereas the dependency scale would identify people who would seek low-status positions as a way to obtain support from others. Further, this assumption leads to the hypothesis, which is congruent with Altrocchi's, that the dominance motive in perceivers should lead them to feel uncomfortable when viewing highly capable other people and quite comfortable when viewing much more submissive people. In contrast, the dependency motive should lead to just the reverse effects in perceivers (cf. Mueller, 1966). Following the main line of thinking since the start of the New Look work on social perception, this experiment tested the prediction that the discomfort experienced by the perceiver would lead to a set of cognitive events that would reconstruct the impression of the other person in ways that would reduce the discomfort.

The difference in status between the people to be observed was conveyed to the perceivers through information about the relative status of these people in the real world. In light of the strong effects of anticipatory sets and a priori labeling on the perception of others (e.g., Kelley, 1950; Kleck, Ono, & Hastorf, 1966; Snyder, Tanke, & Berscheid, 1977), it seemed that clear information would lead the observers to attend to the motive-related information in the way that was intended. The primary perceptual experience was an 18-minute videotape of a male and a female student working at three tasks: an etch-a-sketch game; a discussion of the possible uses that might be made of four objects; and a desert-survival problem in which they had to rank order several objects according to their importance. The two individuals were pleasant in appearance, cordial to each other, and handled the task in a similar and competent way. However, to insure that the dominance and dependency motives of observers would be aroused, one of these two people was identified as a relatively higher status person and the other as a relatively lower status person. In half the groups to whom this videotape was shown, the male was described as the high-status person and the female as the low-status person, with their relative statuses reversed when the videotape was shown to the other half of the groups.

The experiment itself was very simple. Groups of students were assembled to take the personality inventories and view the videotape. After the students had completed the tests, the experimenter introduced the videotape and described the people in one of the two different ways. After the tape was over, in order to obtain a measure on the impressions that these students had formed of the two people on the videotape, students were asked to rate the high-status person and the low-status person separately on a set of semantic differential scales. These responses provided an overall evaluation measure of the impression that the students had formed of each person. In general, it was expected that when the interaction of the perceiver's motives and the observed person's attributes combined to produce a negative subjective response in the perceiver, he or she would construct a significantly less positive impression of the person that had been observed. The major finding of the experiment confirmed the hypothesis: The dominance motive leads people to evaluate the high-status person less favorably than they do the low-status person, whereas the dependency motive leads people to evaluate the high-status person more favorably than they do the low-status person.

This experiment provided a clear demonstration of how the interactive effects of the observer's personality and the social object's attributes affect the impression-formation process. However, these results rest on a set of hypothetical subjective events that are assumed to stimulate the cognitive reconstruction of the social impression. To examine the underlying processes that generate such perceptual biases requires the utilization of psychophysiological techniques that can directly measure the arousal and the reduction of emotion that mediate this defensive process. This is the task set for the next experiment.

The Second Experiment: Defensive Processes in Person Perception.
Throughout this chapter, we have been hypothesizing that certain configurations of stimuli are felt as threatening by the viewer. We have also been assuming that the perception of such threat-provoking stimuli increases the perceiver's state of autonomic arousal to an unpleasant level and that the perceiver then engages in cognitive activity whose purpose is to reduce this level of arousal by diminishing the degree of threat in the stimulus. Through the reconstruction of the impression of the person observed, the perceiver is said to reduce his or her level of autonomic arousal. Although there is sufficient evidence to make the theory of perceptual defense processes plausible (cf. Erdelyi, 1974), there has been no direct evidence on the hypothesized sequence of intervening events. The purpose of this experiment (Assor, Aronoff, & Messé, 1984) was to devise a procedure that would make these hypothetical mechanisms accessible to investigation.

An experiment that might test these hypotheses had to meet the following requirements: (a) identify individuals whose predominant concerns were related to the type of interpersonal events that could be provided in the laboratory; (b) invent an experience that would threaten these concerns; (c) conduct the experiment in a setting that would allow the recording of the perceivers' level of autonomic arousal; (d) demonstrate that the perceivers' level of autonomic arousal was reduced as they were able to institute successfully their defensive cognitive procedures (e.g., to reconstruct their impression of the observed person). These requirements made it necessary to devise a much more complicated experiment than the one just described.

Two experiences were devised for participants in this experiment: The first provided a threat to dominance-motivated people and the second a threat to dependency-motivated people. Based on the results of the first experiment, it seemed probable that dominance-motivated perceivers would be threatened by the prospect of observing (and expecting to evaluate and later working with) a very dominant and competent person. In contrast, dependency-motivated perceivers should be threatened by the prospect of observing (and expecting to evaluate and later working with) a submissive and less competent person. In each condition, either dominance- or dependency-motivated male students were asked to take part in what they were told was an experiment on the "nature of generations" in social groups. They were asked to observe via closed circuit television two members of the present generation of a group, in which they would soon become members, working at their present task. While those two people worked at their task, the person was seated in a comfortable chair and connected by electrodes to a polygraph in order to record his electrodermal activity, or as was explained, to see "how your body responds to problem situations." Each student was told that at the end of the group work session, he would evaluate the person with whom he would be working when he entered into the next generation of the group.

In reality, the television system conveyed a recorded presentation of a staged interaction between two actors who followed scripts designed to create the different threatening experiences. These actors appeared to be fellow students working on an involving discussion task, in which one of them displayed a good deal of dominant/competent behavior and the other a good deal of submissive/less competent behavior. In the dominance threat condition, the student expected to meet the dominant and competent person; in the dependency threat condition, the student expected to meet the submissive and less competent person. All the experimental procedures were quite realistic, and the student believed that he was witnessing a genuine interaction. Finally, after the group completed its task, the two people appeared to leave the experimental room with the experimenter, and the student was left waiting for the evaluation period to begin. During the evaluation, the semantic differential scales were presented on the television monitor one at a time, and the student responded to each scale verbally with the number that he viewed as most descriptive of his future partner.

The degree of emotional responsiveness as a reaction to the perceptual experience was determined by the polygraph record. Autonomic activity was measured by monitoring the student's phasic electrodermal activity, which consists of sudden and transient changes in skin conductance that appear spontaneously or in response to external stimuli. For each student, two measures of autonomic activity were obtained. To test the first hypothesis, the number of spontaneous skin-conductance responses was computed for a number of standard time periods in the experiment. To test the second hypothesis, the amplitude of the skin-conductance response was employed.

In this experiment, the first hypothesis stated that a visual experience that constituted a threat to dominance-motivated perceivers would lead to a significant increase in their level of autonomic arousal. As predicted, the results showed a highly significant interaction between the motive of the perceiver and the type of threatening perceptual experience. The second hypothesis stated that for perceivers who had been exposed to a threatening perceptual experience, the more that the perceiver was able to construct/reconstruct his impression of the stimulus person to remove the threatening attributes, the more his state of arousal would be reduced. The results of this analysis provided strong evidence in support of this hypothesis for dominance-motivated subjects, who showed lower levels of arousal associated with a more unfavorable impression of the prospective dominant/competent partner. This experiment, however, was not successful in confirming the second hypothesis for dependency-motivated perceivers.

The results of this experiment are the first to show that this key internal process does, indeed, occur as hypothesized. This finding is of great supporting value to the many person-perception experiments reported in this chapter, which posit that such a set of subjective events provokes the cognitive reconstruction of the percept. This finding has even greater potential to explain many more complex aspects of the social process. For example, a similar set of subjective events is assumed to account for such social phenomena as the determination of which individuals should serve in different social roles within the group or to explain why certain kinds of people are less productive when working under certain kinds of social conditions. The results of this experiment make such explanations much more plausible.

The Third Experiment: The Interactive Effects of Perceiver, Target, and Situational Influences on Social Cognition.   Throughout this chapter, we have assumed that an impression of a social object is formed through the interaction of the many different components of a social situation. We have also assumed that our understanding of the process will be more accurate the more naturalistic the conditions under which the observation takes place, and the more naturalistic the measures of the cognition. The third experiment we wish to review (Battistich & Aronoff, in press) paid much greater attention than before to constructing an experimental situation in which it was possible to identify more precisely each major dimension of the perceptual field. If individuals attend to those aspects of the social situation that provide them with information that affects their interactional goals, then their motives should help determine which aspects of the entire social situation are most important to them. In other words, perceivers should be most interested in obtaining that information about another person that affects their ability to satisfy or frustrate their interpersonal motives. From this point of view, the behaviors expressed by the other person, as well as the type of situation within which the event is to occur, should be highly important in determining whether the perceiver will believe that his or her goals can be pursued.

Using the same instruments as before, male dominance- and dependency-motivated students were selected to take part in the experiment. These people were told that they would be interacting with another person as part of a study about "how well people with different social orientations work together." Participants were also told that these interactions would be videotaped and that they would be able to see a "get acquainted" tape of their prospective partner. In addition, they were told that they would make such a tape later for their partner to view before they worked together. In order to specify the type of situation in which the experiment would take place, participants were told that their future meeting with these people would occur in either a competitive or a cooperative role relationship.

Following the analysis of interpersonal behavior along the task and the socioemotional dimensions, four scripts were written to vary the level of behavioral assertiveness and affiliativeness that was to be displayed by the person on the videotape who was to become the perceiver's future partner. In other words, the videotaped person displayed behavior that was either assertive–affiliative, assertive–disaffiliative, submissive–affiliative, or submissive–disaffiliative. The second person on the videotapes always played a role that was moderately assertive and affiliative. After viewing the videotape, participants completed a free-response description of their future partner and rated him on a number of scales that included such measures as attraction and the expectation of pleasantness and successfulness in their future interaction.

It is very important to realize how different these tapes are from the one used by Assor et al. (1981). In that experiment, one tape was shown of a competent but not dramatic couple working pleasantly together at a series of tasks. The actual perceptual material (a midrange level of performance) was such that it was possible to engage in some degree of direct perceptual distortion. However, in Battistich & Aronoff (in press) the scripts were written to insure the widest possible degree of difference on the major dimensions of interpersonal behavior. If person perception is measured by the direct rating of the behavior shown on these tapes, then this procedure should be understood to be a task put before the subject in which descriptive accuracy is seen as both required and possible. If the characteristics of the perceiver, the social target, and the social situation interact, then when the stimulus presentation is quite clear, these interactive effects should be seen on measures that are less tied to the information conveyed by the videotapes. In other words, the consequences of the hypothesized set of subjective events produced by this interaction should be differences in the degree to which the person is liked, in the expectation for the pleasantness and the successfulness of the future interaction, and in the set of attributes used to construct the long-term impression (the less situation-bound cognitive representation) that was formed of the observed person.

The major results of this complex experiment were as expected. As predicted, the interaction of the three dimensions of perceiver, target, and situation did not affect the "direct" rating of the behavior that was viewed. Following the principle of complementarity, dominant perceivers liked the submissive targets more than the assertive targets, whereas dependent perceivers nearly always liked the more assertive targets. Expectations as to the results of possible future interactions were a function of the perceiver's motive and the situational definition. Dominant perceivers expected competitive situations to be more pleasant and expected to be more successful in them, whereas dependent perceivers expected cooperative situations to be more pleasant and expected to be more successful in them.

The impression that these perceivers formed of the people they had observed was measured through the free-response descriptions. For each person, the descriptions they wrote of the people they had observed were coded by judges for mention of assertive and affiliative characteristics. The frequencies of these characteristics were then converted to proportions of the total number of characteristics mentioned in the descriptions. From a goal-seeking information-processing point of view, it was reasonable to expect dominance-motivated people to seek information that deals with the assertive properties of the other person, whereas dependency-motivated people seek information that deals with the affiliative properties of the other person. It is very interesting, and theoretically important, that although direct descriptions of the target people on rating scales did not show any type of bias produced by the dispositions of the perceiver, the free-response measure showed these predicted effects very strongly. Because this aspect of the memory of the target people is in line with the other affective (liking) and cognitive (expectancy of future states) outcomes generated by this experiment, it is possible that the free-response measure has captured the characteristics of the longer term impression that are carried into the extended interaction that often ensues following an important observation.

7 Information Processing

The cognitive processes through which social actors perceive others, comprehend the task, and select their goals are among the most important psychological steps they take to enter into complex social activity. Because of the great range of information that any situation provides and the great variability of individual behavior found in most situations, it is possible that personality variables moderate many of the cognitive processes that are essential for all forms of social action. In the previous chapter, we discussed some of the mechanisms that help determine the content of our social cognitions. In this chapter, we review a number of different types of cognitive activity through which these cognitions are generated.

In recent years, personologists have used the term "cognitive style" to describe the regular patterns of cognitive operations through which individuals comprehend their social experiences. Broadly conceived, cognitive style refers to the modes of cognitive activity through which information is obtained, organized, and used. Many personality and social psychologists (e.g., Gardner, Jackson, & Messick, 1960; Klein, 1970; McGuire, 1968; Messick, 1976; Schroder & Suedfeld, 1971; Scott, Osgood, & Peterson, 1979) describe a sizable number of information-processing mechanisms used for these purposes. Our interest in reviewing this work is to identify a set of cognitive variables that has been shown, through significant programs of experimental research, to link dispositional variables to important parts of the social process. Table 7.1 presents eight broad variables that help to form the cognitive base of social action; each of these variables operationalizes different aspects of the broad processes described in chapters 4 and 5.

TABLE 7.1
Stages of Information Processing

Stage I: The Acquisition of Information	Stage II: The Processing of Information	Stage III: Goal Setting
1. Selective attention	1. Conceptual differentiation	1. Level of aspiration
2. Search flexibility	2. Processing flexibility	2. Risk taking
3. Search persistence	3. Processing persistence	

In Table 7.1, we suggest that selective attention, search flexibility, and search persistence constitute three of the most important cognitive activities during the acquisition stage of information processing. During the early phases of information search, a person selectively attends to certain elements and ignores or rejects other aspects of the situation. Selective attention includes the scanning of and attending to limited sets of information that may be encoded for possible later use in guiding the person's response to a situation. During the scanning of the social stimuli, the person's search process can be characterized by the degree of search flexibility (or rigidity) used to extract meaning from the situation. Goldstein and Blackman (1978) define cognitive rigidity during the search process as "a continuation of former behavior patterns when a change in the situation requires a change in behavior for more efficient functioning" (pp. 39–40). This process is similar to another that is called the intolerance of uncertainty (or intolerance of ambiguity), which Goldstein and Blackman define as cognitive activity in which there is "unwarranted imposition of structure" (p. 40). These two related processes can be combined for the purpose of explaining complex and extended social events, because they both describe a mechanism through which the individual limits search by imposing structuring cognitive operations. Finally, the acquisition stage of information processing can also be characterized by the degree of search persistence used to examine the social field. Traditionally, this variable has been defined by the length of time and the number of stimuli examined by the person.

Once the information is obtained, individuals use it to solve the tasks on which they are engaged. As indicated in Table 7.1, the activity in this second stage seems to be comprised of three rather broad variables: conceptual differentiation, processing flexibility, and processing persistence in the work of solving problems. Conceptual differentiation refers to the degree to which information is differentiated into separate components and integrated into organizations. This process identifies the range and width of the cognitive categories used, as well as the person's ability to assimilate the information into an existing conceptual structure. Processing flexibility, as in the acquisition stage, is defined by the degree of flexibility with which the person explores the problem presented by the social field, organizes information into categories, or uses divergent versus convergent thinking. Furthermore, it is likely that conceptual differentiation and processing flexibility also help determine the amount of information an individual can process before reaching a point of overload. Processing persistence, as in the acquisition stage, indicates the degree to which the person persists in his or her attempts to encode, transform, and assimilate any set of information.

If the first stage of information processing can be thought of as an "input" stage and the second stage as a "processing" stage, then the third stage should be seen as the "outcome" stage. Clearly, the quality of the response can vary along several dimensions, which include its complexity, novelty, and effectiveness in aiding adaptation. However, as our interest focuses on extended social behavior, at this stage, we wish to consider primarily the process through which the individual sets the level of achievement in the goals through which he or she plans to respond to the challenges of a specific social event. We choose to examine this aspect of goal setting, from among other possible cognitive "outcome" variables, because it is a clear antecedent of many later forms of unorganized and organized social activity. In more operational terms, the level of goal setting applies to such social phenomena as the amount of prosocial action expressed in an emergency, the attractiveness of the person approached when initiating an intimate relationship, the level of risk assumed in an experimental game, or the degree of entrepreneurial activity established as one's goal over the course of many years of work.

To facilitate our discussion of the relation between personality variables and cognitive style, we have summarized a set of predictions for the level of activity that we expect to appear in each of the stages of information processing (Table 7.2). In each case, we are assuming that environmental stressors are present to only a mild degree. Clearly, the degree of stress present in any particular situation might significantly change the effect of a personality variable upon the level of cognitive activity. We organize this chapter around each of these three main stages. For each discussion, we first outline the major relationships that can be expected between different personality variables and the type of cognitive activity under consideration. We then review the empirical literature in order to estimate the plausibility of these hypotheses. Because there is a great deal of information available on many important topics, we concentrate on those research topics that have been most central to social psychology and report the conclusions of the major reviews of an area, rather than discuss each experiment in turn.

TABLE 7.2
The Level of Activity Expected in Each Information-Processing Category for Selected Personality Variables

Personality Variables	I. The Acquisition of Information			II. The Processing of Information			III. Goal Setting
	Selective Attention	Search Flexibility	Search Persistence	Conceptual Differentiation	Processing Flexibility	Processing Persistence	Aspiration Level, Risk taking
Dependency	H	L	L	M	L	L	L
Abasement	M	L	M	L	L	M	L
Approval	H	L	L	M	L	M	M
Authoritarianism	H	L	L	L	L	M	M
Order	L	L	H	H	L	H	M
Affiliation	M	M	M	H	M	M	M
Machiavellianism	L	H	H	H	H	H	H
Dominance	M	M	H	M	M	H	H
Nurturance	L	H	H	H	H	H	H
Achievement	L	H	H	H	H	H	H
Recognition	M	M	H	M	M	H	H

Note: H = high
M = medium
L = low

153

STAGE I: THE ACQUISITION OF INFORMATION

Selective Attention

Selective attention refers to the tendency to concentrate on some part of a configuration of stimuli to the exclusion of other parts. In general, we expect that as people whose personality structure is organized around the issues of prediction and control begin to experience moderate degrees of stress from their perceptual search, they will utilize a number of different techniques to reduce the discomfort. Selective attention is a way to deal with this discomfort by focusing one's concentration on part of the stimulus field in order to avoid another. For the cluster of personality states based upon the safety needs, we expect to observe relatively high levels of selective attention. In particular, we expect that the high levels of anxiety and need for structure, which characterize authoritarian, dependency, and approval-motivated individuals, will lead them to reduce the breadth of their perceptual search. The compulsivity of the person with a high need for order and the self-defeating aspirations of the person with a high need for abasement should lead them into a wider range of perceptual experience than we might expect simply from their high level of anxiety. Indeed, it is possible that the abasing person will judiciously inattend as part of his or her provocative interpersonal style, rather than as a defense against threatening stimuli. For these reasons, we expect that within this group only the needs for order and abasement will lead to low and moderate levels of selective attention, respectively.

In contrast, we expect that the variables within the affiliative and esteem-needs clusters will be associated with much lower levels of selective attention (i.e., a more evenly balanced search) because individuals with these personality traits are less anxious and possess a broader range of adaptive competencies. Within this group, however, the strong interpersonal orientation of affiliation-oriented people may detract somewhat from their ability to scan both task- and person-related stimuli. Similarly, we expect that the strong task orientation of the dominance-oriented person will be associated with a lack of patience and competitiveness, which will lead to a moderate level of selective attention. We also expect a moderate level from individuals with a strong need for recognition because their striving for praise from other people may cause them to attend to only part of a problem that might otherwise require prolonged investigation for successful accomplishment. On the other hand, we expect low levels of selective attention from Machiavellians because scanning can be a highly critical function through which the Machiavellian can discover opportunities to devise exploitation tactics. For achievement-oriented and nurturant individuals, we also expect low levels because of their desire to demonstrate excellence in performance through competent problem-solving behavior. In other words, we expect the last three variables to lead to the most prolonged and accurate information search.

Search Flexibility

A flexible search of the stimulus field implies that the individual has the ability to use multiple sensory channels, perceptual styles, and problem-solving approaches to the event. In contrast to flexibility, the term "constriction" or "rigidity" refers to a stereotyped or limited style of perceiving, scanning, or approach to a social field, despite informational feedback regarding the ineffectiveness of an incorrect identification of the stimulus. Goldstein and Blackman (1978), in reporting Klein's (1954) important work in this area, write that "individuals who manifested constricted control over the expression of needs were characterized in a manner similar to compulsive people. They were precise and meticulous, overvalued order, were uncomfortable with disorder, and tended to pigeon-hole reality rather than deal with it in affective terms. The characteristics of the flexible person were less clear" (p. 5).

Building upon Klein's (1954) work, it is likely that all of the personality variables within the safety-needs cluster are associated with constriction and rigidity in the way that people search for information. For affiliation-oriented individuals, however, we expect moderate levels of flexibility because of a more relaxed approach to problem solving. We also expect moderate levels of flexibility in information search to be associated with the variables of dominance and recognition. The strongly self-assertive desire to initiate and control activity by dominant individuals should especially reduce their effective processing of cues that fall along the socioemotional axis of social behavior. Similarly, the self-absorbed tendency of recognition-oriented persons to constrict their attention to problem-solving approaches with the most obvious chance of success will limit their ability to perceive other potential problem-solving approaches. Finally, we believe that Machiavellianism and the needs for achievement and nurturance will be associated with high levels of flexibility in information search. Both Machiavellian and nurturant individuals exhibit task and interpersonal flexibility in attending to stimuli, although in pursuit of different goals. The Machiavellian is cognitively flexible in the service of competition and self-enhancement, whereas the nurturant person is flexible in the hopes of effectively meeting the demands of the task in a cooperative and responsible way.

A second aspect of this dimension refers to the individual's ability to tolerate uncertainty, incongruity, ambiguity, or inconsistency in the processing of information. Messick (1970), reviewing cognitive styles, labeled this process the tolerance for incongruous or unrealistic experience. This definition points to the fact that the stimulus event often is either unclear or presents information that is inconsistent with the person's belief structure. We expect that the personality variables that we have been following will lead to the same pattern of information use for related reasons. We expect that because of the anxiety characteristic of these variables, safety-oriented persons will uniformly manifest a low tolerance for uncertainty, whereas affiliation-oriented individuals should show a moderate level of tolerance for uncertainty because of their ability to use uncertainty as a way to create affiliative bonds with others. For dominance-oriented persons, we also expect a moderate level of tolerance of uncertainty because of their rigid approach to problem solving and their impatience when they cannot initiate behaviors that structure the interaction. For the need for recognition, we expect moderate levels because of the need such people feel to identify a goal on which they can succeed. In contrast, however, we believe that Machiavellian individuals will show an unusually high level of tolerance for uncertainty because such conditions permit the widest latitude of interpersonal manipulation. We also hypothesize that the needs for achievement and nurturance will be associated with high tolerance of uncertainty simply because the strong internal locus of control, which characterizes these variables, leads such persons to believe that they can succeed under a variety of conditions by personal effort and skill.

Search Persistence

Search persistence is defined by the degree to which the individual persists in acquiring information. In its simplest form, search persistence is measured by the amount of time the person spends attending to the stimulus event. From the safety-needs cluster of variables, it is likely that only persons with strong needs for order will manifest high levels of search persistence. Clearly, in order to defend against anxiety, these individuals tenaciously focus on many details that can be ordered and understood in highly intellectualized ways (Shapiro, 1965). We expect that the need for abasement will be associated with moderate level of persistence because abasing individuals repetitively engage in behaviors that provoke aversive consequences for themselves. For the variables of dependency, approval, and authoritarianism, we expect low levels of search persistence as a result of their need to impose structure on events as a means of reducing high levels of anxiety.

The tendency of persons with a high need for affiliation to solve problems in cooperation with others should lead them to demonstrate moderate levels of search persistence. From the esteem-needs cluster, we expect all of the variables in Table 7.2 to be associated with high levels of search persistence. The relatively low level of anxiety of people with these dispositions enables them not to feel threatened by unstructured events. Rather, they can carefully examine the stimulus to discern its nature and generate a response that reinforces their feeling of personal control.

THE EMPIRICAL STUDIES

The Need for Approval

There are two studies that help us to understand the process through which approval-motivated persons selectively acquire information about the world. As part of a more complex experiment, Zaidel and Mehrabian (1969) instructed approval- and nonapproval-motivated subjects to encode the expression of a range of positive and negative attitudes through both the vocal and the facial channel. In general, we would expect that it would be more difficult for approval-oriented subjects to encode the more negative attitudes because a possible consequence of negative attitudes might be disapproval from others. The results of this study showed that approval-oriented subjects were better able to encode positive attitudes, whereas nonapproval-oriented people showed superiority in encoding negative attitudes.

Similar results were obtained by Johnson and Gormly (1975), who led undergraduate women to believe that they were participating in a dyadic impression-formation study. As part of this experiment, subjects listened to a confederate describe her attitudes on a variety of issues. On half of these issues, the confederate agreed, and on the other half, she disagreed with the premeasured opinions of the subject. After the confederate left the room, the subject was asked, among other things, to recall the statements that the confederate had made. In this experiment, recall of positive or negative comments was taken to reflect different patterns of attention to the stimuli provided by the other person. The results showed that the need for approval was positively associated with the recall of agreements and negatively associated with the recall of disagreements.

In an interesting contrast to these results which points up the "positivity" defense structure of the need for approval, Johnson and Gormly also measured the anxiety level of these subjects. They expected that without the defense of positivity in perception, anxiety alone would lead people to perceive the negative side of the social interaction. As expected, the results showed that anxiety was positively associated with the recall of disagreements (and negatively associated with agreements). These findings suggest that the characteristic features of these states lead approval-oriented people to appear to attend to the positive information within a situation, whereas anxious persons exhibit the reverse pattern.

Additionally, and especially when subjected to stressful conditions, it seems reasonable that the search procedures of approval-oriented persons will be reduced through the earlier imposition of structuring operations or the earlier termination of search, due to their need to defend against threat. This relationship was shown experimentally by Lefcourt (1969), using the constriction of cognitive expressiveness on the Rorschach test as the measure of cognitive functioning. Another index that would assess this tendency would be the time taken to reach a decision. Jones and Tager (1972) tested this hypothesis in a study in which subjects were asked to evaluate other members of the group under threatening or nonthreatening conditions. Under less threatening conditions, approval-oriented subjects took longer to reach a decision about evaluating a peer than they did in the more threatening condition. On the other hand, nonapproval-motivated subjects took longer to respond in the more threatening condition. In the absence of threat, it would appear that approval-oriented subjects spend more time processing information, which in turn might lead to more adequate or differentiated responses on a particular task, but under threatening conditions they significantly constrained their information search. Indirect support for this concept can be obtained by examining an illustrative study of the effect of the need for approval on some features of the encoding process. In two studies (Brannigan, 1977; Brannigan, Duchnowski, & Nyce, 1974), in which elementary school children were given a simple discrimination learning task, approval-motivated children did better than nonapproval-motivated children, especially when external cues were provided for successful problem solving. As we see elsewhere in this chapter, and at length in part IV, the creation of stress-reducing conditions that are congruent with safety-based motives frequently produces an increment in performance. In this case, children with a desire for approval from adults do well on a simple task to be learned (encoded) in a nonthreatening situation.

Authoritarianism, Dogmatism, and Anxiety

Although the constructs of authoritarianism and dogmatism differ somewhat from each other, both kinds of individuals are thought to be authority oriented, cognitively rigid, and intolerant of beliefs that are not consistent with their value system. The extensive research literature examining the effects of these two variables has been subjected to several thorough reviews (e.g., Christie & Cook, 1958; Ehrlich & Lee, 1969; Goldstein & Blackman, 1978; Vacchiano, Strauss, & Hochman, 1969). Here, we focus our attention on a number of important studies that help us understand more precisely the influence these variables exert on the mechanisms of information processing.

Selective Attention. There is extensive literature demonstrating that high levels of anxiety restrict the range of external cues that the person examines. Both Geen's (1980) and Wine's (1980) excellent reviews of this area summarize a complex set of results on a very complex topic. These reviews provide a great deal of empirical support for Sarason's (1972) and Wine's (1971) conclusion that high levels of anxiety lead the person to divert his or her attention from the task and to focus on matters that bear more immediately upon the self. This generalization will prove to be very helpful in explaining many problems that have been of great importance in social psychology.

Research on the information-search patterns of authoritarian and dogmatic people, in contrast, has been directed toward examining the more limited hypothesis that these traits lead people to pay the most attention to information that is consistent with their existing attitudes. Goldstein and Blackman (1978) review the small number of studies that have examined this hypothesis, using requests for information or selective recall as their measure of selective attention. They conclude that the issue is still unsettled: There are nearly equal numbers of studies that have confirmed or failed to confirm this hypothesis. The problem, of course, may lie in the fact that, as the experimental situation is usually quite arousing, it may lead all types of subjects to a fairly consistent pattern of information search during the experiment. As many of these studies also include an information-processing component, we review this body of work at some length later in this chapter.

Search Flexibility.   The research examining the main hypothesis that the traits of authoritarianism and dogmatism will lead individuals to structure their stimulus field prematurely has received a great deal of support. Goldstein and Blackman (1978) review 17 studies, using a number of different tests to measure these two traits and many different behavioral measures to operationalize premature structuring, nearly all of which confirm this hypothesis. We can indicate the range of this work by describing three different approaches to this phenomenon. The first of these techniques uses the autokinetic effect to measure a person's ability to tolerate an ambiguous situation. In this experimental situation, the person is brought into a dark room and asked to observe what appears to be a moving point of light. In actuality, the light is stationary, and its apparent movement is a perceptual illusion. Capitalizing on Sherif's (1936) early work showing that people establish norms of the distance that they perceive the light to move, Block and Block (1951) found that ethnocentric subjects established personal norms regarding the distance the stimulus light moved sooner than did nonethnocentric subjects. In a similar study, Millon (1957) found the same result using the authoritarianism scale. In other words, in this ambiguous situation, authoritarians "imposed" structure upon the stimulus field (in the form of a norm of apparent movement) more quickly than did nonauthoritarians.

The general tendency of dogmatic and authoritarian individuals to reduce uncertainty has also been shown in decision-making tasks. For example, Taylor and Dunnette (1974) gave subjects a personnel decision simulation task, which required them to assume the role of a business manager, and found that dogmatic subjects made quick decisions following a very limited information search. It is very interesting that dogmatic subjects felt more confident in their decisions; this self-perception is expected if early decision making is based on reducing a sense of discomfort with uncertainty.

A third approach to the study of premature structuring uses perceptual tasks such as the Necker cube illusion. In this illusion, the outline of a cube is drawn in such a way that its orientation in space fluctuates between two positions. In the study of this as well as other perceptual illusions, the assumption is that the alternation between positions creates a discomforting sense of ambiguity in the perceiver. Following this hypothesis, Jones (1955) found that authoritarian subjects tended to reduce uncertainty in this external stimulus by perceiving less frequent reversals than did nonauthoritarians. Sanders (1977) obtained identical results for the trait of dogmatism, using both the Necker cube and another alternating perceptual illusion.

The results of the many studies using these three approaches, as well as several other methods, confirm the major form of the hypothesis that uncertainty in the perceptual field is anxiety arousing to authoritarian subjects and that these people impose structure on the stimulus to reduce their sense of discomfort.

Search Persistence. It is expectable that the inability of authoritarian subjects to tolerate uncertainty, and the corresponding need to impose structure on social events, should also lead them to spend less time in their search of the stimulus field. As noted earlier, Taylor and Dunnette (1974) found that in a decision-making task, dogmatic subjects reached a decision about a hypothetical employee faster than did open-minded subjects. In a similar study testing the same hypothesis, Long and Ziller (1965) used four very different types of cognitive tasks in which subjects could engage in a wide range of predecisional search activity. As expected, there was a negative correlation between dogmatism and the amount of time spent searching for information about the task. A comparable set of results was found by Robbins (1975). In an experiment in which subjects could request information that might be helpful in forming an impression of another person, Robbins found that dogmatic people requested much less information than did nondogmatic people. In each of these studies, the results conform to theoretical prediction. However, because premature structuring does terminate search, additional work, possibly adding measures of effort to those direct measures of requests for information, is needed to establish that search persistence is an independent dimension of information processing.

The Esteem-Needs Cluster

For the set of variables located within the esteem-needs cluster, we expect relatively high levels of performance during the acquisition stage of information processing. We expect that these people will manifest cognitive alertness and persist in attempts at problem solving when such actions are elicited by task or environmental variables that would arouse the motive sufficiently to activate goal-oriented action. Our ability to evaluate the esteem-related hypotheses at this time, however, is limited by the fact that the available research focuses on the study of search persistence. Because these results conform well to theoretical expectations and often seem dependent on a lower degree of premature structuring, it is very likely that parallel studies using esteem-based variables will prove to be successful.

Search Persistence.   In an early investigation of the relation of personality to cognitive style, Block and Petersen (1955) asked subjects, under somewhat difficult conditions, to decide which of two lines was longer. In this experiment, judge's ratings of a wide range of information about each experimental subject were used to identify broad traits with which to characterize each participant. The results of this experiment showed that rapid decision making was associated with the traits of passivity, suggestibility, and conformity, whereas more persistent search behavior was correlated with strong self-assurance and dominance. In addition, Block and Petersen report that in comparison to people who were overly confident (found in people who were dogmatic) or excessively cautious (found in people who were self-abasing), those people who were realistically self-confident had most of the attributes usually associated with high levels of self-esteem.

In a more realistic setting, Dittes (1959) examined the effects of self-esteem on search persistence and decision making in small groups. Measures of self-esteem and intolerance of ambiguity were obtained for the subjects who worked on three different discussion tasks in either a threatening or a supportive experimental condition. The conditions of support or threat were created by providing the subjects with false feedback on how well they were regarded by the other group members (based on questionnaire responses filled out during the group discussion). The strength of search persistence was determined by a combined index that measured the point at which the subject felt that he had discovered the meaning of an ambiguous concept in the three tasks. As expected, the results indicated that low-esteem subjects came to a decision earlier than did high-esteem persons, especially under more threatening conditions. Unlike Block and Petersen's, this experiment had no genuine neutral condition. The results of Dittes' experiment are particularly interesting because they suggest that under supportive group conditions, which parallel those found in a cohesive group, safety-oriented (i.e., low-esteem) persons working on ambiguous tasks may feel more relaxed and defer decision-making responsibility to another group member. We return to this study in chapter 13, when we consider the question of the optimum social structure required by the different personal states in order to reach their most efficient levels of functioning.

The strong information search of esteem-oriented individuals has been shown in several other experiments. For example, in an interpersonal influence study, Davis and Phares (1967) gave subjects the opportunity to ask questions about a target person they were going to meet and attempt to influence. The experimental design also included instructions that systematically emphasized either ability or luck as the determinant of success. The results indicated that people with an internal locus of control asked more questions about the other person than did those with an external locus of control, especially when the instructional set emphasized skill. However, there were no differences in the number of questions asked when the instructional set emphasized chance as a determinant of performance. In a naturalistic replication of this experiment, Prociuk and Breen (1977) examined the number of times students contacted their instructors when encouraged to consult with them in a psychology course. As expected, internals made more contacts with the instructors and requested more information from them than did externals.

Whiteley and Watts (1969) used a mock jury case as a task in which to study the length of information search as a consequence of the interaction of self-esteem and several situational variables. The subjects, all undergraduate educational psychology students, were placed into one of four experimental conditions that varied the cost of information required to make a decision and the consequences of a correct decision. For example, subjects in the high-consequence condition were told that their performance would become part of their permanent academic record. Together, these experimental manipulations created conditions that either aroused or depressed the broad self-estem factor that was measured in these subjects. The most interesting part of this complex experiment was that, in the most arousing experimental condition, there was a strong positive association between the self-esteem factor and information search, whereas in the "unimportant" condition, as we predicted in chapter 5, there was a strong negative relationship. Whitely and Watts' conclusion is congruent with that offered in many other studies: The person's ability to handle the stress associated with the prolonged search for information in a decision-making task is significantly affected by the person's predominant set of dispositions.

The mechanism that may account for the superior information-acquisition ability of esteem-oriented persons has been explored in a number of studies. Pines and Julian (1972) classified subjects into internal and external locus of control groups and gave them a standard learning task under experimental conditions that varied information-processing difficulty by presenting either task-relevant or task-irrelevant cues. The results showed that internal subjects used a different strategy in learning the task than did external subjects; internal subjects attended to task information, whereas external subjects were more likely to attend to social cues concerned with personal evaluation.

These findings suggest the interesting possibility that external subjects engage in more social comparison as a means of reducing uncertainty, whereas internal subjects actively search the stimulus for cues leading to success. Support for this idea has been obtained by Wolk and DuCette (1974), who found that people with a strong internal locus of control demonstrate superiority in a proofreading task and in measures of incidental learning derived from the task.

These findings suggest the possibility that, in contrast to safety-oriented persons, esteem-oriented individuals seem better able to concentrate on task-related stimuli for longer periods of time without being distracted by emotional arousal or the lack of information pertinent to more complex forms of information processing.

STAGE II: THE PROCESSING OF INFORMATION

Conceptual Differentiation

As information is acquired, it can be given meaning in many different ways. Conceptual differentiation is a broad term used to indicate the degree to which a person can make distinctions between concepts and then integrate them in the course of his or her cognitive work. In the field of personology, conceptual differentiation has been studied as category width, as integrative or cognitive complexity, or as certain aspects of a personal construct system (e.g., Bieri, 1966; Harvey, Hunt, & Schroder, 1961; Kelly, 1955; Schroder, Driver, & Streufert, 1967). The complexity of cognitive behavior, of course, is the dimension that has been most actively studied, although it is usually thought to be a structural characteristic of the person. The behavioral descriptions, however, help to clarify how these modes of cognitive activity affect the social process. For the analyses that we wish to make in later chapters it seems helpful for the predictions outlined in Table 7.2 to think of conceptual differentiation as encompassing the more specific modes of cognitive differentiation, integrative ability, and category width.

For the safety cluster of variables, we expect that the need for order will be correlated with high conceptual differentiation because the strong intellectual defenses of this type of person include obsessive insistence on detail, structure, and categorization. For the variables of abasement and authoritarianism, we expect low conceptual differentiation (e.g., wide, undifferentiated categories) due to childhood antecedents which lead these individuals to develop concretistic thinking (e.g., Adorno, Frenkel-Brunswik, Levinson, & Sanford, 1950; Christie & Cook, 1958). Dependent and approval-seeking individuals should manifest moderate levels of conceptual differentiation because they are less rigid characterologically than are need-for-order, abasement, or authoritarian persons. Therefore, they should be more able to encode information in more abstract and differentiated terms.

The personality variables located within the affiliative and esteem-needs clusters should show relatively high conceptual differentiation, partly because of their greater efficiency in acquiring information. Through their greater ability at search persistence, flexibility, and encoding, esteem-oriented persons create the basis by which to differentiate concepts in a more systematic manner. As noted in Table 7.2, however, it is likely that the needs for dominance and recognition will show only moderate levels of conceptual differentiation because of a slightly lower level of information acquisition.

Processing Flexibility

Our predictions for this aspect of cognitive style as it relates to personality variables directly parallel those made for the initial stage of information processing. Although the reasons for both sets of predictions are nearly identical, it should be noted that because we have suggested that safety-oriented persons may acquire less information, this factor should also help to result in a more constricted set of higher order cognitive processes. In addition, we expect that the high level of anxiety that is present should lead to greater rigidity in integrating new sets of information. In contrast, the broader ranges of scanning and persistence in information search enable the affiliation and esteem-oriented individual to explore alternative encoding schemata and ways of integrating experience. However, for the reasons stated earlier, we expect that persons with dominance and recognition needs will show moderate levels of processing flexibility, whereas those with high levels of achievement, Machiavellianism, and dominance concerns will display high levels of processing flexibility.

Moreover, it is very likely that these personological factors should help determine the amount of information that an individual can process without overloading the encoding process. For the safety-needs cluster of variables, we expect that the optimal levels of information are rather low because an increased amount of information is likely to raise anxiety to such a high level of arousal that it would interfere with performance (Sarason, 1980). Thus, to maintain a sense of control, the safety-oriented individual imposes limits on the level of information to be processed. The exception to this pattern is the person with strong order needs, whose defensive structure seems to result in the need to encode large amounts of information as a means of reducing feelings of uncertainty and anxiety. In contrast to the capacity of safety-oriented persons, affiliation and esteem-oriented individuals should have a higher optimal level of stimulation. The Machiavellian should have a high saturation level because processing a large amount of information is necessary in order to construct successful strategies of interpersonal manipulation. Similarly, the strong task orientation and concern with excellence of both the achievement and nurturant individuals should be associated with the ability to process large amounts of information. On the other hand, we expect that the needs for dominance and recognition will be associated with only moderate saturation levels because of their rigidity in encoding and somewhat lower ability levels of cognitive complexity and integration.

Processing Persistence

This aspect of information processing refers to the degree of perseverance an individual exhibits in solving the problems posed by a social task. Within the safety-needs cluster, we expect that dependent persons should have low processing persistance because of their characteristic tendency to shift the burden of responsibility for the task to others. Abasement concerns should lead to moderate levels of persistance because the abasing individual creatively finds the way to behave self-destructively. We expect that the concern for approval and affiliation will also be associated with moderate levels of processing persistance, especially in the absence of threat conditions, because they both seek to meet the demands of the task with active displays of positive social behavior. Similarly, the rigidity of authoritarians and their need to defend their value system should be associated with moderate perseverance in order to discover ways of maintaining motive-congruent social experiences. Finally, the tenacity of individuals with order needs is in large part defined by their intensive encoding operations during this stage of information processing. For the various esteem variables, it seems likely that their usual greater clarity of purpose and their greater sense of control, flexibility, and ease of processing information should enable them to persevere on tasks that engage the predominant peripheral motive.

THE EMPIRICAL STUDIES

Safety-Needs Cluster

Conceptual Differentiation.   Several studies have examined the hypothesis (Frenkel-Brunswik, 1949) that authoritarian and dogmatic people encode information in fewer categories of broader conceptual width. In refining this hypothesis, White, Alter, and Rardin (1965) suggested that it is appropriate only when the authoritarian is dealing with external stimuli that have impact on that trait. After selecting subjects on the basis of their authoritarianism and dogmatism scores, White et al. asked them to perform a sorting task (i.e., to form cognitive categories) of material that either was or was not of personal relevance. The results of this experiment showed that extremely dogmatic groups used fewer and broader categories in making judgments of highly relevant stimuli (with no differences between groups when the material was not personally relevant). This aspect of information processing has not drawn as much attention as has others, nor are the results as clear. Goldstein and Blackman (1978) describe seven studies that are almost evenly divided between those that have confirmed or not confirmed the hypothesis.

On the other hand, there are a large number of studies that have examined the effects of anxiety on cognitive activity in the context of traditional memory or learning experiments (cf. Sarason, 1980). Although the experimental procedures used in these studies are often quite different from those typically used in social psychology, reviewers of this literature (e.g., Mueller, 1979, 1980) conclude that the weight of the evidence supports the hypothesis that high levels of anxiety lead to the encoding of fewer features of the social field. In addition to Mueller's hypothesis that anxiety restricts the range of social stimuli encoded, others (i.e., Craik & Lockhart, 1972) argue that high levels of anxiety cause people to process more superficial characteristics of the stimuli. This levels-of-processing proposal distinguishes between "shallow" stimuli, such as the sound or words, and "deep" features, such as the meaning of words. Mueller's review of this area describes a complex program of work in progress, utilizing experimental procedures that are at least one remove from the typical social psychological experiment. However, as we subsequently argue, the "levels" proposal helps to explain some of the most reliable findings in the field of social behavior.

In addition to encoding strategies, conceptual differentiation includes the mechanisms through which new information is integrated into existing schemata. This definition directs attention to the entire process of cognitive learning, a vast subject well beyond the scope of this chapter. Some aspects of the process of integrating new information, however, help to explain some of the basic features of group process. For example, the social psychological study of persuasion analyzes the factors that lead a person to accept new information and to change existing structures of belief. Our discussion of social influence (chap. 9) examines the social psychological events that seem to be part of the path through which people become sensitized to certain kinds of arguments and persuaded as to their merits. There are two aspects of this social influence process that need to be noted in a review of the cognitive dimension of social events. We begin by briefly examining some evidence indicating that persuasion may, at times, depend on the interaction of the external authority of the source of the information with certain dispositions of the perceiver. Following this, we examine the personological bases that make inconsistent information more or less difficult for the perceiver to tolerate.

The attributes of the people that we observe often indicate that the person is a credible source of information. Some of the attributes most easily understood are those proclaiming that third parties have found the person to be an appropriate source of that information. In other words, the source of the information has been provided with "authority" of one sort or another (e.g., occupational or social rank). By contrast, it is much more difficult to evaluate the quality of the information independently. Thus, there are two separate bases for what Ehrlich and Lee (1969) call the "authority hypothesis." First, external signs of authority are a much more easily comprehended characteristic. It seems quite possible that these attributes are more "superficial," as we have just seen (Craik & Lockhart, 1972), and are more easily comprehended by more anxious people. Second, an independently made decision (e.g., one which evaluates the degree of quality in an argument) possibly needs to examine "deeper," and thus more difficult, features of the social stimulus. For this reason, examination of deeper features may need to be based upon some genuine degree of self-confidence. Cherry and Byrne (1977), Ehrlich and Lee (1969), Goldstein and Blackman (1978), and Vacchiano (1977) review a large number of studies which demonstrate that authoritarian and dogmatic people rely more on the authority of the information source to establish the credibility of the information than do nonauthoritarian or nondogmatic people. Vacchiano, for example, describes 17 studies, all but 1 of which supports this hypothesis for dogmatism. In addition, this relationship has been demonstrated for other safety-based variables, such as external locus of control (cf. Lefcourt, 1976a).

The experiments themselves, on which this support has been found, cover almost the entire range of experimental techniques. Vidulich and Kaiman (1961), for example, used the autokinetic effect procedure to show that dogmatic subjects were more influenced by the norms established by high-status confederates than by low-status confederates. Powell (1962) and Bettinghouse, Miller, and Steinfatt (1970) provided support for the hypothesized association of dogmatism and the greater credibility of authority by having their subjects read and evaluate political statements. Berg and Vidmar (1975) used a mock jury trial to show that authoritarian and dogmatic subjects were more sensitive to, and persuaded by, the status of the defendant than by the quality of the evidence.

Processing Flexibility. In the pioneering work on the authoritarian character, much of the initial empirical attention was given to studying the rigid way that these people seemed to approach their work (e.g., Frenkel-Brunswick, 1949; Rokeach, 1948). In general, for the trait of dogmatism (Rokeach, 1960), as well as for authoritarianism, there is much support for the hypothesis that such people are much more bound to the cognitive set that they bring to work on a problem, much more troubled by inconsistencies in different aspects of the information, and much more influenced by the position taken by an authority who provides any of the direction received in the course of the work. However, in work on this topic as on others, the early successes drew a host of critical responses (e.g., Luchins, 1949), some of which were cogent and some not. Reviews of this area describe these controversies at great length. Among the most important concerns raised by critics was the question of the appropriateness of the experimental operationalization of the concept of "rigidity" itself. As in other areas, the most satisfying solution is to show the range of different social phenomena that the hypothesis helps explain. If we work with an inclusive definition of rigidity, one that focuses on the characteristic of the person continuing a former behavior pattern when the more efficient solution would require a change in approach, we can find many studies whose overall weight is highly supportive of this hypothesis.

In its most commonly studied form, rigidity has been operationalized as the maintenance of an established mode of thinking about the elements of a cognitive problem. In the early work, Luchins' Einstellung problem was often used as the cognitive material upon which people could demonstrate their intellectual rigidity. This task asks subjects to devise a technique that would allow them to measure a specific quantity of water if they had only three containers (of specified capacities) to use in solving the problem. This apparently simple task allows the experimenter to study a narrow form of cognitive rigidity in which the experimenter can pose many different cognitive strategies to the subject. The experimenter is usually interested in determining whether the subject can change his or her approach to working out a solution (if the change is more efficient, in fact) during the course of working on a series of such problems. In one of the early studies, Brown (1953) found that authoritarianism was associated with rigidity on the Einstellung problem. Even more important, this study showed that, in work on this problem as in many other areas of social psychology, this relationship appeared only when the experiment took place under conditions that raised the subject's level of involvement (under relaxed conditions, there was no association). In related research, Ainsworth (1958) found the same relationship for the variable of insecurity, a finding that became common in the work on anxiety (Sarason, 1980). Goldstein and Blackman (1978) review a number of other studies, which set many types of cognitive problems before their subjects, and present a great deal of support (although it is not unanimous) for the association of authoritarianism, ethnocentrism, and dogmatism with problem-solving rigidity.

In the course of subsequent work, cognitive tasks such as tracing paths out of mazes (Riley & Armlin, 1965), comparing objects of different weights (White & Alter, 1965), recognizing the emergence of a new form in a transitional series of pictures leading away from an original form (Kidd & Kidd, 1972), and appreciating new forms of music (Rokeach, 1960) were only a few of the many different cognitive events through which it was possible to show the association between these variables and an apparent reluctance to leave an established way of thinking in preference to a more appropriate one. Similar findings have been reported for related variables such as external locus of control (e.g., Lefcourt, Gronnerud, & McDonald, 1973). For psychologists who wish to rely upon these findings to help explain the intense, complex, and extended interpersonal events that occur in most forms of group process, this range of tasks provides a much more secure foundation for the types of generalizations we hope to obtain.

The type of experimental work on cognitive rigidity that is closest to the more customary social psychological experiment has been done in research studying the ways in which authoritarian or dogmatic people handle information that varies in either internal consistency or in agreement with their existing opinions. For example, in our early scanning of a real social situation, the visible attributes of the other people may be contradictory in some important way or may assert opinions that are in disagreement with those of the viewer. In some of the primary studies in this area, Steiner (1954) and Steiner and Johnson (1963) found that ethnocentric and authoritarian subjects were less able to tolerate trait inconsistency in others. For example, in the first study, subjects were asked to rate trait pairs for the likelihood of their co-occurrence in people. As expected, ethnocentric (as compared with nonethnocentric) subjects were less likely to select pairs that were somewhat inconsistent with each other. Foulkes and Foulkes (1965) continued this approach to the study of rigidity in an impression-formation study using realistic and vivid descriptions of university student life, and they found supporting evidence for the trait of dogmatism. In a study designed to test how this mechanism might affect the acceptance of information that was or was not consistent with the subject's attitudes, Kleck and Wheaton (1967) found that dogmatic subjects were more resistant to information that was inconsistent with their beliefs. These studies illustrate the approach taken by a much larger set of studies, although often with quite inconclusive results (cf. Goldstein & Blackman, 1978). In light of a number of studies which did not demonstrate this effect (e.g., Gormly & Clore, 1969), it does seem that a continuing effort is still needed in this area. It may be, as Crano and Sigal (1968) have shown, that the defensive structure of the authoritarian and dogmatic person is either to accept or reject the inconsistent information in rather extreme ways. We return to this issue in chapter 9, when we deal with the responses of individuals to broader and more realistic influence attempts.

Esteem-Needs Cluster

Conceptual Differentiation.   There are few studies that have examined the relationship of esteem-oriented personality variables to conceptual differentiation. Only in the locus of control program has there been enough work to support even a tentative conclusion, so our discussion focuses on the available information that comes from the study of internal locus of control. Lefcourt's (1976a) valuable review of this area outlines the ways that people with an internal locus of control use information about matters that are of importance to them. In an earlier section, we saw that these people, compared to those with an external locus of control, search the environment much more actively for the information they need (Davis & Phares, 1967; Seeman, 1963; Seeman & Evans, 1962). Of even greater interest, Seeman's results show that these people differentiated much more carefully among this information in order to identify facts that would be especially useful. They also retained more useful information than did individuals with an external locus of control. Phares (1968) focused his attention more directly on how locus of control affects the ways people use information. In this experiment, he used a task that required subjects to learn a set of information about four stimulus persons and then, a week later, to solve another task using this information. Phares was able to show that even though all the subjects had learned a common set of information, when they were asked to use this information a week later, the internal locus of control subjects were able to use much more of it and use it much more effectively. Finally, Hearn and Seeman (1971), using what appears to be a broad self-esteem measure, including the factor of internal locus of control, report that this variable is associated with a much more differentiated set of cognitive categories in forming an impression of people.

Processing Flexibility.   There does not seem to have been any interest in exploring the ways that esteem-based variables might affect cognitive rigidity (or flexibility), as we have seen for the safety-based variables. Only two studies (Mabel & Rosenfeld, 1966; Sorem & Ketola, 1977) for the variables of self-esteem and Machiavellianism, respectively, mirror those discussed earlier and show that more esteem-oriented people are not as uncomfortable with inconsistent information.

Processing Persistence.   Most of the attention in this area has been given to studying the question of the persistence that esteem-oriented people bring to their work on a problem. In large measure, the available research strongly supports the theoretical predictions. In one of the most influential studies examining the effects of locus of control on information processing, Rotter and Mulry (1965) used a fairly difficult angle matching task in experimental conditions that emphasized either skill or chance to measure persistence in work at a task. As expected, the results showed that those subjects characterized by an internal locus of control spent more time on the task under skill instruction, whereas those with an external locus of control were more persistent in the chance condition. These results suggest that those subjects with an internal locus of control take longer on the perceptual task in the skill condition in order to demonstrate their personal effectiveness in controlling the outcome (see also Evans, 1982; Gagné & Parshall, 1975, for related sets of results). It is very likely that in the course of this work, as Pines and Julian (1972) found, such individuals attend more effectively to task-related cues and thus persist in encoding the stimulus in an attempt to reach a correct solution.

In an extension of Rotter and Mulry's (1965) study, Lefcourt, Lewis, and Silverman (1968) tested the hypothesis that situational factors such as a skill condition for performance should lead to greater ego invovlement with the task and therefore result in better recall of the decisions made during the task. To test this hypothesis, they assigned internal and external locus of control subjects to either a chance or skill experimental condition and had them work on a motor coordination game (the Rotter level of aspiration board) that allows participants to estimate their level of performance at rolling a steel ball down a groove in a board. As they expected, Lefcourt et al. found that under skill conditions, internals had longer decision times, recalled more of their expectancies for performance, and recalled more task-relevant thoughts about their performance than did externals. In the chance condition, they manifested less visual attention to the game. Thus, when the motive was aroused by the skill instructions, the internals' scanning and encoding processes were activated in a goal-directed problem-solving manner. In contrast, their behavior in the chance condition was particularly interesting inasmuch as they spent less time scanning the stimulus, presumably because they believed that to exert personal effort would be futile in a randomly controlled event. This factor proves to be very useful in explaining a number of consistent relationships between esteem-based variables and group productivity, which we discuss in the final chapter.

The last set of studies we wish to mention is so extensive, rich, and persuasive that book-length treatments are required to present all the available information. From its inception, the massive program of work on the need for achievement has demonstrated that this motive strongly influences the persistence with which people work on a task. The major summaries of this research (Atkinson, 1958; Atkinson & Feather, 1966; Atkinson & Raynor, 1974, 1978; Heckhausen, 1967; McClelland, Atkinson, Clark, & Lowell, 1953) present an ever-increasing body of evidence showing that the need for achievement motivates greater persistence in solving tasks that engage their sujbects' interest, as measured by nearly every available technique. In fact, the intensity that this motive brings to task work is reflected in virtually every study that has been done in this immense research program, whether the task is as narrow as persistence in solving anagram puzzles (McClelland et al., 1953) or as broad as motivating economic development on a global scale (McClelland & Winter, 1969).

Finally, there is one study (Weiss & Knight, 1980) that claims to show a negative relationship between self-esteem and "performance," as measured by the number of questions asked during work on a problem-solving task. However, because the task used was unusually dull and performed under strongly authoritarian experimental conditions, the results conform precisely to the pattern predicted by most organizational psychologists. In chapter 13, we review a substantial body of work that has identified, as in the studies by Lefcourt et al., Rotter and Mulry, and Whiteley and Watts, described earlier, the specific environmental conditions that depress the level of performance to be expected from esteem-oriented people.

STAGE III: GOAL SETTING

As part of the early experience in a situation, people set the degree of success or excellence they wish to pursue through a particular course of action. As defined by Cartwright and Zander (1968), a level of aspiration is "a level of performance" that individuals or groups "expect to attain at some time in the future" (p. 419). This definition is purposely broad because the goals that people choose and the actions they select to reach these goals can vary dramatically. In the stream of human behavior, the level of aspiration is a key element in the final cognitive steps that select the behaviors through which people meet the demands (and opportunities) of the task. For example, in a social gathering, the person must decide which other people to approach; in an emergency, the bystander must decide how much help should be given; in a factory, the manager must decide the optimum level of production.

The related factor of risk taking is also part of the decision through which a person sets the level of behavioral goals. Whereas in aspiration level a person specifies a level of performance to be desirable, in risk taking the person accepts a probable level of success and failure for the course of action selected. If level of aspiration is defined as a personal preference to seek a certain level of excellence in the task, then the level of aspiration customarily sets a level of difficulty, or possibility of failure, to be accepted as part of seeking that goal. Because accepting the possibility of failure is accepting a level of risk, Heckhausen (1967), following Atkinson (1957) and McClelland (1958), argues that although the behaviors can be defined separately, "the two concepts may legitimately be used interchangeably when a person has to decide about something" (pp. 59–60). Therefore, although the two concepts can be defined independently, it seems useful to think of the final decision, on which action will be taken, as the seeking of a certain quality of the goal based upon a realistic determination of what is possible in that situation.

Each of these variables has been the subject of separate research programs using separate measurement operations. Usually, the level of aspiration is determined before work is undertaken by asking the subjects to estimate the level of performance they expect to attain on a particular task. In the tasks used in these studies, subjects have been asked to estimate their future performance in activities such as the number of puzzles that can be completed, the number of blocks that can be stacked, or the grade that will be attained on an exam. In the broadest program of work on level of aspiration, Zander (1971) used a procedure that asked subjects to estimate the level of success that they, as a team of three to five people, would be able to achieve. The primary task in the experiment was for the team to use a 6-foot aluminum pole to propel a wooden ball down a 12-foot track so that it would stop as close as possible to a predetermined spot. If the team could get the ball to stop at that target, they received 10 points; the further the ball stopped from that goal, the fewer points were awarded to the team. In this situation, level of aspiration was determined by asking each person to estimate the final score that the team would obtain in a set of five trials.

In the area of risk taking, the most widely used procedure has been the Choice Dilemma Questionnaire (CDQ), developed by Kogan and Wallach (1964). The CDQ presents subjects with choices that vary in their apparent level of "riskiness." Briefly, it consists of 12 hypothetical situations; in each situation, a central person is faced with a dilemma involving the choice between two opposing alternatives: a highly desirable but much riskier course of action, or a much less rewarding but much more secure course of action. For example, the vignette will pose an issue such as an undergraduate who must choose between entering a highly prestigious university's graduate program in which few students complete the PhD degree, or a much less impressive university in which nearly every student receives the PhD. The subject reading these stories is shown a form that gives a variety of probabilities (that the chances are 1, 3, 5, 7, 9 out of 10) for the riskier course of action to succeed. The task confronting the subject is to choose the lowest probability of success that he or she would accept in order to recommend the more rewarding course of action. In order to estimate the degree of risk that the subject is willing to accept, his or her scores on the 12 stories are summed to produce a total score of proneness to risk.

With this technique, Kogan and Wallach (1964) introduced what has become one of the most widely studied phenomena in all of psychology (Myers & Lamm, 1976). In general, they showed that if people were first asked to make independent decisions on the CDQ situations and then discussed the questions in a group, usually consisting of five persons, the group would tend to recommend a riskier course of action than would the individual. This change in the level of recommended risk, from the initial individual decision to the final group consensus, was called the "risky-shift."

The great interest aroused by the risky-shift has made available a wide range of information on the factors that determine the level of challenge that individuals and groups are ready to accept. From among this mass of information, our interest focuses on the contribution that dispositional variables make to the level set in the individual's initial decision. In order to use the information that comes from CDQ research, we need to consider more precisely the type of individual tendency that is engaged in responding to this questionnaire. In an excellent theoretical review of this area, Cartwright (1971) questioned whether there was a real shift toward risk because "the average shift per item, expressed in odds, is roughly 6 in 10 to 5 in 10. Groups may be riskier than individuals on the average, but they are not strikingly so" (p. 365). In other words, Cartwright points out that the changes of risk by the subject occur within a fairly narrow band and that both the individual and the group decision could be understood as moderate risk taking. From the subject's point of view, particularly the subject who is not a statistician, scores in the middle range of these apparently absolute values sound quite reasonable and plausible. It is possible that the meaning of the level of risk selected by the subject, within this intermediate band, is that of an index which estimates the level of confidence, optimism, energy, and interest in meeting a challenge that is characteristic of that subject. In this sense, the initial recommendation in these hypothetical situations can be taken to be a measure of the person's subjectively felt willingness to become engaged in social events. If this is true, then the relationship between a dispositional variable and the CDQ recommendation may be construed as an estimate of a level of goal setting under specified situational conditions (Cartwright, 1971).

Our general hypothesis is stated quite simply: We would expect to find that persons who are self-assured, competent, autonomous, dominant, and achievement-oriented would have stronger desires for accomplishment than would insecure, dependent, or rigid persons. Table 7.2 presents the expectation that the safety-needs cluster of variables is associated with low to moderate desires for accomplishment because the anxiety, mistrust, and uncertainty of such persons is likely to be associated with the more cautious attitudes needed to guard against unpredictable events. In contrast, we believe that the greater self-confidence of affiliation and esteem-oriented persons will lead them to set moderate to high levels of aspiration. This prediction is based on the idea that these people enjoy meeting challenges that enable them to engage in mastery behaviors associated with a personal sense of control and feelings of self-worth. As in other areas, of course, specific situational conditions may facilitate or constrain these dispositional effects.

THE EMPIRICAL STUDIES

Anxiety

In a study designed to test the effects of anxiety on aspiration level, Zander and Wulff (1966) had anxious and nonanxious subjects perform a level of aspiration task that required them to estimate how far they (as a team) could roll a wooden ball down a channel. The results show that the anxious subjects reported stronger feelings of tension, and their teams had more variance in their level of aspiration statements and made more "wild jumps" than did nonanxious participants, who seemed better able to attend to the contingencies presented by the task and to raise their level of aspiration when it was appropriate. Hancock and Teevan (1964) also found irrational moves made by anxious people in a gambling situation. Congruent results were reported by Kogan and Wallach (1967), who used the CDQ procedure to study risk preference. Although the focus of their study was on the change in risk level, their results show a more conservative position taken by more anxious persons in setting the level of their initial choice (see also Burnstein, 1963; Rim, 1963; Trapp & Kausler, 1958).

It is interesting to speculate on the results to be expected from the need for approval in this situation. The factor of positivity in the public presentation of self alone should predict a positive correlation with goal setting under relaxed conditions. However, the base of anxiety in this motive would certainly predict a negative relationship if the person subjectively experiences a real degree of threat in setting a level of risk. Strickland (1977), reviewing the effects of need for approval on many aspects of social behavior, concluded that the results of a number of studies (e.g., Efran & Boylin, 1967; Kanfer & Marston, 1964; Thaw & Efran, 1967) demonstrate that this motive leads to risk-avoidant behavior (a tendency to stand closer to the target when throwing darts). In addition, Morrison and Morrison (1978) found a negative relationship between the need for approval and the estimation of future grades (a procedure that may not necessarily be related to goal setting), whereas Lamm, Schaude, and Trommsdorf (1971) failed to find a significant effect of the need for approval on a CDQ task.

There is some interesting evidence that the effects of anxiety may be moderated by certain situational variables. Support for this idea was obtained by Beckworth, Iverson, and Reuder (1965), who selected more and less anxious subjects and assigned them to a discussion group in an introductory psychology class in which the leader presented either task-relevant or task-irrelevant remarks. The subjects' level of aspiration was measured by asking them to state the score they hoped to obtain on an upcoming examination and by an estimate of their performance on a pegboard game. In the task-relevant condition, the leader helped the students focus on questions and concepts relevant to the examination, whereas in the task-irrelevant condition, the leader made remarks unrelated to the course. The results indicated that in the task-irrelevant condition, anxious subjects presented a low level of aspiration. In the task-relevant condition, both more and less anxious subjects presented a higher level of aspiration. Overall, then the results indicated that the nonanxious subjects had a higher level of aspiration than did the more anxious subjects, whose performance goals were modified by the information provided by a goal-directed discussion group, which seemed to reduce the deleterious effects of anxiety on the level of aspiration. This finding is potentially of great importance: If situational variables can reduce the uncertainty of safety-oriented persons, then it is possible to design social environments in which many of these people can function in highly productive ways. In chapter 13, we discuss more fully the relationship between personality and situational congruency as it affects aspiration level and the performance of individuals in groups.

The Need for Achievement

A number of studies has examined the association between the need for achievement and the levels of risk taking and of aspiration. In a classic proposal, Atkinson (1957) derived the prediction of the effects of the need for achievement on risk taking on the basis of purely theoretical reasoning. The hypothesis that individuals with high levels of the need for achievement should show moderate levels of risk taking has become one of the most carefully examined and strongly supported propositions in the field (Weiner, 1978). Studies such as those of Atkinson, Bastian, Earl, and Litwin (1960), Atkinson and Litwin (1960), Brody (1963), McClelland and Watson (1973), Scodel, Ratoosh, and Minas (1959), Smith (1963), and Zander (1971) each makes approximately the same prediction and provides approximately the same pattern of results, using a wide variety of behavioral measures of risk taking. The apparent difference between these results and some of the studies using the CDQ approach to show that achievement-oriented people have higher levels of risk acceptance (e.g., Goldman, 1975; Rim, 1963) is easily resolved by Cartwright's observation that the absolute level of risk acceptance on the CDQ is in the moderate range. The meaning of this finding was extended by Raynor and Smith (1966) who, following earlier work by Littig (1963), showed that the relationship only appeared in tasks that were under the subject's control (cf. Weiner & Kukla, 1970). Raynor and Smith had subjects set the level of their expected goals in a set of skill (puzzles) and chance (gambling) activities. Their results showed that achievement-motivated subjects preferred moderate levels of risk, but only under experimental conditions that emphasized skill as a determinant of performance. These findings are nicely supported by studies such as House (1978), who gave subjects a choice between two tasks varying in their degree of difficulty. The results showed that achievement-motivated subjects consistently chose the difficult task to do first, whereas participants less concerned with this motive initially tended to select the less difficult task.

In addition to the core program on the need for achievement, there are a host of parallel studies using many esteem-related variables, such as internal locus of control, which together provide a strong foundation of support. For example, studies using the CDQ and other measures of risk taking and level of aspiration have shown these personality variables to be correlated with moderate to high levels of initial risk acceptance (e.g., Jackson, Hourany, & Vidmar, 1972; Lefcourt, 1967; Liverant & Scodel, 1960; Morrison &

Morrison, 1978). Similarly, there are a number of parallel studies showing that these esteem-related variables contribute to goal setting only when the task is under personal control (e.g., Brice & Sassenrath, 1978; Cohen, Sheposh, & Hillix, 1979; Kogan & Wallach, 1964; Korman, 1967b; Liverant & Scodel, 1960).

Machiavellianism

The relationship between Machiavellianism and aspiration level is still unclear, with several of the available studies showing nonsignificant findings (e.g., Lamm & Meyers, 1976) and another showing a positive relationship (Rim, 1966). Because Machiavellian persons are primarily concerned with the manipulations of others in relatively unstructured situations, the hypothetical CDQ items may not be the best measure of risk acceptance. However, we would expect that Machiavellian persons would actually manifest higher aspiration levels and risk-taking behaviors in situations involving interpersonal influence. Indeed, Rim (1966) presents evidence that Machiavellian people were effective in persuading other group members to move more toward their risk choice. Goldman (1975) also showed this result for the need for achievement. Goldman's and Rim's studies, as Cartwright (1971) suggests, help to focus this area of research more firmly into the broader issues of social influence within groups.

The Need for Power

There are several studies that have looked into the relationship of power motives to risk acceptance. McClelland and Teague (1975) studied risk taking in a role-playing situation in which individuals, who were more or less concerned with the need for power, acted as board members who would vote on matters of public importance. The results of this experiment indicated that power-oriented subjects tended to select the riskiest of alternatives available with regard to voting on the hypothetical public issue. McClelland and Teague suggest that people with strong power motives become so engrossed in influencing others in a competitive way that they actually distort the probabilities of accomplishing their goal and become willing to take extreme risks. This tendency was noted by LaFollette and Belohular (1982), who found that power-motivated individuals made large shifts in risk acceptance in a CDQ procedure. However, this risky tendency appears to hold true only for public situations that enable power-oriented people to set high levels of aspiration for the impact that they can have on others (Cameron & Meyers, 1966; McClelland & Watson, 1973). In this sense, the Machiavellian and the power-oriented person are similar in their goal-setting behavior: Both motives are activated by the perceived opportunity to influence others and achieve personal gain in the process of social encounter.

8 Interpersonal Attraction

In the early stages of a social event, the person not only records and reconstructs the information received, but responds emotionally as well to the stimuli of which that situation is composed. Although the person must apprehend a situation before responding to it emotionally, it is difficult to describe a precise point at which person perception ends and interpersonal attraction begins. Clearly, both processes help determine the person's readiness to respond and so both contribute directly to the more formally organized modes of social interaction. This chapter completes the discussion of the initial structuring of social behavior with an examination of what is known about the mechanisms through which personality factors affect our evaluative responses of others.

Although, as Huston (1974) concludes, there have been few efforts to conceptualize the nature of interpersonal attraction, the term does seem to refer to human responses as disparate as the initial feelings of liking toward an attractive stranger to the deep-seated commitments made between colleagues, family, and friends. The research procedures themselves indicate the range of events to which the term applies. Interpersonal attraction is studied by examining an observer's emotional response toward the attitudes of a stranger—as described on a questionnaire, by laboratory experiments in which the behavioral interaction between people allows them to respond to each other in some emotional way, by the measurement of the nature and degree of physical contact between people, and by the assessment of the bonds that exist between individuals who have chosen to spend a major portion of their lives together. Although this breadth of human relationships makes a common definition difficult, there seems to be a consensus that the term refers to a state composed of three major elements. In Huston's (1974) words, these include:

> (a) an evaluative component, which refers to the quality and strength of one's sentiments toward another person; (b) a cognitive component, which refers to the belief or beliefs that one has about another person, as well as the cognitive processes by which these beliefs are developed; and (c) a behavioral component, which refers to one's tendency to approach or avoid another person, as well as to the manner in which these behavioral tendencies are manifested. (p. 11).

Based on this broad definition of interpersonal attraction, we turn to the major question of this chapter: How does the array of personality variables that we have been considering interact with the array of situational, task, and group variables to affect the evaluative responses that we make to those we encounter in our daily lives?

Among the many scientists who have studied the nature of attraction from a reinforcement point of view, Donn Byrne's (1971) program of research stands out as a model of the systematic exploration of an unusually clear result. Put simply, Byrne (1969) proposed that similarity in attitudes between people leads to attraction between them because perceived (or actual) similarity is likely to be rewarding:

> [The] most general explanatory concept used to account for the effect of attitude similarity–dissimilarity on attraction is reward and punishment. When one individual receives positive reinforcement from another, positive affect is elicited and, through simple conditioning, becomes associated with the other individual. Subsequent evaluative responses directed toward that other individual will be positive. . . . [The] relative strength of rewards and punishments associated with a given individual determines the strength and direction of attraction toward him. (p. 70)

In attempting to explain the relationship between attitude similarity and attraction, Byrne (1971) argued that the perception of agreement between the attitudes of another person and our own validates the correctness of our own opinions. Because he assumed, following first Festinger (1954) and then White (1959), that people feel a need to test the correctness of their opinions, the perception that opinions are supported (and, therefore, correct) should be rewarding. Perhaps even more important, the perception of dissimilarity between the sets of opinions may be experienced as a form of punishing disagreement, raising the possibility that the person is incompetent, unintelligent, or unsafe.

To test the reinforcement theory of attraction empirically, Byrne and his associates developed a laboratory technique that became one of the most successful procedures in social psychology. In this experimental approach, students were first asked to state their opinions on a number of issues and then, at a later period, were give another copy of this test, which they were told had been completed by a different student in the class. Students were asked to read these completed tests in order to learn about each other. Actually, each student received a test form that had been completed by the experimenter so that it expressed opinions that were either all similar or all dissimilar to those held by that student. Experiments using this and related techniques have shown consistently that the proportion of similar attitudes expressed by the stranger is positively related to the degree of liking for the stranger.

Using a much broader reinforcement model, other theorists attempted to understand the attraction process from a variety of psychological bases (e.g., Cattell, 1950; Centers, 1975; Murstein, 1976; Winch, 1958). The most influential of these theorists was a group led by Winch (1958) who, with his colleagues, hypothesized that interpersonal attraction and mate selection are determined by a pattern of complementarity of needs between partners. Winch (1958) argued that "in mate selection each individual seeks within his or her field of eligibles for that person who gives the greatest promise of providing him or her with maximum need gratification . . . based on different and complementary rather than similar needs" (pp. 88–89, 96). We can take as one illustration of the many comparisons offered by Winch the example that attraction can develop when the assertive needs in one partner are balanced by the submissive needs in the other partner. These proposals generated an industry of research, fiercely competing over whether attraction is based on similarity or complementarity of personal attributes.

For the personologist, the major findings on the effects of personality variables on information processing permit these hypotheses to be expanded in a number of interesting ways. As we saw in chapters 6 and 7, research suggests that certain personality variables are associated with the ability to perceive another person's characteristics less accurately (e.g., Kelley & Stahelski, 1970). If some personality variables are associated with perceptual accuracy and others are associated with perceptual distortion, is it possible that "distorting" personality variables (e.g., authoritarianism) increase the degree of "perceived" similarity in the perceiver's cognitions? Thus, this fact would reduce the "actual" similarity-attraction relationship. Would this line of reasoning suggest that those personality variables associated with more accurate perception (e.g., self-esteem), curiously, sometimes be associated with stronger similarity-attraction relationships?

Second, Byrne implies that dissimilar strangers are disliked, not only because dissimilar attitudes are negatively reinforcing, but because these cues contain less information about the person. Recall that in the last chapter we saw strong support for the positive relationship between anxiety and easier information-processing demands. An important consequence of perceiving another person as being similar to oneself is that the perceiver can use this belief to generate what is apparently a great deal of information about the other person, simply by inspecting that area in him- or herself. When another person is "perceived" to be dissimilar, this source of apparent information is not available. In fact, it is possible to generalize from this small area of disagreement to a much wider area of unpleasantness. Thus, dissimilar strangers should be perceived as threatening to the anxious person in a Byrne-type laboratory study, whereas those variables that we have seen to be associated with the greater ability to tolerate ambiguity should be related to less dislike of a dissimilar stranger.

Many of these reasonable, but contradictory, hypotheses can be resolved by a longer view of the acquaintanceship process. It has been frequently observed that individuals progress through a course of different stages of liking and intimate relations (e.g., Altman & Taylor, 1973; Centers, 1975; Kerckhoff & Davis, 1962; Levinger, 1974; Murstein, 1976; Secord & Backman, 1964). For example, Murstein proposed a mature form of the stage approach, which he called the Stimulus-Value-Role theory of marital choice. Murstein suggested that the initial experiences that people have with each other (the Stimulus stage) come in the form of brief observations of the most accessible external cues that each person can provide. Based on the individual's response to these preliminary sets of information or the way they balance their perception of these assets and liabilities, the person selects those individuals whom they wish to explore further, primarily through conversation designed to elicit information on the other person's most general value orientations (the Value stage). Finally, with the determination that they share compatible value systems, Murstein proposed that the couple attempts to discover if they can function well together in the different roles that they believe they will assume (the Role stage).

These stage models help us organize much of the research that has been done in the area of interpersonal attraction. A stage model, such as Murstein's, suggests that we explore how dispositional and environmental variables may interact to determine at least three distinct stages in the attraction process: (a) attraction in the initial period of acquaintance; (b) attraction based upon the search for compatible modes of interpersonal exchange; and (c) attraction in enduring interpersonal relations. This approach is similar to that of Altman and Taylor (1973), who suggest that social penetration is a process of discovering compatible modes of interpersonal bonding and developing role structures that permit harmonious relations to occur. These approaches need greater specification about both the types of behaviors that individuals emit and the structures that underlie permanent relationships. The theoretical discussion of group process presented in part I should help to provide such clarifications.

STAGES OF INTERPERSONAL ATTRACTION

Initial Attraction

Each of the stage theories argues that the first experiences that people have with each other are dissimilar from those that follow. For this reason, the determinants of the first set of evaluative responses are thought to be quite different from the ones that affect attraction at later points in the acquaintance process. In the natural stream of social behavior, we can expect to observe initial attraction at such events as a party when people mill about a room, exchange glances, return greetings, and engage others in conversations for the first time. The experimental situation that captures this phase of the attraction process best is, undoubtedly, the one used in the extensive research program of Byrne and his associates.

In the first phase of the attraction process, the salient features of the interpersonal experience are the highly evocative cues presented by the other person. Typically, these visible social cues include the other person's clothing, possessions, posture, voice, style of gesture, eye gaze, smile, and physical attractiveness. In the laboratory, as Byrne has shown, the interpersonal meaning of these external cues can be captured by a summary report of the opinions of the person. Much of the empirical work in the field of attraction (e.g., Byrne, 1969; Walster, Aronson, Abrahams, & Rottman, 1966) has concentrated on exploring the effects of this set of antecedents.

For the personologist, the consistency with which the "similarity" effect can be demonstrated across such a variety of dispositions is surprising because differences among dispositions typically lead to different social consequences. For example, based on the definition of these motives, it is plausible to expect that an affiliation-motivated person would respond positively to the description of another affiliation-motivated person. However, it is far from obvious why a dominance-motivated person would respond positively to the description of another dominance-motivated person, as has been demonstrated by Palmer and Byrne (1970). From the earliest work on the role of dominance motivation in the area of person perception (e.g., Jones & Daugherty, 1959), it has been assumed that this combination of perceiver and observed's attributes should be negatively arousing. Indeed, in chapter 6, we reviewed a substantial set of results showing that this expectation is, in fact, accurate (Assor, Aronoff, & Messé, 1981).

An intriguing solution to this problem is available by comparing the correspondences between the research done under the heading of person perception with that done under the heading of interpersonal attraction (cf. Posavac & Pasko, 1971). Recall that from the very first studies by Postman, Bruner, and McGinnies (1948) a research approach was developed whose results are remarkably congruent with that developed by Byrne. In each of those studies, across a variety of motivational states as different as hunger, affiliation, and achievement, experimentalists confirmed the prediction that individuals are most sensitive to those features of the world that are similar to their predominant concerns. In these studies, it seemed satisfactory to postulate that individuals brought to a social situation a readiness to respond that would lead them to possess a lower recognition threshold for stimuli related to their dispositions and a tendency to restructure ambiguous stimuli into disposition-related forms. Given the strength of this tendency, it is highly plausible that this attribute of a disposition would also lead to a positive emotional response.

However, as in the case of dominance, there are clearly specifiable circumstances in which the combination of perceiver–observer similarity leads to states of highly negative emotional arousal. Recall that in chapter 6 we presented evidence to show that this can occur in highly involving situations. As a general rule, there is little reason to expect a disposition to affect social behavior unless it is aroused by that particular situation. In the case of the early scanning of a social situation, under nonthreatening conditions, it is likely that a disposition leads the person to respond positively when recognizing social stimuli whose meaning is similar to itself. This is the task that is usually used in research on interpersonal attraction (i.e., by Byrne's group), and it is one which, by limiting information to sharply contrasting choices, removes the ambiguity and so reduces the level of threat inherent in all experiments. This task is also an extremely appropriate representation of the early stages of a conversation in which we respond positively when we hear similar opinions or values expressed by our partner. There is every reason to assume that the major consequence of this positive emotional response is that we continue to pursue the conversation with the other person. However, under more arousing conditions, which engage the specific features of the disposition, we can expect a more varied set of results. The consequences of this interaction, in which the attributes of the other person may be perceived as appealing, arousing, or aversive, depending on other features of the situation, should determine whether or not the social contact will be continued.

It should be clear, however, that the focus of this discussion on the similarity principle does not exhaust the early stages of an encounter. Our description of a situation (in chap. 4) includes a wide array of possible stimuli with which the person becomes engaged. The similarity principle, it must be recognized, deals with only one characteristic (the distribution of attitudinal or personality characteristics) of the people who are part of that social environment. There are, of course, many other features of that environment that significantly affect the outcome of any set of human activity. Studies such as those of Griffitt (1970), Griffitt and Veitch (1971), or Hines and Mehrabian (1979) show how environmental stressors affect the degree of attraction to a social situation. Because systematic research on these aspects of the initial phases of a social encounter has yet to be done, our discussion must be limited to those findings from programs that have been substantially completed.

In summary, these considerations suggest that under nonarousing conditions, a reinforcement model predicts that a fairly direct similarity principle governs the initial evaluation of the other person. Under these conditions, the initial stage can be viewed primarily as an information-processing event in which attraction is most affected by the cognitive processes associated with dispositional variables, rather than the disposition itself. In contrast, under dispostion-arousing circumstances as described in part I, a much more disparate set of factors is likely to control the course of the emotional response, following the direction of the most reinforcing solution possible in that situation. The outcome of this stage of attraction determines whether or not the person will engage in approach behavior that will lead to further involvement in the acquaintanceship process.

The Acquaintanceship Process: The Search for Compatible Modes of Interpersonal Behavior

Stage theories, such as Murstein's, maintain that as individuals move beyond their initial feelings of attraction, they undertake an extended behavioral exchange with another person in which they inquire about values and practice role-related behaviors. Through these behaviors, people express all the characteristic modes of social behavior that are described in part I. These major elements of social interaction seem to appear in most kinds of social events, whether they are a purely social encounter between potential friends, an occupational undertaking between co-workers, or a competitive engagement between experimental subjects in the laboratory.

In the second stage interpersonal attraction occurs within the context of a genuine interaction. How, then, do individuals discover compatible modes of interpersonal response with the other person? If the dispositional attributes lead people to respond to a social situation with concrete interpersonal behaviors, then these events should affect the other people involved in ways that are more or less congenial to the other people's behavioral preferences. The general hypothesis in stage theories is that when interpersonal contact involves people in modes of social activities that are compatible with their preferred style of interaction, the resulting degree of attraction to the other people will be strong. In contrast, when the acquaintanceship process leads to response incompatibility, then dislike for the other person should develop. If successful, the outcome of the acquaintanceship process is the discovery of overall congruence between the individual modes of social interaction between people, so that a high degree of need satisfaction is provided. This should not imply that a perfect match must exist for each separate dimension of interpersonal behavior. Rather, as Centers (1975) maintains, it is likely that the overall degree of response compatibility results in mutual need satisfaction, feelings of equity, and the potential for long-term commitment to another person. When this is achieved, it forms the basis for the enduring relationship between individuals. On the other hand, failure to achieve congruence should lead to the eventual termination of the relationship. Therefore, the second stage of the acquaintanceship process is defined by the act of engaging with another person long enough to evaluate whether response compatibility is possible.

What makes this process so complex to describe is that it encompasses many different levels of psychological and social interaction, all occurring simultaneously between the individuals. As there are too many predictions to outline at this point, our hypotheses are based on the detailed discussion of group process presented in chapter 5 (e.g., Table 5.4). We can illustrate how these interpersonal dynamics operate by examining a hypothetical relationship between two persons, one of whom is authoritarian and the other nurturant in character. We have chosen two personality variables that are not usually studied together in laboratory experiments in order to illustrate that it is possible to deduce from the theoretical framework presented in part I how these inputs to the attraction process can be operationalized easily in testable form. In order to visualize the course that their relationship might take, let us briefly recapitulate our expectations of how their characteristics influence the major dimensions of social behavior that we have just outlined.

The authoritarian person is a cold, often disaffiliative, and task-oriented individual who is rigid in solving problems and easily swayed by persons of higher status and power. Authoritarians often try to "take control arbitrarily or unrealistically, try to control what should be considered right or wrong in the group, try to restrict others, make demands, give commands, show disapproval or moral indignation, or assume a pose of moral superiority" (Bales, 1979, p. 360). Further, they like hierarchical role structures with clear separation of role function and prefer to use their position in the group to intimidate others. Interpersonally, they are often exploitative in this mode of social behavior because of their mistrust of others and their need to control events around them. In contrast, the nurturant person is a warm, mature, flexible, and task-centered individual who "takes the initiative in protecting or nurturing others, gives unconditional praise or reward, boosts the status of the other, gives approval and encouragement, gives warm acceptance — without regard to the excellence or failure of performance of the other, or gives support, comfort or consideration" (Bales, 1979, p. 365). Additionally, they are not easily persuaded but, rather, are open to influence from others of proven competence and sensitivity. They function best in egalitarian groups in which there are integrated role relationships.

With these kinds of social behaviors associated with an authoritarian and a nurturant person, what course should we expect their acquaintanceship process to take? Initially, we would expect that the authoritarian would search for status and power cues, perceive the accepting posture of the nurturant person, and feel somewhat threatened by the open, integrative style of conversation that he or she reveals. If so, the authoritarian might then begin to change the perception of the other, either by increasing the degree of "perceived" similarity or by denigrating the other person's character. However, as the acquaintance process is one of extended contact, this perception might change as the authoritarian progresses through the initial stage and becomes involved in interaction likely to lead to conflict. This might happen because the integrative mode of behavior of the nurturant person is sharply opposed to the exploitative style of the authoritarian. Thus, in this example, the self-assurance of the nurturant person is not compatible with the preferred style of the authoritarian and so is likely to cause the authoritarian person to seek a structured set of role relations even more forcefully in order to make their interpersonal transactions more predictable. However, by doing so, the authoritarian individual creates an incongruent situation for the nurturant individual. At this point, the response styles of both individuals are fundamentally incompatible with each other. Paradoxically, the qualities of generativity in nurturant people will enable them to receive more gratification than will authoritarian individuals from this relationship, because they can enjoy to some degree the process of caring for authoritarians.

Unfortunately, in the field of attraction research, there is little work that has been done on the response of individuals to this stage of behavioral interaction. On the other hand, in the course of the extensive work on the interpersonal process, small group experimentalists have amassed a good deal of evidence on the preferred behavioral styles associated with the different individual dispositions. This presents a problem as to the most appropriate place to review that work. It is awkward to discuss the results of the studies that bear on attraction without discussing the issues reserved for part III. But, it is equally awkward to break up a theoretical discussion of attraction by distributing parts of it to different parts of other chapters. The solution that seems least inconvenient is to continue the theoretical discussion in this chapter and reserve a discussion of the empirical literature on interpersonal activity for its proper place in the book.

Enduring Attraction: Commitment and Stability in Interpersonal Relations

The emergence of behavioral congruence between people leads to a set of structured role relationships that support their interaction over significant periods of time. Our conception of this stage is consistent with the position taken by Kerckhoff and Davis (1962), Secord and Backman (1964), Murstein (1976), and Duck (1973), who suggest that value consensus, role compatibility, self-acceptance, and perceived similarity are important variables in determining whether the relationship will be maintained. With a relatively strong degree of response compatibility, there should also be the appraisal and clarification of role compatibility so that participants have a better understanding of their own dynamics as well as that of the other person. The more clearly sociological focus of chapters 4 and 5 helps to define terms such as "role compatibility" with the more specific social features of hierarchy, status, power, and reward. This broader organizational point of view also enables us to encompass occupational as well as social relationships. Although most of the work on long-term attraction has been undertaken in terms of the marital relationship, it is just as important to consider the nature of the affective bonds between individuals in the workplace as well as other kinds of groups. Thus, the central feature of the third stage suggests that as relations develop over time between members of most kinds of groups, supportive social structure emerges to maintain the nature of that relationship.

The detailed theoretical discussion of the relationship between dispositions and supportive social structures, provided in chapter 5, applies to the acquaintanceship process among friends as much as among co-workers. Although the many publications on enduring attraction, for the most part, examine patterns of dispositional similarity or complementarity between partners in the marriage relationship (Huston, 1974), they do not examine the nature of the social structure that supports that relationship. However, evidence of this sort is provided by the discussion of group process and group structure in chapters 11, 12, and 13 of this book. In those discussions, a substantial empirical fund is available with which to explore the permanent role relationships that are most congruent for the dispositions that we are following.

PERSONALITY MODERATORS OF ATTRACTION

This section outlines a set of hypotheses about the way in which personality variables moderate the attraction process, based on the theoretical discussion in chapter 5. This discussion and the review of the research on interpersonal attraction concentrate on the types of events that may take place in the first stages of a social encounter.

The Safety-Needs Cluster

The personality variables that fall within the safety-needs cluster all share the common factor of anxiety. It is important to recognize how strongly this anxiety component affects the attraction process and the degree to which it creates the tendency to structure predictable relationships with other people.

Recall our earlier argument that the safety-oriented person actively searches for cues that signal it is safe to approach other people. When interacting with others, especially during the initial stages of the attraction process, the safety-oriented person attends to a wide range of behaviors in the other person that, on the basis of past experience, provide reliable external cues as to the probable sequence of events that will follow if they risk making contact. In particular, we expect that safety-oriented people will quickly note external attributes in the other person such as status, sex-role expectations, age, or nonverbal behaviors that offer cues suggesting approval, friendliness, trust, familiarity, or comfort. When the experimental procedure utilizes an easily understood presentation of similar opinions as the technique to represent another person (i.e., the technique developed by Byrne), we expect to find that most safety-oriented people respond positively.

Similarly, because ambiguity is a strong threat to safety-oriented individuals (as we saw in chapter 7), the lack of emotional expressiveness and facial cues indicative of the attitudes and emotional state of the other, the lack of clarity in the other person's gestures, a simple disagreement in expressed opinions, or even the lack of agreement by the other with one's own opinions will likely be perceived as threatening and generate an avoidance response. Therefore, we expect that the perception of similarity between the individual and the person that he or she observes will increase the initial feelings of attraction. Moreover, if the other person is perceived as someone who can initiate activities and control interactions in ways that enhance feelings of comfort, security, and predictability (i.e., create for the observer the anticipation of the familiar and preferred patterns of modes of interaction), there will result a strengthening of the motivation to approach the person. In summary, the personality variables in the safety-needs cluster should be associated with positive liking for another person when there is perceived: (a) attitude and personality similarity; (b) verbal and nonverbal cues which are anxiety reducing; and (c) initial acts suggesting that the future behavioral interchange is likely to be rewarding. If the initial attraction results in an ongoing acquaintanceship process, then the second stage of attraction should follow the predictions described in Table 5.4 in a search to discover whether or not congruency can be created in the different modes of social behavior.

The Affiliative-Needs Cluster

The affiliatively oriented person seeks to experience warm, friendly, and congenial relations with other people. These motivational characteristics imply that they should be strongly attracted to others who manifest behavior that falls primarily on the affiliation axis of social behavior. In particular, we expect that they would be unusually sensitive to nonverbal acts in another person, such as smiling, eye contact, attentiveness to gesture indicative of emotional states, as well as overt facial cues signaling acceptance, friendli-

ness, and affection. Additionally, we expect that they would be quite perceptive of behaviors indicating the future appearance of tolerance and
cooperation, integrative modes of interdependence, and egalitarian role
relationships.

Although we can predict a general similarity-liking effect for the affiliation
motive, particularly in the early stages of the attraction process, it is also possible to predict that affiliation-oriented persons would be least attracted to
authoritarian, cold, overly task-oriented, hostile, nondisclosing, and exploitative individuals. We believe that, for affiliation-oriented persons, the presence of cues that signify future incompatible modes of interdependence
would generate strong avoidance tendencies. Thus, we predict dislike for the
incongruent dissimilar stranger, rather than simply the dissimilar stranger, as
we do for the safety cluster. In addition, it is also possible for the affiliation-
oriented individual to distort the degree of actual positivity present in another person displaying many superficial indications of sociability. In response to the apparent affability of the other person, the affiliation-oriented
person might initiate the attraction process only to discover, later and with
disappointment, response incompatibility during the second stage of the acquaintanceship process.

Esteem-Needs Cluster

The esteem needs contain a common factor that seeks to enhance feelings of
self-worth through a variety of task and social motives. Esteem-oriented
people are not characterized by strong anxiety or the pressing need to affiliate
with others, so they can find many kinds of people interesting, attractive, and
enjoyable. For the attraction process, this sense of competence seems to enable these people to perceive and utilize a broad range of behavioral cues
more accurately in becoming attracted to another person. Stated simply, we
expect that esteem-oriented persons are often good judges who can effectively identify the stimulus properties in others that are associated with a variety of rewarding modes of social behavior. Additionally, it seemed clear
from the evidence reviewed in chapter 7 that esteem-oriented persons are less
bothered by ambiguity and uncertainty in social situations. When this evidence is applied to the phenomena of person perception and interpersonal attraction, it is quite reasonable to hypothesize that the basic sense of security
of esteem-oriented people would lead them to be attracted to a variety of
other complex and vigorous people who might differ greatly in values, attitudes, and behavior. These characteristics in others should promise a
stimulating and rewarding relationship, especially if the acquaintanceship
process would uncover congruent styles of social interaction. However, all
things being equal, we expect that esteem-oriented persons will be attracted
to others who display verbal and nonverbal cues that indicate confidence and
competence in task and social activity. Although these are obviously desira-

ble attributes valued by most people, the character traits of personal competence are especially valued by esteem-oriented persons because they seek to display the skills resulting from these characteristics in order to gratify their own sense of worth.

Although esteem-oriented persons should respond well to behavioral cues indicating that the other person is relatively strong, it should also be recognized that some of these motives lead people to certain forms of perceptual distortion. As described in chapter 6, Assor et al. (1981) found that dominant individuals evaluated a person of high status less favorably than they did one of low status. In later research, Assor, Aronoff, and Messé (1984) found that the dominant perceiver actually experienced more negative emotional arousal in the presence of another dominant individual. These results would seem to suggest that when a threat is perceived to exist, dominant perceivers are less likely to be attracted initially to the individual posing the threat, presumably because they would assume that the acquaintanceship process would be one of conflict and incompatibility. Thus, although esteem-oriented persons generally are superior judges of character, because they are less anxious, possess a broader repertoire of coping mechanisms, and have a stronger sense of personal efficacy than safety- or affiliation-oriented persons, some of them may also be subject to environmental conditions that might result in avoidance responses or feelings of dislike. Moreover, chapter 5 describes other situations in which the perception of certain environmental demands should lead to competitiveness, achievement behaviors, interpersonal manipulation, strivings for recognition, or mature problem solving and conflict resolution.

THE EMPIRICAL STUDIES

In this section, we review the pertinent research that has attempted to study how personality variables moderate the attraction process; we utilize only those studies that provide information on the first stage of the social process. More specifically, we concentrate on the results provided by research that primarily uses Byrne's approach to the study of attraction. Not only does this choice simplify the nature of the material that must be evaluated, but more important, the procedure closely approximates the very early stages of the attraction process in which a limited range of cues in the other person generates the attraction response.

Insecurity, Social Avoidance, and Anxiety

It is a common observation that insecure individuals are prone to difficulties in their intimate relationships with others. In the earliest stages of a social encounter, we would expect such people to take a guarded and self-protective stance toward the people they are about to meet and show great selectivity in their choice of social contacts. An extremely useful device to limit the degree to which social experiences might be dangerous is to approach only those people whose attributes indicate an apparent high degree of attitude and personality similarity. By using this basis of interpersonal choice, insecure people attempt to reduce the ambiguity and uncertainty in the situation and establish a relationship characterized by a high level of predictability.

There are a series of studies that, taken as a whole, support the major premises of this hypothesis. Although they raise many other questions, the scope of these studies does indicate the directions that are needed in order to complete our understanding of the relationship of anxiety and attraction. In a study using the classic Byrne paradigm, Smith (1972) created two experimental groups of undergraduate women, consisting of those who scored in the upper third and those who scored in the lower third of the distribution on a self-report social anxiety scale. Three weeks after they had completed a 24-item attitude questionnaire, they returned to the laboratory where they were asked to participate in an impression-formation experiment. In a low-similarity condition, these undergraduates received a completed questionnaire in which the answers disagreed with their own on 22 of the 24 items. In the high-similarity condition, the answers to the questionnaire agreed with their own on 22 of the 24 items. Following the procedure developed by Byrne, the task set by the experiment was to read the answers, supposedly produced by another student, and indicate the amount of attraction felt to that other person. For us, the major result of this experiment is that the anxious women disliked the person whose opinions disagreed with their own much more than did the nonanxious women. This experiment used a neutral task condition, and both anxious and nonanxious women equally liked the other person whose opinions were similar to their own. However, in a somewhat less extreme contrast of similarity and dissimilarity, Reagor and Clore (1970) found a more complex result in that the more anxious people were less extreme than the less anxious people: The more anxious people were not as negative to the dissimilar stranger but also not as positive to the similar stranger.

A result similar to Smith's was obtained by Touhey (1976), who modified the basic procedure in an extremely interesting way. Each of the undergraduates and an experimental confederate, tested as a dyad, were asked to complete and then exchange a 12-item attitude questionnaire. Touhey arranged to have the confederate's answers either totally agree or totally disagree with those produced by each participant. In this face-to-face situation, anxiety did not have much of an effect on the amount of attraction felt toward a disagreeing other person; however, anxious people were much more attracted toward another person who agreed with them than were nonanxious people. Similar results, demonstrating that those preferring dissimilar others were more secure than those preferring similar others, as tested in a fairly realistic circumstance, were also shown by Goldstein and Rosenfeld (1969), although only for women.

There are a few studies that help to make some of the mechanisms through which these effects are produced clearer. In the last chapter, we discussed a study by Johnson and Gormly (1975) which directly tested the hypothesis that, because anxiety should lead people to be vigilant to social threats, the more people were anxious, the more they should be sensitive to information which disagreed with their attitudes and the more they should dislike the disagreeing person. In an extremely important variation on the Byrne experiment, they arranged for undergraduate women to hear a statement of attitudes from another person (actually an accomplice of the experimenter) that agreed with half of her opinions and disagreed with the other half. After the accomplice left the room, each student was asked to estimate the number of topics on which they agreed and disagreed, to identify each of them, and to signify the degree of attraction that she felt for the experimental accomplice. As predicted, the results of this experiment showed that the more anxious women, in comparison to the less anxious women, had paid most attention to the areas of disagreement they had experienced in their interaction and felt less attracted to their partially disagreeing partner.

Two other studies provide some additional evidence on the motivational components associated with anxiety. These studies are also interesting because they indicate how useful it would be to examine the impact on attraction of a wider range of variables. In an interesting experiment using a different method, Smith and Campbell (1973) provide some evidence that anxious people are looking for reassurance and protection from those with whom they come into contact. Among the results of this experiment, Smith and Campbell report that nonanxious people want other people to match their own level of liking, whereas anxious people want the amount of liking they receive to exceed the amount of liking that they have for other people. In reviewing the implications of these results, Smith and Campbell believe the desire on the part of anxious people to receive an "over-match" of liking indicates that they wish to avoid possible disapproval from others. It also shows that anxious people are seeking highly specific interpersonal capacities in those with whom they interact. In what is possibly a much more specific form of this result, Mehrabian and Ksionsky (1972) carried out an experiment that supports one of the basic relationships described throughout this book. For all of the reasons already discussed, safety-oriented people find the external social characteristic of higher status to be reinforcing. The study by Mehrabian and Ksionsky is one of the few attempts to examine this hypothesis in the area of attraction. Using a measure of insecurity that they call "sensitivity to rejection," they showed that people with high scores on this test are much more attracted to higher status associates than those with low scores.

We return to what is possibly a more general use of this study later in this chapter.

The results of these studies help to explain how anxiety can influence the attraction process. Given the chronicity of their anxiety, insecure people seek out cues in those they observe who signal a predictable outcome in the interaction and a high probability of response compatibility. The perception of strong attitude similarity in the person who is observed leads to attraction because these cues indicate to observers that the interaction is not going to be unpredictable in ways that would raise their level of anxiety. Thus, the attribution of similarity may also signal the potential for a rewarding encounter, with a reduction of anxiety and a relief from the fear of rejection. Given that this cognitive and emotional sequence occurs, it is also likely to include a behavioral approach toward the person. In the absence of such anxiety-reducing signals, we would expect that anxiety would lead to a greater distancing effect.

Authoritarianism and Dogmatism

Because authoritarian personalities are rigid, moralistic, and overly concerned with status relationships, they should be strongly attracted to others perceived as holding similar values, at least initially. As Byrne (1965) reasoned:

> disagreement on the part of others about various topics should create an ambiguous and threatening situation that the authoritarian would be expected to resolve by rejecting the holder of dissident opinions. On the other hand, individuals low in authoritarianism should be much more flexible in the attitudes they hold, more tolerant of and less threatened by the possibility of being incorrect, and less likely to reject another individual because he expresses dissimilar opinions. (p. 252)

Based on the evidence presented in chapter 7, it is also possible that under conditions of perceived threat evoked by a dissimilar target, the authoritarian will distort the perception of the individual in order to accentuate the areas of perceived differences in values and personality. On the other hand, in the absence of a threatening other or through the denial of individual differences, it is possible that authoritarians would enhance their evaluation of the other person by perceiving more attitude similarity that actually exists.

Five studies have examined the effects of authoritarianism or dogmatism on interpersonal attraction. Byrne (1965), Gormly and Clore (1969), Sheffield and Byrne (1967), as well as two studies by Baskett reported in Byrne (1971) have each sought to demonstrate a similarity effect for the trait of authoritarianism. It is puzzling that none of these studies were able to find support for these hypotheses. Because these results are so inconsistent with those described in chapters 7 and 10 (e.g., the results in areas such as the intolerance of ambiguity, as well as the severity of sentences given in mock jury experiments), it is difficult to accept that there is no similarity effect for authoritarianism. It remains possible that the lack of experimental results is due to the influence of another aspect of the trait of authoritarianism. Following Kelley and Stahelski (1970), it is possible that this trait so distorts social cognitions that perceived and actual attitudes may be discrepant in the Byrne situation, and therefore, the measured attitude-attraction relationship might be weak. It may be that this effect can be found only in those circumstances that force the authoritarian to attend to the attitudinal discrepancy (e.g., Mitchell & Byrne, 1973).

The Need for Approval

The individual with a strong need for approval seeks to defend against a basic sense of anxiety by creating an admiring relationship with a protective superior. Therefore, it is expectable that they would want to be liked by others and would be especially sensitive to social cues that signal liking and acceptance. Yet, as we see in later chapters, their underlying anxiety leads to self-protective security operations in which they attempt to ingratiate themselves with others by being cooperative but not self-disclosing about their true feelings, attitudes, and opinions. With this form of interpersonal relationship as their goal, we expect that the need for approval would lead individuals to desire a highly positive interpersonal climate in which people like each other and avoid areas of disagreement.

Overall, the research on the relation between the need for approval and interpersonal attraction conforms to the pattern that we would expect to find associated with this motive. Several studies have demonstrated that these people appear to possess a strong tendency to make positive evaluations of others. For example, Ettinger, Nowicki, and Nelson (1970), in a standard Byrne-type experiment, found that approval-motivated people expressed more overall attraction to a stranger, without regard to the degree of similarity that was arranged to appear between the subject and the stranger's attitudes. In a face-to-face experimental situation, Touhey (1976) found that subjects who were most attracted to a stranger with similar attitudes were much more approval-motivated than were subjects who were least attracted to that similar stranger. In this study, there were no personality effects for the dissimilar stranger. Posavac (1971), using a wider range of similarity-dissimilarity relationships, found a moderately positive relationship between the participants' need for approval and their attraction to a similar stranger. A study by Holstein, Goldstein, and Bem (1971) provides some evidence for the relationship between the need for approval and positivity of attraction, and a study by Goldstein and Rosenfeld (1969) provides additional evidence of its moderating effects on the similarity-attraction relationship. In both cases, however, the effect was found for males but not for females. Finally, the study by Johnson and Gormly, described in the previous section on anxiety, also provides valuable evidence for the mechanism that seems to underlie the effect of the need for approval on attraction. In this study, not only was there a reasonably strong association between the need for approval and attraction for the person who agreed with half of the subject's opinions (and disagreed with the other half), but more important, there was a positive association between the need for approval and the recall of agreeing opinions and a negative association between the need for approval and the recall of disagreeing opinions (for a related finding, see Zaidel & Mehrabian, 1969).

There are also several studies which show that strongly approval-motivated people orient toward those who are expressive and potential protectors. For example, Holstein et al. (1971) found that approval-motivated women were more sensitive to facial cues than were women unconcerned with this motive. Similarly, Brundage, Derlega, and Cash (1977), in a study on the amount of self-disclosure presented to an attractive stranger, found that approval-motivated subjects disclosed less about themselves than did nonapproval-motivated individuals. These studies support the hypothesis that approval-motivated persons are both ingratiating and unusually sensitive to social cues that might enhance initial approach responses. The implications of these studies in terms of the stages of attraction would appear to be twofold. First, during the initial stage of interaction, all the studies that we have reviewed indicate that the approval-motivated person actively scans the target person for cues that might signal it is safe to approach (e.g., smiling, friendly tone of voice, etc.). Second, the anxiety and defensiveness of these people seem correlated with the tendency to control the amount of self-disclosure or emotional expressiveness they manifest to a target person. This action seems to be a self-protective maneuver designed to buy time in order to scan further for cues which would indicate that it is safe to begin the acquaintanceship process without an intensification of anxiety and the fear of rejection.

In contrast to the deferential and cautious stance of the approval-motivated person, there are several studies indicating that the nonapproval-motivated person may use different criteria when evaluating the relative attractiveness of a stranger. Dion and Dion (1975) report findings suggesting that nonapproval-motivated high self-esteem people are less cautious (than individuals with a strong concern for the need for approval and low levels of self-esteem) to involve themselves in emotional relationships during the acquaintanceship stage, which might not lead to response compatibility in modes of behavioral interchange. The need for approval may lead people only to be able to demonstrate liking for another when there is a clear, unambiguous, and predictable outcome in the relationship. Thus, if approach behaviors result from the initial stage of attraction, the approval-motivated person may need a relatively constant amount of positive feedback and reward in order to remain involved during the acquaintanceship stage. Support for this idea was obtained by Hewitt and Goldman (1974), who found that those people with strong approval needs and low esteem showed increased liking when they received positive evaluations from a confederate (compared to when they received negative evaluations), whereas individuals with the opposite characteristics did not show a significant change in their liking of either a positive or a negative evaluator of the self.

In summary of the work on the initial stages of attraction and in anticipation of the more complex events of group process, these results suggest that approval-motivated persons exhibit a cooperative, friendly, and positive facade when initially interacting with strangers. They seek to be liked but are both guarded and ingratiating while searching for cues in the target that might indicate it is safe to approach others without undue fear of rejection. To accomplish this, they may generate a series of positive evaluations, comments, and opinions very early in the social encounter in order to elicit either verbal or nonverbal cues from the target, which would provide preliminary information as to the personality characteristics of the other and whether or not a potential exists for response compatibility.

The Need for Affiliation

Most personality variables predispose an individual to be attracted to particular types of people, but the need for affiliation is a variable that should be associated with strong and general approach tendencies toward others. We would expect that people characterized by this motive would find other people likable, approachable, and exhibit a greater degree of tolerance for irksome character traits. For these reasons, we would expect to find that, as with the need for approval, the literature would report a generalized positivity effect that would manifest itself in the initial stages of acquaintance in a reduced motive-similarity relationship. This predicted positivity effect assumes that the real or hypothetical situation is neutral, at worst, because we can expect that individuals concerned with affiliative needs are also sensitive to the possibility of rejection. In that case, we would expect the affiliative person to "dislike" a potential rejector quite quickly.

As we see in every area of the social process, there is little information available on the social consequences of the need for affiliation. In fact, there are only three studies in which individuals whose affiliative needs were measured were asked to respond emotionally to the kinds of information that are available in the early stage of aquaintanceship. Although the results of these experiments are not congruent with our expectations in all respects, their overall thrust provides some evidence that a similarity effect can also be established for this motive. Byrne (1961), early in the course of developing his program of work on attraction, ran an experiment in which the need for affiliation, as measured by the TAT, was used as the basis for selecting subjects and opinions. The results of this experiment showed that there was no effect of the need for affiliation in responding to a person with similar attitudes. However, in responding to the dissimilar stranger, participants with higher needs for affiliation disliked that person more than did those unconcerned with affiliative needs. As Byrne speculated, this result might indicate that an affiliative person feels that strong disagreement about attitudes might imply an emotional as well as an intellectual confrontation. In a second study, Byrne (1962) examined a wider range of attitudinal similarity and categorized his subjects' affiliation scores into three groups. Not only did Byrne find a large similarity-attraction effect for all three motive groups, but the greatest effect came in the medium affiliation group (for reasons that are still quite unclear). Finally, Seyfried and Hendrick (1973), using a self-report measure of affiliation, report a more substantial set of results more completely supporting the similarity hypothesis.

Dominance

Perhaps because of the association of dominance with the study of leadership, little is known about the way this motive contributes to the process of attraction. Nevertheless, there is one study that has obtained results consistent with the definition of this motive. Palmer and Byrne (1970), modifying Byrne's procedure in an important respect, sought to use the contrast of dominance and submissiveness as a direct test of the hypothesized similarity versus complementarity explanations of attraction. In this experiment, the hypothetical strangers were not defined by their attitudes on current topics, but rather behaviorally, on the basis of Leary's Interpersonal Checklist (Leary, 1957). Considering the nature of the task presented by this procedure, a task in which subjects rate adjectives that represent interpersonal behaviors rather than opinions, it is interesting that both the dominant and the submissive people claimed to be more attracted to the representation of highly dominant people than to the representation of submissive people.

We can assume that Palmer and Byrne's experimental situation presented a fairly neutral state of arousal in which dominant people were asked to respond to their idealized sense of self. In a natural setting, we can assume that this experimental procedure represents the observation of a set of active and authoritative behaviors in a nonthreatening other person. However, when these results are contrasted with those of Assor et al. (1981) and Battistich and Aronoff (in press), described in chapter 6, we can see just how drastically dominance can affect the individual's emotional response to the perception of other people. Recall that when the subject's motives were threatened by the experimental procedure (the observation of an authoritative other person), defensive processes were instituted that resulted in strongly negative emotional responses. Taken together, these studies allow us to conclude that when a dominance-motivated person observes an authoritative person under neutral conditions, there will be a strongly positive evaluative response, whereas under involving conditions, there will be a strongly negative emotional response.

Locus of Control

Four studies provide additional evidence for the similarity effect for the locus of control in this fairly relaxed social setting. The results of studies by Johnson and Cerreto (1975), Korte, Kimble, and Cole (1978), Phares and Wilson (1971), and Nowicki and Blumberg (1975), in spite of some discrepancies, show that internally oriented people tend to respond more positively to the description of the "internal" stranger, whereas externally oriented people tend to prefer the description of the "external" stranger. Beyond this general tendency, however, not much more is known about how the characteristics of this trait interact with other attributes of the environment.

Self-Esteem

Several studies have examined the effect on interpersonal attraction of a group of variables that can be described broadly as self-esteem. In general, for all the reasons discussed in the last chapter (e.g., greater tolerance of ambiguity, etc.), we would expect that persons with high self-esteem would be much more accepting of dissimilarity in the opinions of others (as long as the opinions were interesting) than would persons with low self-esteem. For this reason, we would expect that high-esteem individuals (at least in comparison to low-esteem people) would either be more attracted to dissimilar people or not distinguish between similar and dissimilar people. In contrast, we would expect that persons with low self-esteem would be threatened by disagreement and so find more pleasant those people whose opinions are similar to their own. On the other hand, the more usual hypothesis concerning the relationship between self-esteem and similarity on attraction, as it would be phrased by Byrne's group, is represented by Griffitt (1966) who suggested that there would be a strong similarity effect for self-esteem. Unfortunately, the results of the few studies available at present are quite contradictory to these theoretical expectations.

First, we need to note that Griffitt (1966, 1969) did not report any relationship at all. Second, in contrast to our expectations, there are several studies which seem to indicate that high self-esteem people are more discriminating, extreme, and rejecting of dissimilarity in their response to the personal attributes of other people. For example, Hendrick and Page (1970) used the Byrne technique and found that high self-esteem people were much more negative in their reaction to a dissimilar stranger. Nearly identical findings were obtained by Johnson, Gormly, and Gormly (1973), Leonard (1975), and Olczak and Goldman (1975). As Hendrick and Page suggest, this unexpected pattern of results may be due to the way the experiments were constructed, which made the subjects feel that their positions were under assault, rather than that they were about to meet an interesting, if dissimilar, stranger. If this interpretation of the experimental context is correct, then it is possible that the strength and self-confidence of the high-esteem person would lead to an easier rejection of the threatening figure. All the evidence presented in chapter 7 makes it difficult to believe that discrepant opinions would be perceived as threatening. The evidence presented in chapter 9 shows that high-esteem persons do not find it difficult to form their own opinion. The puzzle is why esteem-oriented people reject the person along with the idea.

Although most of the experiments described in this chapter appear to capture that moment in the social process when the person recognizes that the other people possess opinions, behaviors or traits that are more or less similar to his or her own, there are a few additional experiments that indicate some of the other variables that need to be studied. These results need to be noted briefly, if only to indicate a promising direction for future research. We have seen that the competence and status attributes of the people to be observed can have significant social consequences. The only study to have examined the effect of these variables (Helmreich, Aronson, & LeFan, 1970) indicates how promising this direction might be. Among the many interesting findings of this experiment, one of the results demonstrated that high-esteem individuals were most attracted to the competent stimulus person. In discussing the effects of anxiety on attraction, we have seen that there is a direct complement to this study from the safety-needs cluster. Recall that Mehrabian and Ksionsky demonstrated that the more anxious person is most attracted to the higher status person. These two studies, taken together, provide another confirmation for one of the major relationships that can be seen in nearly every aspect of the social process.

The other people who are part of a social situation possess attributes beyond those that indicate the level of their status and competence. As a final illustration of interesting lines for future research, we can ask how personal dispositions guide the level of responsiveness to the different stances that other people bring to a social encounter. For example, Jones, Knurek, and Regan (1973) show that low-esteem people (as compared to high-esteem people) are more attracted to those who like them and less attracted to those who dislike them. Other work, notably by Hewitt and Goldman (1974) and Izzett (1976), indirectly helps to support this position. These results are similar to those of Smith and Campbell, which were discussed in the section on anxiety. One of the strengths of the model presented in chapter 5 is that it helps identify many more of these variables, which surely play a significant role in determining the early attraction responses in the acquaintanceship process.

Readiness to Engage in Social Activity: Attraction, Risk Taking, and Task Commitment

Each of the topics examined in part II helps to identify the elements that determine an individual's readiness to engage in social activity. The final discussion in chapter 7 dealt with the factors that entered into the setting of goals. In our discussion of information processing, we explored how personality factors moderate the individual's decision to reach a particular level of task commitment. In this experimental work on interpersonal attraction, the related phenomenon of physical contact can help to extend the analysis of the personality moderators of interpersonal attraction as well as task commitment. The final discussions of both chapters provide remarkably parallel sets of results, which together provide a great deal of evidence on the individual's readiness to engage in a social activity.

A number of interesting reviews (e.g., Argyle & Dean, 1965; Byrne, 1971; Patterson, 1976; Sundstrom & Altman, 1976) survey a great deal of empirical evidence examining the utility of behavioral indices of interpersonal attraction. As Sundstrom and Altman (1976) conclude: "Perhaps the best-supported general proposition about personal space is that positive affect, friendship, and attraction are associated with close proximity" (p. 50). The use of the subjective and the behavioral channels as alternative measures of attraction has characterized many of the primary programs of work in this area. For example, Byrne, Ervin, and Lamberth (1970), in a naturalistic computer dating study of the effects of attitude similarity on attraction, showed that more attracted couples stood closer together than less attracted couples. Similarly, in a controlled experimental situation, Mehrabian (1968) demonstrated the same relationship between attraction measures and a number of proximity measures, as did Rubin (1970), who demonstrated that the more couples reported being attracted to each other, the more they looked at each other. Although we do not explore the communicative function of proxemic behavior (e.g., Duncan, 1969), it is important to realize that even the most gross indicators of physical contact (e.g., distance maintained or degree of eye contact) provide important social stimuli that are used by others in forming their own impressions. We have already mentioned that LeCompte and Rosenfeld (1971) and Patterson and Sechrest (1970) have shown that behavioral cues such as gaze aversion or physical distance are used by observers to form their own impressions of the worthiness of the person.

There are several features to the typical method used in these experiments that create a somewhat different social experience for the participants and provide additional kinds of evidence on the individual's readiness to become engaged in social activity. First, in contrast to the extreme clarity of the information provided about people in the usual Byrne-type study, a person is asked to interact with a real stranger in these experiments. In other words, they are asked to approach an individual about whom they have no information. In fact, occasionally the task set in the experiment is to find out some information about the other person. Second, these experiments typically require a genuine emotional response to be created between participants. We should assume, therefore, that most of the responses produced in these experiments were generated under moderately threatening experimental conditions. Although these differences in method represent a significant departure from Byrne's approach, and so do make some of the most important findings not directly comparable, they do significantly increase the range of social events from which the information is obtained. Our overall expectations are relatively easy to present. For all the reasons described in part I, our broad expectation is that most of the safety-oriented people will use their self-protective defenses to reduce the level of their involvement with other people, that affiliation-oriented people will desire to become involved with other people, and that esteem-oriented people will find it relatively easy to become involved with other people if it is necessary to demonstrate their competence at a task.

Interpersonal Distance

Although there has not been extensive research studying the personal characteristics that lead some people to approach other people more closely, the available studies are unusually consistent in their conclusions. A number of different personality variables, which indicate greater psychological strength, each appear to lead people to bring themselves closer together. A well-known study (Dosey & Meisels, 1969) that experimentally manipulated people's emotional state can serve as the theme for this entire group of studies. Dosey and Meisels showed that as people felt increasing stress, they remained increasingly distant from other people. This experimentally created psychological state is representative of a host of clinical studies, in which a wide range of clinical variables is associated with increased distance responses (Evans & Howard, 1973). Studies of this type have typically used one of two different procedures. The more restrictive type (e.g., Duke & Mullens, 1973; Frede, Gautney, & Baxter, 1968; Smith, 1954) shows that a more disturbed population utilizes a simulation of an interaction (e.g., arranging models) to distance themselves from another person. The more realistic procedure (e.g., Carducci & Webber, 1979; Cavallin & Houston, 1980; DeJulio

& Duffy, 1977; Sanders, 1976) shows that more disturbed individuals approach another person less closely in order to conduct a conversation. In these studies, people are asked to engage in such interpersonal activities as selecting one of several chairs from which they will have a conversation with another person. Factors such as high scores on a neuroticism scale are associated with the choice of the more distant seat.

A similar pattern of results has been discovered for the type of variable with which we are concerned. A number of studies (Cozby, 1973; Gifford, 1982; Hammes, 1964; Patterson, 1973), using a behavioral test of attraction, have each provided evidence to confirm the hypothesis that the more anxious person is more reluctant to approach another person. As we would expect, in the one available study for the related variable of authoritarianism (Frankel & Barrett, 1971), the more authoritarian person similarly was more reluctant to approach another person. Among the safety needs-related variables, we would predict the opposite pattern of results for the need for approval and dependency. Unfortunately, there is no work of which we are aware that has examined the social effects of these variables. The study most similar to this type was done by Rosenfeld (1965). In this experiment, female students were asked to play an approval-seeking or approval-avoiding social role. The results showed that when a woman tried to be friendly with another woman, she approached her much more closely than when she was trying to indicate disapproval.

Of course, it is possible that Rosenfeld's experimental manipulation aroused an affiliative need rather than simply stimulated the women who took part in his experiment to act out a set of approval-related behaviors. The prediction that the need for affiliation should lead to increased levels of interpersonal attraction (i.e., physical contact) has received some support in two studies by Mehrabian and Diamond (1971a, 1971b), as well as an extra bit of corroboration from a study on the effects of extroversion by Williams (1971). Additional support for this relationships becomes available when we discuss eye gaze, the next behavioral channel. Finally, several studies (Cozby, 1973; Fromme & Beam, 1974; Pedersen, 1973; Stratton, Tekippe, & Flick, 1973) indicate that a set of variables such as dominance and self-esteem are associated with people assuming closer interpersonal distances. Although the definition of such variables makes it unlikely that these individuals desire greater intimacy with other people, it is reasonable to conclude that they do feel comfortable coming closer to others. In other words, what these studies probably show is that when high-esteem people need to be together with other people (e.g., when there is a task such as an experiment to complete), they can respond quite comfortably to the requirements of the situation.

Eye Contact

Psychologists can become quite poetic describing how the behavior of the eyes reveals the innermost secrets of the soul. When we consider that we have to look at an object in order to see it, it does seem expectable that the length of time an individual spends looking at an object should reveal its importance to that person. Even more interesting are the suggestions that we communicate with our eyes: to dominate, flirt, or submit by the way that we choose to stare, flutter, or avert our eyes. Although much more work is needed to clarify all the ways in which eye contact contributes to social interaction, there is still a reasonable number of experiments whose results conform quite well to theoretical expectations.

It is expectable that most of the safety-related variables would lead people to avoid interpersonal contact and intimacy. Campbell and Rushton (1978), Kendon and Cook (1969), Rutter and Stephenson (1972), and Williams (1974) have all shown that maladjusted people look at other people's faces much less than do better adjusted people. Within the range of the personality variables that we follow, Daly (1978) showed that more anxious people held eye contact for shorter periods of time than did less anxious people. Similarly, in one of the few available empirical studies on the effects of the need for abasement on any aspect of the social process, Libby and Yaklevich (1973) showed that this variable was very much involved with gaze aversion. In fact, their self-abasing subjects consistently looked away in a leftward direction. Although Libby and Yaklevich offer an extended discussion of the social, psychological, and neurological meaning of looking to the left, the fact that the room's only door was on the left side makes it easiest to conclude that the need for abasement leads to a desire to leave the entire situation. When an individual's characteristics are such as to make interpersonal involvement difficult, it is expectable that he or she would look away in the direction of the best escape route.

Finally, the need for approval seems to be a safety-related motive whose defensive structure is organized around strong approach tendencies. In the initial stages of a nonthreatening social encounter, the approval motive should lead people to approach others with a highly positive set of expectations; this motive should lead people to be attracted to, and draw close to, the average other person. Efran and Broughton (1966) performed just this experiment and demonstrated that the need for approval was related to the tendency to make eye contact. Unfortunately, Efran (1968) failed in an attempt to replicate this finding, although he did make significant changes in his method.

In the area of affiliative needs, a moderate number of studies that have used a variety of tests and procedures all generate the same result: Those individuals who desire to affiliate with others also desire intimate physical involvement such as eye contact. If it is accurate to view the extroversion scale as revealing sociability tendencies, then a number of British studies (Argyle & Ingham, 1972; Kendon & Cook, 1969; Mobbs, 1968; Rutter, Morley, & Graham, 1972) have shown a clear connection between extroversion and eye contact. Libby and Yaklevich showed that the need for nurturance is associated with eye contact, as did Exline, Gray, and Schuette (1965) using the inclusion and affection scales of the FIRO (Fundamental Interpersonal Relations Orientation). In addition, using French's Test of Insight, Exline (1963) provide a valuable demonstration of the need to specify a number of different social dimensions when making personological predictions. He formed three-person all male or all female groups, either homogeneously all affiliation- or nonaffiliation-oriented, which he asked to discuss a problem under two conditions of competitiveness. The major result of this study was that affiliation-oriented women spent more time looking at each other when the discussion was not especially competitive. Under more competitive conditions, the amount of mutual eye contact declined considerably, and there was no influence of the need for affiliation. In other words, Exline's experiment provides clear evidence for the proposition that although the need for affiliation leads individuals into greater contact with other people, threatening circumstances will provoke defenses that will greatly reduce this approach tendency in these people.

Finally, there are just a few indications (Ellyson, Dovidio, Corson, & Vinicur, 1980; Exline, Thibaut, Brannon, & Gumpert, 1961; Fromme & Beam, 1974; Lefcourt & Wine, 1969) that esteem-related variables are associated with eye contact. For the variables of power, Machiavellianism, dominance, and internal locus of control, respectively, these studies showed the capacity of such people to make easy contact with other people. The study by Lefcourt and Wine, in particular, showed that for individuals with an internal locus of control, eye contact increased when the person observed was more difficult to understand. Although the available research provides parallel sets of results, it is likely that a more highly differentiated research program could easily identify the different social circumstances that lead affiliation and esteem-motivated people to become intimate with other people in these ways.

Touch and Smiles

The wide range of other physical means through which people contact others has barely begun to be studied by social psychologists. We mention one study on touch and another on smiles more to indicate the possibilities for research than to present convincing evidence of this effect. First, Silverman, Pressman, and Bartel (1973) demonstrated that their subjects' level of self-esteem correlated positively with their use of touch in a dyadic experiment. As before, it is likely that such findings do not mean that high self-esteem people wish physical intimacy. Rather, these findings probably should be understood to mean that people with more self-esteem are better able to draw close to others if the task calls for that form of behavior. Second, Rosenfeld (1966) showed that undergraduate women with higher levels of the need for approval smiled more at their partner in dyadic interaction than did those women less concerned with approval needs.

Thus, for each of these channels, this small fund of information on interpersonal contact matches the predictions that can be drawn from theory. Although these findings do not yet constitute a sufficient body of information to allow us to understand the relationship between personality, attraction, and interpersonal contact very well, they do constitute a sufficiently large node of results to confirm that interpersonal contact is another situation to which the theory presented in chapter 5 seems to apply. Perhaps more important, these results point us toward the fact that the subjective responses lead directly to behavioral consequences. This is the direction toward which we now turn in an analysis of the behavior of individuals in groups.

III Complex Forms of Social Interaction

We are now able to begin our examination of the human being as a genuinely social creature. The previous chapters described a number of important psychological events that prepare the person to initiate a course of action. As these actions usually involve another person, the response of the other person leads to patterns of behavior that can be understood only as resulting from the joint influence that each person exerts upon the other. Whether the other person is a prospective "co-worker," "friend," or "victim," as soon as the second person acts in response to the first person's overture, each successive act is affected by all the earlier events that have ensued between them. Out of the preliminary social interchange, a bond quickly develops to govern their complex social interactions. In the chapters of part III, we explore the usefulness of our model to explain the interpersonal events that are often referred to as "group process."

Chapters 9 and 10 present a coordinated discussion of the ways that people use the primary coordinates of interpersonal space. In response to the recent strong convergence of empirical results and theoretical analysis (Hogan, 1982; Wiggins, 1980), which argues that two orthogonal dimensions seem to account for many of the responses made to broad batteries of personality tests, we begin the discussion of group process with an analysis of these major orientations of interpersonal behavior. These two factors are also seen as being similar to those identified earlier by Leary (1957) as the fundamental coordinates of interpersonal space (Dominance–Submission and Love–Hate). Further, these reviews offer a way to distinguish theoretical representations of personality processes (which are usually represented as sequential stage models) from empirical representations of behavior (which are frequently represented as circumplexes). Hogan offers an elegant way to account for the origin of the circumplex, which is also congruent with the approach taken by a number of other psychologists (Bales, 1950; Bennis & Shepard, 1956; Cattell, 1948). Combining the terminology used by these different theorists, it seems useful to suggest that social behavior is addressed to meeting two separate demands inherent in a social task. These are the issues of: (a) control over the task and (b) bonding between group members. By locating the source of the circumplex in the task, rather than in the person, we can more easily explain why many quite different motives and traits lead to similar forms of interpersonal behavior, especially under limited situational circumstances.

Chapter 11 continues the analysis of group process by examining the modes of interdependence through which people pursue their goals. This aspect of group process has been intensely investigated, resulting in a large number of alternative constructs to describe the emerging relationships. Owing to the variety of this work, in order to reach even preliminary conclusions on the ways that personality variables affect group process, it is necessary to concentrate results from parallel programs of research, as well as from studies of more distantly related social phenomena. Therefore, in chapter 11, we examine a wide range of studies in hopes of accumulating sufficient empirical evidence to examine the plausibility of the hypotheses offered in chapter 5.

Finally, in chapter 12, we suggest that significant aspects of the emerging group structure can be understood to result from the forms of interaction that group members seem to create. Although there has been little work undertaken on the personological sources of group structure, it is important to review what is known, if only because these discussions indicate the forms of social structure that are preferred by different kinds of people. Substantial theoretical and empirical programs, examining the effects of personality–group structure congruence, are based upon these assumptions. In part IV, we undertake an extended examination of this principle of congruence based on the preferred forms identified in part III.

9 The Initiation–Concurrence Dimension of Group Process

As a complex social event begins, individuals exchange greetings and quickly express their preferences for the kinds of behavior that they expect from other people. Just as energetically, they also try to insure that their preferences shape the allocation of each person's task and role responsibilities. In other words, the social influence process is at the heart of people's earliest efforts to coordinate their activities. Although these events are often referred to as having been done by "leaders" and "followers," with the implication that the first role is active and the second passive, from the individual's point of view, both roles produce highly desirable outcomes. More important, the behavior that is required to bring about both outcomes is highly active and goal oriented.

A simple solution to the apparent paradox that both leaders and followers are active, rather than passive, is to identify different ways of being active that still fit with the ordinary meanings of the words leader and follower. Chapter 4 describes how the extensions of the Bales' (1950) system by Borgatta and by Leary (cf. Borgatta & Crowther, 1965) define both the leader and the follower roles in just this way. As the participants in an event begin to deal with its requirements, whether during an informal social experience or, more obviously, when assigned a task by an employer, together they produce concrete acts that express the initiation and the concurrence poles of the "task" dimension. Both kinds of behaviors can move the group toward its goal.

This chapter begins the analysis of group process by examining the social influence mechanisms of initiation and concurrence. More specifically, the major task of this discussion is to determine if there are personality variables that motivate some people to initiate behavior that solves the problems presented by the task and other personality variables that motivate people to be receptive to such suggestions and eager to follow task-related direction. A simple example from everyday life should help clarify this relationship of personality to social behavior. It is not difficult to visualize the activity of a dominance-motivated person, who forcefully directs the activity of other people by outlining the work, proposing solutions, giving orders, and bestowing compliments on deserving helpers. It is difficult to envision such a person accepting any direction from another without quite assertively testing the value of the suggestions and the competence of the person who dares make them. On the other hand, although it is difficult to imagine a highly dependent person taking such an assertive stance with regard to the work of the group, it is very easy to visualize him or her contributing to the success of the group by asking for direction and complying with the requests made by others. This simple example represents the questions that this chapter poses: Can we extend the reasoning developed in part II to understand the more complex form of social behavior that is represented by the initiation-concurrence dimension of group process?

INITIATION:
THE ATTEMPT AT SOCIAL INFLUENCE

In his comprehensive review, Stogdill (1974) proposed a functional definition of leadership in hopes of integrating the many approaches in the research literature: "Leadership is defined as the initiation and maintenance of . . . role structure and goal direction, necessary for effective group performance" (p. 411). In particular, phrasing the definition in functional terms proves to be extremely useful for clarifying an important element of group process. Leadership refers to all behaviors that initiate or maintain those "structures" that lead to effective group process and members' satisfaction with the quality of their performance and relations with one another. More specifically, in this definition, the term "leader" is used to identify the activity of the person who develops and maintains structures that organize the behavior of other people as they work together toward some goal. The concrete categories of initiation behavior presented in Table 5.4 seem to summarize quite well the range of leadership behavior that is of concern to Stogdill.

In the field of leadership studies, researchers have always been eager to identify the personal characteristics that cause an individual to take charge of the group's activities. The assumption in this line of research has been that if one could isolate the characteristics that separated leaders from nonleaders, then the practical problem of selecting individuals to fill the leadership positions in organizations would be greatly advanced. As a consequence of this hope, hundreds of studies were conducted in which the correlation between some measurable personality trait and some measurable leadership function was computed. There is now an impressive number of studies available that identify those traits that characterize a leader.

In order to understand the value of this kind of research, as well as its limitations, we briefly review the simple research strategy that has been used in these studies. In general, the most common method of assessing the relationship of personality characteristics to leadership has been to determine the level of association between scores on a personality scale and scores on some measure of leadership. In the majority of studies, samples of existing leaders and nonleaders from some real organization are identified and then compared on the basis of their scores on one or more personality tests. Political, business, educational, and religious organizations have all been studied in research of this kind. In somewhat more difficult research, a set of individuals is given personality tests, asked to work together at some task, and finally, asked to rate each other's performance. These peer evaluations serve to identify the leaders and nonleaders within the group whose scores on the personality tests can then be compared. The last method used in this research area is for the experimenter to specify a set of actions that define leadership, and observers of the group can then use these definitions to rate the participants on their level of leadership displayed. More rarely, these definitions can form a coding system that allows the observers to record the frequency of occurrence of some set of behaviors believed to define the different roles within the group. These behaviorally determined leaders and nonleaders can then be compared on the basis of their personality test results.

What is especially impressive about this approach to leadership is that, despite the wide range of personality scales that has been used and the wide range of procedures for determining the identity of the leader, there is a remarkable degree of consistency in the pattern of results. To summarize the results of these studies in a simple way, esteem-related characteristics are associated with leadership activity across many different types of situations, whereas safety-related characteristics are rarely associated with leadership activity, except under very special and limited conditions. The cluster of esteem-related variables seems to constitute the personality attributes necessary to initiate and maintain group structure, direct the group process, and facilitate group members' achievement of their personal goals from the group. At the global level, at which most of this research is done, it is not surprising to find that persons who are assertive, stable, confident, and competent are more likely to actively initiate task activity by effectively producing procedural suggestions, suggesting solutions to problems, coordinating member efforts toward the goal, and manifesting consideration for member's needs.

Stogdill (1974), the authoritative reviewer of leadership studies, has summarized the research evidence that examines this broad generalization. His review indicates that there were 44 studies in which there was a positive relationship between sets of personality variables such as self-confidence and leadership; there were no negative cases. Similarly, there were 43 positive findings for dominance-related variables, with only 6 negative or null findings. Likewise, there were 24 positive findings for emotional stability, against 8 negative ones. In total, Stogdill's review revealed that out of 125 studies involving esteem-oriented personality characteristics, 111 were positively associated with leadership, whereas only 14 of them were not.

The research that examines this relationship is especially easy to report. As we have noted, the question underlying the research is a simple one, the studies tend to use the same design, and the results are remarkably consistent. For this topic, as for none other reviewed in this book, a listing of studies in a table is the most efficient way to present the evidence. The selection of studies presented in Table 9.1 is based heavily on Stogdill's review of this area. We have not included a number of esoteric publications, monographs, and technical reports because they were usually not available to us. However, we have supplemented Stogdill's review with as many subsequent publications as we could discover. Finally, a convenient system for presenting and discussing these studies is not obvious. On the one hand, there are nearly as many scales and trait names as there are publications. On the other, considering the similarity in results obtained from all these scales, it is not impossible that they measured some common leadership factor. We have grouped the studies into six broad categories, mainly following Gibb (1969), which we can feel fairly comfortable calling self-esteem, dominance, achievement, sociability, adjustment, and authoritarianism. This organization allows us to sort the evidence by different features of personality structure and to deal with potentially very different psychological mechanisms underlying initiation behavior.

Self-Esteem

There is a large number of studies in which known leaders and nonleaders were asked very general sets of questions about the degree of positive opinion that they have of themselves. By asking people to reflect about themselves, these tests seem to be tapping the cognitive precipitates of their success in the world. More precisely, these tests seem to be measuring those broad features of people's self-image that are accessible through self-reflection and likely result from the developmental process described in chapter 3. Although these questions are typically variants of "How good do you feel about yourself?" the scales are called by many different names, such as self-assurance, self-confidence, self-sufficiency, self-esteem, and so forth. Given the similarity of most of these studies, there is no reason to believe that the tests discriminate meaningfully among different personality variables, despite their many titles. We suggest that the results of this group of studies be thought of as the most global measure of positivity of self-image that is associated with fairly high levels of self-esteem.

It is not surprising to find that with such a general definition of the personality variable, these studies show leaders to be more self-confident, self-assured, and self-sufficient than the nonleaders in the group. This variable should have the widest degree of association with many different types of leadership situations precisely because it is not a narrow motive or trait. Rather, this broad variable seems to be associated with many of the different, more situationally specific, motivational processes that emerge from esteem motivation. Considering the behaviors that Stogdill describes as constituting the leadership role, we would expect to find that the more confident and assured person is the one most likely to initiate and maintain the movement of the group toward its goal. It certainly would be difficult to explain why more uncertain and insecure persons would emerge in a leadership position. Although certain types of less confident persons are chosen as leaders in a few restricted conditions (i.e., authoritarians), such safety-based characteristics do not generally manifest the same cross-situational consistency of leadership behavior.

Table 9.1 records 22 studies in which self-confidence, self-assurance, self-sufficiency, and so on were found to be positively related to leadership. The impact of this finding is strengthened even further when the characteristics of the sample populations are considered. The subjects of these studies include college students, police cadets, athletes, middle- and upper-level managers, entrepreneurs, sorority candidates, factory foremen, and military personnel. Clearly, the fact that these samples represent such a broad cross-section of the population makes the finding especially robust.

Dominance

Although many personality variables have been associated with various measures of leadership, none has seemed more obviously related than the motive of dominance. If dominance is a need to establish one's self-worth through demonstrations of directing, influencing and persuading others, the dominance-oriented person should find leadership activity most congruent with his or her personality dynamics. Indeed, if the dominance-oriented person's sense of self-worth is largely based on behavior designed to influence others to act in certain ways, it seems almost imperative for such people to assume positions of influence in the group. Clearly, if individuals need to direct others, then they will by necessity produce acts aimed at structuring the interactional sequence among group members. Moreover, unless other equally assertive people resist, it is likely that they will persist in attempts to maintain their position of influence.

Because the research literature on dominance motives and leadership behavior shows such consistently positive results, a full-scale review of the individual studies is not necessary. In Table 9.1, we record 35 studies that found

TABLE 9.1
Studies Examining the Relationship of Personality to Leadership

Personality Characteristic	Reference	Personality Characteristic	Reference
1. Self-Esteem			
Self-confidence	Bass, 1954	Internality	Hiers & Heckel, 1977
Self-reliance	Bass, McGehee, Hawkins, Young, & Gebel, 1953	Self-acceptance	Hogan, 1978
Self-confidence	Bass, Wurster, Doll, & Clair, 1953	Self-sufficiency	Hunter & Jordan, 1939
Self-acceptance	Beer, Buckhout, Horowitz, & Levy, 1959	Self-confidence	Kiessling & Kalish, 1961
Self-confidence	Cattell & Stice, 1954	Self-confidence	Martin, Gross, & Darley, 1952
Internality	DeBolt, Liska, Love, & Stahlman, 1973	Self-esteem	Messé, Aronoff, & Wilson, 1972
Internality[a]	DeBolt, Liska, & Weng, 1976	Internality	Phares, 1965
Self-assurance	Ghiselli, 1963	Self-confidence	Richardson & Hanawalt, 1943
Self-confidence	Gibb, 1947	Self-confidence	Richardson & Hanawalt, 1944
Self-confidence	Grant & Bray, 1969	Self-confidence	Richardson & Hanawalt, 1952
Self-assurance	Harrell, 1969	Self-confidence	Zeleny, 1939
2. Dominance			
Dominance	Aries, Gold, & Weigel, 1983	Dominance	Hanawalt & Richardson, 1944
Dominance	Armilla, 1967	Dominance	Hanawalt, Richardson, & Hamilton, 1943
Ascendance	Bales, 1970	Ascendance	Hare & Bales, 1963
Ascendance	Bass, 1954	Dominance	Harrell, 1969
Ascendance	Bass, McGehee, Hawkins, Young, & Gebel, 1953	Dominance	Hogan, 1978
Ascendance	Bass, Wurster, Doll, & Clair, 1953	Ascendance	Hunter & Jordan, 1939
Dominance	Beer, Buckhout, Horowitz, & Levy, 1959	Power	Kaess, Witryol, & Nolan, 1961
Dominance	Blake & Mouton, 1961	Dominance	McClelland & Boyatzis, 1982
Assertiveness	Borg, 1960	Dominance	Megargee, 1969
Ascendance	Borg & Tupes, 1958	Assertiveness	Megargee, Bogart, & Anderson, 1966
Assertiveness	Borg, Tupes, & Carp, 1959	Ascendance	Miner, Rizzo, Harlow, & Hill, 1974
Ascendance	Carter & Nixon, 1949	Dominance	Moore, 1935
Dominance	Cattell & Stice, 1954	Dominance	Richardson & Hanawalt, 1943
Assertiveness	Cleveland & Fisher, 1956	Dominance	Richardson & Hanawalt, 1944
Assertiveness	Cleveland & Morton, 1962	Dominance	Richardson & Hanawalt, 1952
Assertiveness	Gordon & Medland, 1965	Dominance	Rychlak, 1963
Assertiveness	Grant & Bray, 1969	Dominance	Scioli, Dyson, & Fleitas, 1974
		Dominance	Smith & Cook, 1973

3. Achievement

Trait	Reference	Trait	Reference
Achievement	Andrews, 1967	Achievement	Mussen & Porter, 1959
Achievement	Beer, Buckhout, Horowitz, & Levy, 1959	Achievement	Rychlak, 1963
Achievement	Burke, 1965	Achievement	Sorrentino, 1973
Achievement	Hornaday & Bunker, 1970	Achievement	Tripathi & Agrawal, 1978

4. Sociability

Sociability	Armilla, 1967	Sociability	Gibb, 1947
Empathy	Bass, 1954	Sociability	Guilford, 1952
Sociability	Bass, McGehee, Hawkins, Young, & Gebel, 1953	Sociability	Kaess, Witryol, & Nolan, 1961
Empathy	Bell & Hall, 1954	Affiliation	Mussen & Porter, 1959
Extroversion	Borg & Tupes, 1958	Extroversion	Richardson & Hanawalt, 1943
Sociability	Cattell & Stice, 1954	Extroversion	Richardson & Hanawalt, 1944
Empathy	Chowdhry & Newcomb, 1952	Affiliation	Sorrentino, 1973

5. Adjustment

Ego strength	Armilla, 1967	Ego strength	Hicks & Stone, 1962
Stability	Bass, McGehee, Hawkins, Young, & Gebel, 1953	Adjustment	Holtzman, 1952
Ego strength	Cattell & Stice, 1954	Autonomy	Hornaday & Bunker, 1970
Anxiety[b]	Cattell & Stice, 1954	Anxiety[b]	Richardson & Hanawalt, 1944
Independence	Cleveland & Morton, 1962	Anxiety[b]	Sarason, 1973
Maturity	Fitzsimmons & Marcuse, 1961	Ego strength	Schiller, 1961
Adjustment	Guilford, 1952	Independence	Vroom, 1960
Anxiety[b]	Hare & Bales, 1963		

6. Authoritarianism

Authoritarianism[c]	Bass, McGehee, Hawkins, Young, & Gebel, 1953	Authoritarianism[b]	Marquis, 1973
Authoritarianism[b]	Borg, 1960	Authoritarianism[b]	Masling, Greer, & Gilmore, 1955
Authoritarianism[b]	Hollander, 1954	Authoritarianism[b]	Rohde, 1952

[a]No relationship reported.
[b]A negative relationship reported, as predicted.
[c]A curvilinear relationship reported.

leadership activity to be associated with dominance motives and related constructs (e.g., ascendancy and assertiveness). Once again, these studies cover a wide range of populations, ranging from Peace Corps volunteers to senior executives in business organizations, and suggest that the relationships are ecologically valid and remarkably robust.

It is probably difficult to visualize just what is represented by the list of studies reported in Table 9.1, so a brief account of one of the more interesting studies should help make this type of research more understandable. Smith and Cook (1973) formed dyads composed of a high- and a low-dominant college woman and set before them the task of playing a game that required a great deal of physical coordination. The game was the popular Labyrinth puzzle, in which the two players each manipulated a knob in order to tilt the puzzle so that a steel ball would go through a maze. In order to create what appeared to be two different social positions for that dyad, one of the chairs was labeled "leader" and the other was labeled "follower." The students were told that, because each of them had independent control over their own knob, the person in the leader's chair would direct the actions of the follower verbally. They were also told that they should decide who would be the leader. As Smith and Cook expected, it was the more dominant woman who usually took the leadership chair and directed the work of the less dominant woman. The most interesting part of the experiment was that observers were able to determine how the high-dominance person came to take the leadership seat. In addition to the more dominant woman often simply nominating herself for the leader's position, Smith and Cook found that it was just as likely for the less dominant woman to turn to the other and ask her to take over the group. This action by the less dominant woman raises the important question of how the characteristics of the follower help to determine the selection of the leader. We return to this issue later in this section.

The more usual study listed in Table 9.1 can be illustrated by Borg's (1960) study of the psychological correlates of leadership in Air Force officers. As part of a training program, officers were administered a battery of personality tests, which included the FIRO test, the F-scale, an anxiety scale, an extroversion scale, and the Guilford Opinion Inventory. The responses to the tests were factor analyzed and produced four factors: Assertiveness, Power, Rigidity, and Nonconformity. The leadership scores were based on nominations by the participating officers. Correlations between the four factors and the leadership score showed the factor of Assertiveness to be the best predictor of nominations to the leadership role.

There are several studies in this group that should be described briefly, because they allow us to establish directly the link between personality and initiation behavior. As noted earlier, Stogdill (1974) defined leadership in terms of concrete task-oriented behaviors, which he derived primarily from Bales (1950). Recall that these are the behaviors that we used to construct the definition of initiation behavior in chapters 4 and 5. Stogdill also reviewed a great many studies that demonstrate, across many areas of social activity, the value of operationalizing leadership in terms of sets of concrete behaviors. The vast body of research that Stogdill reviewed provides a convincing demonstration that personality is related to the rated role (or the elected position) of leadership; it is equally convincing in establishing the relationship between rated (or elected) leadership and initiation behavior. However, in order to make the larger inferential net more convincing, it is essential to report a few of the studies that directly measure the relationship between personality and initiation behavior.

In the type of experimental study needed to examine this link directly, Scioli, Dyson, and Fleitas (1974) formed college students into a number of small laboratory groups. Students were given several abbreviated personality tests and asked to reach a group consensus about how to resolve a discussion problem. Groups were asked to agree on the problem in either a condition that required group consensus or in a condition that allowed individual dissent to be recorded as well. Each session was videotaped and later scored using the Bales IPA scoring system. In this study, the instrumental leader was defined as the person in a group who produced the highest percentage of initiating task responses, such as giving suggestions, direction, evaluation, analysis, orientation, information, and clarification. The major result was a marked association of high-dominance scores with the high-instrumental-leadership score in a group, particularly when the decision-making structure limited the participant's expression to just the common group position.

Scioli et al.'s study is useful in several different ways. First, it provides direct evidence of the link between a personality variable (and the one most commonly cited as related to leadership) and the use of concrete initiating behaviors to direct a task-oriented group. Further corroboration of the association between dominance-related personality variables and initiation behavior can be found in Bales' (1970) book on personality and interpersonal behavior. Bales, who has been the creative center of the field of small-group research, reanalyzed several of his associates' studies in order to illustrate a new theoretical model of interpersonal behavior. Although the findings that he presents do not come from experiments specifically designed to test the relationships between dominance-related personality variables and initiation behavior, he does report a number of similar correlations that provide another instance of support for this relationship. In addition, several of our own experiments (Aronoff & Messé, 1971; Messé, Aronoff, & Wilson, 1972; Wilson, Aronoff, & Messé, 1975), which are discussed in depth in later chapters, similarly use a behavioral approach to identify the leader of the group. These studies, which examine a range of group processes as a function, in part, of the personal attributes of group members, all use the Borgatta modification of Bales' IPA coding system. The positive results obtained with this approach further confirm the usefulness of a behavioral definition of leadership functions. Finally, Stogdill (1974) presents a great deal of evidence that the person nominated by the group as the leader, in almost all cases, was also the person who produced the highest percentage of initiating behaviors.

Scioli et al.'s results provide another demonstration of how the motive of dominance interacts with characteristics of the situation to produce leadership activity. Dominance was associated with leadership more strongly when the decision-making structure forced the group to produce only the limiting consensus. With the opportunity for more individual expression by members, the personality-leadership relationship was attenuated. A somewhat similar result was found by Megargee, Bogart, and Anderson (1966), who formed dyads composed of a high- and a low-dominant person. When the instructions to the group emphasized the task, the high-dominant person did not assume the leadership significantly more than the low-dominant person. However, when the instructions emphasized leadership, the more dominant person nearly always became the leader. These two studies are helpful because they indicate that dominance is not a "general" factor that will always be associated with social leadership. Rather, these studies, whose results follow quite well the definition of dominance motivation provided earlier, indicate that this motive will produce its effects primarily when the working structure clearly indicates how initiation behavior by one of the group members can successfully provide dominance rewards.

The conclusion that emerges from all of the studies examined in this section is that the dominant person acts verbally and nonverbally throughout the group process to influence, persuade, and direct others. It is clear from these studies that the motive of dominance is associated with: (a) the initial use of physical space (e.g., seat selection) to indicate the dominant position; (b) the initial choice of leadership role; (c) high frequencies of verbal and behavioral acts; (d) the emergence of task-oriented leadership; and (e) persistent attempts at structuring the interaction sequence among group members. Interestingly, there are indications in these studies that once the procedures of the group become well defined, the dominant person may play a less active behavioral role in maintaining a hierarchical relationship among group members. The results suggest that once the dominant person has established an organization, he or she does not have to exert continuing direct influence, unless challenged by other members. We return to this issue in later chapters because it raises the important question of the point at which the emergent group becomes an organized group.

The Need for Achievement

Sorrentino (1973) has noted the surprising fact that relatively few studies have examined the association of the need for achievement and leadership. It is possible that the precision of the need for achievement construct (McClelland, Atkinson, Clark, & Lowell, 1953) directed the attention of researchers into much more sharply defined research topics than is the case with most motives. It is, of course, true that the extensive research by McClelland (e.g., 1961) and others (e.g., Atkinson & Raynor, 1974) strongly suggests that achievement-oriented people are vigorous problem solvers and realistic risk takers in situations that permit this motive to affect behavior. However, acts of this kind, no matter how vigorous, are not the ones that indicate either leadership or initiation behavior.

If we ask how the need for achievement might appear in the kind of studies that we are examining presently, it is reasonable to expect that achievement-oriented persons would be skillful at initiating those structures that help group members accomplish the task and attain the goal. All eight of the studies that we examined revealed significant positive associations between the need for achievement and leadership. These findings are consistent with previous research (cf. Heckhausen, 1967) that portrays these people as highly task-oriented, active, persistent, and concerned with the proper accomplishment of tasks. Given these well-established results, it is quite reasonable to expect that these people will wish to initiate the tasks being done within a group and see them through in a competent fashion. In fact, considering the high degree of task commitment associated with the need for achievement, it is possible that they, in contrast to dominance-oriented people, will show much more obvious leadership behavior throughout the length of the task. Unfortunately, we were not able to find research that would test comparisons of this kind.

By and large, the results of the studies listed in Table 9.1 parallel those that have been discussed for other personality characteristics and support this association in a fairly simple way. The one unusually intriguing experiment in this area (Sorrentino, 1973), which even includes a behavioral measure of leadership, is too complex to be summarized briefly at this point. Although the results of this study are broadly congruent with our expectations, Sorrentino's most important finding is that the need for achievement affects the emergence of leadership only in conjunction with specific levels of other personality states (e.g., anxiety and the affiliation motive) and the characteristics of the situation (e.g., whether future activity was or was not contingent on success at the experimental task). Much research could be stimulated by this provocative study, because the importance of the specific combinations of variables still remains to be investigated.

Sociability, Empathy, and Extroversion

There are a few studies suggesting that what can be loosely thought of as a set of interpersonal contact characteristics is associated with leadership. In general, these personal attributes are supposed to be those that help the leader understand the other members of the group and increase his or her ability to respond to their concerns. Stogdill (1974) briefly reviews a set of studies that seem to show that these psychological elements help the leader to be more alert to the social environment and better able to evaluate the situation and the thoughts, feelings, and actions of the other group members. Abilities such as these should assist the leader in gaining and maintaining control of the group. It is probably reasonable to assume that these personality variables are somehow involved, because there is a larger number of studies, which Stogdill also reviews, showing that leaders actually do exhibit these valuable social skills.

Table 9.1 presents 14 studies that all report significant positive relationships between empathy, sociability, and extroversion and the elected or rated position of leadership. The easiest way to understand these studies is within the context of the other studies that have been discussed. It seems useful to see these studies as identifying sets of cognitive and emotional skills that increase the capacity of motivational variables to direct initiation behavior. From this point of view, such variables should show their greatest power to affect individual performance in conjunction with the other esteem-related characteristics.

However, it is possible that the instruments used to measure empathy, sociability, and extroversion are really tapping some of the attributes of affiliation motivation. If this were true, it would lead to investigations of such interesting questions as the alternative types of leadership that such people should exhibit. For example, it is possible that people who are strongly concerned with affiliation would be active group members who engage in many acts of a socioemotional nature. They might facilitate the movement of group members toward the goal through behavior that is supportive of others, increases group solidarity, or coordinates member effort. In other words, affiliative characteristics should be more associated with the socioemotional categories of behavior than has been seen to be the case for the other motives under review. Unfortunately, there are no empirical studies to report that would confirm these expectations. Even more interesting is the possibility that the more mature types of affiliation and esteem motives might produce an integrated form of active task and socioemotional behavior. A preliminary version of this approach was carried out by Borgatta, Couch, and Bales (1954) under the title of the "great man" theory of leadership. More recently, a number of studies that, so far, only deal with the behavioral side of this approach have appeared under the label of "androgyny." It is probable that there will soon be studies of the complex forms of leadership that individuals, as concerned with affiliation as they are with ascendancy, are likely to produce.

Adjustment, Ego Strength, and Emotional Stability

From the earliest work in this area, it has seemed obvious to a large number of psychologists that the more psychologically healthy person should find it easier to take on the leadership functions than the person who is significantly less well adjusted. Because this proposition has seemed so plausible, there is a fairly extensive amount of literature demonstrating that healthier people possess the capacity to be realistic problem solvers and effective in working with others on common tasks. Both the theoretical and the empirical literature seem to show that these alternative trait names for mental health simply state that cognitive and emotional structures are available to the person to pursue his or her specific interests within that group. Note that this conclusion does not argue that a person who is somewhat healthier than another is likely to become the leader of the group, as was seen in the discussions of such motivational variables as dominance.

Thus, in the leadership context, the well-adjusted person is the one who has the ability to: (a) realistically assess the concerns that need attention; (b) postpone immediate personal gratification in order to manage group responsibilities effectively; (c) work constructively with other group members to reach shared goals; and (d) prepare for future social needs. Although these personal characteristics should not, in themselves, lead people to assume initiating behavior in the group process, they should make it easier for the other motivational variables to exert their influence. Similarly, although there are many well-adjusted people who do not become leaders, it should be more difficult for a person who does not have these abilities to reach and maintain that position.

Given the argument that healthier individuals are more capable of leadership, it follows that maladjusted, neurotic, anxious, or emotionally unstable people should be less capable leaders in most conditions. Clearly, anxious individuals, who are primarily concerned with reducing their own levels of discomfort, should not find it easy to perform the tasks demanded of the leader. If these people typically respond to their emotional state by withdrawing from the field or by attempting to structure events compulsively, they are much less ready to generate the social structures necessary for effective group process.

In 14 of the 15 studies listed in Table 9.1, there was a positive relationship between a variety of ego-strength measures and leadership. As has been seen in earlier discussions, these studies ask a simple question of many diverse populations. At the level at which the research question has been asked, the association seems to be clearly supported. The interesting questions, at this point, are the ones that build on this finding.

Authoritarianism

As we mentioned at the beginning of this chapter, there has been little expectation that safety-needs-related variables would substantially affect the emergent leadership within a group. Few psychologists would find it easy to explain why insecure, dependent, or anxious people would assume a leadership function in most of the situations that have been described. The evidence that was just reviewed on the relationship between adjustment and leadership showed that the least healthy people typically are the least likely to become leaders. One last small cluster of studies shows that the more precisely defined safety-related characteristic of authoritarianism usually shows the same negative relationship to leadership as well, at least in the kind of social settings that have been used in most of this research. Table 9.1 reports a few studies that examine this association. In virtually all of these studies, leadership is negatively related to authoritarianism, although one study (Bass, McGehee, Hawkins, Young, & Gebel, 1953) found a curvilinear relationship in a discussion group. However, social psychologists would expect to find that authoritarians would become the leaders of a social unit in certain precisely defined social situations. There is a set of classic experiments by Haythorn and his associates that examined how the trait of authoritarianism affects the social behavior of both leaders and followers. We turn to these interesting studies in several later chapters.

The studies that we have just examined allow us to answer our original question: Are there personality variables that lead some individuals to assume an initiating mode of behavior in the group? Working within the limitations of the existing studies, there seems to be a set of characteristics that distinguishes the person who assumes the leadership role in groups from individuals who do not.

Before concluding this discussion of leadership, it is necessary to state that this review did not uncover a substantially new set of facts. Most of the research reported in Table 9.1 has been considered in the major reviews of this field. However, many reviewers of this literature, such as Gibb (1969), Shaw (1981), and even Stodgill (1974), seem troubled by this range of parallel correlations and feel that "numerous studies of the personalities of leaders have failed to find any consistent pattern of traits which characterize leaders" (Gibb, 1969, p. 227). Gibb continues, in apparent contradiction: "there is abundant evidence that member personalities do . . . affect . . . leadership" (p. 227). The problem, of course, is represented by the word "consistent." As long as social psychologists deal uncritically with the names of poorly validated personality scales, there will be "too many" parallel correlations. From the standpoint of the conclusions reached in chapter 3, there is great consistency in the traits that seem to be related to leadership. We have seen that the person who contributes the most to moving the group toward its goals, and is perceived as the most influential by other group members, is described in some measure as self-confident, dominant, achievement-oriented, well-adjusted, and/or empathic. This configuration of results is neither contradictory, equivocal, nor random in nature. Rather, these states are some of the most important adaptations of esteem-oriented people. From this review, it would seem quite clear that the weight of the evidence from widely varying populations and institutional settings unequivocally suggests that the cluster of variables associated with esteem needs is consistently associated with this type of leadership activity.

There are major limitations in this program of research that must be noted before turning to the question of followership. Within this extensive literature, there are few studies that specify the types of people who would become leaders in only certain types of situations or study the role that different types of followers play in determining the type of person who becomes the leader. There are also few studies that specify the type of person who becomes the most effective leader in certain situations or identify the concrete types of activity that such an effective leader would use. These questions not only are interesting extensions of the personality/leadership issue but are the critically important next steps required in a theory of the psychology of leadership.

It is possible that the personality/leadership studies have always disappointed reviewers because their conclusions are so limited in comparison to what is needed. To provide an answer for these needs, it is helpful to examine other literatures that ask different questions and use different methods. It may be that the literature just reviewed is more valuable for explaining the limited construct of the psychological bases of initiation behavior (i.e., the first behavioral phase of group process) than it is for describing the larger sets of behaviors that are part of leadership. The achievement of the present review is that it demonstrates there are general psychological foundations for initiation behavior. For these purposes, this literature is a massive foundation for the later examinations of group process. With this accomplished, let us turn to review what can be discovered about the psychological foundations of concurrence, or followership, behavior in the social process.

CONCURRENCE: THE RESPONSE TO SOCIAL INFLUENCE

Although a serious effort has been made to understand the characteristics of people who assume the leadership role, it is remarkable how little attention has been paid to the other members of the group. Perhaps the leadership role is so visible that the significant contributions made by other group members are easily overlooked. As a consequence, little is known about these people other than the fact that nonleaders usually score low on those scales on which leaders score high. Yet, in order to understand the relationship between group members or to work out a more complete model of the dimensions of group process, it is necessary to know why people assume the other roles in the differentiated group.

To call these people nonleaders is to fail to recognize their essential social role. There cannot be a leader if there is not another person who responds to the leader's procedural suggestions, proposed solutions, and orders by attending to, agreeing with, and carrying out these directions. Unfortunately, with the exception of a few studies, such as Elms and Milgram's (1966) research on the dispositional bases of obedience, there is little information to explain these important social functions within the context of the group.

The behaviors just listed help to define the leader–follower relationship as reflecting the twin components of the social influence process: initiation and concurrence. From the viewpoint of social influence as a basic underlying dimension of social events, it is possible to specify the follower role as constituting behavior that responds to the direction provided by the influence agent. If it is meaningful to define the followership role in this way, then there is a substantial amount of literature available on the personal dispositions that underlie the individual's acceptance of attempts at social influence.

Two major programs of research in social psychology have studied the psychological bases of the susceptibility to social influence. The first program, originated by Sherif (1936), Asch (1956), and Crutchfield (1955), sought to discover the dispositional factors underlying conformity in a quasi-group setting. The second program sought to understand the dispositional factors underlying persuasibility (e.g., Hovland & Janis, 1959). Happily, these two large research programs provide a coherent view of the characteristics that lead people to attend to, accept, and follow the leader's suggestions.

The experimental approach used in both programs was to create a laboratory situation in which one or more people, with whom the person was involved in some way, presented an opinion that differed from that person's judgment of some aspect of the world. The experimenter's assumption was that these discrepant opinions (or incorrect judgments) create a norm that the person feels pressed to accept. The goal of these experiments was to discover which combination of social conditions and individual dispositions lead people to yield to the social pressures. Although a great many variations on the basic experiments were devised, the overall weight of these studies confirms the original insight. To summarize the early hypothesis in a general way, it was thought that with an increased level of psychological maturity, a person becomes less easily influenced by the opinions, desires, and behaviors of others. The years of work that followed have overwhelmingly supported the hypothesis that certain dispositions make people more subject to influence, as well as determine the specific situational conditions under which these effects can be reversed.

In an extended essay, McGuire (1968) presented an illuminating description of the way dispositional factors affect the concurrence aspects of the social influence process. It is valuable to begin this discussion of concurrence with a summary of McGuire's proposal, because it allows us to understand more easily the mass of studies that have been done using what purport to be dozens of personality variables, standard and unusual tests, and the nonsystematic use of a wide range of social conditions. His intriguing hypotheses help us to understand the many results that are apparently inconsistent and bring a fair amount of order into a field that is critically important for social psychology.

McGuire (1968) began by noting that the Yale group (i.e., Janis & Hovland, 1959) maintained that opinion change was not a simple response but rather a series of different kinds of behaviors: "(a) attention to the communication, (b) comprehension of its contents, and (c) yielding to what is comprehended" (p. 1140). For the sake of simplicity of exposition, McGuire combined the attention and the comprehension stages into a single reception stage. This sequence allowed him to propose that a personality variable may have very different effects on each of the two main stages. For example, it is reasonable to expect that anxiety may make a person more ready to yield to a message. However, anxiety should also make the person inattentive to the message. Therefore, the nature of the message and the situation may have a strong bearing on which part of the influence process may be affected by anxiety. In a relaxed situation with a simple message (or command), anxiety may lead to greater yielding. In a stressful and complex situation, anxiety may lead to defensive inattention, which prevents the person from receiving the message. Therefore, as a consequence of the specific situational conditions of that demanding situation, an anxious person would refuse to receive the message and so would not appear to yield. The opposite set of events should occur for the dispositional variable of self-esteem. The self-esteem variable should make a person be more attentive to and understanding of the message and hence, all other things being equal, more influenceable. However, such a person is more independent and so should appear to be less yielding. McGuire proposed that the specific characteristics of the situation interact with self-esteem to determine when that person will conform most. In other words, if influenceability is a tendency of a person to change in the direction desired by an influence agent, then there is no general trait that will predict concurrence in a simple linear way. A great many variables, from both the safety and the esteem-needs clusters predict concurrence. But, as McGuire proposed and as empirical research partially demonstrates, these different kinds of variables do so in very different and highly predictable circumstances. Our understanding of the nature of these contrasting psychological clusters helps to explain the specific form of the person-by-situation interactions that do appear.

With a general model of the response to social influence outlined, this is an opportune point to return briefly to the criticisms of the interactionist approach raised by Bem (1972) and Mischel (1973). Recall that both were concerned that specifying all the situational and dispositional factors needed to account for a social event, in the absence of a general theory, indicates that the investigator is not predicting but rather describing the attributes of the specific event under study. As they warn, this is a tautological statement. We are now in the position to see if there is a way to meet these objections. McGuire's elegant proposal, which suggests an efficient way to account for the effect of situational variables on dispositional variables, together with our proposals in chapter 3, which permit the many dispositional variables to be subsumed under relatively few, appear to produce such a compact set of theoretical statements. In reviewing the extensive research on the dispositional bases of concurrence, it is possible to see how well this synthesis handles the data.

Influenceability in the Conformity Experiment

Asch (1956) and Crutchfield (1955) devised a simple laboratory technique for placing a person's judgment in conflict with that of other people. This type of experiment asks people to match a particular stimulus with one of a set of other stimuli (e.g., people might be judging the length of a line). The experimenter arranges for the subject to give his or her judgment only after hearing the judgment of a group of other people (who are, in fact, really part of the experimental team). On some of the trials, the group (whose opinions the experimenter controls) unanimously asserts that a clearly incorrect stimulus is the correct choice. The question is: Will the subject agree with the judgment of the group? In the Asch-type of situation, subjects announce their judgment publicly before all the members of the group. In the Crutchfield situation, all subjects — each believing he or she is the last to report — are seated in separate stalls and communicate more discreetly, and somewhat more privately, by way of light switches. An interesting contrast between this method of studying conformity and the opinion-persuasion approach is that, in this case, the other people involved, whose responses construct the group's position, merely announce their judgment. There is no overt attempt at persuasion or conscious effort at coercion. It is an influence attempt simply by creating and presenting a group norm (Crano, 1975).

Anxiety. In a fairly relaxed and simple situation, anxious people should conform more because conformity is the easiest way to impose structure. Vaughan (1964) defined a high- and low-conforming group of people by examining the level of conformity that they had demonstrated on four very different tasks and subsequently had them complete a battery of objective tests. These tests showed the high-conforming people to be much more anxious than the low conformers, a finding similar to the marginal result noted by DiVesta and Cox (1960) and the significant result found by Steiner and Rogers (1963) for women. We return to Vaughan's study later in a discussion of other variables that distinguished between the two groups. Meunier and Rule (1967), using very mild initial success and failure experiences, reported that highly anxious people conform more than less anxious people; there were no interactions with the mild stress or success conditions. Steiner and Vannoy (1966) compared scores on the Manifest Anxiety scale for: (a) subjects who conformed in a laboratory situation and then later reaffirmed their conforming responses in a private situation with (b) those initially conforming subjects who later renounced their conforming responses in the follow-up private session. They showed that the more stable, conforming subjects had higher anxiety scores than did those whose conformity behavior was more transitory.

A very interesting experiment on conformity under pressure was done by Mangan, Quartermain, and Vaughan (1960). They modified the usual Asch procedure by having the first confederate hesitantly give a correct answer, only to be criticized strongly by the remaining confederates who argued for the incorrect response. Although this argument burst forth on only 6 of the 20 trials, we can imagine that the hostilities colored the emotional climate of the entire session. The results showed that the highly anxious subjects gave many fewer yielding responses than did the low-anxious subjects, who conformed at about the usual rate for subjects in the Asch situation (Asch, 1952). This apparent contradiction in the results, which we just discussed, is handled easily by McGuire's model. The discrepancy between sets of results disappears with the realization that the strong stress in the Mangan et al. study led the anxious people to institute defensive manuevers, which very likely caused them to reject the influence situation. In McGuire's words, the dispositional variable, which under relaxed conditions affects the yielding stage, under stress conditions affects the reception stage. This pattern not only extends throughout the research on social influence but is extremely valuable for understanding how anxious people function more generally in different types of groups.

Authoritarianism.   From the earliest work in this area, the complex trait of authoritarianism was thought to be an important personal disposition underlying influenceability. The description of the authoritarian personality syndrome, as portrayed by Adorno, Frenkel-Brunswik, Levinson, and Sanford (1950), emphasized the component of conformity and argued that this personality type is highly dependent on the structuring of events by others. Many studies have examined the effect of authoritarianism in the standard conformity situation and have produced an impressive collection of results that show all possible kinds of relationships. For example, in the study by Vaughan (1964) just discussed, both authoritarianism and dogmatism characterized the high conformers more than the low. Essentially similar results were reported by Beloff (1958), Canning and Baker (1959), Crutchfield (1955), Malof and Lott (1962), Nadler (1959), Smith, Murphy, and Wheeler (1964), Vaughan and White (1966), and Wells, Weinert, and Rubel (1956).

In a more complex experiment, Steiner and Johnson (1963) reported that authoritarians conformed more to two confederates who took the same position, as well as to one of the confederates in a condition where the confederates disagreed markedly. In a condition where the confederates disagreed only moderately, the nonauthoritarians agreed more with the confederate who gave the usually correct answer. Steiner and Johnson argued that it is unusual in the real world to find a situation where everyone else is in agreement. Their study shows that, in the face of strong disagreement, authoritarians select one person on whom to rely rather than trust their own judgment. No relationship was reported by Steiner and Vannoy (1966), discussed earlier, or by Gorfein (1961), Hardy (1957), and Weiner and McGinnies (1961).

Vidulich and Kaiman (1961) varied the status of the person making the judgment and, using dogmatism as a measure of authoritarianism in an autokinetic effect situation, found that closed-minded people agreed more with the higher status person, whereas open-minded people did not make a status distinction. Continuing this line of research, Moore and Krupat (1971) examined the finer distinction between two levels of positivity of the source. Comparing the levels of agreement produced by a mildly positive versus a highly positive source, they expected, following McGuire (1968), that authoritarians, who see the world in contrasting terms, would make less of a distinction between the two levels than would nonauthoritarians. Their results clearly reveal that nonauthoritarians respond much more strongly to this informational distinction than do authoritarians. This interaction between authoritarianism and source characteristics is discussed further in the section on personality and persuasion (cf. Nisbett & Gordon, 1967).

Self-Abasement.   Costanzo (1970) argued that people who think poorly of themselves or harshly evaluate their own behavior are more likely to conform to the standard set by the group. In an interesting developmental study using four groups of subjects ranging from a 7–8-year-old group to a 19–21-year-old group, he examined the relationship between scores of a self-blame test and performance in a Crutchfield-type apparatus. Costanzo found an extraordinarily high correlation between self-blame and conformity in all four age groups. Although Costanzo located his ideas on self-blame in terms of the characteristics of the low-self-esteem person, it is worth noting that his self-blame scale uses direct self-blaming statements rather than the usual absence of self-esteem statements. This procedure increases the likelihood that self-abasement is a peripheral personality variable in itself.

Two other studies offer minor support for this relationship. Appley and Moeller (1963), using a battery of objective tests, reported a positive correlation between scores on the self-abasement scale and conformity in a simple perceptual judgment task only for women (as did McDavid & Sistrunk, 1964). Endler (1961), however, did not find such a relationship. Finally, Hoffman (1953) examined the psychodynamic factors that underlie motivated conformity and found strong evidence of self-critical and self-punishing tendencies, along with many of the attributes of authoritarianism.

The Need for Approval.   The approval motive defends against anxiety by constructing a relationship in which the value of the other person is emphasized. Therefore, it is reasonable to expect that in most influence situations, a person concerned with the need for approval should yield to the judgment of others. This relationship was reported by Moeller and Applezweig (1957) in one of the earliest of the Asch-type studies. It was also seen to be one of the primary studies needed to validate the approval construct and scale. Strickland and Crowne (1962) used a tape-recorded version of the Asch situation to generate a conflict over the number of auditory stimuli heard and announced by three confederates and the subject's own judgment. As expected, people strongly concerned with the need for approval were found to yield more to the confederate's judgment than were people less concerned with this motive (see Crowne & Marlowe, 1964, for a review of related work). Back and Davis (1965) and Linton (1955), using the related constructs of other-directedness and field dependency, respectively, found a similar pattern of association. These results are especially striking because they require a low level of personal involvement. It is reasonable to expect even stronger levels of conformity in genuine face-to-face interactions in which the approval motive is more directly aroused.

The Need for Affiliation.   One important conclusion reached by many studying the process of social influence was that conforming behavior may be produced by many different individual factors. In the case of the variables from the safety-needs cluster, yielding to the group satisfies the individual's need for structure and thus temporarily reduces the subjective feeling of anxiety. On the other hand, for affiliation needs, a different motivational base appears to be involved. Those who have studied the effects of the need for affiliation stress the purposive nature of conformity and imitation. Overall, they argue that the need for affiliation includes a greater sensitivity to the opinions of others and a desire to be accepted by the group and be included in their activities. Such a person should yield more to the group judgment. Therefore, in many situations, the need for affiliation should predict the same kinds of results as the safety needs.

What appears to be the simplest and most reliable study was performed by McGhee and Teevan (1967). In a Crutchfield situation, they found that affiliation-motivated subjects conformed much more than did those not so motivated. This result confirms the earlier finding by Hardy (1957) that affiliation-motivated subjects conform when their judgment is set against that of the group. McDavid and Sistrunk (1964) found, in the experiment discussed earlier, that the high affiliation scores on the EPPS and the Guilford–Zimmerman test were associated with high levels of conformity. In a follow-up study, Sistrunk and McDavid (1965) also found that affiliation was positively related to conformity, as did Tuddenham (1959). However, Samelson (1958), in a TAT study that he felt might be flawed methodologically, did not find this relationship.

An interesting variation of this experiment was done by Hardy (1957). Together with the usual condition of setting the subject's judgment against that of the group, he added a condition in which, of six confederates, the confederate speaking two turns before the subject agreed with the previously determined position of the subject. Thus, when the subject had, in effect, an agreeing partner, the high-affiliation person was significantly less conforming than were those who were less concerned with this motive. In other words, the special social sensitivities of the affiliation-motivated person allowed him or her to focus on the one agreeing confederate and, perhaps through a limited coalition, to find a satisfactory way out of the dilemma that the Crutchfield situation produces. It is interesting to speculate, from the results of this single study, that the special concerns of the affiliation motive might lead to a much greater concern for coalition formation in a larger group situation.

Assertiveness.   In much of the early work on personality and social influence, there was the expectation that a number of variables reflecting psychological strength would make the person more independent of group pressure (e.g., Crutchfield, 1955; Tuddenham, 1959). We have seen an elementary form of this position in the study by Back and Davis, where the opposite end of the other-directedness scale was the global variable of inner-directedness. A number of more specific variables, most notably self-esteem, were included in many social influence studies and, by and large, confirmed this basic insight, especially on resistance to the yielding process. When additional aspects of the human environment were brought into the laboratory, the results became more complex. We review many of these studies in the next section on persuasion.

Two of the studies already presented (McDavid & Sistrunk, 1964; Vaughan, 1964) included a wide variety of self-report tests that purport to measure many different esteemlike variables. Although there are many inconsistencies by sex, test, and condition, the overall thrust of their results is quite clear: There is a reasonably strong negative relationship between the dominance, ascendancy, assertiveness type of variable and conformity. The results of studies by Helson, Blake, Mouton, and Olmstead (1956), deCharms and Rosenbaum (1960), Izard (1960), Moore and Krupat (1971),

Rosenbaum, Horne, and Chalmers (1962), and a marginally significant result by Kelman (1950) are also in line with this global finding. A few studies, which are reviewed in the next section (e.g., Gergen & Bauer, 1967), anticipated McGuire's line of reasoning and found a curvilinear relationship between levels of esteem and conformity under low and moderate levels of task difficulty.

The Need for Achievement.   From the earliest work on the need for achievement, independence training and independence of judgment were considered to be important parts of the motive syndrome. In the first book on achievement motivation (McClelland et al., 1953), a greater resistance to social pressure was considered to be part of the necessary validational work on the construct and the test. From his own studies, Asch made available the TAT records of a group of yielders and nonyielders which McClelland et al. then scored on the need for achievement. The results showed that nearly all the subjects above the median in need for achievement score were nonyielders. Samelson (1958) reported an unpublished study by Clark that found similar results, although he failed to replicate this finding in the usual Asch situation. Krebs (1958), using the TAT measure of the need for achievement, and DiVesta and Cox (1960), using a self-report achievement scale, both found a negative relationship in the Crutchfield situation. Sistrunk and McDavid (1965), using the same self-report achievement scale, also found the same negative relationship in the Crutchfield situation with easy tasks and, as McGuire would predict, found a positive relationship with difficult tasks.

In a more complex study, Zajonc and Wahi (1961) examined conformity to the content of the norm that is being stressed, rather than simply the general process of resistance to influence. They were able to demonstrate that when conformity is directly instrumental to achievement purposes, individuals concerned with the need for achievement show greater levels of conformity. Although there are few studies that examine the instrumental value of accepting an influence attempt, it is extremely likely that this aspect of the group process is very important in a real group.

Influenceability in the Persuasion Experiment

In the Asch and Crutchfield type of experiment, an influence attempt is made by simply presenting a group norm to different kinds of people. Janis (1954) undertook a series of studies on the psychological bases of persuasion using the more active technique developed at Yale (Hovland & Janis, 1959) to change people's opinions. The logic behind this type of experiment is exceedingly simple. A group of people is given several personality tests as well as attitude scales on some topic. They are then asked to read or listen to a statement about that topic, after which they again indicate their attitude. The change in opinion from the first to the second measurement is taken as the measure of susceptibility to the social influence attempt. This technique brought into the laboratory a very simple aspect of this group leader's role: the capacity to tell the membership what to believe about some particular topic. This more realistic approach to the study of those personality characteristics that make individuals susceptible to a direct influence attempt led to a pattern of results that is essentially similar to those obtained with more direct approaches.

Anxiety. An early study by Janis (1954) outlined many of the ideas that were to underlie the later work on personality and persuasibility. Based on work with a clinical group, Janis hypothesized that people who felt inadequate or depressed would be more disposed to be influenced than those who felt more capable in a social situation. Janis argued that the disturbed group would be more influenced because they would be less able to tolerate disapproval for disagreeing with the opinions held by others. However, Janis also believed that when anxiety appeared in a more acute form, associated with such disturbances as hypochondriacal complaints or obsessional ideas, a set of defenses would be used to protect the individual from contact with intruding social stimuli. These defenses, he believed, worked by reducing the attention, comprehension, and acceptance that they give to the communications received from others. Janis tested these ideas with a nonclinical group of college students, using a questionnaire as his measure of personality and the customary persuasion technique as his measure of susceptibility to influence. His results showed that what he called low esteem (which was essentially an anxiety measure), as well as depression, predisposed people to be more influenceable, whereas the strong defensive structures associated with acute anxiety led people to be more resistant to influence. These results were essentially replicated in a follow-up study (Janis, 1955), which showed neurotic anxiety to have some dampening effect on persuasibility, social anxiety to lead to greater degrees of persuasibility, and low test anxiety (which might be low self-confidence) to lower degrees of persuasibility (cf. Janis & Feshbach, 1954; Janis & Rife, 1959). Additionally, McGuire (1968) reported the results of a brief experiment which demonstrated that depression is negatively related to opinion change due to the effects of poor message reception. Janis' two hypotheses were integrated by McGuire (1968), as discussed earlier, to predict that the greatest amount of opinion change would occur at intermediate levels of anxiety, a theoretical prediction that has been demonstrated by Millman (1968) and Lehmann (1970).

Authoritarianism. The theoretical expectations concerning the way authoritarianism affects influenceability generally follow those outlined in our discussion of person perception. Individuals strongly dominated by authoritarian tendencies are expected to be especially sensitive to the status attributes of the people with whom they interact. This differential sensitivity is thought to lead authoritarians to be more readily influenced by authority figures, a prediction supported in an early experiment by Wagman (1955).

An early experiment by Berkowitz and Lundy (1957) attempted to explore whether people who are influenced more by authority figures than by peers differ in their personality characteristics. Berkowitz and Lundy expected that, by definition, authoritarian people would be influenced by higher status figures, whereas affiliation-oriented people would be influenced more by their peers. In addition, recognizing that cognitive structures as well as motives may be involved, they argued that people with a simple cognitive structure would be influenced more by authority figures as a means of more easily categorizing the information provided by the world. Their lucid discussion of the expected effects of these three personality characteristics on the influence process briefly stated the thinking that was to underlie much experimentation in this area of social psychology, as well as others. However, their results are exceedingly complex and serve to introduce the issues rather than resolve them.

Other studies continued to find an absence of a simple relationship between authoritarianism and persuasibility. A set of studies (Harvey & Beverly, 1961; Johnson & Steiner, 1967; Johnson, Torcivia, & Poprick, 1968; Mischel & Schopler, 1959) showed that low rather than high authoritarians were persuaded by credible information. The expected positive relationship between authoritarianism and persuasibility seems to occur only when the message is easy to comprehend (Johnson & Izzett, 1969; Klein, 1967) or when the authoritarian person is directly engaged in a personal encounter (Centers, Shomer, & Rodrigues, 1970; Harvey & Beverly, 1961), which is the closest persuasion situation to that devised by Asch to study conformity. Overall, however, the results of the authoritarianism programs are handled well by McGuire's model.

Predictions derived from elements of cognitive structure follow most of those for authoritarianism. This is to be expected because elements of closed-mindedness and cognitive simplicity are likely to be part of the cognitive element of the trait of authoritarianism. Results from several studies on dogmatism (e.g., Gold, Ryckman, & Rodda, 1973; Miller, 1965; Rotton, Blake, & Heslin, 1977) and cognitive complexity (Harvey, 1965) are often complex but follow, overall, the major outlines of McGuire's model. Miller and Rokeach (1968), Ehrlich and Lee (1969), and Bieri (1968) have written useful reviews of the research on the effects of these variables on persuasion.

Need for Approval.   People who are concerned with obtaining approval from others should be likely to agree with reasonable requests made upon them. Even more, they should look to external factors for the definition of socially acceptable beliefs, norms, and behavior. In the persuasion situation, especially if it is pleasant and nonthreatening, it is reasonable to expect that the need for approval will lead to relatively higher levels of acceptance of the opinions and attitudes suggested by the experiment.

In a complex and interesting experiment, Klein (1967) demonstrated that people who were consistently conforming (e.g., accepted the influence attempt) across a variety of tasks and situations scored higher on the Crowne–Marlowe test than did those people who accepted less degrees of influence. Smith and Flenning (1971), Buckhout (1965a, 1965b), and Martin and Greenstein (1983) similarly found the need for approval to predict susceptibiliity to influence, as did Centers and Horowitz (1963) for the related variable of other-directedness, continuing a line of research begun by Linton and Graham (1959) for field dependency. Skolnick and Heslin (1971), in a thoughtful study that showed great sensitivity to the situational parameters of the experiment, also showed that people with high scores on the Crowne–Marlowe scale are more persuasible than those with low scores. In addition, as part of the persuasibility complex, they showed that approval-oriented people do not distinguish between good and bad arguments (or high- and low-credible sources), whereas low-approval-oriented people do make the distinction. As McGuire's model suggests, there are situational conditions where the most rational response is to be persuaded. We should expect that more psychologically mature people can discriminate among situations in which it is appropriate to be persuaded.

Skolnick and Heslin's explanation of an apparently contradictory result by Miller, Doob, Butler, and Marlowe (1965) seems satisfactory in attributing it to the relatively unpersuasive nature of their experimental situation. This result also can be handled by McGuire's model, for there is no reason to expect nonapproval-oriented people to be influenced in an unpersuasive situation. A careful analysis of the characteristics of the situation permits this general model to handle two other apparently reversed sets of results reported by Greenbaum (1966) and Silverman, Ford, and Morganti (1966). For example, Greenbaum found that the most persuaded type of person (classifying people on the basis of approval and esteem sources) was the person with low need for approval and high self-esteem. This result appears to be directly opposite to our assumptions of the type of behavior expected from these variables. However, in a difficult, complex, and threatening experimental condition, such as existed in Greenbaum's experiment, it is just this type of person that McGuire proposed is able to receive the message best. If we extrapolate from this experiment to a real small group working under difficult conditions, it is possible that it is the more mature person that can join best with others in meeting the realistic demands of the task and, least defensively, accept legitimate direction from an authority.

Locus of Control.   The definition of external locus of control leads to a set of predictions that are very similar to those for the need for approval. In fact, the measurement of external locus of control, or the expectation that external events determine the course of one's life, is based on the person agreeing to statements that he or she is responsive to direct influence attempts. Thus, within the range of nonthreatening situations, we would expect that externals would be more affected than internals by attempts at persuasion.

This simple prediction was demonstrated by Hjelle and Clouser (1970) and Jenks (1978). In a straightforward precommunication–postcommunication comparison of attitudes, they showed that externals changed more than internals in the direction of the communication. In a somewhat more complex study, Biondo and MacDonald (1971) found essentially the same result, with an interesting trend in their results indicating that internals seemed to show a reactance effect in a strong influence condition. If this reactance trend is substantiated in future research, it may confirm the suggestion that a motivational "esteem" factor is also associated with the cognitive components of internal locus of control (cf. Phares, 1976).

More complex examinations of the effects of locus of control on persuasibility follow the overall pattern of results on personality and persuasion and show how important it is to know the situational context in which the influence attempt is made. Ritchie and Phares (1969) studied the effect of the prestige of the source in creating opinion change among internal and external people. In a straightforward experiment, they showed that externals were influenced more by high-prestige sources than they were by low-prestige sources. Similarly, they showed that externals were more influenced than were internals by the high-prestige source. In coordinating the results of this experiment with those already cited, it is important to realize that this experiment created a low-involvement context in which to respond to the task. It is very likely that more involving or more difficult situations — an experimental context that has not been used, to our knowledge — would complete the parallel set of results to match those for the other variables.

Affiliation.   Our review of the personality and persuasion literature failed to discover any substantial study in which the need for affiliation in the Asch–Crutchfield approach to conformity (a heightened sensitivity to the opinions of others) should lead to even greater degrees of persuasion, at least under nonthreatening conditions. Under such conditions, the need for affiliation probably would lead to results that parallel those for the need for approval, as indicated by the results of Burdick and Burnes' (1958) preliminary study. Within a threatening context, it is possible that affiliation-oriented people might function as do esteem-oriented people. In any case, we can speculate that the procedure usually employed to study persuasion might be too impersonal and not engage the need for affiliation, for the simple pre- to postcommunication comparison usually does not require personal contact.

Self-Esteem.   The early speculation that strong feelings of competence would make a person more resistant to influence (Hovland & Janis, 1959) stimulated a good deal of research whose contradictory results led to McGuire's (1968) model of personality and persuasion. A simple listing of results in this area would include nearly every form of relationship possible between self-esteem and persuasion, and an examination of the experimental procedure used in each of these studies allows them to be handled rather satisfactorily by McGuire's model.

Although systematic examination of the model has not yet been performed, the pattern of results seems fairly clear. The most direct test of parts of McGuire's theory was done by Nisbett and Gordon (1967), who examined the persuasive effects of two types of influence attempts. The first type provided a message that was easy to receive but difficult to yield to. In terms of events in a real group, the message was similar to the group's leader simply asserting, without proof, that some norm or procedure was true. The second influence attempt provided a message that was difficult to receive but easy to yield to. This message was similar to a leader outlining and evaluating, in full detail, all the reasons for adopting a procedure. In the first message, the reception and yielding properties were designed to achieve maximum influence on low-esteem people, whereas these properties in the second message were designed to achieve maximum influence on high-esteem people. Therefore, Nisbett and Gordon expected, and found, that most opinion change occurs at a lower level of self-esteem for the first message and at higher levels for the second. The basic logic of this approach is then clear: When the communicator uses an easily understood message, based on assertions of opinion rather than fact, from a nonobviously expert communicator in a fairly relaxed setting, a negative relationship is found. When these situational characteristics are reversed, a positive relationship is found. When intermediate levels are used, a curvilinear relationship is found (cf. Gergen & Bauer, 1967).

Additional pieces of evidence for this generalization are provided by Eagly (1967, 1969), Dabbs (1964), Greenbaum (1966), Lehmann (1970), Leventhal and Perloe (1962), Maile (1977), Silverman (1964), and Silverman et al. (1966). These experiments differ in certain respects, and although not all the results are precisely congruent with the model, a close reading of the procedure followed usually allows the experiment to be understood in terms of McGuire's model. For example, Dabbs showed that high-esteem people are influenced more by highly competent communicators, whereas low-esteem people are influenced more by the less threatening, less competent communicators. Even studies that show no relationship (e.g., Zellner, 1970) are often understandable when the nature of the experimental sample is considered. This experiment used high school boys who answered an advertisement in *The New York Times*. High school boys who even read *The New York Times* are hardly a representative sample of the population. In other words, when the subject population provides a restricted range, skewed to the high end of the self-esteem distribution, we should not expect to find the self-esteem variable predictive of different levels of persuasibility.

Machiavellianism. Studies comparable to those for esteem have not been done to examine the mediating effects of Machiavellianism on persuasibility. A few studies (cf. Christie & Geis, 1970) have generally supported the expectations that high scorers on the Machiavellianism scale are less persuasible than low scorers. If we think of Machiavellianism as part of the esteem cluster, then all else being equal, Machiavellians should be more certain of their own position and thus more resistant to influence attempts. A study by Burgoon, Lombardi, Burch, and Shelby (1979) provided an additional piece of evidence, similar to the esteem pattern, showing the non-Machiavellians could be threatened by authority-based assertions and resist influence under this condition.

Two additional studies (Burgoon, Miller, & Tubbs, 1972; Epstein, 1969) examined a more extended form of this hypothesis in experiments using counterattitudinal role playing. In both studies, Machiavellians seemed more persuaded by factual arguuments, and non-Machiavellians seemed much more affected by the dissonance-producing characteristics of the role playing. All of these studies focus on the self-certainty characteristic of Machiavellians. Although this is very important for understanding their behavior in social interaction, the defining quality of deceit and manipulativeness in Machiavellians is discusssed in later chapters as it affects broader aspects of group process.

Responses to More Active Sources of Influence

In a real group, the simplest issue underlying members' responsiveness to a leader is whether they accept direction. Examination of other issues (e.g., which member becomes the follower, the way a directive is carried out, or the contribution that followers make to the outcomes of the group) all assume a clear understanding of the mechanisms through which social influence is accepted. In each of the studies using the procedures reviewed in this chapter, a social norm is presented to people, and the experiment examines the conditions under which they follow this elementary form of social guidance. At this point, the weight of the evidence from these studies provides a reasonably clear picture of the mechanisms through which dispositional characteristics contribute to the acceptance of social influence.

Before turning to the larger forms of social interaction that are based on this process, it is useful to review the small number of high focused influence studies that are closer in nature to the kind of events that take place in a real group. These conformity studies use more active forms of social interaction, examine more behavioral responses to the influence attempt, and so provide a useful bridge from the rigor of the conformity laboratory to the actual form that responses to social influence take in more extended social events.

Modeling.   The behavior of other group members is a powerful source of information on how the task is to be completed. Whether we think of such behavior as providing cues that indicate the type of behavior that will be successful or as establishing normative patterns that must be followed, each mechanism reduces uncertainty by defining the situation for the viewer. The social influence processes already discussed seem adequate to explain the somewhat larger set of events studied under the heading of modeling and imitative behavior.

An experiment by Sarason, Pederson, and Nyman (1968) shows how the observation of others influences social behavior. They hypothesized that anxiety leads people to become more active cue users because they do not have a satisfactory repertoire of adaptive responses. Because earlier work (Sarason & Harmatz, 1965) on the role of reinforcement in verbal learning showed that highly anxious subjects were more favorably affected by praise from the experimenter, Sarason et al. felt that the performance of anxious people would be facilitated by opportunities to observe a model. Their results, using a large number of experimental conditions, showed that the most anxious subject's performance was the one that benefited most from the modeling cues provided in the observational conditions.

Although the Sarason et al. experiment specifically examined the effect of modeling on the level of performance, two other experiments investigated its effect on the content of the imitated behavior. Brannigan and Duchnowski (1976) studied the effects of the need for approval on the imitative behavior of fifth-grade children. They asked each child to watch a short film in which a model (either a child or an adult) used building blocks to construct a farm scene and then asked the child to use the same kind of blocks to build anything the child wanted. Imitative behavior was determined by counting the frequency with which each child used the behaviors provided by the film. Results of this experiment showed that high approval-motivated children were more imitative than low, although only in the peer model condition. In a somewhat similar experiment, Akamatsu and Thelen (1977) found that highly anxious people imitated more than less anxious people under low-information conditions. There was no difference due to anxiety in the high-information condition. In addition, in chapter 10 we describe an experiment by Wilson (1976), which showed that safety-oriented men and women model active bystanders in an emergency situation against their usual predilection to remain passive.

Taken together, these four experiments fit nicely into the larger picture of the social influence process and bring that framework somewhat closer to events in real groups. However, their conclusions are only suggestive, and they make it apparent that a wide range of studies is needed in order to understand the relationship between personality and modeling more fully. It would be especially useful to have a series of studies that examines the conditions under which variables from the esteem cluster affect the modeling process (see Wilson & Petruska, 1984, which is described in chap. 10).

Obedience.   The clearest form of leadership is the statement of a direct instruction; the simplest form of followership is compliance with that command. It is difficult to study this isolated element in the fluid sets of interactions that take place in real groups. A few studies, however, approximate this aspect of a natural situation. A study by Elms and Milgram (1966) followed upon a round of the basic research in Milgram's classic studies of obedience. Men who had proven themselves to be either obedient or defiant to an authoritative command to give high-voltage shocks were asked to return for a follow-up interview at which they were administered a set of personality scales. The most interesting result of this analysis was the clear picture of the obedient person as much more authoritarian than the defiant person. In many ways, Elms and Milgram's study is also a fine validational study of Adorno et al.'s claim of the authoritarian's tendency to submit to authority. In a similar study, Larsen, Lancaster, Lesh, Redding, White, and Larsen (1976) found the same results for dogmatism, low self-esteem, and approval motivation, although not for locus of control. A minor note in Elms and Milgram's paper indicates something of the paradoxical nature of this syndrome and the need for a broader interactional model: All the subjects who declined the request to return for the interview had been classified experimentally as "obedient" subjects.

Several other studies show that certain dispositions lead individuals to be highly influenced by another form of instruction, namely, the definition of the situation provided by the experimenter. McLaughlin and Hewitt (1972) formed discussion groups with two high- and two low-approval-motivated members in each group. Half of the groups were given instructions that defined "being open" as the optimum form of interpersonal behavior. In the course of the 45-minute discussion, approval-motivated people who had received these instructions were the only type to show an increase in emitting this type of behavior. Somewhat similar results were found by Cohen and Teevan (1974) and Wright and Harvey (1965) for the variables fear of failure and authoritarianism, respectively. All these studies show that a broad range of safety-related variables leads people to be extremely sensitive to the demand characteristics of the experiment and to utilize the cues or instructions provided to guide their efforts at impression management. Unfortunately, we know of no study in which an esteem-related variable (e.g., the need for recognition), which could be expected to produce a similar effect, has been used.

Opinion Change.   We are aware of three experiments that study the effect of individual characteristics on the process of opinion change after the course of an extended interaction. Although the results of these studies fit nicely into the general persuasion framework, it is useful to classify them separately in order to bring the persuasion studies a bit closer to the events in a real group. Frye and Bass (1963) had groups of five subjects discuss a set of human relations problems. Before the discussion, subjects ranked five alternative solutions to each problem; following the discussion, they came to a group consensus and then ranked their individual preferences a second time. The results of this experiment showed that within a group, the high scorer on the social acquiescence scale tended to accept the group's decision more readily. In a somewhat related experiment, Jones and Shrauger (1968) found essentially similar results for external locus of control.

In a much more extended interaction, Ward and Wilson (1980) had women resolve a difficult moral dilemma either alone or in a three-person mock jury group. Each group was arranged so that one confederate initially argued for acquittal and a second confederate argued for conviction. Later, both confederates argued against the subject. This experiment was interested in the degree to which motives affected the degree of adaptation to social pressure. Subjects were classified by safety or esteem needs, as well as by their level of moral development (as defined by Kohlberg's theory). They were formed into four comparison groups by combining safety and esteem needs with stage three (conventional) and stage five (postconventional) levels of moral development. Subjects in each of the four comparison groups were asked to resolve the moral dilemmas either by themselves or by debating them within the group. Within the group setting, both confederates used level two (instrumental exchange) characteristics of moral reasoning. The pressure from the confederates was expected to cause safety-oriented people to imitate the level of reasoning used by the confederates much more strongly than would esteem-oriented people. The major finding was that esteem-oriented people consistently used their typical style of moral reasoning, whether they were alone or under attack in a group. In contrast, safety-oriented people under social pressure changed the type of moral reasoning that they used when they were alone so that it would conform more closely to the type of moral reasoning used by the source of social pressure. These results showed that when people were confronted with the problem when alone, their motives were not engaged, and so they used their typical style of moral reasoning (i.e., either pre- or postconventional). It was only when their motives were engaged by the situation that motives had a mediating effect on the nature of their reasoning. Thus, although not the usual attitude-change study, these results show that when confronted by strong social pressure in a face-to-face situation, safety-oriented persons may change the nature of the cognitive schema they use in order to reduce unpleasant states of emotional arousal.

SUMMARY

We have reviewed a great deal of evidence in this chapter to reach a simple conclusion. As human beings grapple with the demands of the task, they try to establish a way of relating to each other that is congruent with their psychological needs, the demands of the task, and the characteristics of the situation. Our early summary phrase — that some of the members of a group attend to, agree with, and carry out the suggestions or directions given by other members — captures the first important dimension of the group process needed to accomplish the group's goals. The extended sets of research that have been presented seem to confirm the theoretical position that there are consistent dispositional foundations to the initiation–concurrence dimension of group process. Under most conditions, esteem-related variables seem to lead people to produce behavior that initiates social events, whereas safety-related variables seem to lead people to produce behavior that encourages and supports these initiatives. In addition, this review has shown that this dimension, especially the concurrence category of behavior, is susceptible to marked interaction effects with situational and task variables that can change the outcome dramatically.

However, this generalization falls short of the complexity of initiation or concurrence behavior that can be predicted on theoretical grounds. In chapter 5, we predicted that a different combination of concrete behaviors — of the kind listed in Table 5.4 — could be expected from each of the personality variables. It is possible that if a satisfactory base of research describing these performance styles was available, we would not be in the position of predicting global forms of initiation or concurrence behavior from a host of apparently different antecedents. How much more interesting it would be to contrast the type of social directions that are given by a dominance-oriented person with those given by an achievement-oriented person. Similarly, how much less simplistic it would be if we knew the different ways that an achievement-oriented person encourages and supports the leader as compared to a dependencey-oriented person. There are two classic studies, by Haythorn, Couch, Haefner, Langham, and Carter (1956a, 1956b) that provide a first set of data for the types of emergent social roles created by authoritarian or nonauthoritarian people. From the beginnings of modern small-group research (e.g., Borgatta, Cottrell, & Mann, 1958; Carter, Haythorn, Meirowitz, & Lanzetta, 1951; Carter, Haythorn, Shriver, & Lanzetta, 1951), information at this level of precision has seemed to be the best way to define the social roles in the group. If these kinds of data were available, we would not only be able to define many different kinds of leaders and followers clearly, but many other social roles as well (cf. Benjamin, 1984; Wiggins, 1980).

10 The Affiliative–Disaffiliative Dimension of Group Process

Most theories of interpersonal behavior describe the affiliation–disaffiliation axis as the second important dimension of social behavior (Wiggins, 1980). The kinds of activity that Borgatta (see Table 5.4) and others identified as the behaviors that comprise this dimension range from affiliative acts (e.g., social sensitivity, altruism, warmth, friendliness, love, compassion, loyalty, nurturance, cooperation, generosity, and kindness) at one pole to the other extreme of disaffiliative behavior (e.g., hostility, brutality, aggression, derision, cruelty, refusal to provide assistance, avoidance, and withdrawal from the common task). Our goal in this chapter is to identify which characteristics of the person influence the interpersonal behaviors that make up this dimension of social interaction.

In social psychology, affiliative behavior is usually studied in the research programs on cooperation and prosocial behavior. Staub (1978), the authoritative reviewer of studies on prosocial behavior, notes that positive social behavior is simply defined as "behavior that benefits other people. To behave in such a way a person has to understand another's needs, desires or goals and acts to fulfill them" (p. 2). Similarly, cooperation in the experimental context is often broadly thought of as interpersonal behavior that is beneficial to others as well as to oneself (Cartwright & Zander, 1968). In using these definitions, it is important to recognize the distinction that needs to be made between the act and the intent of the act. For example, affiliative behavior may appear as the result of a person's desire to be protected by, be intimate with, dominate over, or solve tasks with another person. Although the motivational determinants of acts on the affiliative–disaffiliative dimension may vary greatly, this chapter focuses upon this common set of behaviors to which these different dispositions may contribute.

In describing the empirical work on the affiliative dimension of interpersonal behavior, it is important to recognize that most of the research on affiliative behavior comes from the study of prosocial behavior. There is comparatively less written on the relationship of personality variables to disaffiliative actions or to the wider range of affiliative acts that Borgatta describes. Of necessity, we base much of our discussion on the results from the analysis of prosocial behavior. Wherever possible, we examine disaffiliative acts, the most common of which is the absence of responding in situations where action could have produced a positive interpersonal outcome.

Based on a comprehensive review of the literature, Staub (1978) attempted to develop a theoretical framework that could include both personality and situational variables in an interactional model of prosocial behavior. Unlike the important theoretical models of Latane' and Darley (1970) or Schwartz (1977), which focus on the sequence of mechanisms involved in an individual's recognition and response to an emergency, Staub did not propose a detailed decision-making scheme. Rather, with his point of departure being that personality characteristics underlie most forms of social behavior, Staub maintained that "to make accurate predictions [of positive behavior] we have to measure (a) the intensity and/or relative importance of personal goals and (b) the activating potential of situations for personal goals" (p. 50). As we have argued, an interactionist model of behavior must have as clear a conceptualization of situations as it has of personality. After reviewing the research literature on prosocial behavior, Staub (1978) proposed that the stimulus dimensions of situations can be conceptualized according to their effects on persons. In applying his classification of stimulus dimensions to helping situations, Staub identified 10 relevant situational attributes: (a) ambiguity of need for help; (b) type of help required: responsive or self-initiated; (c) severity of need; (d) stimulus intensity or "impact" of stimulus for help; (e) material costs for helping; (f) responsibility focus on bystanders; (g) situational rules; (h) competing task demands; (i) role relationship to victim and others; (j) psychological state in bystanders.

Staub argued that these situational attributes interact with the personal goals of the bystander to determine the relative degree of prosocial action. It is interesting to see how close Staub's description of the set of situational variables needed to explain prosocial behavior comes to those that we argued constitute the social situation that affects all social activity (see part I). This detailed analysis of the situation allows us to approach the examination of affiliative–disaffiliative behavior in a more complex, interesting, and hopefully, accurate way. More specifically, we can use this discussion to illustrate a point of view that is likely to be applicable to many other kinds of social events. Rather than view prosocial behavior (as well as many other forms of behavior) as the consequence of a specific disposition, we can explore the much more detailed pattern of interaction between specific features of the person and the situation.

Staub's model provides a general paradigm for the study of affiliative behavior and, together with the seminal work of Latane' and Darley (1970) and Schwartz (1977), which describes the decision-making stages through which a prosocial act is selected, allows us to construct a more accurate person-by-situation model of affiliative behavior. In coordinating Staub's analysis of the emergency situation with the general model of a situation presented in chapter 4, we need to focus on: (a) the level of stressors present in the physical environment; (b) the status, competence, role relationship, and level of prosocial action of others; and (c) the dimensions of the task. As operationalized for the emergency situation, the task dimensions include their: difficulty (the various material and psychological costs for involvement); complexity (the type of action required and the number of competing task demands and personal goals); ambiguity (the lack of clarity in the need for help); and importance (the severity of the need).

When examining research in this area, it is useful to consider the way each of these situational and task variables is brought into the social context of the experiment. This is especially important because it has been found that high levels of stress or threat can depress prosocial responding in persons with different personality characteristics. For example, Staub (1978) has noted that prosocial action is significantly reduced when there are high levels of cost, threat, ambiguity, difficulty, and complexity in a situation. Fortunately, most events in the real world do not possess such high levels of stress. In most, although not all, of the experimental studies as well, the overall degree of threat is usually set at no worse than a moderate level. Although the forms of distress range from a minor need (e.g., a lost contact lens) to a major medical concern (e.g., an apparent epileptic seizure), these studies typically occur in laboratories located in academic buildings on attractive campuses where the subject participates with fellow students of about the same status and background. There are generally few competing tasks to do when an emergency occurs within a moderately ambiguous situation (e.g., a smoke-filled room) which is of relatively low cost to the bystander (in terms of time, energy, well-being). In these studies, the subject can respond easily and quickly in the proximity of an experimenter on whom rests the ultimate responsibility and legal liability for the experimental situation. In the absence of overpowering situational presses, it is likely that the typical experimental situation is of sufficient intensity and realism to engage, but not overpower, motives within the person that are theoretically relevant to prosocial action.

THE PATTERN OF INTERACTION

As with most forms of social activity, the person must perceive a need for action, form a set of attributions about the other people involved in the situation, and process varying amounts of information about likely outcomes before deciding whether or not to act. By beginning our analysis of affiliative behavior with a review of these mechanisms, we can use the analysis presented in part II to help explain a significant aspect of group process. The evidence reviewed in part II strongly supports the types of interactive propositions made possible by the detailed sequential decision-making models of prosocial behavior such as Schwartz's (1977). These models, together with Staub's, help us understand how motives influence the decision-making steps activated by those external events and lead to positive or negative socioemotional behavior. Even more, the analysis to be presented can be extended to most other, more long-term interactions that compose group process.

Let us examine a likely course of events that would lead to such activity. First, many situations are sufficiently interesting, challenging, or novel to create some degree of emotional arousal. Thus, during the activation stage (Schwartz, 1977), the person begins an active information search by scanning the environment for cues to use in problem solving. If others are present, the person may engage in a process of social comparison, especially in ambiguous situations where there is a lack of clarity about the event. By observing the behavior of others, the person may obtain information that can clarify how they are to respond to the event.

The activation stage of decision making may have properties that can arouse the bystander's motives or emotions. For safety-oriented people, the recognition that helpful behavior may be required is likely to arouse anxiety to the point where it can inhibit the person's willingness to act. In many cases, this recognition may lead them to experience great conflict, because they may also be aware of a normative obligation to intervene on behalf of someone else. However, because their anxiety may outweigh their sense of responsibility, they may feel it safer not to respond, even though they might possess the physical ability to do so. Thus, it is likely that the negative emotional arousal and the perceived uncertainty of proper action will activate a motive-specific response pattern. The safety-oriented person searches for the set of responses that will bring relief from the discomfort caused by anxiety. In Schwartz's (1975) terms, the perceived potential costs for helping may be high even if a prosocial norm is activated and made salient to the individual.

The psychological costs for safety-oriented people come from the experience of an uncontrollable and unpredictable situation, which can be created by such events as a strange environment, an injury to a stranger, or the need for immediate action. From this perspective, such psychological costs can be thought of as stressor variables that are cognitively processed in defensive ways, reviewed in chapter 7, in order to reduce the perceived situational threat. If bystanders provide easily understood cues as to response alternatives that seem effective in coping with the situation, the safety-oriented individual is likely to attend to them as a means of deciding on their own response. By modeling other's actions, they can reduce anxiety and uncertainty about the consequences of responding in a particular way. Further, the perceived cost for helping may be offset by a high degree of environmental or social structuring such that rendering assistance requires minimal risks. Thus, well-defined roles and norms and easy access to people or things that facilitate helping responses all reduce the perceived unpredictability and uncontrollability of a given situation. Under these special conditions, we would expect moderately higher rates of prosocial behavior from safety-oriented individuals.

In contrast, the affiliation- and esteem-oriented individual does not feel overly anxious when confronted with a situation in which help is needed. Instead, the emotional arousal seems to be effectively channeled into a problem-solving strategy. For affiliation-oriented individuals, their involvement in others makes them both more sensitive to the needs of others and more rewarded by helpful or cooperative behavior. The esteem-oriented person, who has a greater degree of certainty about his or her own ability to initiate some action that will be efficacious, may view the multiplicity of choices not as a set of unpredictable factors, but rather as alternative modes of task-related responding. Because esteem-oriented people believe that they can act to influence the outcome of the situation, they are less likely to model bystanders in a situation, unless the bystanders were demonstrating superior competence related to the problem in question. Furthermore, in a somewhat unpredictable and uncontrollable situation, we can expect affiliation- and esteem-oriented persons to seek information actively in order to respond most effectively to the emergency confronting them. As we saw in part II, safety-oriented individuals tend to avoid or approach others cautiously, both verbally and nonverbally, unless the attributes of others, task instructions, or situational cues reduce their fears. In contrast, many of the affiliation- and esteem-oriented motives lead individuals to approach others and actively engage them through smiles, verbal exchanges, friendly nonverbal gestures, physical contact, and collaborative work. These motive-related differences in modes of social behavior will share a strong effect on the range of behaviors the person can exhibit on the affiliative–disaffiliative axis, especially in terms of prosocial behavior.

This analysis of motive-based differences in the potentiality for affiliative or disaffiliative behavior enables us to construct our specific hypotheses. For the set of variables that falls in the safety-needs cluster, we expect that because of their reliance on others for support and direction, dependent persons are likely to be friendly, but also passive and express relatively low frequencies of overt affiliative behavior. The person with a strong need for approval should manifest moderate levels of positive socioemotional behavior in situations where there are clear, explicit cues on how to affiliate without fear of rejection. However, situations that are ambiguous, stressful, and threatening should lead to low levels of affiliative behavior because they would arouse anxiety and defensive operations. For the person with abasement needs, we expect high levels of hostility and disaffiliation in situations where they can command power over subordinates. Further, their character-based rigidity would preclude the empathic forms of relating that could lead to a helpful response under normal conditions. Similarly, because persons with strong needs for order are defensively task oriented and neither actively affiliative nor disaffiliative, we expect that they will be moderately affiliative under conditions of low stress, ambiguity, and when working with others who model competent and efficacious behaviors of an affiliative sort.

The affiliation motive includes both strong concern with interpersonal involvement and strength when confronting at least moderate levels of situational stress. For these reasons, we expect the affiliation motive to lead to high levels of affiliative behavior, low rates of negative socioemotional interaction, and a strong disposition to act prosocially.

As a general hypothesis, we expect psychologically stronger persons to be realistically aware of the range of affiliative behaviors that are possible in social encounters. This implies an ability to appraise events correctly and not to distort or deny aspects of a situation that are unpleasant, emotionally arousing, or threatening. As discussed in previous chapters, a sense of inner control, competence, and self-confidence enables a person to initiate actions that effectively meet the challenges raised by diverse interpersonal events. Also, such people should find successful involvement to be rewarding. We would expect that persons possessing high self-esteem, autonomy, an internal locus of control, dominance, strong needs for achievement, nurturance or recognition, and higher levels of moral judgment to be more affiliative than are individuals characterized by the absence, or opposite, of such dispositions. Thus, we expect self-confident, assertive individuals who are striving for mastery to seek to demonstrate social competence on the affiliation-disaffiliation axis of behavior as well, if the task requires it. The exception to this prediction is for the trait of Machiavellianism, because it is associated with exploitativeness and self-enhancement. However, we believe that Machiavellianism will be associated with affiliative behaviors if such people believe that the appearance of prosocial, affiliative, or cooperative behaviors is in their self-interest.

THE EMPIRICAL STUDIES

Anxiety and Insecurity

As we have seen, anxiety interferes with many aspects of social functioning (Sarason, 1980). Anxious people are especially likely to be vulnerable in situations in which there are unexpected interpersonal events, threats, hostility, or a demand for effective action. Such stressful experiences should cause anxious people to withdraw from the field as the safest response, and when withdrawal is difficult, as in the laboratory, anxious people should retreat into passivity. Thus, anxiety should be inversely associated with the rendering of assistance, unless the situation is especially calm or there are many explicit cues about how to help at a low psychological cost to the person.

This relationship has been shown in many ways. Turner (1948), in a field study of adolescent boys, found that a number of maladjustment indicators were negatively related to altruism (which, in this study, was operationally defined to include a wide range of positive affiliative behaviors). Similar results were found by Cattell and Horowitz (1952), who found that paranoid tendencies were negatively associated with altruism among college women. In an experimental investigation of this hypothesis, Wagner, Manning, and Wheeler (1971) assigned anxious and nonanxious naval recruits to experimental conditions that varied a number of different situational factors, such as the cost for helping. In this study, cooperation was defined as the recruit's acting to assist a peer to correct a malfunction on a submarine simulator board. Consistent with expectations, when costs were high, anxious recruits were less helpful than they were when costs were low. Nonaxious recruits, in contrast, were much less affected by the different levels of cost provided in the experiment. In a later experimental study extending these ideas, McGovern (1976) also found that anxious people were much less willing to help than were nonanxious people.

Gergen, Gergen, and Meter (1972) offer a complex set of results examining the hypothesis that the nature of the intrinsic rewards provided by different types of altruistic behavior determines which dispositional factors become involved with any particular type of altruism. The results of this study demonstrated many of their predicted relationships, such as the fact that the need for abasement was negatively correlated with volunteering to counsel high school students, whereas dependency (in men) was positively related to this form of giving help. Overall, the results of this study do not lead to an easy generalization, which was the theoretical intent of the study.

Four recent studies have been designed to test aspects of a complex interactional model. In these studies, the influence of safety (and esteem) needs, broadly defined, has been examined as they affect helping behavior in bystander-intervention situations. These studies are discussed in detail at the end of this chapter. However, it should be noted here that in each of the studies the subject was required to render direct help to a victim who had either dropped books, lost a contact lens, or been exposed to an apparent laboratory accident. Overall, the results confirmed the hypothesis that: (a) the anxiety of safety-oriented persons inhibited prosocial behavior, and (b) if provided with bystanders during the emergency, they would imitate the behavior of the bystanders in either an affiliative or disaffiliative way.

Authoritarianism

The definition of the trait of authoritarianism has generally included the tendency to displace hostility onto moral outgroups as well as to defend against anxiety by establishing deferential attitudes toward high-status authority figures. For these reasons, authoritarian persons should manifest a general disaffiliative orientation: We expect them to generate acts of aggression, criticism, and moralistic judgment. Further, we expect that when the nature of the situation reduces stress, reduces the costs for acting positively toward others, or includes active and competent high-status models, the authoritarian individual will be better able to act in empathic, considerate, and prosocial ways. Unfortunately, we have not been able to locate studies that have systematically tested the conditions that increase or decrease the affiliative behaviors of authoritarians. However, there are several studies that do examine the interpersonal behavior of authoritarians in a variety of experimental situations, and together, these studies help us to understand their response tendency on this axis of behavior.

Prosocial Behavior.   We have found few studies that examine the relationship of authoritarianism to prosocial behavior. Friedrichs (1960) reported that authoritarianism was positively correlated with self-report measures of altruism among college students. However, in this same sample, because ethnocentrism was negatively correlated with this measure of prosocial tendencies (ethnocentrism and authoritarianism are usually highly correlated), the results appear puzzling, as Krebs (1970) notes. In addition, in their classic study of a simulated epileptic seizure, Latane' and Darley (1970) also failed to obtain a significant correlation between authoritarianism and intervention in an emergency situation, although in this case, the personality variables were measured after the gripping experimental procedure.

Disposition to Aggression.   There have been only a few studies reported which examine the prediction that authoritarianism leads to a generalized expression of hostility. For example, in an experimental learning task, Dustin and Davis (1967), show that authoritarians are much more likely than nonauthoritarians to use negative sanctions rather than rewards to improve the performance of a follower. Friedell (1968) and Raden (1980) also report that authoritarianism increases a subject's tendency to be aggressive in an experimental situation. Lipetz and Ossorio (1967), however, report only minor indications of support for a related hypothesis. Other studies have typically located this hypothesis in terms of a specific social condition. In an interesting experiment concerned with the effects of pain on learning, Epstein (1965) investigated the effects of authoritarianism on a subject's willingness to administer painful electric shocks to people who varied in social status. The results of this study showed both a general tendency of authoritarians to be more aggressive than nonauthoritarians, as well as a tendency for authoritarians to give stronger electric shocks to the low-status learner than to the high-status learner. In contrast, the low-authoritarian subjects displayed more aggression to the high-status participant. In a second, more complex study, Epstein (1966) also found that authoritarians were more aggressive than nonauthoritarians and imitated more the level of aggression set by a higher status model. It did not, however, replicate the original finding that authoritarians were more aggressive to lower status targets. Similar patterns of results were reported by Roberts and Jessor (1958) and Thibaut and Riecken (1955), who suggest that authoritarians inhibit their expression of aggression toward high-status persons and direct it to low-status individuals.

Punishment of Deviants: The Mock Jury Experiments. The disaffiliative tendency of authoritarians has also been studied in mock jury experiments. In these studies, interest has focused on the hypothesis that authoritarians would tend to find defendants guilty in legal cases and impose a more severe sentence for a crime. Mitchell and Byrne (1973) had students read a case involving a fellow student who was accused of stealing an examination from the duplicating room of an academic department the day before the class examination. In constructing the description of the student, based on pretesting of the subject's attitudes, the Byrne interpersonal attraction paradigm was used to create the impression that the defendant was either entirely similar or dissimilar to the subject. The results indicated that when the accused student was portrayed as dissimilar to them, authoritarians were more likely to convict and recommend a more severe punishment. However, when the student was perceived as similar, the more authoritarian student did not recommend a more severe punishment than did the egalitarian students. It is interesting that this is the one study in Byrne's program that showed an effect for authoritarianism (see chap. 8). In commenting on this fact, Mitchell and Byrne conclude that this effect may appear in this situation because there is an acceptable target and an arousing set of information. It is also possible that this situation makes the attitudinal information so salient that it is difficult for the authoritarians to distort, as we speculated in chapter 8.

Berg and Vidmar (1975) continued this line of research, using the same basic procedure as Mitchell and Byrne, but varying the status attributes of the defendant. As described in chapter 7, Berg and Vidmar also tested the hypothesis that authoritarians would show selective recall of information about the defendant's character rather than the situational context of the alleged crime. In support of previous results, they found that authoritarians were generally more punitive toward the low-status defendant. The selective recall hypothesis was also supported, and confirmed the tendency of authoritarians to scan others for information pertaining to status and moral character. Nearly identical results were reported by Garcia and Griffitt (1978b), who asked students to write down what they could recall from media accounts of the Patty Hearst trial. They found that authoritarian subjects remembered more of the evidence that supported the contentions of the prosecution than did nonauthoritarian persons. Taken together, the results of these two studies suggest that authoritarians may be hypervigilant in searching for cues in others which provide information regarding status and the degree to which the person adheres to conventional values.

Similarly, Bray and Noble (1978) found that authoritarians were more punitive when functioning as jurors in a simulated trial and that they reached guilty verdicts more often than did the less authoritarian people. Moran and Comfort (1982) reached similar conclusions in a follow-up study of members of real juries. Parallel findings were reported for dogmatic subjects by Foley and Chamblin (1982). In a more complex analysis of the authoritarian's disposition to condemn and punish deviants, Garcia and Griffitt (1978a) presented subjects with two cases for deliberation. The first case described an unambiguous depiction of deliberate sexual abuse of a child by an adult. The second case depicted the physical abuse of a child who was repetitively disobedient to a parent. The authors hypothesized that the authoritarian would be punitive to the incest offender because such conduct would be considered immoral and condemnable. However, in the case of physical abuse, it was predicted that the authoritarian would not be punitive because obedience to authority and the use of corporal punishment are attitudinally congruent with authoritarianism. The result supported the hypothesis and provides an excellent illustration of the interaction between authoritarianism and the selective use of situational variables to determine the level of punishment expressed in an interpersonal context.

Disaffiliative Behavior in Groups.   Although authoritarianism has been studied in relation to many forms of interpersonal and group behavior, there is only one study that has specifically assessed the affiliative and disaffiliative behaviors of authoritarians in active, task-oriented groups (Haythorn, Couch, Haefner, Langham, & Carter, 1956a). This study was composed of groups that varied the distribution of participants' level of authoritarianism. Using Carter's (1951) behavioral coding scheme, Haythorn et al. found that the authoritarian groups had fewer positive acts (e.g., fewer agreements, more acts of self-isolation and withdrawal, less group participation in decision-making, and more tension). The findings of this study provide a good illustration of the natural interpersonal behavior of authoritarians in a situation that placed few experimental constraints on their behavior and provide us with concrete evidence of the activity of authoritarians along the affiliation–disaffiliation axis of interpersonal behavior.

The Need for Approval

Because the definition of the need for approval states that such people seek to reduce their anxiety by establishing an admiring relationship with others, this variable should be associated with many forms of affiliative behavior. In terms of the specific behaviors presented in Table 5.4, the approval-oriented person is expected to exhibit high levels of friendliness, empathy, consideration, social sensitivity, and understanding. However, we also hypothesize that they do not possess the ability to ameliorate situations of interpersonal conflict. Thus, low-stress and low-threat conditions should lead approval-motivated persons to be most responsive to cues that would signal it is safe to initiate affiliation actions. In contrast, they should not feel comfortable in situations of potential threat, especially because they tend to deny anxiety-provoking experiences or hostile impulses. (See Strickland, 1977, for a valuable discussion of the possible mechanisms by which the need for approval may inhibit the expression of hostility.)

The available research of the kind being considered in this chapter elicits affiliative behavior in moderately stressful conditions and indicates that the need for approval is unrelated to intervention in emergencies (Benson, Wright, & Riordan, 1978; Midlarsky & Midlarsky, 1973). In an interesting study with fourth-grade children, Staub and Sherk (1970) showed that the need for approval was negatively correlated with sharing candy. Their conclusion identifies the specific type of disaffiliative behavior that can be expected from approval-motivated people: "In a situation where the norms for appropriate behavior are not clear, such children may remain inactive in order to avoid disapproval" (p. 251). There is one study which tested the hypothesis that situational cues that facilitate prosocial action at low cost will increase the helping behavior of approval-motivated subjects. Satow (1975) found that approval-oriented women donated more money to a research fund in a public as opposed to a private condition. Further, the donation of money was made possible on a "no cost" basis, because the subjects received $1.50 in cash for working on three puzzles. Thus, the solicitation of contributions by the experimenter after the experiment made salient the cues for helping ("placing it in the jar on the table") at little cost to the subject. Interestingly, what distinguished the public from the private condition was the existence of a one-way mirror in the experimenter's office, which afforded a view of the experimental room. There was no mirror in the private condition. Clearly, the possibility that observers might view the subject's behavior creates conditions that the subject can see as conducive to receiving approval for acting prosocially (or, we should note, disapproval for not following the social direction).

The Prosocial Personality

Staub (1974) has suggested the value of taking a broader perspective to the study of the personality antecedents of prosocial behavior. This approach asks if there is a personality structure (or a set of motives, traits, values, and beliefs) that makes the person more likely to behave in a prosocial way. To illustrate how these personality processes may combine to form the personality structure of the altruistic individual, we first examine the original set of studies conducted by Staub and his associates. We then review much larger bodies of research evidence that examined separately the major dimensions that comprise the prosocial personality (i.e., empathy, moral responsibility, and a set of motives and traits).

To assess the prosocial personality orientation, Staub (1974) gave a battery of personality tests to male undergraduates. Through factor analytic procedures, a composite score was derived which Staub believed reflected the degree of these subjects' prosocial orientation. To examine how this broad prosocial personality orientation might affect helping behavior, Staub exposed these students to a low, moaning sound of distress, which came from the room adjoining the experimental room. Helping was measured by whether or not the subject entered the room of the distressed confederate within 135 seconds. Overall, the results indicated that the students with higher levels of the prosocial orientation were more helpful. Indeed, in this study, these subjects showed a tendency to help in many ways, which included entering the victim's room and taking action to fill a prescription for the confederate, as well as in the total number of helping acts.

In a follow-up dissertation study, Feinberg (described in Staub, 1978) took the same broad approach and administered a number of personality scales to undergraduate women. The test scores were factor analyzed and produced two factors for prosocial and for achievement tendencies. The procedure used in the study involved exposing subjects to a distressed confederate who confided that she had separated from her boyfriend. A situational variable, the recency of the need for help, was also included. In the high-need condition, the breakup supposedly occurred the day prior to the experiment, whereas in the low-need condition it was reported to have occurred the year before. Feinberg predicted that the achievement-motivated women would focus their attention on the task, whereas prosocial women would show concern for the distressed student. In partial support of the hypothesis, the results indicated that women with a strong prosocial orientation and achievement needs spent the most time with the woman and worked relatively little on the task, especially in the high-need condition. Across the experimental conditions, achievement-oriented women were found to be highly task oriented, which may account for the finding that they disliked the confederate more in the high-need condition. The least helpful women were those who were low on both the prosocial orientation and the need for achievement. In a later study, Grodman (described in Staub, 1978) used many of the same procedures as Feinberg and found results that were consistent with those obtained in the earlier studies.

In summary, the series of studies carried out by Staub and his associates provides an initial demonstration of the utility of conceptualizing the prosocial personality to be a structure of elements that can combine to affect positive social behavior. Also, the related work by Marks, Penner, and Stone (1982) in studying the effects of sociopathy — a broad variable which appears to be the inverse of Staub's concept of the prosocial personality — demonstrated that sociopathy is inversely related to helping behavior. Most of the work in this area, however, examined the effects of individual elements of the structure. Therefore, we present this information in the form in which it has been investigated in social psychology. Future research will determine if this broader structural approach is appropriate when studying the effects of these variables on affiliative behavior.

Empathy

Although not easy to define (Hogan, 1975), empathy is generally thought of as the ability to apprehend the inner state of another person, as well as the factors that might have produced that emotional state. Among its capacities, empathy is often thought to include cognitive role-taking ability, or the observer's ability to identify accurately the way another person feels in a particular situation. Because empathy includes the ability to understand and perhaps identify with the needs of another person, it seems reasonable to examine its involvement in effective functioning on the affiliative axis of social behavior. In Table 5.4, the categories that make up the affiliative pole of socioemotional activity (e.g., increases group solidarity) all seem to involve empathic ability. Clearly, persons with high degrees of empathic ability should be capable of prosocial responding, especially in situations in which another person is experiencing emotional distress. On the other hand, the lack of empathy should be associated with more disaffiliative behaviors, because the lack of feeling for others and minimal role-taking ability should lead to tendencies to ignore the needs of others or to see them as objects for the satisfaction of personal needs.

Using measures of sympathetic (i.e., empathic) and instrumental orientations, Liebhart (1972) studied the effects of these orientations on helping behavior by arranging to have subjects hear the experimenter experience an accident in an adjoining room. The apparent accident occurred in a room that was separated from the subjects by a curtain, and the measure of help was the time it took the subject to pull open a curtain-divider between the experimental rooms. The results showed that persons with a high sympathetic orientation tended to be more helpful than those who were low; persons scoring high on both instrumental activity and sympathetic orientation were even more responsive. The least responsive subjects were those who were low on both orientations. Liebhart suggests that the person with a strong sympathetic orientation responds quickly in a prosocial manner to reduce his own empathic distress produced by the cries of the lady in distress. These findings are especially interesting because they suggest that a person with a disposition to respond on both the affiliation and initiation axes of social behavior will act most prosocially in those situations that elicit such behavior.

Mehrabian and Epstein (1972) explored the relationship of empathy to both disaffiliative and affiliative behaviors. On the basis of scores from an empathy questionnaire, they selected subjects for two studies in which they sought to determine the relationship between empathic tendencies and the willingness of the subject to act aggressively or prosocially. In the first study, a Milgram-type paradigm was used in which a "teacher" was instructed to shock a "learner" for failing to answer correctly. In addition, the learner was either 8 feet away and fully visible or out of sight in another room. Aggression was measured by computing the average shock level the subject administered to the learner. In the second study, women worked on a task with a confederate who became emotionally upset and requested the subject's help in conducting "an experiment for a class." In these two experiments, the results clearly demonstrated that, when the potential victim was visible, high levels of empathy are associated with the tendency to act prosocially as well as to refrain from disaffiliative actions of an aggressive nature. In contrast, the reverse pattern seems to be the case for persons with low levels of empathy, who act aggressively when situational variables facilitate that behavior and fail to respond prosocially when asked for help.

In a series of studies, Hogan (1975) and his colleagues have shown that persons who score high on an empathy scale also exhibit a broad range of social competence on the affiliative axis of interpersonal behavior, such as social sensitivity, role-playing ability, tactfulness, good communication skills, considerateness, humanistic values, acceptance of individual differences, and ethical sensitivity. Other studies provide additional supportive evidence that empathy is also correlated with a wide range of helpful and cooperative behavior (Barnett, Mathews, & Howard, 1979; Buckley, Siegel, & Ness, 1979; Davis, 1983; Eisenberg-Berg, & Mussen, 1978; Mathews, Batson, Horn, & Rosenman, 1981; Mills & Bohannon, 1980).

In contrast to the affiliative activity of empathic individuals, Hogan (1975) has also shown that the unempathic person manifests many disaffiliative interpersonal behaviors, such as insensitivity, coldness, tactlessness, and antisocial tendencies. Additionally, when scores on the empathy scale are combined with those on the socialization scale of the CPI, even more precise predictions of interpersonal behaviors can be made. Consistent with Staub's (1974) conception of the prosocial personality, persons with high empathy and socialization scores on the CPI are characterized by moral maturity, conscientiousness, and responsible action, whereas at the other end of the spectrum, unempathic and undersocialized persons are prone to delinquency, aggression, and antisocial behavior.

Values and Moral Judgment

An individual's moral system was the second major component of the prosocial personality postulated by Staub (1974). Clearly, it is reasonable to assume that persons with a more articulated sense of morality, as well as those who believe in values that emphasize the individual's integrity, dignity, equality, justice, and responsibility for others' welfare, would act positively and helpfully toward others. In this area, Kohlberg's (1973) theory of moral development has been the most influential in guiding the research that has examined how moral reasoning can influence a person's capacity to act prosocially in situations of interpersonal conflict. The theory of moral development proposed by Kohlberg and his associates delineates a sequence of well-defined stages in which the primary elements are the cognitive structures that the person uses to think about moral conflict situations. In addition to its structural nature, a stage of moral reasoning also includes certain concrete values. For example, individuals at the postconventional level typically are concerned with universal ethical principles in which they maintain beliefs in individual integrity, dignity, and moral justice. This aspect of Kohlberg's theory permits the incorporation of other work that is based less on a developmental perspective (Rokeach, 1973).

Because persons with higher stages of moral reasoning are capable of producing abstract principles of morality, it is reasonable to hypothesize that there should exist a general willingness to behave prosocially in situations that would arouse concerns with fairness, well-being, equity, and human rights. Blasi (1980) reviewed the extensive literature that has examined this hypothesis, including a large number of difficult to obtain unpublished dissertations and technical reports. One cannot help but be impressed by the overall body of evidence that is available to support the general form of the hypothesis. In addition, one of Blasi's conclusions is that it is necessary to consider a host of methodological and theoretical factors carefully before the results from any one study can be accepted. Overall, Blasi's conclusion is that there is a great deal of evidence to support the hypothesis that lower levels of moral development are associated with disaffiliative behavior, a conclusion that is based upon a comparison of delinquent and nondelinquent youth, and "clear but less striking [support] for the hypothesis that higher moral stage individuals tend to be more honest and more altruistic" (p. 37).

Personal Norms

The ways that personal norms moderate the decision-making steps that underlie many forms of affiliative and disaffiliative behaviors have been explored in a continuing series of studies by Schwartz (1977) and his associates. Recently, Schwartz and Howard (1981) offered a model of altruism which suggested that situational factors activate personal norms, values, and social motives. In addition, they proposed that the individual cognitive mechanisms of "awareness of consequences" and "responsibility denial," which they see as personal attributes indicating the degree to which people recognize the potential consequences of actions and the degree to which they deny responsibility for events, moderate many forms of prosocial behavior.

In an early test of this theory, Schwartz and Clausen (1970) replicated Latane' and Darley's (1968) epileptic seizure study, conceptualizing responsibility denial as a personality variable. Subjects who did not deny responsibility were found to be more likely to assist the seizure victim than those who denied responsibility. In a later study, Schwartz and Ben David (1976) examined the effects of responsibility denial in a situation in which a rat "accidentially" escaped while the study was in progress. During the course of an apparent training program in the laboratory, the experimenter left the room and spoke to the subject over the intercom. After the second series of training procedures had begun, an accident occurred in which there was a crash and an announcement that the rat escaped. Consistent with the results of the earlier study, this study showed that subjects who tended to deny responsibility took much more time to open their door to investigate the crash than did people who were low on this trait.

In their review, Schwartz and Howard proposed that responsibility denial is a psychological defense that affects the attribution process of moral responsibility for prosocial action. In reanalyzing data from Schwartz's previous studies, they found that persons with stable value structures and internalized personal norms were more prosocial (e.g., willing to donate bone marrow; read to the blind, etc.) when they scored low on responsibility denial. In this regard, these results are compatible with Staub's description of the prosocial orientation, in that a person with a prosocial set of attitudes and moral values, and the lack of a tendency to deny anxiety-provoking events, is more likely to attend to a need, to become motivated to act because of humanitarian values, and to act prosocially, if the costs are not too great.

MOTIVATIONAL DETERMINANTS OF AFFILIATIVE-DISAFFILIATIVE BEHAVIOR

In this section, we explore how motives influence cooperation, altruism, and other behaviors that make up the affiliative axis of social interaction. We begin with a discussion of the need for affiliation as a motive state that is clearly involved in generating affiliative behavior, and then we discuss the effects of a variety of esteem-related variables. We conclude with a presentation of four studies designed to test some of the central predictions of the model outlined in part I.

Affiliation

Even in the area of affiliative interpersonal behavior, there are few studies examining the social consequences of the need for affiliation. As indicated in Table 5.4, this motive should by definition be associated with very high levels of affiliative behavior and low degrees of aggression, hostility, and other disaffiliative activity. In the area of prosocial behavior, the person should show high levels of activity, except when in highly stressful situations. Thus, following Bales (1970), we expect that the need for affiliation will lead individuals to be strongly concerned with behaving as "good" group members who seek to occupy supportive roles in many situations.

In an interesting examination of the influence of the need for affiliation on affiliative behavior, Fishman (1966) had undergraduate women meet in a four-woman discussion group for a 1-hour period. During the discussion, their behavior was scored using a modification of Bales' IPA technique to produce a measure of affiliative behavior that is quite similar to that presented in Table 5.4. Fishman showed that for the group of women who believed they could find satisfaction for their affiliative goals through group interaction, the measure of affiliation correlated strongly with their use of affiliative behavior (see also Mehrabian & Ksionsky, 1972, for a similar finding). This additional "expectancy" factor is rarely included in empirical studies on social behavior, although it has been central to Atkinson's (1957) theory of motivation since its inception. McClelland (1981) returned to this issue recently in an extremely valuable theoretical consideration of the factors that enter into behavioral selection.

Exploring the effects of a number of different motives on prosocial behavior in a group meeting over an extended period of time, Kolb and Boyatzis (1970) examined the effects of achievement, affiliation, and power motives on the performance of advanced students participating in T-group training. Eight small groups were formed in which ratings were taken on individual performance as well as effectiveness in responding to others. Interestingly, the results indicated that the most effective helpers scored moderately high on all three motives. These people were also characterized as self-confident and empathic, and they tended to use more positive than negative feedback. In contrast, the ineffective helper scored high on both achievement and power motives but low on affiliative needs. These ineffective helpers, however, did exhibit task-oriented leadership qualities and were described as organized, impatient, open, superior, and prone to give negative feedback. It is also interesting that nonhelpers were concerned with affiliative needs but were low on the needs for achievement and power. In other words, in the complex and extended instance of group process represented by this experiment, the need for affiliation required the support of the other needs, which contribute most directly to behavior on the initiation–concurrence axis, in order to render a reasonable amount of assistance.

In an experimental study, Schwartz, Feldman, Brown, and Heingartner (1969) explored the relationship between moral judgment, achievement, and affiliation motives to helping behavior and cheating. Undergraduates first were placed in a situation that could evoke cheating; they were asked to work on a vocabulary test that contained the correct answers printed on the reverse side of the page. A few weeks later, most of the subjects participated in a second study designed to assess helping behavior on a task that required them to assist an incompetent accomplice with a puzzle. To elicit helping behavior, an accomplice indicated that he was experiencing difficulty in completing the puzzle and eventually asked the subject for assistance.

This experiment had a number of interesting results. Subjects with a high level of morality and subjects with a high level of achievement motivation did not cheat as much as subjects lower in these attributes. As predicted, the need for affiliation was unrelated to cheating. In the helping situation, level of morality was not related to helping the incompetent confederate. In contrast, 75% of the high need for affiliation subjects and 78% of the low need for achievement subjects helped the frustrated and incompetent accomplice.

These results are especially interesting in several ways. First, the request for help by the confederate afforded the subject with affiliative needs an opportunity to interact with the perplexed accomplice actively. Second, the low rate of helping by highly achievement-oriented subjects is consistent with the task-orientation of such persons. However, we can speculate that the achievement-oriented person's concern with meeting a standard of excellence would predict prosocial behavior in some situations, such as where the person's need for help was due to misfortune, but not in situations such as created by Schwartz et al. (1969) where the need for help was due to incompetence. In this situation, the low rate of prosocial responding may be a manifestation of disdain for the anxious confederate who does not persist at working toward a solution.

Machiavellianism

Several studies (e.g., Harrell & Hartnagel, 1976; McLaughlin, 1970) show how easily Machiavellians will use wide-ranging disaffiliative behavior when it is in their interest. Similarly, Geis (1978) concludes (see chap. 11) that the Machiavellian is much less person-oriented and, interpersonally, is more deceptive than a non-Machiavellian. For example, there is evidence to show that in a group setting, the person that members believe they can understand best is the member who scored highest on Machiavellianism. However, irrespective of their sense of confidence, group members' judgment of a Machiavellian was actually much more inaccurate than their judgment of a non-Machiavellian. Finally, in two studies involving distressed persons and in one on jury decision making, Machiavellianism was not associated with affiliative behavior (Foley & Chamblin, 1982; Latane' & Darley, 1970; Staub, 1974). Because the trait of Machiavellianism is defined by an opportunistic, self-enhancing orientation to social interaction, we would not expect it to be consistently associated with prosocial behavior.

Locus of Control

In earlier chapters, we reviewed a good deal of evidence demonstrating that individuals who possess an internal locus of control are effective in influencing many aspects of their interpersonal activity. This tendency to initiate behavior in the service of a task suggests that internality should be associated with high rates of affiliative behavior when that kind of act appears to be needed. In general, the available research does not yet provide a clear answer. Some studies show that internality is positively related to providing assistance. For example, it has been found to be correlated with a willingness to become actively involved in civil rights efforts (Gore & Rotter, 1963; Strickland, 1965), to receive electric shocks from a cohort in a laboratory study (Midlarsky, 1971; Midlarsky & Midlarsky, 1973), or among children, to share candy (Fincham & Barling, 1978). On the other hand, a number of studies have found no relationship (Burke, 1982; Schneider, 1977; Schwartz, 1974; Schwartz & Clausen, 1970; Yakimovich & Saltz, 1971). At this point, the involvement of locus of control in affiliative behavior must remain an open question.

Achievement

As discussed earlier, Schwartz, et al. (1969) found that achievement motivation was unrelated to helping an incompetent student complete a jigsaw puzzle, but it was significantly associated with resistance to cheating (i.e., a reluctance to behave in a disaffiliative way). In this study, it is quite likely that the simplicity of the task and the demands for help by the confederate did not engage the achievement-oriented person's motives. Support for this idea was found by Kolb and Boyatzis (1970), who found that the most effective helpers scored moderately high on achievement, affiliation, and power motives. This finding is especially interesting because the combination of moderate levels of the three motives parallels much of Staub's (1974) prosocial personality orientation. That is, a person with these dispositional attributes is very likely to emit the relatively high levels of behaviors that define the initiation and affiliation axes of social behavior. Thus, if task or situational cues made salient the need for effective interpersonal behaviors of an affiliative nature, the individual with power, affiliation, or achievement motives can flexibly initiate activity as required by the demands of the task and gratify all three motives in the process. However, as Kolb and Boyatzis found, persons with prepotent power or achievement needs are more likely to emit behaviors that fall predominantly on the initiation axis of social behavior by being overly task centered or concerned with organizational leadership.

These studies serve to introduce the very interesting questions of the personal and situational factors that lead to effective and combined patterns of interpersonal functioning. Future research may more clearly show that achievement motivation may lead to high degrees of affiliation behavior: (a) if affiliative behavior is instrumental to the accomplishment of the task; (b) if there are few competing task-oriented activities; and (c) if the person possesses, in addition, the motive to affiliate or prosocial values (Staub, 1974) which enables the person to make effective helping the standard of excellence by which to direct the motive.

Self-Esteem, Ascendancy, and Nurturance

A number of studies have investigated the expected positive relationship of self-esteem (and related constructs) to different forms of prosocial behavior. Turner (1948), Cattell and Horowitz (1952), and Form and Nosow (1958) report the results of naturalistic studies suggesting that such persons are outgoing, warm, competent, trusting, empathic, capable of role taking and active caring for others. Similarly, Schneider (1977) found that undergraduates who score higher on the trait of ascendancy (although not internality) were more willing to read to the blind.

The definition of nurturance as "the need to establish self-worth by responsibly caring for the successful development of persons, generations and institutions" (see chapter 3) clearly predicts that this variable should lead to strongly affiliative behavior. There are two interesting studies that begin to explore this question. Pandey and Griffitt (1977) selected undergraduates on the basis of their nurturance scores and brought them into the laboratory to participate in what they believed would be a Byrne-type impression-formation experiment. After that experiment appeared to be over, they were asked to volunteer to help another person assemble questionnaires. Although there were a number of interesting situational variables tested in this experiment, our interest lies in one striking result. Each person was asked to answer a few questions about his or her willingness to help. If subjects were willing to help, they were brought into another room where they found six stacks of questionnaire pages and a stapler. The experimenter provided instructions and then left the subject alone in the room. The behavioral measures of prosocial activity were the actual number of minutes helped and the number of questionnaires stapled together. The results showed a strong relationship between nurturance and the stated willingness to help, but there was no relationship with the actual help given. This finding leads to many speculations. It is possible that the verbal measures were similar to an aspiration-level type of measurement, a purely cognitive judgment, or a characteristic estimate of potential achievement. However, once engaged in the task, as Pandey and Griffitt conclude, the physical absence of a person needing help and the dullness of the task probably did not engage the nurturance motive sufficiently. Similar findings were reported by Gergen et al. (1972), who found that nurturance needs were significantly correlated with volunteering to counsel others, but not for a variety of routine and impersonal tasks.

INTERACTIONAL STUDIES OF PROSOCIAL BEHAVIOR

In this section, we present a series of studies that examines the effects of safety and esteem motives on prosocial behavior. We describe these studies in detail because, taken together, they allow us to examine the effects of many more variables than can be handled in a single experiment and permit us to examine an extended set of hypotheses within a consistent interactional approach. To permit greater cross-situation comparisons, the same assessment instrument (Aronoff, 1972) was used in all four studies to measure safety and esteem motives among undergraduate students.

As a general hypothesis, we expected that the characteristics of safety-oriented persons would reduce prosocial behavior in many situations because their feelings of anxiety, uncertainty, and insecurity would tend to generate avoidance responses, whereas esteem-oriented persons would be likely to initiate prosocial behavior across situations because of their desire to demonstrate mastery and competence. Beyond these general orientations, as we have seen in earlier chapters, these variables are significantly affected by the characteristics of other people in the situation. Therefore, following the evidence presented in part II, we expect that the safety-oriented person should be especially attentive to external attributes of a bystander (e.g., sex, status, activity level) that would provide salient cues for use in evaluating response alternatives in a situation of need. In contrast, because the research on esteem-oriented people has shown that they tend to rely less on external social cues and more on information related to effective task performance based on ability and effort, we would expect them to be influenced by others who exhibit personal competence and efficacy in their behavior.

Each of these studies explores the ways in which safety and esteem motives interact with environmental variables to influence prosocial behavior. In the first study, the effects of these motives are examined in a simple situation in which an undergraduate woman drops her books in the presence of passive bystanders. In the second study, a direct request is made to help search for a lost contact lens while the apparently needy person leaves the experimental room to go to a pressing appointment. In the third and fourth studies, undergraduates are exposed to an explosion that ostensibly injures the experimenter. In these studies, the activity level, status, and competence of the bystander are varied systematically in order to examine the effects of these social variables on the dispositional readiness to respond prosocially.

The First Experiment: The Effects of Safety and Esteem Motives on Helping Behavior.   This experiment (Michelini, Wilson, & Messé, 1975) and the three others to be reported in this section used the same sentence completion test (Aronoff, 1972) scores to select undergraduate subjects. We hypothesized that strongly safety-oriented individuals would not act to help in the usual bystander-intervention situation because their chronic anxiety and sense of personal inadequacy would generate a tendency toward passive withdrawal when confronted with even a modest emergency. In contrast, we expected that esteem-oriented persons would be more likely to render assistance because their personal sense of competence and desire to gain the recognition of others would motivate helping in a situation where a small act of assistance is needed.

Undergraduate men were led to believe that they would be participating in a four-man study of group interaction. Upon arrival, the subject and two confederates went to the experimental room to fill out some preliminary forms while waiting for what was represented as the remaining person to arrive. By arrangement, the confederates entered the room in front of the subject and occupied the chairs such that the subject always sat between them. The chair apparently reserved for the fourth "subject" was stacked with papers. About 3 minutes after the experimenter left the room to look for the fourth subject, an attractive undergraduate woman entered and inquired about a different experiment. Appearing confused and indicating that she had entered the wrong room, she hastily turned to leave and in doing so spilled the materials that she was carrying, which included a box of computer cards, onto a section of floor near the doorway. The two confederates were instructed to remain passive and offer no assistance unless the subject began helping the flustered woman. The results of this experiment are simple and clear. Over 80% of the esteem-oriented individuals helped pick up the materials as compared to 45% of the subjects with equal scores on both motives and 30% of the safety-oriented persons. Thus, in the presence of passive confederates and in response to a mundane accident, esteem-oriented subjects were significantly more helpful than were their safety-oriented counterparts.

The Second Experiment: A Direct Request for Assistance.   In the second study, Haymes and Green (1977) examined the effects of a direct request for assistance on the prosocial behavior of safety- and esteem-oriented persons. The subjects were brought to the laboratory to work on a task. A confederate, who was ostensibly waiting to participate in the study, reported to the subject that he had lost a contact lens. After searching for it for 6 minutes, he said that he was "frantic to get to his other appointment." The direct request for help was arranged by asking the subject to leave a note describing the problem to the experimenter (who was briefly absent from the room), so that no one would step on the lens.

In this experiment, esteem-oriented subjects, in comparison to safety-oriented subjects, spent about twice as much time searching for the lost lens. Thus, with results that are similar to those of our first study, Haymes and Green (1977) found that in response to an indirect but legitimate request to render assistance, esteem-oriented persons responded more helpfully than did safety-oriented persons. In this study, however, it is important to realize that the prosocial activity occurred when the person was alone in the room. The strong motivational effects found in these two studies can introduce the third study in which we examined prosocial behavior in response to an apparently serious accident in which the subjects were alone or interacted with either passive bystanders or an active helping role model.

The Third Experiment: The Effects of Motivation and Model Characteristics on Altruism.   This study (Wilson, 1976) was an extension of our previous research on role differentiation in task-oriented small groups (Messé, Aronoff, & Wilson, 1972), which indicated that safety- and esteem-oriented persons attend to different social cues in determining the role allocation of group members. In that study, to be described in chapter 12, we found that safety-oriented persons used external cues (e.g., status) as the basis of role differentiation, whereas esteem-oriented individuals used manifest competence at the task as the basis for allocating group roles. This finding suggested that a similar interpersonal process might occur in an ambiguous bystander-intervention situation. In the absence of certainty about an emergency, we hypothesized that safety-oriented persons would look externally to others and engage in a social comparison process leading to high levels of imitative behavior as a means of reducing uncertainty in the situation. In contrast, we expected that the emergency event would provide the esteem-oriented person with an opportunity to demonstrate personal competence by behaving in an efficacious problem-solving manner across situations.

The subjects were selected on the basis of their scores for safety and esteem motives and assigned to one of three experimental situations. In the first condition, the subjects completed the study alone. In the second condition, they participated with two confederates who served as passive role models. In the third condition, they also participated with two confederates, one who was to become an active helping model and the other who was to remain a passive, unresponsive bystander. The subjects were told that the purpose of the study was to learn about the relationship of personality to heart disease, and they were asked to complete a detailed questionnaire on this subject. As the subjects worked on the questionnaire, an apparent explosion occurred in the next room where the subjects had seen the experimenter working with what appeared to be an impressive set of electronic equipment. In comparison to the experimental situation used in the first and second experiments, this experiment increased the need for assistance and the potential costs for helping, and provided a variety of other participants who could be used to help determine the affiliative response.

Consistent with our hypotheses, esteem-oriented people helped more frequently and more consistently across all the situations. On the other hand, although safety-oriented persons helped a moderate amount when alone, they tended to model the behavior of the bystanders in the passive and active model conditions. The results of this experiment corroborate the findings of the earlier studies and show that esteem-oriented persons become actively involved in prosocial activity across many different kinds of situations. Safety-oriented persons also show some prosocial tendencies in such a personal situation but appear vulnerable to stressors (e.g., an explosion), which seem to heighten their anxiety and intensify the need to engage in social comparison as a means of determining their own response to the situation. For the reasons that we have described in chapters 7 and 9, safety-oriented people seem able to reduce their level of anxiety by modeling the behavior of other group members. Thus, it is extremely interesting that, under the special circumstances of facing an emergency with an active "other" person, the safety-oriented person will join the types of prosocial activity that are usually felt as too anxiety provoking when the person is alone.

The Fourth Experiment: The Effect of the Status, Competence, and Activity of the Model.   In the fourth experiment, Wilson and Petruska (1984) extended the findings of the earlier studies to examine the hypothesis that the comparison process can be used in even more complex and interesting ways by these two kinds of people. In general, we felt that safety-oriented persons use different cues and social comparison targets as the basis of modeling an active or passive bystander in an emergency situation. Specifically, we predicted that safety-oriented persons would demonstrate a higher degree of imitation when the bystander has been shown to have high status, and we expected that esteem-oriented persons would demonstrate higher rates of modeling when the bystander was a highly competent individual.

This experiment replicated the procedure used in the third experiment, with only a few changes in the task to make the experimental manipulations more salient. The subject was led to believe that he would be working on a creative decision-making task with another person whose status and competence were varied through the experimental instructions. In the high-status condition, the confederate indicated that he was a PhD program student who held prestigious degrees from nationally prominent institutions. In the low-status condition, the confederate presented himself as a part-time undergraduate student who was unsure of his career goals and worked on campus in the plant service division. The competence of the confederate was established during the initial period of the experiment through the success that the confederate demonstrated on the task. Subjects had been asked to begin their work by drawing up plans for the ideal urban university. In the high-competence condition, the confederate worked briskly, expressed many signs that he found the work interesting and easy, and received strong praise from the experimenter on the quality of his work. In the low-competence condition, the confederate worked slowly, expressed many signs of inadequacy, and was confirmed as not very capable after the experimenter read through his work.

As the subject began to work on the task, the experimenter indicated that he would be in the control room working on videotape recordings made of previous groups. Once in the control room, the experimenter increased the volume on the TV monitor to convey the impression that he was observing a videotape. In a replication of the third experiment, an ambiguous accident was created by simulating an "explosion" that ostensibly injured the experimenter. In half of the groups, the confederate actively intervened within 7 seconds by going into the control room. In the other half, the confederate remained seated and ignored the emergency. Thus, half of the subjects confronted the emergency with an active model and the other half with a passive model. This experimental design created eight experimental conditions: Subjects were assigned to either an active or a passive model condition, in which they worked with a person with the social attributes of high or low competence and high or low status.

The results of this experiment were strongly consistent with the results from many other studies: Personality and situational variables had strong effects on prosocial behavior. Across the experimental conditions, esteem-oriented people rendered more assistance to the distressed victim than did safety-oriented people. Second, a strong situational effect was found in that more help was given when the confederate was an active helping model than when he was a passive model. Third, an interesting interaction effect was found which confirmed one of the central hypotheses of this book: Esteem-oriented people tended to model the actions of the competent co-worker, whereas safety-oriented people tended to model the behavior of the high-status confederate.

There were many other findings in this complex study, such as the fact that many esteem-oriented people intervened within the 7-second period before the confederate could act or the fact that safety-oriented people were especially responsive to the active model, which is the most easily grasped observable characteristic of the co-worker. At this point, however, the range of results from these four experiments leads to several general conclusions about how personality factors may influence affiliative behavior in the kinds of emergency situations constructed in our laboratory. First, it seems clear that a safety-oriented person alone is quite reluctant to help, even when the help needed or requested is not difficult to provide. In comparison, the esteem-oriented person is quite willing to be helpful, even when there are several unresponsive bystanders present. Second, safety-oriented people seemed to be greatly affected by a range of situational cues, the most important of which is the activity and status level displayed by other people who are present; they will imitate the bystander's behavior in either the affiliative or disaffiliative direction. In contrast, esteem-oriented people may be influenced by the known competence of the other people present and be willing to imitate disaffiliative behavior, even if it contravenes their usual willingness to offer help. Thus, consistent with their cognitive and interpersonal styles, safety- and esteem-oriented individuals seem to attend to, and be affected by, different sets of cues in the social environment.

In this chapter, we have seen how these two motives form a core around which related peripheral motives, traits, and values affect the person's investment in the affiliative dimension of social life. In the next two chapters, we examine how these individual tendencies combine to affect the interpersonal units of the social process.

11 Negotiation Processes

In most daily situations, we are faced with interpersonal transactions that demand some form of extended interaction. The previous two chapters established which personality variables lead people to be assertive, accommodative, affiliative, or disaffiliative. As with all social events, the continued use of each of these major poles of interpersonal space assumes a significant response from the other people who are involved. For example, an individual cannot continue to play some form of the follower role without complementary leadership responses from another person. The purpose of this chapter is to examine the nature of the relationship that develops between people as they devise ways to maximize opportunities available in a situation.

The activities through which individuals confront the demands of a task are often referred to, quite loosely, as "group process," with a vast array of constructs offered to explain the different types of interpersonal events. Although we have been arguing throughout the book for a fairly compact set of constructs, the need for parsimony is even greater in the case of those ongoing activities through which individuals form and maintain their longer term relationships. Our purpose in exploring these complex transactions is to identify the most important dimensions of the relationships that human beings invent as they pursue a common goal and to explore the influence of personality variables on the use of these social features.

In the earlier chapters, we reviewed a set of social dimensions that allow us to explain much that is usually included under the heading of group process. In order to make it easier to visualize a person's interpersonal style, we have combined all the elements of group process into a single presentation, which is displayed in Table 11.1. In this table, each of the columns represents a dif-

TABLE 11.1
Elements of Group Process Associated with Selected Personality Variables

Personality Variable	Performance Styles		Negotiation Styles			
	Initiation–Concurrence	Affiliation–Disaffiliation	Firm–Yielding	Rigid–Flexible	Cooperative–Competitive	Revealing–Concealing
Dependency	Concurrence	Disaffiliation	Yielding	Rigid	Cooperative	Concealing
Abasement	Concurrence	Disaffiliation	Firm	Rigid	Competitive	Concealing
Approval	Concurrence	Affiliation	Yielding	Rigid	Cooperative	Concealing
Authoritarianism	Initiation	Disaffiliation	Yielding	Rigid	Competitive	Concealing
Order	Initiation	Disaffiliation	Firm	Rigid	Cooperative	Concealing
Affiliation	Initiation	Affiliation	Yielding	Flexible	Cooperative	Revealing
Machiavellianism	Initiation	Affiliation	Firm	Flexible	Competitive	Concealing
Dominance	Initiation	Affiliation	Firm	Rigid	Competitive	Revealing
Achievement	Initiation	Affiliation	Firm	Flexible	Cooperative	Revealing
Nurturance	Initiation	Affiliation	Firm	Flexible	Cooperative	Revealing
Recognition	Initiation	Affiliation	Yielding	Rigid	Competitive	Revealing

ferent aspect of the characteristic means through which the individual seeks to obtain reward from the social encounter. Notice that in the first two columns, we list the variables that were just discussed in chapters 9 and 10. We repeat them here because, in order to visualize the entire range of group process, it is also important to include the extent to which the task dimension (or the degree to which the person uses initiation–concurrence behavior) and the socioemotional dimension (or the degree to which the person uses affiliation–disaffiliation behavior) jointly form his or her major coordinates of interpersonal space.

Extending from these primary performance styles are additional features of the interaction that we have called the negotiation styles. The first characteristic represents the firmness with which individuals maintain the initial requests that they make during an interaction. To us, the degree of firmness that group members use when they coordinate their requirements with other participants usefully accounts for activities as varied as a person maintaining an initial bid in a bargaining experiment, the selection of which form of entertainment to choose in a purely social encounter, or the extended discussion through which other people become convinced that the person's solution should be chosen by the group. The second interpersonal characteristic seems to be the degree of flexibility that individuals exhibit as they execute the interpersonal task. This characteristic focuses on the information-management techniques that people use to persuade other members, to survey potential solutions, or to readjust initial solutions in the face of new evidence or powerful opposition.

As with performance styles, we are interested in how the members of a group use those negotiation styles that are most congruent with their predominant personality orientation. Thus, with respect to a task that permits a range of responses, we are interested in how personality variables influence the degree to which an individual assumes a firm or yielding bargaining stance. In a negotiation, we expect that a firm bargainer does not waiver very much from his or her initial position relative to the stand taken by another person, whereas a yielding individual generally shifts away from the initial bargaining position. Similarly, we are interested in how the predominant personality orientation of group members influences the way that they explore the informational opportunities available to them in that situation. The flexible individual should employ a wide range of potential solutions and be able to overcome unpredicted changes in the direction of the negotiation. In fact, some people (e.g., Machiavellians) may turn such unscheduled events to their personal advantage by shrewd manipulation of the bargaining process (Geis, 1978). In contrast, the rigid individual is more limited in his or her cognitive problem-solving techniques, which leads to a more fixed pattern of problem solving that is employed in widely different situations. When faced with uncalculated changes in the bargaining task, the rigid person may become stymied because he or she will not explore alternative opportunities. This sense of helplessness may lead the person to insist on maintaining an unsuitable position or to become reluctant to proceed further in the negotiation.

The third and the fourth elements of negotiation styles identify the types of problem-solving strategies that people prefer to use in their interaction with other people. These characteristics are the degree to which individuals choose to maximize their own or joint outcomes (to stress competition or cooperation) and the degree to which individuals are frank or guarded in sharing their purposes with others (to reveal or conceal information). As we reviewed the social psychological research on negotiation processes (cf. Rubin & Brown, 1975), which has been the area in which most of the work on group process has been performed, it seemed to us that the combination of these two social elements could account quite well for a great deal of the most interesting and important work. We can use familiar language to identify these four modes of interdependence that have been of such interest to so many social psychologists. It seems reasonable to refer to these four interpersonal relationships as: adversarial (competitive and information-revealing); exploitative (competitive and information-concealing); ingratiating (cooperative and information-concealing); and integrative (cooperative and information-revealing). Each of these relationships seems easily applied to a wide range of the dynamic activities that take place within a group.

If it is useful to view group process as the resultant of these elements of social interaction, what programs of research are available to evaluate the predictions presented in Table 11.1? Once again, there are extensive amounts of material at hand to deal with some questions, scattered results obtainable to explore others, additional sources of evidence that can be seen as related indirectly to these processes, and finally, no data at all to examine some highly important matters. Surprisingly, in the case of the topics with which we are concerned in this chapter, it is easy to decide how to proceed.

Let us first consider how best to handle the body of indirect evidence. For whatever reason, most of the work in the area of group process does not deal with "process," but rather with the types of decisions that are made or the degree of success of some experimentally manipulated aspect of group process. We have virtually no work to measure the actual rigidity or flexibility of information use and only a scattered body of studies to measure the degree of firmness or yieldingness used to maintain an individual's initial position throughout the time that it takes to reach a decision. At a minimum, Table 11.1 is useful because it can help us to identify important research to do in the future. However, by examining these predictions, we are also able to recognize the correspondences between this area and the significant body of related work that we have already reviewed. In chapter 7, we examined a sizable body of research on information processing at the individual level that is highly supportive of the predictions outlined in Table 11.1 on the personality variables associated with the rigidity or flexibility of information use. Notice that this evidence is only indirectly related to our interest in measuring the ongoing use of information during an interpersonal negotiation. Still, the available data on how these processes operate when a single person responds to a certain type of stimulus or makes a certain type of decision are quite congruent with our predictions.

In addition, although we have only scattered information available on the personality variables that lead individuals to be firm or yielding in their efforts at social influence, in chapter 9 we reviewed a massive body of evidence that indicates which personality variables lead individuals to be accommodating to the direction provided by others. In fact, the predictions on yielding presented in Table 11.1 are identical to the results of the research discussed in chapter 9. However, in order to evaluate the predictions on the personality bases of firmness in interpersonal negotiation, we are forced to rely on the few scattered studies that are found in the area of interpersonal bargaining.

Fortunately, there is a sizable body of carefully executed experimental work available through which we can explore the topics that interest us the most. Although the conception of four major modes of interdependence is more detailed than is most of the work on group process, the quality of the existing research should generate greater confidence in the conclusions it permits us to draw. In order to examine the hypothesis presented in Table 11.1, which view the major forms of negotiation as the result of the joint combination of a cooperation–competition dimension and an information-concealing–revealing dimension, we review and attempt to integrate two very different programs of research. We believe that combining the evidence from these apparently different programs of research can provide a substantial basis of support for many of the major hypotheses.

Rubin and Brown (1975) maintain that most bargaining experiments characteristically involve two or more parties who are voluntarily joined in a sequence of negotiation over the use of some resource. As studied by most social psychologists, the investigation of such negotiation processes typically focuses on the cooperative or competitive choices that previously unacquainted individuals select during the early phases of an interaction. In the experimental laboratory, these negotiations are usually studied in the form of a highly structured task in which a person must decide between cooperation or competition with an opponent, without knowledge of the opponent's choice. However, the rules of the game are such that it is the conjunction of the choices by both players that determines their degree of success. A wide variety of approaches has been used to study this aspect of negotiation, ranging from the very clear cognitive choices demanded by the widely used Prisoner's Dilemma game to much more open-ended games that require some behavioral activity as well, such as the Trucking Game. For all the criticism raised against what often appears to be a too highly structured and artificial procedure (Rubin & Brown, 1975), the work on experimental games still provides a vast body of reasonably clear, plausible, and useful information on the factors that govern the cooperative or competitive approach to interpersonal relations.

Possibly because the negotiation researchers find the cooperative or competitive choice to be the most interesting representation of the more naturalistic forms of group process, they have not typically examined the degree to which the participants are open or guarded in revealing their purposes to each other. To obtain information on the information-revealing–concealing dimension of interpersonal life, we must turn to a program of research that may, at first, seem a surprising partner to pair with experimental games. Under the title of "self-disclosure," which has been defined as "a person's voluntary revelation of personal information that a receiver could not learn from any other source" (Chelune, 1979, p. 80), this program of research has used self-report, observational ratings, and experimental procedures to produce a fairly sizable body of interesting information. Based on the original observation by Jourard (1958) that psychologically troubled people could neither know nor reveal important information about themselves, a substantial experimental research program has amassed a broad set of reliable findings on the personal and social antecedents of self-disclosure (Chelune, 1979). We can integrate quite easily the main features of the results that have been obtained from the self-disclosure literature with those drawn from the literature on experimental games.

FOUR MODES OF INTERPERSONAL NEGOTIATION

In this section, we describe the main features of each of the four negotiation styles. This discussion should help to account quite parsimoniously for many of the complex, fluid, and extended human events that are called group process. Among its other possible merits, this set of constructs makes it possible to present quite easily the ways in which the major personality orientations influence an individual's style of relating to other people.

The Adversarial Mode

The adversarial mode of relationship is one in which individuals are able to define their social purposes in highly competitive as well as straightforwardly open ways. Not only does this mode of interdependence permit individuals to attempt to maximize their own gain from the situation, but it allows them to choose to do so as an open and fair competition. In carrying out this form of relationship, individuals see themselves in a "fair" fight in which they are guided by rules known to all participants, as well as one in which they are permitted to use the entire range of openly understood forms of interpersonal intimidation. We would expect individuals using this form of negotiation to exhibit a broad set of dominance gestures (e.g., staring or touching), interpersonal strategms (e.g., criticism or the one-upmanship types of giving help that define which opponent is the weaker), as well as the more blunt forms of questioning, teasing, joking, taunting, sparring, or jockeying for status. However these power displays are carried out, their major purpose is to permit the individual to succeed in open combat against another person who is defined psychologically as an opponent.

The dominance-oriented person seems most likely to use this form of negotiation. In general, dominant individuals seek to demonstrate competence (to themselves) by successfully influencing, directing, or persuading others. These people satisfy such esteem-related desires through attempts to establish control over an organization or a domain of activity as well as the more direct engagement of others in open competition. Clearly, such people should view compromise as a defeat, because giving any amount of ground defines a symbolic loss of that amount of power.

Table 11.1 demonstrates how the larger analysis of group process can be used to predict the remainder of the dominant individual's interpersonal activity. Notice that we predict (and demonstrated in chaps. 9 and 10) that in extended interactions the dominant person will use a great deal of the initiation form of behavior and will be relatively uninvolved in using affiliative behavior. Recall that in Table 5.4 we used the Borgatta system to define the specific behaviors that we can expect to characterize the dominant person's use of each of these axes. That table portrays the dominance-oriented person as a task-directing individual who can use all of the many types of initiation behavior. In addition, although not disaffiliative in actively hostile ways, he or she is simply unconcerned with unnecessary pleasantries or social amenities. Table 11.1 also predicts that dominance-oriented people should assume a firm stance in their attempts at bargaining with other people, but their success is limited by the rigid way they handle the information needed to solve problems. However, as they are skilled at influencing others and have easy use of most modes of power, they make formidable opponents. Clearly, the combination of an open, competitive interpersonal style, an intensely task-oriented (and nonaffiliative) performance style, and a firmness of bargaining stance results in a strong and effective negotiation style.

The need for recognition shares many of the attributes of the dominance motive and directs the individual to many of the same features of negotiation. However, as the purpose of the interpersonal competition is to confirm the individual's worth by coercing praise from the opponent (rather than the dominant person's simpler need for success at the task), this complex requirement necessarily leads to less intense competition with other people. This apparent need for praise from competitors leads the person to assume a more affable and conciliatory stance, factors which lead the person toward compromise and a more maleable bargaining position. Furthermore, as they are also rigid in their problem-solving techniques, they are vulnerable when their attempts at influence fail. Thus, when challenged in a way that exceeds their ability to respond, persons with a need for recognition first tend to become hostile but then reluctantly become compromising in their negotiating style. Overall, they could be characterized as moderately strong and effective negotiators whose initially strong demands are not pursued throughout the course of an intense negotiation with a determined opponent.

As we review the total number of studies that have been undertaken in the area of group process, it is interesting to note that the vast majority of them are of the exploitative mode of interdependence. Although there might be many reasons for this concentration of effort, it is probable that most investigators focus on the personality variable that appears to be most involved with the most dramatic feature of the social phenomenon being considered. Thus, for example, we have seen that dominance is most often studied in the area of leadership, the need for approval in the area of conformity, anxiety in the area of rigidity of cognitive processing, and so forth. In the case of the resolution of interpersonal conflict, the focus has been on the frequently melodramatic forms of deceptive competition practiced by Machiavellians. Fortunately, for the motive of dominance, which has played such an important role in other areas, we have just enough empirical evidence to sketch out what appear to be its effects across all the features of the group process.

Let us begin by briefly summarizing the conclusions that we reached in earlier chapters. A massive collection of studies supports the hypothesis that dominance is involved in the initiation form of activity (Table 9.1). It is also interesting that there are virtually no published studies that have examined the effects of dominance on the behavioral use of the affiliation-disaffiliation axis of interpersonal space (chap. 10). Recall that we predict a neutral position in the use of this axis by dominance-motivated people. The only supportive bit of evidence for this comes from the study by Kolb and Boyatzis (1970), which showed that the need for power was associated with intense task concern rather than with interpersonal concern. Similarly, we could find no published results to examine the prediction that dominance-motivated people are more rigid in their use of information.

There is one study (Assor & O'Quin, 1982) demonstrating that dominance is related to the expected firmness of an individual's bargaining stance. Assor and O'Quin report the results of an experiment in which they examined the association between a number of personality variables and several behavioral measures of bargaining firmness, such as the number of bids and the level of the final agreement. After an initial testing session in which the CPI dominance scale was included, along with tests for internality, need for approval, and dependency, male and female undergraduates were invited to participate in a subsequent experimental session. In the second session, in a dyadic face-to-face encounter with another undergraduate across a table, they were asked to bargain until they reached agreement on the price of a landscape painting. In this fairly realistic situation, which postsession questionnaires demonstrated successfully involved the participants, scores on the Dominance scale were significantly related to a number of the measures of bargaining firmness. We return to additional results from this study as appropriate in later sections. In light of the types of research that we would expect to discover in the literature, it is surprising that there are so few examinations of the effects of dominance, or related states, on the toughness of bargaining stance. If we can assume that "winning" at a bargaining session is a measure of firmness of bargaining stance, then two studies by Uleman (1971, 1972) on the related state of the need for influence provide some evidence to support the conclusion that this variable frequently affects the individual's intention, expectation, and degree of success at interpersonal bargaining.

Notice that there has been no discussion of the empirical network of behaviors associated with the need for recognition. As we have seen throughout the book, the lack of interest in this variable has resulted in the lack of a proper measure for studying this motive. This is unfortunate because the normal population probably contains many more people concerned with this motive than with dominance or power, and the social effects of the need for recognition are probably nowhere more interesting than they are for understanding the flow of group process.

Our major purpose, however, is to describe and evaluate the utility of this approach to the study of group process. In the case of the adversarial mode of interpersonal relations, there is one study that confirms the prediction that dominance is associated with a tendency to reveal information, as well as several others that indicate its association with a primarily competitive stance to conflict resolution. In the area of information management, Rosenfeld and Plax (1976) report the results of a study using self-report techniques to establish the personality correlates of self-disclosure. They asked students to complete a battery of standard psychological instruments and two questionaires that identify the degree of willingness to reveal information about oneself. As expected, scores on the Dominance scale were positively associated with this self-report index of the openness of information use. Much more research is needed, however, before we can feel secure in this particular feature of group process.

On the other hand, there is just enough information to determine that this motive is related to competitive forms of negotiation. In a rather straightforward experiment designed to identify the personality factors that contribute to competitive interpersonal behavior, Sermat (1968) selected individuals who had scored either quite high or quite low on the Dominance scale in an earlier testing session and brought them into the laboratory to play an experimental game. On this highly structured task, which offered players the usual incentive to win by choosing the cooperative as well as the competitive strategy, Sermat predicted, and found, that those participants who had scored high on the Dominance scale selected a much more competitive basis for relating to the other player than did those who had scored low on the test.

In the most influential of the studies on personality and negotiation strategy, Terhune (1968) used the TAT measures of the need for achievement, affiliation, and power to select individuals to play a series of Prisoner's Dilemma games. In this carefully planned experiment, Terhune was able to demonstrate a variety of interesting effects that we describe as each motive is considered. Although Terhune is extremely sensitive to the mechanisms through which situational and task variables affect the personality-negotiation relationship (see Terhune, 1970), in this monograph-length report he demonstrated a number of important ways that motives influence negotiation behavior. To state one of his major findings briefly, Terhune provided clear evidence that the need for power is associated with a highly competitive orientation to interpersonal relations. Finally, Rubin and Brown (1975) suggest that an unpublished study by Higgs and McGrath (1965) and a brief report by Marlowe (1963) provide some corroborating pieces of evidence in support of the power-competition relationship, as does, possibly, part of a study by Williams, Steele, and Tedeschi (1969).

The Exploitative Mode

The exploitative mode of relationship is one in which individuals are as competitive in seeking to enhance their own opportunities from a relationship as they are in the adversarial mode. It can be distinguished easily from the adversarial mode, however, because it is one in which information is concealed in order to maximize the individual's personal gain. Individuals who assume this mode of interdependence will adhere to rules only as long as it is expedient; they will lie, deceive, ingratiate, bluster, and in general, seek to circumvent the rules if it contributes to their own gain. Unlike the individual who assumes the adversarial style of "clean" competitive encounter, the exploitative style permits the individual to assume a manipulative approach to the vulnerabilities of others. This may range from the display of a pseudonurturant consideration for the welfare of others to the more obviously aggressive, tormenting, or retaliative behavior needed to enhance their own egocentric pursuit of their own welfare. Thus, the individuals who assume this approach have the opportunity to use the many varieties of deceit as they stealthily pursue their own ends.

It is interesting that quite different kinds of people can use this mode of relationship. The most important difference between these types of people is the way in which they conceal information. Possibly, this may be due to the fact that although an open stance to an encounter directs the attention of the participants to the actual materials of the social situation, a deceitful stance permits the participants to develop a much wider range of invention. The preeminent personality variable associated with this mode is the trait of Machiavellianism, because the Machiavellian seeks to enhance his or her own gain by the opportunistic manipulation of others. Machiavellian individuals represent an interesting form of adaptation because they are fundamentally cynical and yet enormously skilled interpersonally. They present the fascinating combination of a public representation of self that mimics psychological health, but their intentions border on psychopathic exploitation. For the Machiavellian, the personal gain found in an interaction is the opportunity to manipulate others (Christie & Geis, 1970). It is not surprising that these attributes lead to success in negotiations because the Machiavellian often can enact with great fluency those behaviors necessary to play whatever role will maximize personal gain.

Table 11.1 outlines many of the additional features of the behavioral process through which the Machiavellian becomes successful. First, they are highly energetic initiators of the task and the socioemotional activity required by that social situation. They are skilled at both defining the nature of the activity and orchestrating the flow of events. Second, with their great clarity of purpose, they are clear and firm in their bargaining stance. Third, their flexibility in problem solving leads them to more easily select the most promising direction to take in the course of a negotiation. This includes the ability to withhold or reveal information in ways that solidify their position and attack the Achilles' heel of their adversary. It also includes the ability to obtain and use any form of power that they believe will be effective in controlling their opponent. In sum, the Machiavellian is a strong and effective negotiator.

Authoritarianism is a second trait that directs the individual to select the exploitative style of negotiation. Together with the Machiavellian, the authoritarian shares a mistrustful view of people. They, too, selectively manipulate the information that they reveal about their purposes. However, in contrast to the Machiavellian, it is a serious lack of self-confidence that leads the authoritarian to disclose as little information as possible in order to retain as much freedom of action as the negotiation permits. Similarly, the mistrust component of this trait should make it more difficult for authoritarians to believe that cooperation is a viable mode of interdependence. Rather, their self-protective nature should lead them to assume a competitive stance toward peers that focuses on personal gain. In addition, the analysis of performance styles presented in Table 5.4 describes an individual who is fairly active on the initiation axis in order to minimize his or her level of anxiety by rigidly controlling the flow of events. However, Table 5.4 predicts that the authoritarian selects a very narrow band of behaviors through which to accomplish his or her effects. The table also represents the authoritarian as highly disaffiliative. We expect this type of performance style because, as we argued earlier, anxiety over issues of prediction and control leads to egocentric utilization of external sources of support. For the authoritarian, this support is usually found in the task. The hostility component associated with this trait leads the authoritarian even more strongly into the disaffiliative orientation, especially when negotiating against those individuals of lower status and power.

Let us return to Table 11.1 in order to complete our review of the interpersonal behavior that we expect to find from the authoritarian. As we have seen in earlier chapters, authoritarians possess rigid problem-solving strategies, which lead them to become quite anxious when workable solutions do not quickly materialize. This factor, together with their lack of self-confidence, leads the authoritarian to be more compliant in the course of bargaining. Moreover, as the negotiation process continues, authoritarians rely on their position of authority as a major source of their attempt to exert influence over others. In the event that reliance on social rank fails to be influential in helping them achieve their bargaining goal, authoritarians may become hostile and attempt to control the flow of information, the allocation of tasks, and group decision making. If these attempts fail, the theoretical analysis of the authoritarian personality suggests that he or she may become completely recalcitrant or else completely submissive, depending on the rank of the opponent. Overall, we expect that the authoritarian's fairly successful externally oriented defensive structure will lead to a moderately strong and effective negotiation style.

The need for abasement is a third dispositional characteristic that leads individuals to use interpersonal transactions to maximize their own gain through highly nondisclosing maneuvers. From the ordinary observer's point of view, the self-abasing individual is not an effective negotiator because of the self-defeating nature of the behavior that is produced by this motive. Behaviorally, these individuals are neither task nor interpersonally competent. They do not initiate significant amounts of activity but rather are compliant and, especially, disaffiliative in order to evoke dissatisfaction from others. They attempt to draw the contempt of others by their plaintive displays of worthlessness and maintain a firm bargaining stance in defense of their self-deprecating maneuvers in order to irritate others even further. These people present an interesting contrast to Machiavellians in that, from their point of view, they are extremely active and highly flexible in selecting the particular interpersonal approach that is sure to displease. Behaviorally, they appear to be rigid in maintaining a narrow problem-solving approach, but across interpersonal "opponents," they may be highly intelligent in modifying the particular technique of ineffectiveness that they choose to display.

Once again, we begin our empirical examination of this view of group process by summarizing the relevant research presented in earlier chapters.

For both authoritarianism and Machiavellianism, we predicted a more complex pattern than usual in the use of the initiation–concurrence dimension, determined by the presence or absence of additional situational variables. In the research at hand, we have virtually no information on the degree to which authoritarians and Machiavellians exhibit leadership behaviors in a task group. However, in the next chapter, we examine the few studies that show the limited social conditions under which authoritarians assume the leadership of a group. In addition, the research on experimental games shows the Machiavellian to be a strong, controlling, and manipulative individual. These characteristics all fall on the initiation side of interpersonal space.

The information on concurrence is a bit clearer. Just as theory predicts, authoritarians are much more yielding to higher (as compared to lower) status influence agents, whereas Machiavellians have been shown to be much less agreeable in response to attempts at influence. In the last chapter, we saw that, on the affiliation–disaffiliation axis, authoritarians are unhelpful, critical, and punitive in their judgment of others. Although Machiavellians have been shown to be interpersonally sensitive, in the few studies that are available (Geis, 1978), their self-interested focus shows them to be neither helpful nor involved in the concerns of other people. In contrast to these scattered results, we have reviewed a major body of evidence describing the rigidity with which authoritarians use information. Again, Machiavellianism has not drawn the attention of those experimentalists who study information processing in the usual way. We soon see that they are extremely flexible in devising ways to control the outcomes of the interaction during experimental games. Considering the nature of Machiavellianism, however, we would predict that in the typical cognitive-processes laboratory they would emerge as highly rigid in their performance because they would find few incentives in that task to arouse their more flexible information-processing capabilities. Such experiments, contrasting the incentives inherent in the task, should be quite easy to perform.

We have found enough evidence to make plausible Jourard's observation that more neurotic individuals are less disclosing of information about themselves. Four separate studies (Pilkonis, 1977a, 1977b; Post, Wittmaier, & Radin, 1978; Wheeless & Grotz, 1977), using self-report and behavioral techniques, demonstrated that safety-related variables are negatively associated with an individual's tendency to reveal information about him- or herself. A variety of indices of less successful personal adjustment (e.g., anxiety, neuroticism, and mistrust, which are among the primary components of the trait of authoritarianism) have all established that such a relationship does exist. A fifth study (Worthy, Gary, & Kahn, 1969) attempted to examine this relationship in a highly structured experiment that made frequent demands for publicly broadcast self-disclosure. Unfortunately, this interesting experiment was less successful, although their approach might be useful if a way could be found to reduce the overwhelming impact of the experimenter's requirement of public self-disclosure on demand. It is likely that this methodological factor made the subjects quite apprehensive and so dampened the expected effect.

On the other hand, there is now a substantial body of research to support the assumption that authoritarian people attempt to maximize their own gains during a negotiation. As part of his larger program studying the antecedents of cooperation, Deutsch (1960) hypothesized that the authoritarian individual will perform in mistrustful, competitive ways. In an experiment that became the model for many others, Deutsch measured the authoritarianism of undergraduates and, several weeks later, asked them to participate in an experimental game that offered each player the usual choice between the cooperative and the competitive alternative. This initial experiment presented strong evidence that the authoritarian individual will make the more competitive choice.

The major features of this study have been repeated many times. Although there has been some variation in the selection instrument used, dispositional variable identified, type of game played, and interpersonal strategy selected, the main thrust of the hypothesis has been substantially supported. Studies that have reported similar results using the authoritarianism scale or related instruments and variables are: Berkowitz (1968); Bixenstine and Douglas (1967); Bixenstine, Levitt, and Wilson (1966); Bixenstine and O'Reilly (1966); Bixenstine, Potash, and Wilson (1963); Bixenstine and Wilson (1963); Bloomfield and Blick (1975); Druckman (1976); Friedell (1968); Kuhlman and Marshello (1975); Lutzker (1960); McClintock, Gallo, and Harrison (1965); McClintock, Harrison, Strand, and Gallo (1963); McKeown, Gahagan, and Tedeschi (1967); Rim (1979); Schlenker, Helm, and Tedeschi (1973); Tedeschi, Hiester, and Gahagan (1969); and Wrightsman (1966). However, it must be cautioned that not all of these studies neatly confirm Deutsch's original finding. Some of them provided only marginal support (i.e., Schlenker et al.) or found that the relationship appears in more or less complex patterns of interaction (i.e., McKeown et al.; Wrightsman). Finally, we need to note three additional studies that did not demonstrate this relationship: Bixenstine, Chambers, and Wilson (1964); Wilson and Robinson (1968); Wood, Pilisuk, and Uren (1973).

The overwhelming weight of all the evidence obtained in these studies follows Kelley and Stahelski's (1970) influential discussion of the interpersonal negotiating techniques used by the authoritarian person. This theoretical review concluded that the authoritarian person behaves in consistently exploitative ways, whereas the nonauthoritarian person realistically determines the most appropriate strategy to fit the negotiation. All of this work, then, describes the authoritarian person as consistently guarded and uncooperative because he or she is suspicious of the intentions of other people and concerned to structure an interpersonal relationship in highly self-protective ways.

In contrast to the shared set of experimental procedures and the quiet language used to study the interpersonal strategies of the authoritarian, work on Machiavellianism seems to be highly stimulating to the psychologist's methodological inventiveness. In fact, the range of experimental situations that have been used and the liveliness of the discussion seem only surpassed in social psychology by the work on prosocial behavior. If the accounts of the Machiavellian's tactics of lying, cheating, and stealing seem reprehensible, it may satisfy our sense of fairness to realize that, in a very high proportion of these experiments, psychologists have in turn used confederates to deceive Machiavellians in highly imaginative ways.

There are several excellent reviews (Christie & Geis, 1970; Geis, 1978) that describe the major studies of this program in great detail. The most important conclusion that emerges from all of this work is that "the Machiavellian individual is one who, among other things, thrives in situations where manipulatory possibilities abound" (McLaughlin, 1970, p. 115). The Machiavellian reports a greater willingness to use deceitful strategies or to select more information-concealing tactics from an array presented in a simulated interview (Domelsmith & Dietch, 1978; Falbo, 1977; Pandey & Rastogi, 1979). In role playing as well as in naturalistic settings, the Machiavellian is more capable of modifying his or her behavior in ways that lead to the most personally desirable set of outcomes (Blumstein, 1973; Singer, 1964), a finding that is supported by more traditional experimental procedures that study cheating and other information-management tactics (Cooper & Peterson, 1980; Jones, Nickel, & Schmidt, 1979).

From the point of view of the disclosure of information as a weapon in the interpersonal struggle, it is important to realize that Machiavellians lie more easily and more capably (Braginsky, 1970; Geis & Moon, 1981). They are also much more willing to trick, injure, or interfere with another person (Harrell & Hartnagel, 1976). For example, McLaughlin (1970) devised an experiment in which he asked Machiavellian or non-Machiavellian people to attempt to distract another person (actually, a confederate) who was attempting to learn a list of words on a tachistoscope. Subjects were given a list of suggested interventions, such as whistling, interrupting, telling the "learner" that he was doing poorly, or they could invent any other device that might be distracting. It is interesting that not only did Machiavellian people use much more distracting behavior, but in the course of disrupting the activity, they also showed much less incidental learning of the list of words than did non-Machiavellian people. Therefore, these results show that not only are Machiavellians more manipulative, but their attention is much more highly focused on this aspect of a social situation.

The opportunistic and amoral nature of this trait, even with children as young as 10 years old who lied and even bribed in order to deceive their partner (Braginsky, 1970), has been demonstrated in many interesting studies. If, in fact, the Machiavellian is less moral, then we would expect such people to be less troubled after committing an unethical act. This has been demonstrated both behaviorally and cognitively in situations that involved a case of cheating. Exline, Thibaut, Bannon, and Gumpert (1961) found that, after being implicated in such an act, the non-Machiavellians decreased visual contact with the experimenter much more than did the Machiavellians. Further, in a comparable situation, Bogart (1971) found that non-Machiavellians showed a dissonance effect that led them to change their attitudes in the direction of their immoral behavior. In contrast, Machiavellians, presumably because this behavior was not dissonant with their self-image as a moral person, did not change their attitudes in this direction.

Underlying the many different strategies that Machiavellians may employ in negotiating with other people is the fixed pursuit of their own personal ends. What makes this type of group process so fascinating, and so difficult to study, is that Machiavellians may, in one situation, use bluntly competitive maneuvers and yet, at other times, appear to be deeply concerned with their opponent's welfare. In Geis' (1978) words, the Machiavellian may "appear quite aware of others' concerns . . . [and] use them to their own advantage — for example, to strike a bargain ensuring themselves the lion's share of the payoff. . . . [They] are the ones who get others to help them win in such a way that the others feel grateful for the opportunity" (p. 354).

In addition to evaluating the more accessible material dealing with the effects of Machiavellianism on interpersonal strategies, Rubin and Brown (1975) examined the results of a number of dissertations and other unpublished studies. The preponderance of the 16 studies that they reviewed supports the hypothesis that Machiavellians bargain more competitively than do non-Machiavellians. For example, in an attempt to extend the research on authoritarianism and competition in the Prisoner's Dilemma game, Uejio and Wrightsman (1967) had undergraduate women take part in an extended series of experimental games after completing a set of personality and attitudinal measures. In the part of this experiment that parallels the studies done on authoritarianism, Uejio and Wrightsman found a strong positive association between Machiavellianism and competitive choices. In one of the most dramatic and informative of the early experiments on the behavioral consequences of the trait of Machiavellianism, Geis, Christie, and Nelson (1970) devised a game to be played by three people, in which they were assigned different degrees of power to be used in playing the game and in which they could form coalitions to improve their chances of winning. In this game, a Machiavellian, an intermediate, and a non-Machiavellian person were the three players, and the rules allowed them to form and to dissolve coalitions at any time as long as the players agreed on how the final winnings were to be divided. Additionally, the game was played under conditions in which all players were either ignorant (the ambiguous condition) or knowledgeable (the unambiguous condition) of the power assigned to the other players. The results of this game were quite clear. Machiavellians consistently outbargained the other players, particularly in the setting that was the most ambiguous (the condition in which they were most able to manipulate the flow of information). Even more important than the mere fact of winning were the tactics used by the Machiavellian. In this experiment and in others reported by Geis (1978), it is clear that Machiavellians are much more determined to succeed in obtaining the goal that they define as their self-interest. They are more focused on the task, more inventive in devising tactics that might lead them to prevail, and more unscrupulous in their relationships with their adversaries.

The Ingratiating Mode

The ingratiating mode is defined by a cooperative and information-concealing pattern of interaction. Although a cooperative relationship is selected, if possible, individuals who use this form of relationship are not concerned with the joint welfare of all participants as much as they are concerned with devising a secure means to mimimize any further losses. Partly because of their more extreme form of insecurity, these people attempt to develop a stable relationship with clear-cut bases for sharing resources, in which they can expect to receive care from more capable people. In return for the care that they desire, people who require this form of relationship are willing to appear to be deferential, even servile, toward the caregiver. In addition, as their level of insecurity leads them to be mistrustful of others, they are quite cautious about revealing personal information. Thus, in attempting to minimize losses, the ingratiating individual is cooperative in response to social demands, guarded in disclosing his or her thoughts and purposes, and in general, anxious to seek an ameliorating and nonconfrontational resolution to the appearance of interpersonal conflict.

The ingratiating mode is most congruent with the requirements that the need for approval brings to interpersonal behavior. Individuals concerned with this disposition tend to exhibit a variety of task and socioemotional behaviors as their performance style, omitting only those initiating behaviors, such as "gives procedural suggestion," that direct the work of others. Table 5.4 suggests the set of specific behaviors through which such individuals convey their cheerful participation in an activity controlled by others. The negotiating styles suggested by Table 11.1 further reveal the activity through which these individuals make agreements to remove what they perceive as an interpersonal threat. They are yielding in their bargaining stance, rigidly focused on what might appear to be the most promising route to a cooperatively protective relationship with a stronger group member, and although overtly anxious to be seen by others as good-humoredly participative, they are, in fact, highly guarded about revealing their true thoughts, feelings, and purposes. After all, these people are attempting to obtain a desperately needed resource through the construction of a deferentially cheerful public image. We might wonder about how high an inner toll such a difficult interpersonal task must take and how carefully such people protect what they perceive to be their extreme vulnerability.

The need for dependency is a second disposition that leads individuals to attempt to reduce their high levels of anxiety through the use of these group-process mechanisms. The major difference in their interpersonal behavior is that the defensive structure that generates the dependency needs does not lead to such highly participative levels of task or social activity. Table 5.4 suggests a much more passive individual who waits for others to take the lead in organizing an activity and whose fairly high disaffiliative score is produced by withdrawal rather than by aggressive activity. A comparison of the behaviors resulting from the defensive structures of these two dispositions predicts that the personal benefits of the interaction for the other people in the group is likely to be much higher in the case of the need for approval than it is for dependency.

The need for order is a third dispositional variable that uses the ingratiating mode. At first, this prediction might appear to be surprising because the discussion of this characteristic portrays an annoying, if not unpleasant, individual. However, reviewing a key aspect of this person's defensive structure explains why we feel that these people's tendencies are in the direction of overall cooperation (and thus why we do not predict that this person uses the exploitative mode). Recall our assertion that this person controls anxiety by a significant investment in task activity. This factor, together with his or her mistrust of others, leads the individual concerned with the need for order to define the task as one in which he or she is responsible for the success of the joint activity. However, as long as this person retains effective control over the activity, it is not necessary to maximize personal gain. In other words, the overall task and the benefits of accomplishing it are seen as a joint venture of the group, even though the direction is provided by this person. In addition, we expect that they will be quite guarded in their disclosure of information, because such caution helps to assure that they will retain control. However, because they prefer a highly structured rule-bound procedure, in the course of working on the task, they become firm bargainers who may get locked into a preconception of how the task is to proceed. Consequently, this rigidity may interfere with their ability to consider other negotiating strategies. Finally, because their defensive structure is formed around an investment in task competence, it is quite possible that these individuals will produce large amounts of impressive technical detail, which should help them become fairly effective bargainers with most opponents.

Of these three personality variables, there is a substantial amount of research available only on the behavior associated with the social consequences of the need for approval. Therefore, we are forced to limit our discussion only to that motive. In general, the research that we reviewed in earlier chapters provides a great deal of support for several of our more obvious theoretical expectations. The bulk of the research that has been done on the level of activity to be observed on the initiation–concurrence dimension centers around the degree to which the need for approval is associated with compliance, conformity, persuasibility, obedience, modeling, and imitation. There seems to be little doubt that this disposition can be involved in a person's yielding to social influence attempts. Unfortunately, the types of information that would help us to develop a richer view of group process are not yet available. In Table 5.4, we use the more differentiated set of behaviors provided by Borgatta to inquire into the range of behaviors that we might expect to observe from an individual concerned with the need for approval. Theoretically, we would expect such an individual to be fairly active in his or her use of many of the initiation types of behavior, such as suggesting solutions or giving opinions or information, that allow the person to be an active participant in the work of the group. We would not expect these people to direct or evaluate the work of others. Similarly, we know that these people will not be engaged in affiliative activity with other people in fairly stressful circumstances. However, we have not been able to find any research to examine our belief that they will respond affiliatively to others in nonstressful circumstances.

We know from a number of sources (e.g., Larsen, Martin, Ettinger, & Nelson, 1976) that individuals strongly characterized by the need for approval tend to report many positive comments about other people, the task, their performance, and the experimenter. One would think that people who are so positive in their apparent perceptions would be quite sociable, talkative, and self-disclosing in their interactions with other people. However, recall that the definition we prefer to use emphasizes that the interpersonal approval-seeking behaviors are designed to reduce these people's levels of anxiety, rather than confirm the quality of their performance. For this reason, we would expect, as did Strickland and Crowne (1963), that approval-oriented persons would act defensively by disclosing less information about themselves. A number of studies (Brundage, Derlega, & Cash, 1977; Buhrenne & Mirels, 1970; Cravens, 1973; Efran & Boylin, 1967; Kopfstein & Kopfstein, 1973; Matloff & Doster, 1976; Rosenfeld & Plax, 1976), using role-playing, experimental, free description, and self-report techniques, report results that confirm this hypothesis. One of these studies (Cravens, 1973) extends this idea in an interesting way. Drawing upon the mainstream of work on approval motivation, Cravens suggested that although this relationship should appear in the normal private communications between individuals, the strength of the conformity response of highly approval-motivated people would lead them to be more disclosing if a public task required them to be more open. Cravens study, which confirmed his two hypotheses, is an important addition to the conclusions that we may draw from this group of studies.

Once again, enough studies are available to make plausible the hypothesis that the need for approval leads individuals into cooperative relationships, and there is a larger number available to examine the mechanism that may underlie this choice. First, in a study correlating scores on a number of tests with reported preferences for different forms of negotiation, Jones and Melcher (1982) provide some evidence that approval-motivated people state a desire for cooperative modes of conflict resolution. Putting this hypothesis to an experimental test, Marlowe (1963) and Tedeschi, Burrill, and Gahagan (1969), using a modified Prisoner's Dilemma game, provide experimental evidence that approval-motivated people seek the cooperative choice in an extended, highly structured negotiation.

In support of these three studies are the results from several programs of work on a closely related problem: How do approval-motivated people handle their responses to frustration? The central hypothesis in a number of different studies is that, in reaction to frustration, individuals who are highly motivated to gain approval would inhibit their less socially acceptable behavior toward the frustrator and substitute positive and cooperative attitudes in its place. In other words, the overall thrust of these studies (Berger, Levin, Jacobson, & Millham, 1977; Conn & Crowne, 1964; Dies, 1970; Fishman, 1965; Larsen et al., 1976; Millham, 1974; Millham & Kellogg, 1980; Palmer & Altrocchi, 1967) allows us to point to the substitution of cooperation for anger as an impression-management device used by the approval-motivated person in order to avoid rejection. In the next section, we examine two additional motivational bases for forming a cooperative relationship.

The Integrative Mode

The integrative mode is defined by a cooperative and information-revealing pattern of interaction. Just as the exploitative style is the one that most emphasizes self-interest, the integrative style is the one that most emphasizes the joint welfare of all parties. Thus, this mode provides the most cooperative and democratic interpersonal relationships, in which the process of the negotiation is nearly as important as the outcome. The individuals who manifest this mode of interdependence are confident of their ability to work well with other people on the task, and so are both disclosing of their purposes to others, as well as able to recognize their rights to a successful outcome. Thus, in most of our experimental situations, we expect negotiations that stress persuasion rather than intimidation and solutions that recognize the joint welfare of all participants.

There are three dispositions in our group of personality variables that seem to use the central features of the integrative mode. We have described the affiliative person as one who seeks mutually satisfying and egalitarian involvement in social transactions. By definition, these people are highly invested in the affiliative, rather than the initiation, axis of interpersonal life. In fact, it is possible that task activities merely provide the means through which these people become involved with other members of the group. This motivational feature predicts that the need for affiliation leads the person directly into cooperative and information-revealing relationships. Although they can be quite flexible in searching for possible solutions, they do not appear to be as firm in their bargaining stance, because the feared loss of mutual involvement creates a vulnerability that a more demanding negotiator can seize upon during a negotiation. In sum, the person with strong needs for affiliation appears to be a most pleasant and conscientious group member who steadfastly adheres to group norms and goals. However, should he or she be threatened by loss of group support (e.g., experience hostility or exploitation), the affiliative person will tend to withdraw from the field.

The need for achievement should lead to a cooperative and information-revealing style for the same type of reason. Achievement-oriented people are highly invested in the goal of task accomplishment, just as individuals with strong affiliation needs are highly invested in interpersonal activity. Their focus on the outcome of the task, rather than on using the task to affect their relationship with others, reduces the benefits that might come from concealing their purposes from others, just as it increases the value of obtaining the cooperation of other participants. We expect that cooperation is not sought as an end in itself, as with affiliation-oriented people. Rather, if it is a reasonable choice to make in responding to a task, then there are few personal barriers to its selection. In the course of working on a task, these individuals are highly active initiators of events, and if socioemotional activity is part of the task description, they can perform along that dimension, too. Furthermore, we expect that their deeply rooted sense of personal competence enables them to be firm in bargaining with an opponent and flexible in surveying possible solutions to a bargaining task. Overall, we expect that they are strong, effective negotiators who can clearly articulate their goals and skillfully organize their resources to achieve success.

With the single exception of their strong involvement on the affiliative axis of social behavior, we expect that the need for nurturance should lead individuals into a similar type of group process as the need for achievement. If we have been correct in describing this need as representing "generativity," in the Eriksonian sense, we can predict that these people will desire to work with others as an end in itself. Therefore, we expect them to value the cooperative relationship highly, as well as the process of disclosing information. Specifically, they should enjoy working with others in jointly valued projects and assisting them to be successful. In the course of the group's work, we expect that they will be flexible in surveying solutions, firm (although not insistent) in maintaining their opinions, skillful and tactful in directing co-workers, and perceptive, unthreatened, and persistent in negotiating with adversaries. In sum, for these people, satisfaction from the group process is derived most from the success and growth of all participants involved.

Although one would expect to find a rich treasury of empirical studies relating affiliative needs to self-revealing and cooperative processes, we are once again puzzled by the absence of work on the behavioral correlates of affiliative variables. In previous chapters, we saw that there are a moderate number of studies confirming the prediction that the need for affiliation will lead individuals into a substantial amount of affiliative behavior. On the other hand, there is virtually no information with which to evaluate our other predictions. We are in a similar position in searching for evidence on the modes of interdependence. There are only two studies (Rosenfeld & Plax, 1976; Tuckman, 1966) indicating that this variable is associated with a tendency to be more self-revealing in social situations. Even more surprising, there are only four studies (Bennet & Carbonari, 1976; Kilmann & Thomas, 1975; Noland & Catron, 1969; Terhune, 1968) that have examined the preferred relationships sought by affiliation-oriented individuals. As predicted, these studies demonstrate that a cooperative relationship is selected, at least in the context of an experimental game. Terhune makes an extremely important contribution to our understanding of the context within which the affiliative person behaves in cooperative ways. Terhune was able to show that as the choice became riskier, the affiliative person became more suspicious, defensive, and uncooperative. This fact, showing that the need for affiliation does not lead to an unrelentingly cooperative posture, should stimulate a much broader set of hypotheses on the nature of group process to be expected from this variable. We can conclude, with Rubin and Brown, that affiliation-oriented people will behave cooperatively as long as other people reciprocate. However, it is likely that their lack of a firmer sense of self, which we expect to find associated with esteem-related variables, makes them feel more threatened by the lack of trustworthiness in other people, and so leads them to behave more vindictively in their own self-defense.

When we examine the empirical support for the hypotheses related to esteem needs (see Table 11.1), the situation is similar to one encountered in some of the earlier chapters. We have found a good deal of support for certain broad statements on the relationship of personality to group process, but our ability to make theoretical distinctions far outstrips our ability to marshall empirical support. In this area of group process, although some of the research has been performed using tests for variables such as the internal locus of control or the need for achievement, it seems most reasonable to see the similarity of the results of these studies as the consequence of a broad self-esteem factor. However, the advantage of focusing on the similarities in the studies is that it permits us to combine studies across variables and instruments into a reasonably strong collection of evidence with which to examine the core of our predictions.

Let us quickly summarize our earlier discussions of group process and then proceed to examine a set of new information that is available on the modes of interdependence. As we saw in chapter 9, there is an enormous, if totally undifferentiated, amount of literature to support the hypothesis that self-esteem is positively related to the initiation of, and negatively related to the concurrence to, social influence attempts. Similarly, as we saw in chapter 10, there is evidence to support the hypothesis that certain self-esteem variables (e.g., the need for achievement) make possible substantial functioning on the affiliation dimension, if needed to complete a task successfully. In addition, in chapter 7, we saw another major body of evidence to support our hypotheses on the flexibility with which these people approach their solutions to the task.

The new information on group process that can be added to these earlier discussions evaluates the hypotheses on the firmness with which these people deal with social negotiations, the degree of informational openness they demonstrate, and the degree to which they prefer to use cooperative forms of interpersonal relationship. In the course of establishing their position in an experimental negotiation, these much more confident individuals are much more likely to take a firm course to their goals. During these experiments, in comparison to those individuals who score lower on these tests, they are more likely to: make a realistic appraisal of their relative strengths as compared with that of an opponent; set a higher initial negotiating position; bargain through an extended process of realistic concessions; and be more successful. The experiments that have studied this topic have used a variety of measurement techniques, such as self-report measures of achievement motivation, internal locus of control, and semiprojective measures of self-esteem. These experiments have used an even wider variety of experimental tasks within which to study the negotiation process, ranging from highly structured forms of negotiation such as the Prisoner's Dilemma game, to fairly unstructured bargaining over a real object, to behavioral studies of some of the forms of assertive behavior among newly married couples, to the characteristics of expert bridge players. The results of the studies in this area (Amidjaja & Vinacke, 1965; Assor & O'Quin, 1982; Bigoness, 1976; Capage & Lindskold, 1973; Chaney & Vinacke, 1960; Doherty & Ryder, 1979; Harnett, Cummings, & Hamner, 1973; Phillips, Aronoff, & Messé, 1971; Reznikoff, Bridges, & Hirsch, 1972; Watts, Messé, & Vallacher, 1982), which examine different aspects of the behaviors through which these people maintain their initial position in an interaction, provide reasonably clear evidence that self-esteem is associated with firmness in interpersonal negotiations.

Much of what we expect to find when we review the available research on self-esteem and the separate components of the integrative mode of interdependence has been anticipated in many of our earlier discussions. As we have seen so often, tests of anxiety or mistrust frequently identify people who are more secure and trustful as well. Discussions on the exploitative mode reviewed several studies (e.g., Kuhlman & Marshello, 1975) that contrasted authoritarian with nonauthoritarian people and were able to show the more cooperative orientation of the nonauthoritarian individual. The studies that have used esteemlike variables are similar in form and in quality to those that have been discussed to this point and confirm the broad outlines of the major hypothesis that has guided the research of many people since Deutsch and Jourard. Several studies (Ellison & Firestone, 1974; Hekmat & Theiss, 1971; Lefcourt, Sordoni, & Sordoni, 1974; Lombardo & Fantasia, 1976) provide evidence to support the hypothesis that more psychologically mature individuals are better able to reveal important information about themselves. Similarly, a number of studies (Haythorn, 1953; Norem-Hebeisen & Johnson, 1981; Terhune, 1968) reveal the preference of these individuals for more cooperative forms of relationship.

As we have seen before, Terhune's (1968) observations are especially valuable. The need for achievement was the third personality variable included in Terhune's study, and he was able to demonstrate that this variable was associated with the most cooperative choices made in his Prisoner's Dilemma game. It is interesting that Terhune explains the expected behavior of individuals concerned with the need for achievement with an argument based on the types of cognitive processes to be expected from these kinds of people. Rather than using a directly reward-seeking explanation, Terhune argues that it is achievement-motivated peoples' ability to make realistic assessments of their situation and to use cooperative relationships, if it promotes their self-interest, that underly their cooperative choice. We have discussed this explanation in the previous chapter as the source of the achievement-oriented individual's affiliative behavior. It is likely that such capacities serve equally well as the bases through which these people form their more enduring forms of interrelationship.

12 Group Structure

In the course of the kinds of negotiations that we have just described, individuals assume responsibility for the different components of the task. Over time, such task-based interactions become regularized as relatively stable patterns of interpersonal behavior. The form of these interchanges is composed of many of the structural elements that were described in chapter 4: the system of interrelated positions; the bases for rank between positions; the types of power used by the different positions; and the nature of the rewards distributed. In other words, a differentiated group with a fully articulated structure can emerge from this type of group process. In this chapter, we consider how dispositional factors may contribute to the emergence of these elements of group structure.

On the theoretical level, it is highly unusual for a social psychologist to state the problem in this way. We are most accustomed to consider the structure of the group as a primary independent variable within which we typically examine some psychological consequence. Throughout the book, we have described experiments in which individuals have been given instructions to interact within highly structured role relationships. Indeed, the next chapter describes extensive programs of research that specify the effects of variations of group structure upon the level of performance to be expected from different kinds of people. Yet, by extending the analysis that we presented in the last chapter, we can illustrate why it is worth investigating the possibility that features of group structure may have evolved, in part, from the characteristics of those individuals who participate in the interaction.

Thus, for example, it is rather easy to argue that the forces that produce the integrative mode of interdependence will also support an egalitarian type of group. The open and cooperative interpersonal orientation provided by individuals predominantly characterized by the needs for affiliation, achievement, or nurturance should lead these people to value the contribution made by other people as well. Such individuals should encourage other group members to participate actively in the group's work and not attempt to force distinctions among the different kinds of activity that occur within a group. In contrast, it seems highly unlikely that the forces producing the exploitative mode of interdependence would lead to an egalitarian group. The need to manipulate others in order to control the course of the group's work for personal gain is not best satisfied in an open form of social interaction. Rather, the structure that permits individuals such as authoritarians or Machiavellians to maximize their personal gain by manipulating decisions, persons, and resources is a hierarchically arranged group with clear distinctions of power that can centralize decision making. The interpersonal steps that such people take to conceal their purposes and maximize their gains also include the capture of whatever power is available and the isolation of the contributions advanced by the other group members. In other words, these individuals seek to organize a differentiated and hierarchical group.

These examples illustrate how the forces that underlie group process also contribute to significant aspects of group structure. Although there has been little work on this topic, it is important to review these social mechanisms, not only for their intrinsic interest, but also because of their extreme practical importance. We need to know if there is a force within the members of a group to devise a social structure that matches their predominant dispositions, because this form of congruence may seriously affect a group's level of productivity. In chapter 13, we review a great deal of evidence in support of an interactional theory of group productivity which argues that congruence between personality and situational variables creates the social environment that optimizes group output. In order to establish this principle, we must begin by indicating the nature of the social organization that is most congruent with the main forms of dispositional tendencies that members bring to their social activity.

ROLE DIFFERENTIATION

In chapter 4, role differentiation was defined in terms of the allocation of tasks across the members of the group. With this functional definition, one extreme form of role differentiation is the condition in which each member is allocated only a few tasks to perform. We termed this most differentiated role structure "role separation" in order to refer to the lessened degree of overlap among the tasks assigned to each position. At the other extreme, we used the term "role integration" to characterize groups in which the members each assume responsibility for many different tasks. In these groups, the roles are defined by a good deal of amalgamation of function.

We can recapitulate the bases for the predictions presented in Table 5.7 quite easily. Because of the pervasiveness of anxiety, we expect that most of the motives and traits based on the safety needs will lead the individual to desire as little responsibility for the work of the group as can be arranged. This aspect of the safety-based variables should lead them to develop narrowly construed social roles, with as few tasks assigned to each as is possible. For the same reason, these dispositions should lead to the additional feature of unequal ranks, or a condition of hierarchy between positions, being established in the group. Only the need for approval, with a defensive structure centering around participation in the work of others, should lead to a more integrated and egalitarian role structure. The affiliation motive, by definition, should also lead to more participative and egalitarian relationships with other group members. In contrast, most of the variables based upon esteem needs should lead individuals to assume responsibility for a wide range of activity in order to demonstrate their level of competence. With this desire to accumulate areas of responsibility, these dispositions should generally create pressure to establish an egalitarian group with broad roles based on amalgamation of function.

Only Machiavellianism and dominance seem to lead in somewhat different directions. Both of those variables lead to egocentric concentration on personal control of the group's work, and so should result in divided areas of responsibility. However, the Machiavellian seeks to use the task for personal displays of relative competence, which should result in a group with unequal ranking. As the dominance needs seem to be more task oriented, we expect that as long as there is division of control over the task, it is less necessary to rank the positions as well.

Although it is not difficult to predict the features of group structure that are the most likely outcomes of the various dispositional tendencies, marshalling a satisfactory base of supportive evidence is another question entirely. Only in the area of role differentiation has enough research been done to provide the empirical base on which we can form a tentative conclusion. There are two kinds of evidence that we can cite in evaluating these hypotheses. The first type is derived from the stated social preferences of the different kinds of people that we have been studying. The second is derived from observation of the actual social structures that some of these different kinds of people create when they have the opportunity to interact in the absence of an externally imposed social structure. Let us examine each source of information in turn.

The Stated Preference for Role Differentiation

Authoritarianism.   In one of the earliest of the studies that provides evidence on dispositionally related social preferences, Sanford (1950) assessed the ways in which authoritarians perceive leaders. In this study, Sanford found that authoritarians state that they prefer a strong, directive, high-status leader who would be active in making decisions and in initiating action. Similar results were reported by Medalia (1955) in a study of Air Force enlisted men. He found that authoritarian crew members were more accepting of their commanding officers than were nonauthoritarians and were more likely to reenlist, a fact that may indicate a greater need for a well-defined hierarchical group structure. In an industrial setting, Vroom (1960) found that authoritarian workers disliked participative decision making and tended to prefer hierarchical relations.

Dogmatism.   In an educational setting, Kuhlman (1976) found that dogmatic teachers expressed a desire for hierarchy, as measured by their strong endorsement of organizational control over decision making, subordination to authority, and rigid reliance on rule-oriented action. Nearly identical results were obtained by Zagona and Zurcher (1964), Talley and Vamos (1972), and Frye, Vidulich, Meierhoefer, and Joure (1972), who studied dogmatic students in small-group discussions. In a laboratory study, Weed and Mitchell (1974) found that dogmatic subjects prefer a highly structuring leader. In general, dogmatic persons in each of these studies became anxious in the unstructured group situation and stated a preference to have it changed.

Anxiety.   There are several studies that have examined the relationship between anxiety and a desire for a structured relationship. Tannenbaum and Allport (1956) found that the more anxious and insecure clerical workers in a large business preferred a hierarchically organized structure in which management closely controlled the decision-making powers. In contrast, employees with higher levels of self-esteem preferred to work in a structure that placed decision-making authority upon the workers. Nearly identical results were reported by Wispé and Lloyd (1955), who found that among life insurance agents, whose occupational success was often based on factors that they found difficult to understand or control, the more anxious agents preferred highly structured interactions with their supervisor as a way to make their outcomes more predictable.

Reviewing the information that these different studies produce, it seems quite clear that individuals who can be characterized as safety-oriented all seem to prefer hierarchical group structures with well-defined and separated role structures. This conclusion is further strengthened by the fact that this information is obtained from naturalistic organizations in a wide range of industrial, military, and educational settings. Additional information of this kind is provided in the parallel discussion in the next chapter. The stated preference obtained from these people is sufficiently strong to suggest that they would evolve this form of group structure as a way to manage their high levels of anxiety.

Behavioral Tests of the Relationship

In a classic study, Haythorn, Couch, Haefner, Langham, and Carter (1956b) studied the behavior of authoritarian and nonauthoritarian leaders in groups that were either homogeneous or heterogeneous in the authoritarianism level of the members. In groups that were composed of authoritarian individuals, the emergent leaders (as identified by the group members) were autocratic, interpersonally cold, and directed most of the group's activities. In contrast, groups composed of nonauthoritarian individuals had emergent leaders who were democratic, interpersonally sensitive, and requested participation from the other members. In a parallel study, Altman and McGinnies (1960) report that groups composed of ethnocentric subjects developed hierarchical group structures, whereas groups composed of nonethnocentric subjects developed more egalitarian structures. In a similar study, Slater (1955) found some evidence for the association of authoritarianism and the separation of function. Using a much more structured coalition-formation game, McGaffey (1976) found that more anxious subjects selected the low-risk game strategy in which they could transfer responsibility for success in the task to a stronger partner. In contrast, people with strong achievement needs resisted this tendency in favor of a more moderate risk strategy in which they retained responsibility for the play of the game. In summary, both the reported preference and the behavioral form of investigation provide a moderate amount of support for the conclusion that safety-oriented people prefer and, when possible, evolve the more hierarchical form of group structure with well-defined and separated role functions.

However, there are few studies to guide our understanding of the preferences of esteem-oriented people. Several studies that we review in other chapters provide indirect support for the prediction that the motive of dominance is associated with role separation and hierarchy. As we have seen, many studies show that dominant individuals seek the leadership role. Although this fact by itself would not confirm the prediction, other studies (Ashour & England, 1972) indicate that dominance-oriented subjects seek to limit the amount of control over the task that co-workers might possess, and in chapter 13, we describe a number of studies which indicate that these people do best in groups with divided function. Similarly, although there have been no studies directly examining the preference of individuals characterized by the need for achievement or internal locus of control for egalitarian groups with integrated roles, we describe a number of studies in chapter 13 that provide a substantial amount of evidence showing that persons with these characteristics are much more productive when they work in such groups.

Personality Influences on the Differentiation
of Social Groups

In a series of studies on natural and experimental groups, we were able to obtain enough evidence to show that it is plausible to believe there is an association between the dominant motives of the members of a group and important features of its structure. Using a common theoretical framework, these studies triangulate upon the relationship, each one trying to capitalize on the strength of a particular method as a way to make up for the limitations inherent in another method. Together, they yield a coordinated attack upon the problem.

The first study (Aronoff, 1967) was a naturalistic investigation of the relationship between personality and social structure among two occupational work groups on an island in the West Indies. This book-length report compared what appeared to be two somewhat different subcultures organized around work on the sugar cane plantation and around work in offshore fishing. One main finding from this study provides a significant piece of corroboration of our hypothesis. On the basis of a study which measured the socialization history, adult personality, and sociological structure of the work group, there emerged a strong association between the personality of the personnel in the group and the structure of the group itself. In one type of group, personality tests revealed that most of the members could be characterized as safety-oriented, and survey techniques revealed that the work structure was strongly authoritarian, with separated and hierarchically arranged social roles. In the other type of group, the research revealed that the members were esteem-oriented, with a strongly egalitarian work structure composed of broad and integrated roles.

This association between personality and social structure does not provide evidence on the possible causes for the correlation. Considerable effort was devoted to testing more traditional alternative hypotheses that might account for the finding. In each case, no other source could be found that might explain the effect. Still, from the point of view of the concerns of this chapter, the finding ultimately remains that of a simple correlation. However, the value of the study is that the correlation was obtained from real groups in which the strength of the separate factors that might have contributed to the interaction is not under question. Thus, although this study is not a conclusive investigation of the hypothesis, it is the appropriate first study in the series.

Four years later, after learning that there had been significant changes in the sociological structure of the first type of work group, a follow-up study (Aronoff, 1970) was conducted to determine the probable sources of the changes. This study replicated the procedures of the first and provided a significant part of the evidence that is needed to confirm the hypothesis. The main findings of this study were that: (a) there had been a substantial turnover of personnel in the work group; (b) the new personnel were predominantly esteem-oriented; and (c) the new members successfully demanded that the work organization be changed from an authoritarian to an egalitarian structure. As a second study of this series, this research represents a naturalistic experiment in which one component of an interaction was changed and its effects observed upon the other elements. This study retains the benefits of being a naturalistic examination of the personality/structure relationship, and it adds one of the ways in which a causal relationship can be determined. Yet, the results still need to be interpreted cautiously. Not only is the subject matter just one type of work group, but as a naturalistic study, it is difficult to make certain that the source of the effect is not some other as yet undetermined variable.

This particular aspect of the investigation is best conducted in the laboratory. As part of a triangulating scientific process (Crano, 1981), an experimental group adds to the confidence that the antecedents have been identified correctly. To further test the validity of the results obtained in the naturalistic research, a third study (Aronoff & Messé, 1971) replicated the study in the small-groups laboratory. Subjects were selected with the same assessment instrument used in the field and were asked to work in five-member groups that were homogeneous for either safety or esteem needs. The groups were given a set of quite involving tasks, lasting 2 hours, which required a wide range of task and socioemotional behavior. In the movement from a natural to an experimental group, it was necessary to operationalize social structure as the distribution of task-oriented communicative acts among group members. The activity of each group was videotaped, and later, the Borgatta Interaction Process Score system of behavioral analysis (Borgatta & Crowther, 1965) was used to code the entire course of group process. The results of this study showed that safety-oriented groups tended to establish hierarchical social structures, because most of the task-oriented leadership acts were consistently concentrated in a few individuals. In contrast, the distribution of such behaviors was spread much more evenly among the members of the esteem-oriented groups. Thus, the results of this study provide direct experimental evidence that careful control of the motivational input to an emerging group makes it possible to establish that group members attempt to develop motive-congruent properties to their groups (see Tuckman, 1964, for a related set of results).

The fourth study of this sequence (Wilson, Aronoff, & Messé, 1975) will be described in chapter 13. Briefly, this study tested the hypothesis by having safety- and esteem-oriented individuals work in groups whose structures were either congruent or incongruent with their motives (i.e., half the groups of each kind worked under an imposed hierarchical structure and the other half worked under an imposed egalitarian structure). The results of this study provide further confirmation of the hypothesis by demonstrating that, under carefully controlled conditions, both safety- and esteem-oriented groups can be highly productive when working under congruent structural conditions (and unproductive when working under incongruent structural conditions).

Each of these four studies contributes an additional type of evidence that the dispositions of the members of a group can affect the nature of the group's structure. Taken together, as well as when seen in the context of the research reviewed earlier in the chapter, these four studies make it plausible to maintain that member motivation is one of the antecedents of group organization.

THE BASES OF RANK

In chapter 4, we described the characteristics that a group can use to establish distinctions of rank between its different internal positions. We noted that many attributes that individuals and groups can use to rank group members seemed to fall into two major clusters. The first, termed the "external" bases of rank, included the wide variety of easily perceived attributes, such as occupation, sex, or class, which are derived from their place in the larger social system. The second, termed the "internal" bases of rank, included the more difficult to evaluate personal attributes, such as intelligence, competence, or courage, which are the functional properties of the individual. These two groups of attributes rather closely resemble those that are more traditionally termed "ascribed" versus "achieved" sources of status.

In chapter 5, we argued that as a group structure emerges, the dispositional characteristics of the members of the group may contribute to the type of prestige system that becomes part of that group. To recapitulate that discussion briefly, we argued that because of the high degree of anxiety that is present, the social comparison processes engaged in by safety-oriented people should focus predominately upon the highly salient external cues in determining rank among individuals. In contrast, we hypothesized that the lower levels of anxiety, and the concern for task and socioemotional achievement, should lead affiliation and esteem-oriented individuals to use social comparison processes that attend to personal qualities associated with some form of mastery behavior.

Throughout this book, we have witnessed a wide variety of social effects that are produced by the interaction of dispositional factors with the external and internal attributes of a social situation. From the early work in social cognition to present work in prosocial behavior, we have seen that many psychologists were concerned with demonstrating that safety-related personality variables lead individuals to use "social status" consistently as the most important cue when evaluating others, whereas esteem-related variables serve the same function with "competence" cues. However, although we have reviewed a substantial body of work that has demonstrated this relationship in other areas of social psychology, there is virtually no work suggesting that a similar mechanism would operate in forming the structure of small groups. One indication of this relationship is provided by the naturalistic study described earlier (Aronoff, 1967), which revealed that the men in the hierarchical work group reported external characteristics to be the basis of prestige within the group. In contrast, the men in the egalitarian work group reported internal characteristics to be the basis of prestige within that group. Interestingly, the follow-up study (Aronoff, 1970) showed that as the first group changed from a hierarchical to an egalitarian form, the bases of prestige within the group similarly changed from an external to an internal kind.

Because these preliminary results from the naturalistic studies were so intriguing, we decided to replicate them in the laboratory, as we had done with the study of role differentiation. In this study (Messé, Aronoff, & Wilson, 1972), we selected subjects as we had earlier and formed them into three-person groups that were homogeneously either safety- or esteem-oriented. However, as we wished to test the hypothesis that safety-oriented people would use external cues in allocating individuals to the higher positions in the group, whereas esteem-oriented people would use internal cues for this task, we organized the groups so that each group was composed of two women and one man. Our expectation was that, if safety-oriented people used external cues in selecting the group's leader, such a group would focus on gender and select the male member to be the leader. On the other hand, because we expected esteem-oriented people to use internal cues, we predicted that gender differences would be much less salient in such groups, which would rather use task competence as the basis for allocating a person to the leadership position.

As in the earlier experiment, we asked these people to work at an involving task for 2 hours while we videotaped the course of the group's activity. At a later time, coders used the Borgatta IPS system to score the tapes for task-oriented behavior in order to obtain precise measures of the acts through which we operationalize leadership. The results of this experiment strongly confirmed the relationship obtained in the field studies. Men emerged as the leader in 75% of the safety-oriented groups, and in 33% of the esteem-oriented groups (just as they should have, considering their number in that type of group). Moreover, in the esteem-oriented groups, the person who became the leader was the one who, irrespective of gender, demonstrated the strongest level of task competence (as measured by the IPS). The results of this single experiment provide strong preliminary support for the hypothesis that dispositional factors contribute to the determination of the bases of prestige within the group.

POWER AND REWARD

The final subjects to consider are the sources of power that regulate the conduct of group members, the norms that define the types of activity that will be rewarded, and the principles through which rewards are distributed. In chapters 4 and 5, we described the ways in which these structural features shape the functioning of the group, as well as the ways in which the member's personal concerns contribute to the particular configuration of these features within a group. There is little that we can now add to that discussion, as our ability to speculate theoretically far outstrips the research with which we can assess its validity. The tables in which we present our hypotheses (Tables 5.8, 5.9, 5.10, and 5.11) primarily consist of deductions drawn from theory. Because only a few studies of this kind are available, it is unnecessary to repeat any substantial part of that theoretical analysis.

The few studies that are available for review on personality and power do not constitute a broad enough spectrum of research on which to build a serious review. Essentially, these studies confirm just a few of the predictions outlined in Table 5.8. The largest group examines how authoritarians exert power in an interpersonal context. In experimental games, in examinations of classroom behavior, and in experimental studies of the control of interpersonal behavior, this set of studies consistently demonstrates that authoritarian people are prone to wield coercive power, particularly if they occupy a higher status position within the group (Dustin & Davis, 1967; Epstein, 1965; Haythorn, Couch, Haefner, Langham, & Carter, 1956a; Lipetz & Ossorio, 1967; Nachtscheim & Hoy, 1976; Smith, 1967; Thibaut & Riecken, 1955). The few existing studies on dominance and power motives tend to show that these people reward ingratiating subordinates and use both their position and their expertise to exert strong personal control over the activities of the group (Fodor & Farrow, 1979; Watson, 1971). Finally, the more insecure person is more reluctant to use coercive power in preference for legitimate power (Kipnis & Lane, 1962), whereas the more confident internally controlled person is more likely to use expert power (Goodstadt & Hjelle, 1973). Because these studies reveal results that are strongly in accord with the pattern predicted by a broad theory of the social process, they encourage a continuing exploration of the involvement of dispositional factors in the social influence process.

The conclusions that we can obtain from the research that we have reviewed in this chapter are quite clear. The results of a significant number of studies show that variables within the safety needs are consistently associated with the preference for hierarchical structures with separated roles. Several studies show that these variables are associated with the tendency to rank group members on the basis of external attributes such as status. In contrast, variables within the esteem-needs cluster are consistently associated with the preference for egalitarian structures with broad, inclusive roles. Further, there is some evidence that these variables are associated with a tendency to rank group members on the basis of internal attributes such as competence. The only conclusion that we can draw on all the critically important issues of social control is that this area is greatly in need of further study. Finally, we need to note that our knowledge of the relationship of personality to reward structures is remarkably limited.

In summary, although the study of the relationship of personality processes to group structure is not a traditional topic in social psychology, enough is known to raise the question of the congruence between the two classes of variables and to test whether the congruence between the person and his or her work environment contributes toward the satisfaction, cohesion, and productivity of individuals in group settings.

IV

THE OUTCOME OF GROUP PROCESS: TESTING THE MODEL OF THE PERSON IN THE SITUATION

13 The Performance of Individuals in Groups

Each chapter in this book focuses on a different phase of the group processes through which people pursue their goals. The task of this chapter is to consider if the events that occur within a group lead to different levels of personal satisfaction, group cohesiveness, and task productivity. This discussion considers how much our theoretical perspective contributes to clarifying the complex interactional processes through which personality, situation, task, and group-structure variables determine the level of group performance.

THE PRINCIPLE OF CONGRUENCE

For theorists of organizational behavior (e.g., Katz & Kahn, 1966; Porter, Lawler, & Hackman, 1975; Stogdill, 1974), it is well established that each of these classes of variables exerts a significant impact on the most important outcomes of organizations. At this time, the most important theoretical requirement seems to be the need for principles that specify the sets of conditions that maximize satisfaction, cohesion, and productivity for different types of persons. In this effort, we expect that the principle of congruence will help greatly to predict the conditions that maximize group performance. Stated simply, the principle of congruence proposes that it is necessary to match the characteristics of the person and the situation in order to provide the most productive environment within which to work. More specifically, the principle of congruence suggests that many kinds of people and organizations can be quite effective and that the optimal situation is one in which the personal and the social characteristics are matched so as to enhance personal satisfaction and group productivity.

The principle of congruence implies that conditions failing to reach this kind of match will lead to a state of incongruence that will have a negative effect on the outcomes of human groups. In a useful generalization, Steiner (1972) maintained that "actual productivity = potential productivity minus losses due to faulty group process" (p. 9). He further defined group process as "the actual steps taken by an individual or group when confronted by a task. It includes all those intrapersonal and interpersonal actions by which people transform their resources into a product, and all those nonproductive actions that are prompted by frustration, competing motivations, or inadequate understanding" (p. 8). Using Steiner's definition, incongruence between member personality and the social situation should lead to ineffective group process and, therefore, to a decrement in group performance.

All of the many topics that have been reviewed to this point are the specific events in the group process that can be affected by incongruence between psychological and social variables. For example, incongruence of this kind can negatively affect group process through such effects as: (a) distortions in perception; (b) reduced levels of aspiration; (c) less effective task identification; (d) disagreement on role structure; or (e) ineffective work organization.

The expectation that congruence between personality and situational factors will optimize performance has long been discussed by students of personality and group dynamics (e.g., Bales, 1970; Maslow, 1970; Murray, 1938; Pervin, 1968; Tuckman, 1965). In the field of organizational psychology, this idea is newer and appears in such works as those of Friedlander (1971), Hackman and Oldham (1976), and Steers (1975a). Friedlander (1971) states the proposal succinctly: "There is growing evidence which suggests that the more congruent the task characteristics, the human needs and values, and the organizational structure, the greater will be the degree of task accomplishment and human fulfillment" (p. 155). Although these proposals are usually phrased quite broadly, it is possible to specify the principle of congruence in much greater detail. In this chapter, our goal is to present the most precisely phrased discussion of the conditions of congruence as can be supported by the research literature at this time.

Congruence Between Individual and Social Characteristics

We propose that when the state of the major social variables is congruent with an individual's predominant personality characteristics, the person will reach his or her highest level of performance. To make this general principle more precise requires that we utilize the conclusions reached throughout this book. Chapter 5 suggested a set of relationships between specific personality and social variables through which the social environment could facilitate or retard the efforts that individuals make to reach their goals. In earlier discussions, a great deal of evidence was presented to demonstrate the social conditions that appear to be most congruent with each of the major personality variables that we have been following. The substantiation, in these discussions, of many of the predictions offered in chapter 5 allows us to construct a table that predicts the specific social conditions that are most congruent with each of these personality variables.

In Table 13.1, the social factors are organized, as before, into the major situational, task, and group structural categories. Following the reasoning used in chapter 4, each of these categories is subdivided into the more precise factors needed to analyze social events. This format allows us to identify the optimal state of each of these specific social dimensions for each of the personality variables that we follow. These relationships are seen to be the optimal conditions of congruence that underlie member satisfaction, group cohesiveness, and task productivity. In addition to these predictions, the table as a whole allows us to envision the optimal state of the entire work environment for a particular type of person. Although it is impossible to examine all features of a work environment systematically in one experiment, Table 13.1 as a whole reminds us that a single study refers to a broader world. This chapter reviews a great deal of empirical evidence from studies that examine the specific predictions, and the table as a whole allows us to integrate the results of each study with those that come from all the others. It should help the reading of Table 13.1 to review briefly the major features of the social environment that seem to affect social behavior.

1. Situational variables specify the characteristics of the physical and the human environment with which we interact. The physical variables are those nonhuman material features of our lives, such as the temperature or the noise level of the room in which we work, the degree of crowding or the pace at which our work has been set, or the degree of danger that is present. These attributes of our environment can have a stressing effect on at least some of the people who work within that environment. The first column of Table 13.1, then, indicates the optimum level of stress for the performance of the different kinds of people whom we have been tracking. The second column of the table focuses on the status and the competence attributes of the people with whom we interact, that is, the human component of our environment. We expect that the nature of people's dispositional characteristics will lead them to be substantially affected by the status or the competence attributes of the other members of a social event. Theoretically, the degree to which a social event is formed out of individuals who possess these attributes should determine the degree to which the social influence process should work well and, therefore, when the outcome of the group should reach its optimum level.

TABLE 13.1
Situation, Task, and Group-Structure Conditions Required for Optimal Group Performance

Personality Variables	Situational Variables		Task Variables				
	Physical Attributes	Personal Attributes	Difficulty	Complexity	Ambiguity	Importance	
Dependence	Low	Status	Low	Low	Low	Low	
Abasement	Low	Status	Low	Low	Low	Low	
Approval	Low	Status	Low	Low	Low	Low	
Authoritarianism	Low	Status	Low	Low	Low	Low	
Order	Low	Competence	Moderate	High	Low	Moderate	
Affiliation	Moderate	Competence	Moderate	Moderate	Moderate	High	
Machiavellianism	Moderate	Competence	Moderate	Moderate	High	Low	
Dominance	Moderate	Competence	High	High	Moderate	High	
Nurturance	Moderate	Competence	High	High	Moderate	High	
Achievement	Moderate	Competence	Moderate	High	Moderate	High	
Recognition	Moderate	Status	Moderate	Low	Low	High	

TABLE 13.1 *(Continued)*

Personality Variables	Group Structure Variables					
	Role Differentiation	Basis of Rank	Ranking System	Power Technique	Reward System	Basis of Reward
Dependence	Separation	External	Unequal	Reward	Rule 1	Time
Abasement	Separation	External	Unequal	Coercive	Rule 1 & 3	Time
Approval	Separation	External	Unequal	Reward	Rule 1 & 3	Effort
Authoritarianism	Separation	External	Unequal	Legitimate	Rule 2a	Effort
Order	Separation	Internal	Unequal	Expert	Rule 2a & 2b	Ability
Affiliation	Integration	Internal	Equal	Reward	Rule 1 & 3	Effort
Machiavellianism	Separation	Internal	Unequal	Coercive	Rule 2a & 2b	Ability
Dominance	Separation	Internal	Equal	Expert	Rule 2a, 2b, & 4	Ability
Nurturance	Integration	Internal	Equal	Expert	Rule 2b & 4	Ability
Achievement	Integration	Internal	Equal	Expert	Rule 2b & 4	Ability
Recognition	Integration	External	Equal	Reward	Rule 2a	Effort

2. Task variables, similarly, can influence group performance in positive or negative ways. For example, jobs that are difficult because of time pressures, the demand for intellectual ability, or the amount of information required may be stressful to some people and challenging to others. In the same way, the nature of the task will be more or less complex, ambiguous, or important. These features of the task can additionally stress or challenge individuals engaged in dealing with that task. Table 13.1 presents our expectations of the level (indicated as either high, moderate, or low) of each of these dimensions of the task that is required to produce the best performance from each of the different kinds of people whom we have been following.

3. The structural organization of the group is the third source of significant influence on the group's performance. The previous chapters have presented sufficient evidence to demonstrate that different configurations of these structural elements provide very different kinds of rewards. For example, a rigidly structured, hierarchical group reduces the level of uncertainty and stress inherent in most tasks that groups face. However, this social organization also reduces the possibility of individual innovation. We have seen that a loosely organized egalitarian structure produces a reversed set of effects. Based on the evidence provided in previous chapters, it is possible to predict the differential effects on performance of the interaction of all the personal and the structural variables. Table 13.1 presents the type of structural element that is preferred by each of the personality types, which we hypothesize should create the optimum social conditions within which to work.

In order to test these hypotheses, we draw upon many sources within psychology: tightly controlled laboratory experiments; field experiments; and correlational studies within a wide range of organizations. These many different kinds of studies use a wide variety of procedures and outcome measures to examine the predictions outlined in Table 13.1. The breadth of social situations that can be used to test these hypotheses allows us to generalize to a wide range of social events. In this way, the array of available information greatly helps to strengthen the conclusions that emerge from this review.

The discussion of group performance is organized in terms of the three major classes of social variables. As usual, we find a highly uneven distribution of empirical work to report. In some areas, there is such an abundance of evidence that the problem is one of avoiding repetition. For some other topics, there is no research at all. At those times, we simply restate the hypotheses in hopes of stimulating future research. More typically, there are several noteworthy studies to review that, together with several related studies, increase the plausibility of this point of view.

As a final word of orientation to the three major sections of this chapter, it should be pointed out that we discovered no empirical work that has been done on the first set of hypotheses (i.e., the situation). For this reason, we present in its place a brief discussion of a well-established laboratory analog that indicates the pattern of results that might be obtained by more direct studies. The major thrust of the hypotheses of the second section (i.e., the task) receives substantial support from primarily field studies in a wide variety of organizations. In the third section (i.e., the structure of the group), there is substantial support based on many kinds of evidence for the hypotheses that deal with the structural features of role differentiation and ranking among positions. Because of the fragmentary nature of existing information on reward and power, the discussion in this section concentrates on the issues of role differentiation and rank.

THE SITUATION

The Congruence Between Personality and the Physical Setting

It seems obvious that the properties of the physical situation should affect the way individuals work. In the field of human factors, devoted to the study of the interaction of the human body in the physical world, there have been many examinations of questions such as the proper shape of an airplane pilot's seat, the most calming color to paint an elementary school classroom, or the number of square inches of space needed to furnish a research psychologist. Considering how much attention has been given to the design of the technology that human beings use, it is surprising that we have found no studies that attempt to discover the effects of these physical properties on different kinds of human beings. To be more specific, we have not been able to find any studies of the effects of noise level, crowding, heat, or room size on the performance of different kinds of people.

In surveying the range of physical properties of the situation within which people work, the feature that they all seem to have in common is their ability to stress the human being. In general, we expect that physical stressors will raise the anxiety level of people concerned with safety-related characteristics beyond the level required for optimal levels of performance. Therefore, for anxious individuals, a low level of environmental stress is optimal, as anything more intense is likely to raise their anxiety to a level that interferes with effective performance. For people concerned with both affiliation and esteem-related peripheral variables, we expect that a moderate level of physical stress will lead to optimal levels of group performance. We expect that people concerned with affiliation possess sufficient cognitive controls to cope with moderate levels of physical stress. In addition, under moderate stress, such people should be even more eager to seek out others with whom to work. We expect that moderate stress will provide a valid reason for forming stress-reducing modes of interaction that will be personally re-warding, and so improve their task performance. We also expect that esteem-oriented people will be able to cope with moderate physical stress quite well. In addition, we expect that this level of stress will lead to the optimal level of arousal that will facilitate their highest level of performance.

Although there is little research on the topic, there is another group of ex-cellent studies that provides some measure of support for these hypotheses. These studies are not usually presented in discussions of group dynamics, but they do constitute a sufficiently adequate analog to the kind of study desired to make it worthwhile to survey their main conclusions briefly. Although this section is devoted primarily to the relationship between physical stress and task performance, the larger question of how stress and anxiety influence many forms of social behavior has been one of the central interests of psy-chology (see Epstein, 1972; Janis, 1958; Lazarus, 1966; Sarason, 1980; Spielberger, 1972). A full discussion of this work is beyond the scope of this chapter, but a summary of several important empirical studies serves to focus on the key point that may be obtained from this laboratory analog.

Mandler and Sarason (1952) developed a measure (the test anxiety ques-tionnaire) to assess a form of anxiety that seemed to interfere with academic performance. In characterizing this "test anxious person," they wrote: "These responses . . . may be manifested as feelings of inadequacy, helpless-ness, heightened somatic reaction, anticipations of punishment or loss of sta-tus and esteem, and implicit attempts at leaving the test situation. It might be said that these responses are self rather than task centered" (p. 166). Re-viewing the definition given earlier, as well as much of the subsequent re-search (cf. Sarason, 1980), this variable seems to be quite similar to many of the major features of the safety needs. By accepting the equivalence of these definitions, the findings on the relationship of test anxiety to academic per-formance seem to be a reasonable way to estimate how physical stressors may affect the performance of safety-oriented people.

Wine (1971) reviewed the research on test anxiety and noted that the initial description of the test anxious person proved to be valid in experimental re-search for the following 20 years. Further, the early work by Mandler and Sarason stimulated a large set of studies that was designed to understand the conditions that facilitated or interfered with the task performance of anxious and nonanxious people. The study of these conditions introduces a valuable additional feature to this program of research. These stress-reducing social variables, or "stress buffers," provide another analog to the events produced by the broader physical stresses of our environment. From the point of view of congruence between psychological and social states, it is very desirable to identify social conditions that reduce the impact of anxiety on performance. These stress buffers can range from a pleasant room in which to work, to a clear plan for work, to a supportive co-worker whose sense of humor always seems to relieve the tension.

Two experiments from Sarason's program can illustrate the general conclusions that have been established. Using a moderately difficult learning task, Sarason (1961) selected anxious and nonanxious people on the basis of their test scores and randomly assigned them to either a neutral or an achievement-oriented condition. In the neutral condition, the performance of both types of people was about the same. However, in the achievement-oriented condition, which emphasized the importance of the task as the basis for evaluating the person, the performance of anxious people was significantly worse than that of nonanxious people. Later studies have confirmed this conclusion and found that stressors, such as these threatening contexts, produced interfering responses, including high autonomic nervous system arousal and negative attributions about self-worth, ability, and intelligence (cf. Garber & Seligman, 1980; Lamb, 1978; Wine, 1971).

If one of the characteristics of anxious people is that they are prone to excessive worry and react poorly to stress, then it seems possible to design social conditions to buffer the stresses that they find in situations. These stress buffers, by and large, use the other characteristics of group process that we describe in the rest of this chapter. To explore this possibility, Sarason (1972) conducted a study in which anxious and nonanxious people were assigned to learn certain material in either a reassurance or a control condition. In the reassurance condition, the instructions tried to reduce the strain brought about by the evaluatory situation by indicating that the people should work slowly and not worry if they make mistakes in the difficult task. In general, the reassurance condition tried to reduce anxiety by creating a supportive environment that conveyed a sense of acceptance of the person. As predicted, anxious people performed better than nonanxious people in the reassurance condition but not as well in the more stressful control condition. These results, as well as those from other studies (e.g., Sarason, Pederson, & Nyman, 1968), led Sarason to conclude that clear problem-solving information can improve the performance of anxious people. Further, Sarason (1981) reports the results of several studies on the beneficial effects of broader forms of social support on the performance of anxious people. The superior performance of anxious people in the presence of these additional social conditions (whether of reassurance or information) clearly demonstrates that they do best when the situational stress is either at its lowest point or is buffered by additional social conditions. In fact, Wine (1971) reports that training anxious people in "attentional behavior" decreases their anxiety and improves their performance.

Although these studies contain no indication of how affiliation-oriented people might behave in the face of this kind of situational stress, it is likely that the performance of less anxious people is representative of the responses that would be obtained from esteem-oriented people. A few of these studies can be added to this discussion. The superior performance of less anxious people in moderately stressful situations is supported by several studies that measure esteem-related variables more directly. For example, in a major review of the self-esteem and job-performance literature, Tharenou (1979) concluded that low-self-esteem individuals are much more affected by job stress than are high-self-esteem people. Similarly, Schalon (1968) found that low-esteem people had a poorer performance under evaluative conditions than under nonstressful conditions. In contrast, the performance of high-self-esteem people did not differ between the two conditions. Lefcourt (1976a) and Wolk and Bloom (1978) have shown the same effect for the related variable of internal locus of control. These fragmentary results are too few to do more than suggest the pattern of results that a more substantial program would produce. However, these findings do seem to reflect the ability of the high-self-esteem person to concentrate on the task by screening out potentially distracting information or stimulation.

The Congruence Between Personality and Member Attributes

From the earliest discussions of person perception in chapter 6 through the extended reviews of the most preferred forms of group structure in chapter 12, we have followed a far-reaching trail of evidence in support of a broad hypothesis. These very different types of studies seem to show that safety-oriented people are most responsive to the status attributes of those with whom they interact, whereas esteem-oriented people are most responsive to the attributes of others that indicate a high level of competence. Unfortunately, we have not found studies that examine the attributes that lead people to be most effective in stimulating safety- or esteem-oriented individuals to perform most effectively.

Such experiments are not difficult to design or carry out, and their results would be valuable because there are practical consequences to this aspect of the social influence process. The closest approximation to this type of research is a study by Wilson and Petruska (1984), which we discussed in chapter 10. Once again, this study is only a distant analog of the type of research that is needed to evaluate these hypotheses properly. Recall that in this helping-behavior study, Wilson and Petruska showed that safety-oriented people helped a bystander more when they observed a high-status model, whereas esteem-oriented people helped more when they observed the high-competence model. Although this is hardly a satisfactory base of evidence for evaluating the hypothesis, this approximation to an "outcome" study at least provides one model for the research that is needed.

THE TASK

As we analyzed the nature of a social event in chapter 4, it seemed reasonable to expect that the task characteristics of difficulty, complexity, ambiguity, and importance would affect the way people reach their goals. As a simple illustration, tasks can be so difficult that they challenge the most capable person or so easy that they bore even the dullest person. Because tasks vary along these four dimensions and people differ in their strengths and skills, we attempted to predict how a wide range of people would respond to these task characteristics in the course of their work in a group (see chap. 5).

In recent years, organizational psychologists have shown an increasing interest in studying this aspect of the social process. Usually in work settings, although occasionally with experimental techniques as well, the psychologists have tried to explore whether the dominant concerns of group members moderate the way that task characteristics affect a variety of performance criteria. The results of a great many studies on the interaction of person and task variables permit testing the most important hypotheses outlined in chapter 5.

Unfortunately, these studies are not distributed across all the relationships that we would want to examine. Another problem is that these studies often combine several of the dimensions that could be considered separately (e.g., the difficulty and the complexity of a task often are not distinguished from each other). However, viewing this literature as a whole, the basic thrust of our hypotheses seems to be supported quite well. Thus, we review what is known about this relationship, following the major questions that organizational psychologists have actually asked. First, we review how the performance of different kinds of people is affected by the level of task difficulty. Then, we review how the performance of different kinds of people is affected by the degree of ambiguity inherent in the task or work structure.

The Congruence Between Task Difficulty and Individual Characteristics

Our general expectation is that safety-oriented people will feel overwhelmed by demands for sustained effort in difficult and/or complex tasks. Because a successful outcome is more uncertain when the task is difficult, these tasks should be a disincentive to people characterized by safety-related peripheral variables and so should reduce their levels of performance. In contrast, these people should find that low levels of difficulty provide the greatest incentive because such levels insure the greatest gain at the least risk. We expect that affiliation-oriented people should find that a moderate level of difficulty provides the greatest incentive because they possess neither the high levels of personal uncertainty that would cause them to feel overwhelmed nor a concern to demonstrate personal competence that would require a greater challenge. We expect that esteem-oriented people will feel the need to test themselves in this way in order to establish their ability. Easy tasks should be a disincentive to esteem-oriented people, whereas difficult (but solvable) tasks should offer substantial incentive and lead to their highest level of performance.

Considering how important this process is to industry, it is surprising how few studies have examined the optimum task conditions for safety-oriented people. This relationship is probably so obvious to organizational managers that it needs no further examination. Indeed, to the organizational psychologists who originated the job enlargement movement (e.g., McGregor, 1960), the traditional view of the task–person relationship was that industry seemed to view all its employees as safety-oriented and arranged their tasks accordingly. However, there is some evidence on the relationship of anxiety and task difficulty, using laboratory techniques similar to those of Sarason, that should be noted briefly before we discuss the more interpersonal types of social events on which we wish to concentrate. Cronbach and Snow (1977) reviewed a large number of empirical studies that have examined personality-by-treatment interactions on performance. They conclude that anxious and defensive people do better when the task is relatively simple, structured, and provides much feedback. The set of characteristics of learning tasks that they delineate parallels the analysis of the job task in the workplace, proposed by Hackman and Oldham (1976), to which we turn shortly. The similarity of the two conclusions clearly demonstrates the value of expecting a similar structure to underlie apparently very dissimilar tasks.

Similarly, we have found no studies examining the level of task difficulty that provides the optimal conditions for the affiliation-oriented person. The nature of the affiliation motive seems to direct psychologists' attention to the social climate within which such people work rather than toward their response to the task. Although the social area of their work life is certainly important to affiliation-motivated people, it is also necessary to consider that people predominantly concerned with interpersonal involvement are also working at a task for which they want to be paid. However, there is a sizable amount of literature that examines the task conditions that are optimal for esteem-related variables. Organizational psychologists have been quite concerned with showing that esteem-oriented people prefer "challenging" tasks that test their competence and that such tasks lead to optimal levels of performance. We briefly review several different programs of research, which together appear to have substantiated this relationship quite well.

Growth Need Strength.   During the 1950s, a number of psychologists became concerned with the quality of the work experience and began to search for ways to make industry more stimulating for human beings as well as more productive. They found in Maslow's theory of motivation a convenient language to categorize the forces within the person that seemed to be related to the way work organizations operate. From Maslow's distinction between higher and lower psychological needs, they carved out a broad variable which they called *growth need strength*. This psychological dimension, which is seen as the degree to which people are concerned with esteem and self-actualization, provided a general way to categorize both the work organization and the personality of the employees. Their assumption was that most human beings were capable of responding to much more stimulating environments and succeeding at much more difficult tasks. For this reason, they suggested that the nature of work should be changed to enlarge the scope of the job, enrich its stimulating properties, and increase the demands that it makes on the worker.

In an interesting analysis, Hackman and Oldham (1976) proposed that jobs are composed of the dimensions of task variety, completeness, significance, autonomy, and the provision of feedback. With the exception of feedback, these job characteristics have much in common with our four task dimensions. Hackman and Oldham summarize the basic hypothesis of this approach when they suggest that growth-needs-motivated persons prefer jobs based upon the presence of these task characteristics because through them they are able to satisfy their predominant needs. In other words, they suggest that esteem-oriented people would find that difficult, complex, and also, more unstructured and important work provides the optimum arena within which to confirm their talents (a conclusion shared by Cronbach & Snow, 1977, for their narrower range of tasks).

To measure growth need strength, Hackman and Lawler (1971) developed a self-report scale whose content strongly reflects the general esteem-based character of the construct. Their study provides a good example of how this kind of research has been carried out. They incorporated scales measuring both the task and psychological need characteristics into a questionnaire that was distributed to several hundred employees working at 13 different jobs at a telephone company. Hackman and Lawler hypothesized that persons who score higher on the needs scale should respond more positively to enriched jobs (i.e., those that have more variety, autonomy, completeness, significance, and feedback) than should persons who score low on the scale. The results of their study strongly supported the prediction that growth needs moderate the effects of job characteristics on attitudes toward work.

These findings were essentially replicated by a series of later studies (Abdel-Halim, 1980; Brief & Aldag, 1975; Hackman & Oldham, 1976; Ivancevich & McMahon, 1977; Oldham, 1976; Rabinowitz, Hall, & Goodale, 1977; Sims & Szilagyi, 1976; Wanous, 1974). In an important addition to this set of studies, Oldham, Hackman, and Pearce (1976) were able to show that the level of performance of the individual (using the standard effectiveness ratings made by the company), as well as the salary of the employee, was determined by this relationship between task and personality characteristics. The finding that such concrete behavioral outcomes also result from this interaction greatly strengthens the conclusions provided by the earlier studies.

The Need for Achievement.   A second group of studies, focusing on the need for achievement, used a more precisely defined and well-established construct whose relationship to the work setting is quite clear. In addition, these studies incorporated the substantial literature on risk taking and the need for achievement into the broader analysis of group performance. Reviews of this literature, described in chapter 7, indicate that the need for achievement is also associated with the way that job difficulty affects the level of performance at that job.

In reviewing the research on this topic, we hoped to buttress the findings that come from work done in real organizations with comparable results from the laboratory. However, it is difficult to equate the level of difficulty set in the laboratory with that set in real organizations. Because it is easy to vary the difficulty of laboratory problems but much harder to calibrate this range with that presented by real jobs, it is possible that an intermediate level of an arithmetic problem is equivalent to the level seen as difficult in the field studies. These scaling considerations will eventually become extremely important when more empirical evidence accumulates. At the moment, however, there are only preliminary sets of experimental findings to report.

As noted in chapter 7, extensive literature demonstrates that high levels of the need for achievement are associated with preference for moderate levels of risk taking. However, although they are both seen as outcome criteria, the level of expressed preference for risk is not the same as level of performance at the task. Fortunately, there are a few studies associated with the risk-taking literature that address this problem. As part of the early work on the need for achievement construct (McClelland, Atkinson, Clark, & Lowell, 1953), people who had scored high or low on the need for achievement test were asked to work on a set of easy and hard anagram problems. There was no difference in the way both kinds of people handled the easy problems, but there was a clear difference on the difficult problems. People who had scored higher on the need for achievement test improved their performance as they worked at the task, whereas people with low scores did not improve their performance. In this setting, the difficult problem seemed to present an interesting challenge to achievement-oriented people and stimulated them to show greater persistence and success at the task.

It is surprising how little additional work has been done on this problem. A more recent study (Kukla, 1974) provided evidence that not only does the achievement-oriented person do better on difficult tasks than the person less concerned with achievement, but this relationship reverses on easy tasks. Although a few other studies (Entin & Raynor, 1973; Karabenick & Youssef, 1968; Schneider & Delenay, 1972; Touhey & Villamez, 1980) have contributed important additional pieces of information, the conclusive set of studies has yet to be done.

In research that examines this problem in large industrial organizations, Steers (1975a, 1975b; Steers & Braunstein, 1976; Steers & Spencer, 1977) has published the results of a series of studies in support of this hypothesis. These studies all used the same procedures that we just reviewed in the organizational research that uses the growth needs construct. However, Steers generated his hypotheses from the need for achievement literature and developed a self-report measure that focuses much more sharply on need for achievement concerns. Using these procedures, Steers provided an additional set of studies showing that an esteem-related variable moderates the task difficulty–job performance relationship in an industrial organization. Unfortunately, these studies have not taken full advantage of the need for achievement construct. The major contribution of this research is the focus on the individual's expectations for high levels of performance. These studies, as well as several others that use a broader esteem construct (Carroll & Tosi, 1970; Gavin, 1973; Hechler & Weiner, 1974; Kerr-Inkson, 1978; Korman, 1967a; Terborg, Richardson, & Pritchard, 1980), develop the expectation mechanism and argue that it leads to greater success at work because it fosters much more persistent task-related efforts.

Ultimately, these organizational psychologists have not made a convincing case that it is useful to discriminate among these different personality variables. Both the predictions and the results are comparable in all respects. Further, the empirical literature does not even allow us to begin to evaluate the more differentiated predictions outlined for the various esteem-related peripheral variables. At this point, we can only conclude that persons concerned with esteem-related issues expect to succeed at more difficult tasks and work hard to do them well. In contrast, people who seem characterized by low self-esteem tend to give up as the task gets more difficult. However, this general conclusion appears to be fairly secure and worth using in the planning of work practices for individuals.

The Congruence Between Task Ambiguity and Individual Characteristics

If the task environment is composed of sets of people and objects, then the degree of clarity that characterizes their organization should greatly affect group member's efforts to reach their goals. Significantly, this same degree of clarity might also restrict member's opportunities to shape the nature of the outcome. Thus, the task dimension of ambiguity appears as a characteristic of: (a) the objects that constitute the task and (b) the work arrangements that are available to guide the people's interactions with each other.

A few simple examples should make this dimension clearer. If we ask most adults to solve a page of elementary arithmetic problems, some people may not do very well, but virtually everyone will know the rules required for the solution. That task is both easy and unambiguous. If we ask the same people to solve long division problems, the task would be more difficult but not much more ambiguous, for the rules of arithmetic remain the same. However, if we ask people in the laboratory to discover the attribute that several objects have in common, they will be much less certain of what questions to ask. If we train these people to ask the right questions (as they are trained in the principles of arithmetic), then the task will become less ambiguous because they will possess the rules needed to explore and solve the task. Similarly, if a number of people are asked to solve a problem together, they may not understand at first how to coordinate their efforts. If we appoint one of them to be the leader and instruct everyone in the group to take direction from that person, then we have provided that group with a fairly clear work structure. To expand this example, we can also be more or less detailed about the type of activity that we expect from the positions of leader and member. To the extent that we provide this kind of information or impose these kinds of rules, we have made the work organization that coordinates the activity of all group members that much less ambiguous. On the other hand, to the extent that we do this, we restrict the range of activity that each member is able to display.

We expect that the level of ambiguity in the task should exert the same effect on the performance of people concerned with each of the different safety-related variables. By definition, these people desire predictable and orderly environments. With greater task ambiguity, many more options need to be considered, many more decisions need to be made, and therefore, many more risks need to be taken. We expect that ambiguity in the task will raise the anxiety level of safety-oriented people and set up defensive processes that will interfere with their performance. In contrast, clear and highly structured tasks should offer the greatest degree of predictability possible in that situation. For this reason, the more clearly defined task should reduce the anxiety level of these people and permit them to become engaged with the tasks to the limits of their abilities. We expect that the affiliative needs will not be related to the dimension of ambiguity in any interesting way. It is likely that these people will work just as well in a moderately ambiguous task as they will in a clear one. Probably, the more ambiguous situation will lead to a decrement in performance, but only because it makes greater information-processing demands on the person. For the esteem-related variables, when the element of competence validation is aroused, the highly structured task can be quite restrictive. If this is the case, then the clear task structure would lead to subjective feelings of frustration. Obviously, a clear structure in itself is not a negative element to esteem-oriented people and only leads to feelings of frustration when it interferes with the desire to use the task to display their abilities. When this occurs, the clear structure should serve to lower the level of performance expected of them. Similarly, we would expect a less restrictive task environment would give esteem-oriented people the widest latitude for selecting the most suitable goal-seeking behaviors. This type of environment should lead to the highest levels of performance for persons concerned with esteem-related characteristics.

We have a wide range of research available to explore the validity of this hypothesis. Many different kinds of problems have been posed to people taking part in laboratory experiments, and many kinds of organizations have been provided to them as they have worked at their tasks. This and related hypotheses have been examined in many different sites, such as industrial, educational, psychotherapeutic, and experimental settings. A fairly large number of variables have been used in this research which, unlike our review of the moderating effects of task difficulty, has been produced by many different research groups. Yet, despite the breadth of research and researchers, the major proposal has been substantiated quite well.

Anxiety.   In the field of education, there has been considerable interest in the most effective classroom approach to use with different kinds of children. Among these programs is a set of studies on the effects of structured versus unstructured educational programs on the classroom learning of anxious and nonanxious children. In this work, the clarity of information flow provided by a structured classroom is seen as similar to the clear task-related information provided by researchers such as Sarason, which is designed to reduce the effects of evaluative stress on anxious people.

A very interesting study by Grimes and Allinsmith (1961) illustrates the results of a number of similar studies. They measured both the level of anxiety and compulsivity (a variable that is nearly identical with Murray's definition of the need for order) in a large population of third-grade children in two urban school systems. In one system, all schools used a highly structured approach to learning in the first 3 years. In the other system, all schools used an unstructured approach. Grimes and Allinsmith's (1961) definition of structure, "the clarity of procedure to be followed in a given task and the explicitness of the connections between one task and the next" (p. 251), is not only compatible with our definition of the dimension of clarity–ambiguity but extends it as well. The results of this study were based on the children's performance on a battery of standard achievement and intelligence tests. In order to measure only the effects of the school's program on the child's progress, Grimes and Allinsmith used the discrepancy between the child's achievement score and the hypothetical achievement score that would be expected from the child's IQ. The most important result of this study was that highly anxious (as well as compulsive) children learned much more in the highly structured school than they did in the unstructured school. Grimes and Allinsmith (1961) conclude: "Apparently academic challenge in the structured setting creates an optimum of stress so that the child with high anxiety is able to achieve because he is aroused to an energetic state without becoming confused or panicked" (p. 260).

The most successful type of child in this study was the one that studied in the structured school and was both highly anxious and highly compulsive. The authors speculate that compulsivity is a valuable adaptational defense for the anxious child in the right environment: "Apparently, when the school systematizes the learning experience for such children in accordance with their need for orderliness, their anxiety is facilitating rather than disorganizing" (p. 264). This result is interesting from both the theoretical and the practical points of view. Theoretically, it indicates the need for the interactionist approach to social behavior. Practically, it indicates that it is possible for anxious people to produce good quality work, in the right setting.

After reviewing the experimental research on the relationship of anxiety (and similar constructs) to performance in the classroom, Cronbach and Snow (1977) conclude that much more research is needed before the optimal level of structure required for good performance from anxious people is established. However, they do note that a variety of research (e.g., Domino, 1968, 1971; Dowaliby & Schumer, 1973) suggests that anxious persons perform better under the several different components of more structured organization (e.g., directive instruction, immediate feedback, etc.).

Dogmatism.   A few studies have examined how performance is affected by the interaction of dogmatism and the degree of task ambiguity. These studies provide some support for Rokeach's (1960) belief that dogmatic individuals find the lack of structure in an environment threatening because it appears to increase the degree of unpredictability of future events. Therefore, we can expect dogmatic individuals to perform best in situations or on problems that are fairly clear. Vacchiano (1977), reviewing the research literature on the performance of dogmatic people, concludes that the results of many narrowly focused laboratory experiments (e.g., Restle, Andrews, & Rokeach, 1964) indicate that dogmatic people will perform at their optimum when the task environment is most structured. Informal studies of classroom (Zagona & Zurcher, 1964) and clinical (Frye, Vidulich, Meierhoefer, & Joure, 1972; Talley & Vamos, 1972) behavior showed that dogmatic people were threatened by lack of structure, made great efforts to impose internal structure, and achieved less than nondogmatic people did in that setting. More formally, in a very interesting experiment, Weed and Mitchell (1974) found that when asked to work at difficult tasks, dogmatic people do better when they are able to work with a highly structuring task leader. This type of leader seems to reduce the informational uncertainty inherent in such tasks.

In addition, several industrial studies of a correlational sort buttress this conclusion for the related variable of authoritarianism. It is possible to see a work setting in which employees are permitted to participate in decision making as a task whose structure is relatively ambiguous. Vroom (1960) presented evidence that nonauthoritarian people were more satisfied in more participative work situations than were authoritarian people. Kenis (1978) reviewed the small number of studies that have supported (with some exceptions) Vroom's proposals. In addition, participation can also be understood to indicate a broader definition of the work role. In the next section on group structure, we return to these studies as an indication of the dispositional moderators of the effects of role differentiation.

Concrete–Abstract Cognitive Structure. A number of studies (e.g., Tuckman, 1964) have argued that individuals with increased levels of concreteness in their cognitive structure prefer increased degrees of structure in their task. Recall that Tuckman, stimulated by the seminal work of Harvey, Hunt, and Schroder (1961), demonstrated that groups homogeneously composed of individuals at each of the four nodal points of cognitive complexity would develop group structures that were congruent with their predominant personality structure. For example, cognitively concrete individuals formed highly structured hierarchical groups, whereas cognitively abstract individuals formed flexible egalitarian groups. Based on findings such as these, it seemed reasonable to determine if matching the level of group members' cognitive complexity with the level of task structure would lead to optimal levels of performance. The expectation was that cognitively concrete people should profit from a highly structured environment, whereas cognitively abstract people should profit from less structured environments.

This very straightforward idea of matching the person and the task has been studied in many types of social situations. In the field of education, Hunt and Sullivan (1974) review a number of studies which show that classroom learning is broadly affected by the interaction of the student's cognitive complexity level and the degree of task structure (e.g., Hunt, 1970; Tuckman & Orefice, 1973). Similarly, Stein and Stone (1978) thought that matching the person and the situation should improve the effectiveness of the clinically oriented initial interview procedure. In a well-designed clinical experiment, they studied the effect of two different interviewing styles (more and less structured) on either cognitively concrete or abstract people. On a number of subjective outcomes (e.g., satisfaction with the counselor) as well as behavioral outcomes (e.g., amount of client talk), the match of person and situation was shown to lead to the more effective clinical interview.

In an industrial setting, Morse (1975) examined this relationship among clerical employees at a commercial savings and loan company and at a county government organization. Each of the employees who took part in this study had just entered a new job in the organization. Based on personality tests and analyses of the ambiguity demands of the new job, each employee was identified as being in either a "congruent" or an "incongruent" job. The results showed that after 8 months, employees in new jobs that were congruent with their personality seemed to be much more satisfied than those put into incongruent jobs. Finally, Tuckman (1967) followed up his previously cited experiment with another that tried to demonstrate that congruent groups would outperform incongruent groups. Half of his groups were composed of more cognitively abstract people than cognitively concrete people; the other half had the reverse composition. The groups were given a concrete structured task and an abstract unstructured task to perform. The results of this experiment indicated that groups with more cognitively abstract members outperformed groups with more cognitively concrete members on the abstract task. There was no difference between the two groups on the concrete structured task. Although much more research is needed, these results suggest that the match between cognitive structure and task ambiguity is an important determinant of the performance of people in groups.

Locus of Control.   Individual differences in the locus of control appear to interact with task ambiguity in a way similar to that found for the other personality variables. There is a small set of studies carried out in classroom, clinical, and industrial settings that essentially parallels the other studies already discussed. Typically, these studies argue that the externally controlled person has come to rely upon other people to direct events, whereas the internally controlled person has come to rely upon his or her own demonstrated skill. A task or group that is clearly structured provides more of the external supports desired by "externals," whereas less structure provides opportunities for the individually determined action desired by "internals."

In the clinical setting, there is a series of studies that has tested the hypothesis that internals gain the most from counseling when it is relatively unstructured, whereas externals benefit most from highly structured counseling guided by an expert. It is interesting that these researchers have made the leap of imagination from the locus of control experimental laboratory research situation to the much more extended and fluid experiences in the counseling situation. In these studies, the task is not a short-term problem (e.g., a puzzle) but rather all the complex events that a large number of people can produce in the course of many hours. Typically in these studies, people volunteer for a personal therapy experience, and after completing the personality tests, they are assigned to either a structured or unstructured therapeutic group. At some point after the experience, the participants complete another set of tests and questionnaires. Typically, these studies demonstrate that internals report more personal satisfaction in the unstructured groups, whereas externals show more satisfaction in the structured groups (Abramowitz, Abramowitz, Roback, & Jackson, 1974; Fry, 1975; Kilmann & Sotile, 1976; Kinder & Kilmann, 1976).

It is very interesting that the relationships found in these relatively brief encounters are replicated by the much more substantial demands of the educational and industrial world. In the industrial setting, we have already reviewed a group of studies that examined the interactive effects of the closely related variables of task difficulty and the broad personality variable called growth needs. As we saw, those studies showed that growth needs moderated the effects of task difficulty on employee satisfaction. In nearly all of those studies, the degree of task ambiguity present in the job was measured, and the results for that related personality variable support the broad hypothesis quite well. Mossholder, Bedeian, and Armenakis (1981), Morse and Caldwell (1979), and O'Reilly (1977) also provide additional sources of support using other measures of related personality variables. Returning to the locus of control program, a number of studies (Abdel-Halim, 1980; Arlin, 1975; Kimmons & Greenhaus, 1976; Mitchell, Smyser, & Weed, 1975; Organ & Greene, 1974; Runyon, 1973) combine to make the same general point. From the results of these studies, it seems fairly clear that internals prefer and feel a greater level of satisfaction when they work in less structured work organizations, whereas externals desire the more structured work organization.

GROUP STRUCTURE

We have discussed group process extensively throughout the book, but we have yet to address the fact that people usually work together with others in well-organized social groups. Up to this point, we have worked to develop, as carefully as the empirical evidence permits, each separate piece of the complex social mosaic that needs identification in order to support a genuine theory of person-by-situation interactions. To complete the examination of the person in the social process, we turn to review one body of work, done in many laboratories and using many methods, that allows us to examine the final set of theoretical propositions introduced in part I. This final section concerns a fundamental question: Does the interaction of the members' personalities with the group's social structure affect overall productivity?

The introduction to group structure in chapter 4 focused on four major features of group structure: differentiation of function; ranking among positions; the nature and distribution of power; and the system of reward. Chapter 5 described a detailed set of theoretical propositions to predict the kinds of social behavior expected from each of the personality variables that we follow. In part III (especially chap. 12), we were able to demonstrate that many of these theoretical propositions receive substantial empirical support. This chapter attempts to demonstrate that knowledge of the individual's dispositionally related preferred forms of social organization allows us to identify the combinations of personality and social structure that appear to result in the highest levels of performance.

Although research is not available to examine the effects of each separate facet of social organization, there is fortunately a substantial number of well-designed studies that allows us to test one of the major propositions that we have been following throughout this book. In this final empirical discussion, we examine the effects that result from two types of social organizations: a differentiated, hierarchical structure with unequal degrees of legitimate or reward power assigned to each position versus an integrated, egalitarian structure with equal degrees of legitimate or reward power assigned to each position. In other words, our final discussion centers around the consequences of a classic comparison in experimental social psychology: the contrast between what is called the authoritarian versus the democratic social structure. The more detailed hypotheses in Table 13.1 perhaps may guide more differentiated research in the future.

Although we can visualize many variations of these two primary forms of social organization, each of which is likely to be effective for persons with different personality characteristics, it is premature to become too detailed at this time. Instead, we concentrate on the level of performance that results from the interaction of the two major forms of social organization with the two major personality clusters. Thus, our major hypotheses are phrased in terms of the structural organization that leads to the optimum level of performance for safety- and esteem-oriented people.

Throughout the book we have been able to demonstrate that the safety-oriented person prefers the sense of predictability that comes from knowing rather precisely what each person in the group is expected to do. This level of predictability can be most easily achieved through highly structured situations that feature a hierarchical arrangement of the positions within the group and a clear division of task responsibility. In addition, the external attributes of status provide an easily perceived and understood set of cues upon which to signify the expected role relationship. In this way, external attributes of status greatly serve to reduce the ambiguity of the social situation. All of these features increase the clarity and certainty of group structure, thereby reducing anxiety so as to create the necessary preconditions for effective group process.

Although we have no evidence to present on the performance of affiliation-oriented people in different social structures, we wish, nonetheless, to suggest which structure should be most congruent with this motive. In characterizing the behavior of the affiliative person in small groups (the P and PF role types), Bales (1970) wrote: "He responds to task-oriented attempts of others, but does not take the initiative. He is not submissive, however, nor is he ascendant, but egalitarian. He seems responsible about group agreements" (p. 265). Our assumption that this motive rests on a core desire for intimacy leads to the prediction that the affiliative person functions at an optimal level when he or she is able to work within an integrated role structure with equal statuses among group members. An egalitarian, participative social environment, in which individuals are evaluated on the basis of their internal attributes, affords the maximum opportunity for direct contact and involvement with other human beings.

The central concern of the esteem-oriented person is the demonstration of personal competence. Given the active, self-initiating quality of these people's behaviors and their characteristic tendency to enhance their feelings of self-worth through manifestations of task and social competence, it is to be expected that they will attempt to become engaged in all aspects of the group's work. In the course of such wide-ranging task activity, esteem-oriented persons establish roles within the group that include a large proportion of the group's tasks. In this way, the roles within an esteem-oriented group become complex and integrated. This social condition is not produced because it is a larger plan "desired" by each person for all the members of the group (which is the goal sought by affiliation-oriented people), but rather as the unplanned result of the separate goal-directed actions that each person attempts to achieve for him- or herself. The group also emerges with an egalitarian social organization because each person's desire for a significant place in the group controls the self-aggrandizing tendencies of the other members. Finally, with their greater concern for competence, the esteem-oriented person focuses on the demonstrated abilities of all group members. Hence, to the degree that ranking does occur within the group, it is based upon internal qualities.

The Contrast Between Safety and Esteem Needs

We begin our exploration of personality and social structure by focusing on two classic studies that report the results of a genuine field experiment in an industrial setting. It might help to introduce these studies if we return briefly to some of the material in chapter 12. Recall that we discussed some of our early work (Aronoff, 1967, 1970) that examined this question in a cross-cultural study of two work organizations. At a minimum, these studies demonstrated that safety-oriented people prefer to work in hierarchical organizations with differentiated roles, whereas esteem-oriented people prefer to work in egalitarian structures with integrated roles. In addition, one of these studies (Aronoff, 1970) presented evidence which demonstrated that changing the membership of a natural group from safety-oriented personnel to esteem-oriented personnel transformed the structure of the group from an authoritarian to an egalitarian form. This naturalistic finding was confirmed in a laboratory experiment (Aronoff & Messé, 1971) which showed that constituting groups with all safety-oriented members led to a hierarchical social structure, whereas constituting groups with all esteem-oriented people resulted in an egalitarian structure.

Two classic studies extend our knowledge of person/structure preferences into the area of the determinants of group productivity. The first study

(Morse & Reimer, 1956) experimentally introduced two types of organizational structures (autonomous and hierarchical) into four equivalent clerical units of a large business corporation. In the autonomous program, the members of the work groups were asked to take control of the decision-making process in many significant areas of their work. In the hierarchical program, changes in the work procedure were introduced to reduce the degree of control that employees held over their activities. Measures of employee morale, productivity, and turnover rate were made before, during, and after the experimental changes were introduced into the organization. Morse and Reimer hypothesized that greater participation would increase, and less participation would reduce, employee satisfaction and productivity. As predicted, the results showed an increase in satisfaction in the autonomous condition and a decrease in satisfaction in the hierarchical condition. The results also showed, contrary to prediction, that both experimental innovations raised productivity and that the rise was significantly greater in the hierarchically controlled program.

Tannenbaum and Allport (1956), studying the results of this experimental field study, hypothesized that if an individual's personality was suited for the structure that she worked in, whether it was the hierarchical or the autonomous organization, her level of satisfaction with the organization would be higher than when it was mismatched with the organizational structure. In order to estimate the employee's major concerns, a scale was developed to assess the general tendency toward self-reliance, autonomy, striving for personal competence, and initiative versus tendencies toward dependency, submissiveness, approval seeking, defensiveness, and expressions of inferiority. In other words, this study used a rather simple safety versus esteem contrast in devising sets of self-report questions. Measures of the level of satisfaction with the organization were taken about 1 year after the experimental changes were introduced, which is a rather demanding test. The results of this analysis clearly indicated that the congruence between personality and structure was related to satisfaction with the company. For example, employees whose personalities were congruent with the nature of their organization liked, were satisfied with their roles in, and wished to keep their particular type of program.

From our point of view, these two studies raise many questions. For example, it is not clear if an unexamined personality–structure congruence might account for the nonpredicted result in the Morse and Reimer study or if it was due to some property of the organization or the work force that was not measured. It would also have been valuable to obtain additional behavioral productivity measures. However, as a genuine field experiment, these two studies show how useful it might be to extend this mode of analysis. We want to continue to introduce this point of view with a description of a carefully controlled laboratory experiment (Wilson, Aronoff, & Messé, 1975) that used a clearer measure of group outcome. We present the study in some detail and then coordinate its findings with those from other experimental work that has been done in this area.

Based on the principles established in the earlier study (Aronoff & Messé, 1971), this experiment focused directly on the effects of personality–structure congruence upon the productivity of the group. We expected that group productivity would be greatest when all the negative effects of faulty group process could be avoided. Following the reasoning that we have outlined throughout this section, we expected that we could test the proposition that, for both safety- and esteem-oriented people, we would be able to show higher levels of productivity in congruent as compared to incongruent social structures. We expected that safety-oriented people are most satisfied by the characteristics of a hierarchical social structure and find an egalitarian social structure unpleasant because its relatively unstructured nature raises their anxiety. Conversely, we expected that esteem-oriented people are most satisfied by the characteristics of an egalitarian social structure and find a hierarchical system unpleasant because it frustrates their independence of action.

Male undergraduates were recruited through an advertisement in the university newspaper and given the same sentence completion test used in our earlier work. Based on scores on this measure, safety- and esteem-oriented people were selected for work in three-person groups that were organized homogeneously by motive. There were 12 groups of safety-oriented people and 12 groups of esteem-oriented people. Two kinds of social structures (hierarchical and egalitarian) were imposed upon these groups through two different sets of instructions. For half of the groups (the hierarchical condition), group members were told that, based upon the results of the assessment interview, it was best for one of them (a person who, in fact, was chosen at random) to assume the role of leader and take command of the group. The other half of the groups (the egalitarian condition) were told that, based upon their assessment interview, it would be best for all of them to share the leader's position equally. In this way, half of each kind of group worked in a hierarchical structure and half worked in an egalitarian structure.

We brought the three people who were to compose a group into the laboratory, seated them at a table, gave them their instructions, and asked them to construct the model of a building. Each group was given a photograph of a modern office building and told that their job, as a group, was to construct as much of the building as possible in a 1-hour period. Materials for the model — consisting of about 1,000 small, interlocking pieces of plastic in the shape of blocks, doors, windows, and so forth — were arranged on a side table.

We expected that neither the motives of the people nor the nature of the group structure would determine the extent of the model that each group would be able to complete in the 1 hour that they were given to work at their task. Instead, we expected that groups whose personality–structure properties were congruent in the ways that we predicted would be much more productive than those whose properties were not congruent. The results of this experiment confirmed the predictions dramatically. This study completed a series of studies, each of which provided additional information designed to supplement the inherent limitations in any method. The first study (Aronoff, 1967) revealed the association between motive and structure in two naturalistic work groups. The second (Aronoff, 1970) showed the process of change in the structure of one of these naturalistic groups as the composition, and the dominant personality orientation, of the membership changed over time. The third (Aronoff & Messé, 1971) demonstrated the motive–structure relationship in emerging small groups under the highly controlled conditions of the experimental laboratory. And most important, this study confirmed the hypothesis of motive–structure congruence. Safety-oriented people were much more productive when asked to work in a hierarchical group, as compared to an egalitarian group. Esteem-oriented people were much more productive when asked to work in an egalitarian group, as compared to a hierarchical group.

These results, like so many others that we have discussed, are based upon the assumption that certain disposition–situation relationships are more anxiety arousing than others. Although greatly needed, ongoing measures of emotional states have typically been too difficult to obtain in the fluid events of the group process. Recently, Seeman (1982) reported the results of a study that provides a great deal of evidence to substantiate the type of mechanism typically proposed to underlie the different degrees of congruency in the personality–structure relationship. Seeman assigned anxious and non-anxious subjects to either an autocratic or democratic group structure and asked them to discuss and resolve an involving social problem. Each of the members of the discussion group was connected to a galvanic skin response (GSR) recording apparatus. The major finding from this particular experiment was that the nonanxious subjects showed a substantially elevated level of arousal when working in the autocratic group structure. The results for the anxious subjects did not show the expected elevation in the incongruent condition, although we can easily speculate that the strength of the experimental leader in both conditions reduced their level of arousal. In any case, these results, together with those obtained from the experiment reported earlier (Assor, Aronoff, & Messé, 1984), provide the initial physiological evidence of the subjective events that we have assumed mediate the person–structure relationship.

Additional Studies of Motive–Structure Congruence

Authoritarianism. The early rush of research studying the social consequences of the trait of authoritarianism dealt with almost every type of question, including the effects on productivity of the interaction between authoritarianism and group structure. In the first exploratory study, McCurdy and Eber (1953) predicted that authoritarians would be more successful working in an autocratic organization, whereas egalitarians would be more successful working in a democratic organization. They constructed an elaborate set of lights and switches in the laboratory and had three-person groups use the equipment as a device to communicate with each other about a problem that the group was asked to solve. The instructions to the group instituted either an autocratic (one person in control) or a democratic (each person in control) form of organization. The results, unfortunately, were not clear. There was some indication that placing authoritarian people in a democratic organization reduced their level of performance, but otherwise, there were no important findings.

Shaw (1959) argued that part of the problem with McCurdy and Eber's study was in the way the social organization was created in the laboratory. Instead, Shaw created centralized and decentralized communication structures in which the members of four-person groups communicated with each other via written messages. Shaw formed homogeneous groups with people who were either all authoritarian or nonauthoritarian. The results of this experiment provided the first real experimental evidence on the validity of the hypothesis on motive–structure congruence. Shaw found that, in the centralized type of organization, groups with authoritarian leaders outperformed groups with nonauthoritarian leaders. Conversely, in the decentralized organization, groups with nonauthoritarian leaders outperformed groups with authoritarian leaders.

As we review these results, it seems likely that at least one of their bases lies in the authoritarian individual's desire for the clear task guidelines that the centralized organization is able to provide. This mechanism has been discussed at length in our review of task ambiguity and authoritarianism, as well as in chapter 7. In fact, the phenomenon that Vroom and others term "participation" probably reflects a work structure in which the roles are broad and inclusive (i.e., integrated). Those studies performed in industrial settings should be considered, along with the results from Shaw's experiment, as a demonstration of this relationship in a natural setting. What is missing from this research is the study of the properties that are unique to the authoritarianism variable. For example, we would expect that authoritarianism would be especially sensitive to the hierarchical components of this organization and more affected by the status and power attributes of leadership than might some other, safety-related variable (which might be affected most by the informational flow aspects of these organizations). It would be both interesting and useful to pull apart the different components of these social organizations in order to show how variables within a cluster respond to very different features of the complex social system.

Immature Character Structure.   There is an excellent field experiment by Kipnis and Wagner (1967) that helps explain more about this relationship. The basic form of this experiment replicates all the studies found in this section, but the group structure that was imposed included a more coercive superior position than is usually used in the laboratory. Kipnis and Wagner developed a scale that measured what they termed an active and hostile form of immature character structure. We include this study here because the pattern of scores on this test, correlated with those of other tests, indicates quite clearly that the test was measuring some aspect of the safety-needs cluster. Although the details of the study are too extensive to describe here, for our purposes it is sufficient to state that Kipnis and Wagner were able to construct a real-world experiment in which sailors were asked to work in three different types of social structures. As the authors expected, the results of this experiment demonstrated that immature people reached their highest levels of performance under quite hierarchically structured and coercive conditions. By contrast, mature people were most productive in the least structured, noncoercive condition. Kipnis and Wagner (1967) write: "working for a punitive and powerful leader depressed the performance of mature Ss and tended to elevate the performance of immature Ss" (p. 22).

The Need for Achievement and Internal Locus of Control.   It is perplexing that the need for achievement and internal locus of control, both of which have stimulated far-reaching research programs, have not been used in a major study in this area. It is not difficult to predict that individuals who are highly achievement-motivated (as well as internally controlled) would be more satisfied and more productive in egalitarian, role-integrated work structures in which they would have the greatest opportunity to influence the outcome of events. But unfortunately, there are only a few scattered studies which indicate the need for more research in this area. For example, Fineman (1975) designed a questionnaire-based study of middle-level managers in a number of industrial organizations. The results of his study, which used a variety of outcome measures, including salary, showed that achievement-oriented managers were much more satisfied and productive when their work roles were designed in a broad and inclusive way. In a similar kind of study, Meadows (1980) used several brief assertiveness measures to show that more assertive people were more satisfied by opportunities to work in organizations with greater role sharing, supportive leadership, and participation. In a more unusual type of study, Ghiselli and Johnson (1970) argued that organizations with fewer levels of management (i.e., a flat structure) should provide greater opportunities for individual initiative than those organizations with more management levels (i.e., a tall structure). They found that esteem-oriented managers in the flat structure advanced further and were more satisfied than were safety-oriented managers.

Internal locus of control should follow the same pattern of social relationships. Much like the person with strong achievement strivings, the internally directed person likes to initiate a wide range of activity. For this reason, the most congruent social organization would be the democratic structure. Several studies tend to confirm this prediction. For example, Runyon (1973) studied employees at a packaging plant and found that internally directed people were more satisfied with participative management than they were with directive management. Virtually identical results were obtained by Brownell (1982) and by Faytinger (1978).

The results of the studies that looked at the interaction of locus of control and task ambiguity (recall that of Kilmann and his associates) provide another small piece of evidence that this variable seems to be most suited to more inclusive social functions. The final bit of evidence presently available comes from an interesting experiment by Hrycenko and Minton (1974) who assigned internally and externally controlled people to either a powerful or a powerless position in an experimental dyad. Not surprisingly, the externally controlled men were more satisfied in the low-power position, whereas internally controlled men were more satisfied in the high-power position. Taken together, these results support and extend our earlier discussion in the task section. Where information is available, it seems to support the appropriate part of the larger model. Yet, the model points out just how fragmentary our present fund of information really is.

Dominance.   Throughout the book we have seen a great deal of evidence that identifies the modes of behavior to be expected from the dominance-oriented person. Simply put, such a person needs to establish feelings of self-worth through behavior that directs, influences, and controls others. In the group context, such a person egocentrically seeks personal control over task activity. We saw in earlier chapters that such a person reaches for the more powerful positions in space, assumes the more powerful positions in the group's social structure, and uses a wide variety of means—from cognitive distortions of the meaning of social events to a rather easy use of coercive power—in the service of these needs. Clearly, the dominant person is a competitive, hard-driving, task-oriented individual who likes to see things done well and, preferably, under his or her guidance. As such, the dominant person has been of great interest to social psychology.

This disposition, then, leads to straightforward predictions in this area. The dominant person should function best when he or she has access to the position that controls the group's activity. We expect that when a social structure is available that establishes this sort of control, the dominant person should be more productive than when such social support is not available. Certainly, the worst social position in which to place the dominant person is one in which another person has control over his or her fate. We are not suggesting that this esteem-based variable leads to higher rates of productivity in egalitarian conditions. In contrast to the other esteem-oriented types that we have seen thus far, we expect that dominance-motivated people need to maintain much more control over the task. This requirement should prevent them from doing well in an egalitarian condition.

There is a set of experimental studies (Moos & Speisman, 1962; Shaw & Harkey, 1976; Smelser, 1961; Watson, 1971) that examined these predictions in the laboratory and supports them rather well. Although all of these experiments would reward close study, they take a common form that permits us to present them as a group. In general, the common procedure is to identify dominant and nondominant individuals, place them in a powerful or powerless position in an experimental group social structure, and determine the group's achievement at some common experimental task. In each of these studies, the congruent condition has the dominant person in the high-power position and the nondominant person in the low-power position. In the incongruent condition, the positions of the dominant and the nondominant persons are reversed or are undifferentiated. The results of these studies clearly show, across a fairly wide range of experimental tasks, that congruent groups are more productive than incongruent groups.

Smelser's (1961) study is a good illustration of the way such research is done. Smelser tested male volunteers from university military studies classes with a short form of Gough's (1957) Dominance scale, which he used to identify dominant and submissive individuals. He brought two of these people into the laboratory at a time and asked them, as a group, to run two model railroad trains around a moderately complicated track. Each person had a control panel with which to operate one of the trains. The task emphasized cooperation: The people were asked to operate their trains so that they could produce as many mutually complete trips around the track as possible in a specified time period. In other words, both trains had to complete a circuit of the track for the group to earn a score. Finally, Smelser designed a simple social system with one dominant position (charged with deciding how to coordinate both trains) and one submissive position (charged with following instructions from the dominant person). The feature that makes this experiment so interesting is that Smelser used seven different kinds of conditions to examine the many possible combinations of personality and social system variables that might affect the group's achievement. Not only did Smelser have the two usual congruent and incongruent conditions, but all the additional conditions as well, including the different personality combinations without any social structure.

As we have seen in the other studies, this experiment found that the congruent condition was the most productive and the incongruent condition the least productive way to arrange individual dispositions and social organization. However, in addition to the two conditions upon which we base this conclusion, Smelser also had three conditions in which no role relationships were instituted. In these conditions, the two college students operated the trains without any further instructions, and it seems that an egalitarian condition probably developed inadvertently in the laboratory. We find it very interesting that these three conditions had the lowest level of achievement of any of the conditions, except for the extreme incongruent condition. This result seems to demonstrate that dominance motivation leads to poor levels of performance both in an egalitarian condition and when the dominant person is put into a grossly incongruent condition (the submissive position).

However, the predictions in Table 13.1 go beyond these expectations. We assumed that the dominance-motivated person most requires the opportunity to be an effective agent over the events in his or her life. This can be achieved by a sharp division of labor as well as by a hierarchical social structure. There is even reason to believe that one of the other conditions in Smelser's experiment, in which dominance-oriented people were quite successful, approximated the separated roles condition that is needed to complete the analysis. However, the examination of such hypotheses will require future research designed to address that point.

SUMMARY

Curiously, although a variety of statements on person–situation congruence have been offered by many theorists, it has not been recognized just how much empirical evidence has already accumulated in their support. Even more than was necessary in previous chapters, evaluation of the propositions derived from a theory of congruence requires a more orderly view of the entire scope of a social event. We have seen that there are several important nodes of the social process where a substantial amount of information has been obtained that allows us to confirm significant derivations from theory. However, these nodes typically are focused on a specific aspect of the social process; they are usually identified with a particular researcher and method as well. Because of their focus, these bodies of information customarily have not been used to support general models of the social process. Yet, it is only by raising the scope of the analysis to encompass larger sequences of the social process, including many different types of research, that the amount of progress already made can become evident. With the use of a broad and articulated model, the evidence obtained in each of the focused areas not only supports the conclusions from another, but makes the scattered results obtained in other areas appear to be a more promising avenue for future research.

14 Epilogue

Our goal in writing this book has been to discover a theoretical framework that might explain the coherence in adaptive human behavior. The result of many years of work on personality and social behavior has produced such a substantial body of information that it is now possible to develop a theory of interactions between personality and situational variables that is rich enough to account for a wide range of human behavior and explicit enough to be put to an empirical test. Although few of the basic processes have been completely explored, the findings from many important programs seem ready to be integrated into a broader framework that might stimulate research throughout the discipline. In other words, this seems to be the time to use the generalist's approach to continue to generate broad models to guide the next wave of empirical research.

In seeking to identify the elements that are required by a theory of interactions, our assumption has been that a social event occurs when a person responds to the features of the environment with a set of behaviors designed to achieve a personal goal. With this point of view, it is possible to reformulate the questions typically asked about person-by-situation processes from the vantage point of two separate disciplines into those that consider personality to be an integral part of the process that constructs a social event. As even the most minimalist theories of social psychology make assumptions about human information-processing capacities and as cognitive social learning theories make assumptions about the nature of social reinforcement, it seems more productive to make clearer the assumptions upon which so much informal explanation is based. Not only should explicit use of these variables sharpen the analysis of the effects that they are assumed to produce, but it should allow us to understand their limitations as well.

To generate an interactionist theory, we need to identify concrete elements of the person and the situation, and then identify the types of effects that each class of variables might have upon the other. It has been exciting to explore the theoretical opportunities that became available once these concrete elements were clearly articulated. Although the testable consequences of the theory could have been developed at much greater length, our assumption has been that it is preferable to set the level of theoretical prediction only somewhat ahead of its empirical base and use the available research to evaluate and refine the theory's central assumptions.

In preparing the materials necessary to test a theory of interactions, we confessed that our approach has much in common with that of the paleontologist who uses mere fragments of bone to determine the structure of a dinosaur. In this book, we have sifted through thousands of fragments of empirical data, discovering along the way some especially robust and complete elements, in order to see if our present fund of information allowed us to articulate a coherent view of personality in the social process. A number of important theoretical predictions derivable from the theory could not be evaluated because of the absence of appropriate bases of empirical work, but still, viewing the wide range of results that is available, a unified model materializes whose parts form a remarkably interesting structure. What makes this structure so fascinating is that, despite the use of many different personality measures utilized by researchers with widely diverging theoretical positions in a multitude of experimental and field settings, the empirical evidence that is available consistently supports the major predictions of this model. If personality variables were merely constructs in the eye of the beholder or unrelated to broad social events, the existing literature should not yield such a high level of coherence.

The focus on the personological bases of social responsiveness permits us to link personality and social variables in a manner that reveals the coherence of adaptive behavior across the full spectrum of social processes. These variables lead the person to select rewards from among the array offered by most social events; they also generate the mechanism through which social variables produce their impact upon the person. Following this line of reasoning, personality processes interacting with social variables produce predictable classes of social behavior through a relatively limited number of mechanisms that seem to underlie most social events. When we examine the effect of a personality variable across the major dimensions of social behavior presented in Table 1.1, there emerges an extraordinary amount of coherence in the observed behavior that can be accounted for by a relatively small set of prior information. We use the term coherence, rather than cross-situational consistency, because the goal of prediction is to account for the type of behavior that may occur, considering the nature of the situation. As Bem and Allen (1974) argue, it is neither necessary nor desirable to assume that a particular personality variable should lead to the same set of behaviors, irrespective of the situation.

The social consequences of the dominance motive provide a fine example to show the extraordinary amount of cross-situational predictive power that is contained in a specific theory of interactions. On the bases of the brief definitions of this motive and the different elements of the social situation, we can predict that people strongly concerned with the dominance motive would be relatively unaffected by stress-evoking aspects of situations, but highly sensitive to spatial configurations or the competence (but not the status) attributes of other people. We can predict that task difficulty, complexity, ambiguity, and importance would be an incentive to performance. We can predict that this motive would be associated with moderate levels of selective attention or toleration of ambiguity, yet associated with high levels of persistence in processing information as well as the setting of high levels of aspiration. We can predict that this motive would lead people into strongly assertive, task-oriented, nonaffiliative, styles of performance as well as the frank and competitive adversarial mode of interaction, in which they would negotiate quite firmly and rigidly. Further, we can predict the way such people use and respond to power as well as their preference for differentiated role structures.

All of this information allows us to predict the social conditions under which dominance-motivated people exhibit their highest levels of performance. The use of a unified consensus model of personality allows us to make relatively modest changes in the definition of the dominance motive in order to define the need for achievement, and with the addition of this slightly revised definition, we can generate a markedly different pattern of prediction. Moreover, as we have shown, we can accomplish the same result for a wide variety of personality variables, in each case remaining within the larger model of personality and social variables. Thus, we are able to generate an extraordinarily large amount of cross-situational coherence from this model, and the empirical evidence that we have examined throughout the book provides a reasonable amount of confidence in the accuracy of many of the most important assumptions.

More generally, in this book we have been trying to demonstrate that the fields of personality and social psychology need to recognize that they constitute separate orientations to the study of a common event: All personality processes occur within a social context; all social psychological processes occur within an individual. Each subdiscipline provides the other with just the material that it has been lacking the most. The field of social psychology can provide the field of personality with the interesting range of normal human behaviors and the significant social elements that can lead it away from the limited phenomena obtained from its origin in the clinical tradition. The field of personality, in turn, can provide social psychology with the range of detailed constructs that can explain the power of the social environment to evoke the complex range of behavior with which it has been concerned.

Thus, we suggest that the model described in this book, and the research which supports its major predictions, may point to new levels of behavioral analysis. It is very likely that there are many additional social processes that can be helpfully explained from the perspectives outlined in this book. It is also likely that there are substantial opportunities for more clearly articulated theory. Hopefully, the research described in *Personality in the Social Process* has shown that we need no longer search for fossil remains to find traces of an extraordinarily interesting path of adaptation. There is now more than sufficient evidence to confirm the role of personality in the social process.

References

Abdel-Halim, A. A. (1980). Effects of higher order need strength on the job performance–job satisfaction relationship. *Personnel Psychology, 33,* 335–347.

Abramowitz, C. V., Abramowitz, S. I., Roback, H. B., & Jackson, C. (1974). Differential effectiveness of directive and nondirective group therapies as a function of client internal–external control. *Journal of Consulting and Clinical Psychology, 42,* 849–853.

Adler, A. (1956). *The individual psychology of Alfred Adler.* New York: Basic Books.

Adorno, T. W., Frenkel-Brunswik, E., Levinson, D. J., & Sanford, R. N. (1950). *The authoritarian personality.* New York: Harper & Row.

Ainsworth, L. H. (1958). Rigidity, insecurity, and stress. *Journal of Abnormal and Social Psychology, 56,* 67–74.

Ainsworth, M. D., & Bell, S. M. (1974). Mother–infant interaction and the development of competence. In K. J. Connolly & J. S. Bruner (Eds.), *The growth of competence* (pp. 97–118). New York: Academic Press.

Akamatsu, T. J., & Thelen, M. H. (1977). Observer states and traits and the imitative process: A test of a new formulation. *Journal of Research in Personality, 11,* 165–179.

Allport, G. (1961). *Pattern and growth in personality.* New York: Holt, Rinehart & Winston.

Allport, G. W., Vernon, P. E., & Lindzey, G. (1951). *Study of values.* Boston: Houghton Mifflin.

Altman, I., & McGinnies, E. (1960). Interpersonal perception and communication in discussion groups of varied attitudinal composition. *Journal of Abnormal and Social Psychology, 60,* 390–395.

Altman, I., & Taylor, D. A. (1973). *Social penetration: Development of interpersonal relationships.* New York: Holt, Rinehart & Winston.

Altrocchi, J. (1959). Dominance as a factor in interpersonal choices and perception. *Journal of Abnormal and Social Psychology, 59,* 303–308.

Amidjaja, I. R., & Vinacke, W. E. (1965). Achievement, nurturance, and competition in male and female triads. *Journal of Personality and Social Psychology, 2,* 447–451.

Andrews, J. D. W. (1967). The achievement motive and advancement in two types of organizations. *Journal of Personality and Social Psychology, 6,* 163–168.

Appley, M. H., & Moeller, G. (1963). Conforming behavior and personality variables in college women. *Journal of Abnormal and Social Psychology, 66,* 284–290.

Argyle, M., & Dean, J. (1965). Eye-contact, distance and affiliation. *Sociometry, 28,* 289–304.

Argyle, M., & Ingham, R. (1972). Gaze, mutual gaze, and proximity. *Semiotica, 6,* 32–49.

Aries, E. J., Gold, C., & Weigel, R. H. (1983). Dominance and situational influences on dominance behavior in small groups. *Journal of Personality and Social Psychology, 44,* 779–786.

Arlin, M. (1975). The interaction of locus of control, classroom structure, and pupil satisfaction. *Psychology in the Schools, 12,* 279–286.

Armilla, J. (1967). Predicting self-assessed social leadership in a new culture with the MMPI. *The Journal of Social Psychology, 73,* 219–225.

Aronoff, J. (1967). *Psychological needs and cultural systems.* Princeton, NJ: Van Nostrand.

Aronoff, J. (1970). Psychological needs as a determinant in the formation of economic structures: A confirmation. *Human Relations, 23,* 123–138.

Aronoff, J. (1972). *A scoring manual for safety, affiliation and esteem motives.* Unpublished manuscript.

Aronoff, J., & Messé, L. A. (1971). Motivational determinants of small-group structure. *Journal of Personality and Social Psychology, 17,* 319–324.

Asch, S. E. (1952). *Social psychology.* Englewood Cliffs, NJ: Prentice-Hall.

Asch, S. E. (1956). Studies of independence and conformity: A minority of one against a unanimous majority. *Psychological Monographs, 70*(9, Whole No. 416).

Ashour, A. S., & England, G. (1972). Subordinates assigned level of discretion as a function of leader's personality and situational variables. *Journal of Applied Psychology, 56,* 120–123.

Assor, A., Aronoff, J., & Messé, L. A. (1981). Attribute relevance as a moderator of the effects of motivation on impression formation. *Journal of Personality and Social Psychology, 41,* 789–796.

Assor, A., Aronoff, J., & Messé, L. A. (1984). *An experimental test of defensive processes in impression formation.* Unpublished manuscript.

Assor, A., & O'Quin, K. (1982). The intangibles of bargaining: Power and competence versus deference and approval. *Journal of Social Psychology, 116,* 119–126.

Atkinson, J. W. (1957). Motivational determinants of risk-taking behavior. *Psychological Review, 64,* 359–372.

Atkinson, J. W. (Ed.). (1958). *Motives in fantasy, action and society.* Princeton, NJ: D. Van Nostrand.

Atkinson, J. W., Bastian, J. R., Earl, R. W., & Litwin, G. H. (1960). The achievement motive, goal setting, and probability preferences. *Journal of Abnormal and Social Psychology, 60,* 27–36.

Atkinson, J. W., & Feather, N. T. (Eds.). (1966). *A theory of achievement motivation.* New York: Wiley.

Atkinson, J. W., & Litwin, G. H. (1960). Achievement motive and test anxiety conceived as motive to approach success and motive to avoid failure. *Journal of Abnormal and Social Psychology, 60,* 52–63.

Atkinson, J. W., & McClelland, D. C. (1948). The projective expression of needs. II. The effect of different intensities of the hunger drive on thematic apperception. *Journal of Experimental Psychology, 38,* 643–658.

Atkinson, J. W., & Raynor, J. O. (1974). *Motivation and achievement. New York: Wiley.*

Atkinson, J. W., & Raynor, J. O. (1978). Personality, motivation and achievement. New York: Wiley.

Atkinson, J. W., & Walker, E. L. (1956). The affiliation motive and perceptual sensitivity to faces. *Journal of Abnormal and Social Psychology, 53,* 38–41.

Back, K. W., & Davis, K. E. (1965). Some personal and situational factors relevant to the consistency and prediction of conforming behavior. *Sociometry, 28,* 227–240.

Bales, R. F. (1950). *Interaction process analysis.* Reading, MA: Addison-Wesley.

Bales, R. F. (1970). *Personality and interpersonal behavior.* New York: Holt, Rinehart & Winston.

Bales, R. F. (1979). *Symlog*. New York: Free Press.

Barnett, M. A., Mathews, K. A., & Howard, J. A. (1979). Relationship between competitiveness and empathy in 6- and 7-year olds. *Developmental Psychology, 15,* 221–222.

Bass, B. M. (1954). The leaderless group discussion. *Psychological Bulletin, 51,* 465–492.

Bass, B. M., McGehee, C. R., Hawkins, W. C., Young, P. C., & Gebel, A. S. (1953). Personality variables related to leaderless group discussion behavior. *Journal of Abnormal and Social Psychology, 48,* 120–128.

Bass, B. M., Wurster, C. R., Doll, P. A., & Clair, D. J. (1953). Situational and personality factors in leadership among sorority women. *Psychological Monograph, 67,* 1–23.

Battistich, V. A. (1979). *Personality and situational influences in person perception and social cognition: An interactive model of the impression formation process.* Unpublished doctoral dissertation, Michigan State University, East Lansing.

Battistich, V. A., & Aronoff, J. (in press). *Perceiver, target and situational influences on social cognition: An interactional analysis. Journal of Personality and Social Psychology.*

Beckworth, J., Iverson, M. A., & Reuder, M. A. (1965). Test anxiety, task relevance of group experience, and change in level of aspiration. *Journal of Personality and Social Psychology, 1,* 579–588.

Beer, M., Buckhout, R., Horowitz, M. W., & Levy, S. (1959). Some perceived properties of the difference between leaders and nonleaders. *Journal of Psychology, 47,* 49–56.

Bell, G. B., & Hall, H. E. (1954). The relationship between leadership and empathy. *Journal of Abnormal and Social Psychology, 49,* 156–157.

Beloff, H. (1958). Two forms of social conformity: Acquiescence and conventionality. *Journal of Abnormal and Social Psychology, 56,* 99–104.

Bem, D. J. (1972). Constructing cross-situational consistencies in behavior: Some thoughts on Alker's critique of Mischel. *Journal of Personality, 40,* 17–26.

Bem, D. J., & Allen, A. (1974). On predicting some of the people some of the time. *Psychological Review, 81,* 506–520.

Benjamin, L. S. (1984). Principles of prediction using structural analysis of social behavior. In R. A. Zucker, J. Aronoff, A. I. Rabin (Eds.), *Personality and the prediction of behavior* (pp. 121–178). New York: Academic Press.

Bennet, R. P., & Carbonari, J. P. (1976). Personality patterns related to own-, joint-, and relative-gain maximizing behaviors. *Journal of Personality and Social Psychology, 34,* 1127–1134.

Bennis, W. G., & Shepard, H. (1956). A theory of group development. *Human Relations, 9,* 415–437.

Benson, P. L., Wright, A., & Riordan, C. (1978). Social approval needs and helping behavior. *Journal of Social Psychology, 106,* 285–286.

Berg, K. S., & Vidmar, N. (1975). Authoritarianism and recall of evidence about criminal behavior. *Journal of Research on Personality, 9,* 147–157.

Berger, S. E., Levin, P., Jacobson, L. I., & Millham, J. (1977). Gain approval or avoid disapproval: Comparison of motive strengths in high need for approval scorers. *Journal of Personality, 45,* 458–468.

Berkowitz, L., & Lundy, R. M. (1957). Personality characteristics related to susceptibility to influence by peers or authority figures. *Journal of Personality, 25,* 306–316.

Berkowitz, N. H. (1968). Alternative measures of authoritarianism, response sets, and prediction in a two-person game. *Journal of Social Psychology, 74,* 233–242.

Bettinghouse, E., Miller, G., & Steinfatt, T. (1970). Source evaluation, syllogistic content and judgments of logical validity by high and low dogmatic persons. *Journal of Personality and Social Psychology, 16,* 238–244.

Bibring, E. (1941). The development and problems of the theory of the instincts. *The International Journal of Psychoanalysis, 22,* 102–131.

Bieri, J. (1966). Cognitive complexity and personality development. In O. J. Harvey (Ed.), *Experience, structure and adaptability* (pp. 13–37). New York: Springer.

Bieri, J. (1968). Cognitive complexity and judgment of inconsistent information. In R. P. Abelson, E. Aronson, W. J. McGuire, T. M. Newcomb, M. J. Rosenberg, & P. H. Tannenbaum (Eds.), *Theories of cognitive consistency: A sourcebook* (pp. 633–641). Chicago: Rand McNally.

Bigoness, W. (1976). Effects of locus of control and style of third party intervention upon bargaining behavior. *Journal of Applied Psychology, 61,* 305–312.

Biondo, J. & MacDonald, A. P., Jr. (1971). Internal–external locus of control and response to influence attempts. *Journal of Personality, 39,* 407–419.

Bixenstine, V. E., Chambers, N., & Wilson, K. V. (1964). Effect of asymmetry in payoff on behavior in a two-person nonzero-sum game. *Journal of Conflict Resolution, 8,* 151–159.

Bixenstine, V. E., & Douglas, J. (1967). Effect of psychopathology on group consensus and cooperation choice in a six-person game. *Journal of Personality and Social Psychology, 5,* 32–37.

Bixenstine, V. E., Levitt, C. A., & Wilson, K. V. (1966). Collaboration among six persons in a prisoner's dilemma game. *Journal of Conflict Resolution, 10,* 488–496.

Bixenstine, V. E., & O'Reilly, E. F., Jr. (1966). Money versus electric shock as payoff in a prisoner's dilemma game. *Psychological Record, 16,* 251–264.

Bixenstine, V. E., Potash, H. M., & Wilson, K. V. (1963). Effects of level of cooperative choice by the other player on choices in a prisoner's dilemma game. Part I. *Journal of Abnormal and Social Psychology, 66,* 308–313.

Bixenstine, V. E., & Wilson, K. V. (1963). Effects of level of cooperative choice by the other player on choices in a prisoner's dilemma game. Part II. *Journal of Abnormal and Social Psychology, 67,* 139–147.

Blake, R. R., & Mouton, J. S. (1961). Perceived characteristics of elected representatives. *Journal of Abnormal Psychology, 62,* 693–695.

Blasi, A. (1980). Bridging moral cognition and moral action: A critical review of the literature. *Psychological Bulletin, 88,* 1–45.

Block, J. (1971). *Lives through time.* Berkeley, CA: Bancroft.

Block, J., & Block, J. (1951). An investigation of the relationship between intolerance of ambiguity and ethnocentrism. *Journal of Personality, 19,* 303–311.

Block, J., & Petersen, P. (1955). Some personality correlates of confidence, caution and speed in a decision situation. *Journal of Abnormal and Social Psychology, 51,* 34–41.

Bloomfield, D. R., & Blick, K. A. (1975). Personality correlates of verbal conflict resolution. *Journal of Psychology, 90,* 45–49.

Blumstein, P. W. (1973). Audience, Machiavellianism, and tactics of identity bargaining. *Sociometry, 36,* 346–365.

Bogart, K. (1971). Machiavellianism and individual differences in response to cognitive inconsistency. *Journal of Social Psychology, 85,* 111–119.

Borg, W. R. (1960). Prediction of small group role behavior from personality variables. *Journal of Abnormal and Social Psychology, 60,* 112–116.

Borg, W. R., & Tupes, E. C. (1958). Personality characteristics related to leadership behavior in two types of small group situational problems. *Journal of Applied Psychology, 42,* 252–256.

Borg, W. R., Tupes, E. C. & Carp, A. (1959). Relationships between physical proficiency and measures of leadership and personality. *Personnel Psychology, 12,* 113–126.

Borgatta, E. F. (1968). Traits and persons. In E. F. Borgatta & W. W. Lambert (Eds.), *Handbook of personality theory and research* (pp. 510–528). Chicago: Rand McNally.

Borgatta, E. F., Cottrell, L. S., & Mann, J. H. (1958). The spectrum of individual interaction characteristics: An interdimensional analysis. *Psychological Reports, 4,* 279–319.

Borgatta, E. F., Couch, A. S., & Bales, R. F. (1954). Some findings relevant to the great man theory of leadership. *American Sociological Review, 19,* 755–759.

Borgatta, E. F., & Crowther, B. (1965). *A workbook for the study of social interaction process.* Chicago: Rand McNally.

Braginsky, D. D. (1970). Machiavellianism and manipulative interpersonal behavior in children.

Journal of Experimental Social Psychology, 6, 77–99.

Brannigan, G. G. (1977). Role of approval motivation in children's problem solving. *The Journal of Genetic Psychology, 131,* 139–145.

Branningan, G. G. & Duchnowski, A. J. (1976). Outer-directedness in the decision making of high and low approval motivated children. *The Journal of Genetic Psychology, 128,* 85–90.

Branningan, G. G., Duchnowski, A. J., & Nyce, P. A. (1974). Roles of approval motivation and social reinforcement in children's discrimination learning. *Developmental Psychology, 10,* 843–846.

Bray, R. M., & Noble, A. M. (1978). Authoritarianism and decisions of mock juries: Evidence of jury bias and group polarization. *Journal of Personality and Social Psychology, 36,* 1424–1430.

Brice, D. J., & Sassenrath, J. M. (1978). Effects of locus of control, task instructions, and belief on expectancy of success. *Journal of Social Psychology, 104,* 97–105.

Brief, A. P., & Aldag, R. J. (1975). Employee reactions to job characteristics: A constructive replication. *Journal of Applied Psychology, 60,* 182–186.

Brody, N. (1963). Achievement, test anxiety and subjective probability of success in risk taking behavior. *Journal of Abnormal and Social Psychology, 66,* 413–418.

Brown, R. W. (1953). A determinant of the relationship between rigidity and authoritarianism. *Journal of Abnormal and Social Psychology, 48,* 469–476.

Brownell, P. (1982). The effects of personality-situation congruence in a managerial context: Locus of control and budgetary participation. *Journal of Personality and Social Psychology, 42,* 753–763.

Brozek, J., Guetzkow, H., & Baldwin, M. V. (1951). A quantitative study of perception and association in experimental semi starvation. *Journal of Personality, 19,* 245–264.

Brundage, L. E., Derlega, V. J., & Cash, T. F. (1977). The effects of physical attractiveness and need approval on self-disclosure. *Personality and Social Psychology Bulletin, 3,* 63–66.

Bryant, B. K. (1974). Locus of control related to teacher–child interperceptual experiences. *Child Development, 45,* 157–164.

Buckhout, R. (1965a). Need for social approval and attitude change. *Journal of Psychology, 60,* 123–128.

Buckhout, R. (1965b). Need for social approval and dyadic verbal behavior. *Psychological Reports, 16,* 1013–1016.

Buckley, N., Siegel, L. S., Ness, S. (1979). Egocentricism, empathy, and altruistic behavior in young children. *Developmental Psychology, 15,* 329–330.

Buhrenne, D., & Mirels, H. (1970). Self-disclosure in self-descriptive essays. *Journal of Consulting and Clinical Psychology, 35,* 412.

Burdick, H. A., & Burnes, A. J. (1958). A test of "strain toward symmetry" theories. *Journal of Abnormal and Social Psychology, 57,* 367–370.

Burgoon, M., Lombardi, D., Burch, S., & Shelby, J. (1979). Machiavellianism and type of persuasive message as predictors of attitude change. *Journal of Psychology, 101,* 123–127.

Burgoon, M., Miller, G. R., & Tubbs, S. L. (1972). Machiavellianism, jusification, and attitude change following counter attitudinal advocacy. *Journal of Personality and Social Psychology, 22,* 366–371.

Burke, P. J. (1966). Authority relations and disruptive behavior in small discussion groups. *Sociometry, 29,* 237–250.

Burke, R. J. (1982). Personality, self-image and informal helping processes in work settings. *Psychological Reports, 50,* 1295–1302.

Burke, W. W. (1965). Leadership behavior as a function of the leader, the follower, and the situation. *Journal of Personality, 33,* 60–81.

Burnstein, E. (1963). Fear of failure, achievement motivation, and aspiring to prestigeful occupations. *Journal of Abnormal and Social Psychology, 67,* 189–193.

Byrne, D. (1961). Interpersonal attraction as a function of affiliation need and attitude similarity. *Human Relations, 14,* 283–289.

Byrne, D. (1962). Response to attitude similarity as a function of affiliation need. *Journal of Personality, 30,* 164–177.

Byrne, D. (1965). Authoritarianism and response to attitude similarity–dissimilarity. *Journal of Social Psychology, 66,* 251–256.

Byrne, D. (1969). Attitudes and attraction. In L. Berkowitz (Ed.), *Advances in experimental social psychology* (Vol. 4, pp. 35–89). New York: Academic Press.

Byrne, D. (1971). *The attraction paradigm.* New York: Academic Press.

Byrne, D., Ervin, C. R., & Lamberth, J. (1970). Continuity between the experimental study of attraction and real-life computer dating. *Journal of Personality and Social Psychology, 16,* 157–165.

Cameron, B., & Meyers, J. L. (1966). Some personality correlates of risk taking. *The Journal of General Psychology, 74,* 51–60.

Campbell, A., & Rushton, J. P. (1978). Bodily communication and personality. *British Journal of Social and Clinical Psychology, 17,* 31–36.

Canning, R. R., & Baker, J. M. (1959). Effect of the group on authoritarian and non-authoritarian persons. *American Journal of Sociology, 64,* 579–581.

Cantor, N., & Kihlstrom, J. (Eds.). (1981). *Personality, cognition and social interaction.* Hillsdale, NJ: Lawrence Erlbaum Associates.

Capage, J., & Lindskold, S. (1973). Locus of control, sex, target accommodation and attempts at influence. *Proceedings of the 81st Annual Convention of the American Psychological Association, 8,* 297–298.

Carducci, B. J., & Webber, A. W. (1979). Shyness as a determinant of interpersonal space. *Psychological Reports, 44,* 1075–1079.

Carlson, E. R. (1961). Motivation and set in acquiring information about persons. *Journal of Personality, 29,* 285–293.

Carroll, S. J., & Tosi, H. L. (1970). Goal characteristics and personality factors in a management-by-objectives program. *Administrative Science Quarterly, 15,* 295–305.

Carter, L. F. (1951). Some research on leadership in small groups. In H. Guetzkow (Ed.), *Groups, leadership, and men: Research in human relations* (pp. 146–157). Pittsburgh: Carnegie.

Carter, L. F., Haythorn W., Meirowitz, B., & Lanzetta, J. T. (1951). The relation of categorizations and ratings in the observation of group behavior. *Human Relations, 4,* 239–254.

Carter, L. F., Haythorn, W., Shriver, B., & Lanzetta, J. T. (1951). The behavior of leaders and other group members. *Journal of Abnormal and Social Psychology, 46,* 589–595.

Carter, L., & Nixon, M. (1949). Ability, perceptual, personality, and interest factors associated with different criteria of leadership. *Journal of Psychology, 27,* 377–388.

Cartwright, D. (1971). Risk-taking by individuals and groups: An assessment of research employing choice dilemmas. *Journal of Personality and Social Psychology, 20,* 361–378.

Cartwright, D., & Zander, A. (Eds.). (1968). *Group dynamics: Research and theory* (3rd ed.). New York: Harper & Row.

Cattell, R. B. (1948). Concepts and methods in the measurement of group syntality. *Psychological Review, 55,* 48–63.

Cattell, R. B. (1950). *Personality: A systematic theoretical and factual study.* New York: McGraw-Hill.

Cattell, R. B. (1957). *Personality and motivation structure and measurement.* New York: World Book.

Cattell, R. B. (1966). Anxiety and motivation: Theory and crucial experiments. In C. D. Spielberger (Ed.), *Anxiety and behavior* (pp. 23–62). New York: Academic Press.

Cattell, R. B. (1970). *Handbook of the 16 PF.* Champaign, IL: Institute for Ability and Personality Testing.

Cattell, R., & Horowitz, J. (1952). Objective personality tests investigating the structure of altruism in relation to source traits A, H, and L. *Journal of Personality, 21,* 103–117.

Cattell, R. B., & Stice, G. F. (1954). Four formulae for selecting leaders on the basis of personality. *Human Relations, 7,* 493–507.

Cavallin, B. A., & Houston, B. K. (1980). Aggressiveness, maladjustment, body experience and the protective function of body space. *Journal of Clinical Psychology, 36,* 170–176.

Centers, R. (1975). *Sexual attraction and love.* Springfield, IL: Thomas.

Centers, R., & Horowitz, M. (1963). Social character and conformity: A differential in susceptibility to social influence. *Journal of Social Psychology, 60,* 343–349.

Centers, R., Shomer, R. W., & Rodrigues, A. (1970). A field experiment in interpersonal persuasion using authoritative influence. *Journal of Personality, 38,* 392–403.

Chaney, M. V., & Vinacke, W. E. (1960). Achievement and nurturance in triads varying in power distribution. *Journal of Abnormal and Social Psychology, 60,* 175–181.

Chelune, G. J. (1979). *Self-disclosure.* San Francisco: Jossey-Bass.

Cherry, F., & Byrne, D. (1977). Authoritarianism. In T. Blass (Ed.), *Personality variables in social behavior* (pp. 109–133). Hillsdale, NJ: Lawrence Erlbaum Associates.

Chowdhry, K., & Newcomb, T. W. (1952). The relative abilities of leaders and nonleaders to estimate opinions of their own groups. *Journal of Abnormal and Social Psychology, 47,* 51–57.

Christie, R., & Cook, P. (1958). A guide to published literature relating to the authoritarian personality through 1956. *Journal of Psychology, 45,* 171–199.

Christie, R., & Geis, F. (1968). Some consequences of taking Machiavelli seriously. In E. F. Borgatta & W. W. Lambert (Eds.), *Handbook of personality theory and research* (pp. 959–973). Chicago: Rand McNally.

Christie, R., & Geis, F. L. (1970). *Studies in Machiavellianism.* New York: Academic Press.

Cleveland, S. E., & Fisher, S. (1956). Prediction of small group behavior from a body image schema. *Human Relations, 9, 223–223*

Cleveland, S. E., & Morton, R. B. (1962). Group behavior and body image. Human Relations, 15, 77–85.

Cofer, C., & Appley, M. (1964). *Motivation: Theory and research.* New York: Wiley.

Cohen, P. A., Sheposh, J. P., & Hillix, W. A. (1979). Situational and personality influences on risk-taking behavior: Effects of task, sex, and locus of control. *Academic Psychology Bulletin, 1,* 63–67.

Cohen, R. J., & Teevan, R. C. (1974). Fear of failure and impression management: An exploratory study. *Psychological Reports, 35,* 1332.

Conn, L., & Crowne, D. P. (1964). Instigation to aggression, emotional arousal and defensive emulation. *Journal of Personality, 32,* 163–179.

Cooper, S., & Peterson, C. (1980). Machiavellianism and spontaneous cheating in competition. *Journal of Research in Personality, 14,* 70–75.

Coopersmith, H. S. (1967). *The antecedents of self-esteem.* San Francisco: Freeman.

Costanzo, P. R. (1970). Conformity development as a function of self-blame. *Journal of Personality and Social Psychology, 14,* 366–374.

Cozby, P. C. (1973). Effects of density, activity, and personality on environmental preferences. *Journal of Research in Personality, 7,* 45–60.

Craik, F. I. M., & Lockhart, R. S. (1972). Levels of processing: A framework for memory research. *Journal of Verbal Learning and Verbal Behavior, 11,* 671–684.

Crano, W. D. (1975). *Conformity behavior: A social psychological analysis.* Homewood, IL: Learning Systems.

Crano, W. D. (1981). Triangulation and cross-cultural research. In M. B. Brewer & B. E. Collins (Eds.), *Scientific inquiry and the social sciences* (pp. 317–344). San Francisco: Jossey-Bass.

Crano, W. D., & Sigal, J. A. (1968). The effects of dogmatism upon pattern of response to attitudinally discrepant information. *Journal of Social Psychology, 75,* 241–247.

Cravens, R. W. (1973). The need for approval and the private versus public disclosure of self. *Journal of Personality, 43,* 503–514.

Crockett, W. H., & Meidinger, T. (1956). Authoritarianism and interpersonal perception. *Journal of Abnormal and Social Psychology, 53,* 378–382.

Cronbach, L. J. (1955). Processes affecting scores on "understanding of others" and "assumed similarity." *Psychological Bulletin, 52,* 177–193.

Cronbach, L. J. (1958). Proposals leading to analytic treatment of social perception scores. In R. Tagiuri & L. Petrullo (Eds.), *Person perception and interpersonal behavior* (pp. 353–379). Stanford, CA: Stanford University Press.

Cronbach, L. J., & Snow, R. E. (1977). *Aptitudes and instructional methods.* New York: Irvington.

Crowne, D. P., & Marlowe, D. (1964). *The approval motive.* New York: Wiley.

Crutchfield, R. S., (1955). Conformity and character. *American Psychologist, 10,* 191–198.

Dabbs, J. M. (1964). Self-esteem, communicator characteristics, and attitude change. *Journal of Abnormal and Social Psychology, 69,* 173–181.

Daly, S. (1978). Behavioral correlates of social anxiety. *British Journal of Social and Clinical Psychology, 17,* 117–120.

Davids, A. (1956). Past experience and present personality dispositions as determinants of selective auditory memory. *Journal of Personality, 25,* 19–32.

Davis, M. H. (1983). Measuring individual differences in empathy: Evidence for a multidimensional approach, *Journal of Personality and Social Psychology, 44,* 113–126.

Davis, W. L., & Phares, E. J. (1967). Internal–external control as a determinant of information-seeking in a social influence situation. *Journal of Personality, 35,* 547–561.

DeBolt, J. W., Liska, A. E., Love, W., & Stahlman, R. W. (1973). Status-role consequences of internal–external control of reinforcement. *Psychological Reports, 32,* 307–311.

DeBolt, J. W., Liska, A. E., & Weng, B. R. (1976). Replications of associations between internal locus of control and leadership in small groups. *Psychological Reports, 38,* 470.

deCharms, R. (1968). *Personal causation.* New York: Academic Press.

deCharms, R., & Rosenbaum, M. E. (1960). Status variables and matching behavior. *Journal of Personality, 29,* 492–502.

Deci, E. L. (1975). *Intrinsic motivation.* New York: Plenum.

DeJulio, S., & Duffy, K. (1977). Neuroticism and proxemic behavior. *Perceptual and Motor Skills, 45,* 51–55.

Deutsch, M. (1960). Trust, trustworthiness, and the F scale. *Journal of Abnormal and Social Psychology, 61,* 138–140.

Dies, R. R. (1970). Need for social approval and blame assignment. *Journal of Consulting and Clinical Psychology, 35,* 311–316.

Dion, K. K., & Dion, K. L. (1975). Self-esteem and romantic love. *Journal of Personality, 43,* 39–57.

Dittes, J. (1959). Effect of changes in self-esteem upon impulsiveness and deliberation in making judgments. *Journal of Abnormal and Social Psychology, 58,* 348–356.

DiVesta, F. J., & Cox, L. (1960). Some dispositional correlates of conformity behavior. *Journal of Social Psychology, 52,* 259–268.

Doherty, W. J., & Ryder, R. G. (1979). Locus of control, interpersonal trust, and assertive behavior among newlyweds. *Journal of Personality and Social Psychology, 37,* 2212–2220.

Domelsmith, D. E., & Dietch, J. T. (1978). Sex differences in the relationship between Machiavellianism and self-disclosure. *Psychological Reports, 42,* 715–721.

Domino, G. (1968). Differential predictions of academic achievement in conformity and independent settings. *Journal of Educational Psychology, 59,* 256–260.

Domino, G. (1971). Interactive effects of achievement orientation and teaching style on academic achievement. *Journal of Educational Psychology, 62,* 427–431.

Dosey, M. A., & Meisels, M. (1969). Personal space and self-protection. *Journal of Personality and Social Psychology, 11,* 93–97.

Dowaliby, F. J., & Schumer, H. (1973). Teacher-centered versus student-centered mode of college classroom instruction as related to manifest anxiety. *Journal of Educational Psychology, 64,* 125–132.

Druckman, D. (1976). Dogmatism, prenegotiation experience, and simulated group representation as determinants of dyadic behavior in a bargaining situation. *Journal of Personality and Social Psychology, 6,* 279–290.

Duck, S. W. (1973). Personality similarity and friendship choice: Similarity of what, when? *Journal of Personality, 41,* 543–558.

Duke, M. P., & Mullens, M. C. (1973). Preferred interpersonal distance as a function of locus of control orientation in chronic schizophrenics, nonschizophrenic patients, and normals. *Journal of Consulting and Clinical Psychology, 41,* 230–234.

Duncan, S., Jr. (1969). Nonverbal communication. *Psychological Bulletin, 72,* 118–137.

Dustin, D. S., & Davis, H. P. (1967). Authoritarianism and sanctioning behavior. *Journal of Personality and Social Psychology, 6,* 222–224.

Eagly, A. H. (1967). Involvement as a determinant of response to favorable and unfavorable information. *Journal of Personality and Social Psychology, 7*(1–15, Whole No. 643).

Eagly, A. H. (1969). Sex differences in the relationship between self-esteem and susceptibility to social influence. *Journal of Personality, 37,* 581–591.

Edwards, A. L. (1959). Social desirability and the description of others. *Journal of Abnormal Psychology, 59,* 434–436.

Efran, J. S. (1968). Looking for approval: Effects on visual behavior of approbation from persons differing in importance. *Journal of Personality and Social Psychology, 10,* 21–25.

Efran, J. S., & Boylin, E. R. (1967). Social desirability and willingness to participate in a group discussion. *Psychological Reports, 20,* 402.

Efran, J. S., & Broughton, A. (1966). Effects of expectancies for social approval on visual behavior. *Journal of Personality and Social Psychology, 4,* 103–107.

Ehrlich, H. J., & Lee, D. (1969). Dogmatism, learning, and resistance to change: A review and a paradigm. *Psychological Bulletin, 71,* 249–259.

Eisenberg-Berg, N., & Mussen, P. (1978). Empathy and moral development in adolescence. *Developmental Psychology, 14,* 185–186.

Ellison, C. W., & Firestone, I. J. (1974). Development of interpersonal trust as a function of self-esteem, target status, and target style. *Journal of Personality and Social Psychology, 29,* 655–663.

Ellyson, S. L., Dovidio, J. F., Corson, R. L., & Vinicur, D. L. (1980). Visual dominance behavior in female dyads: Situational and personality factors. *Social Psychology Quarterly, 43,* 328–336.

Elms, A. C., & Milgram, S. (1966). Personality characteristics associated with obedience and defiance toward authoritative command. *Journal of Experimental Research in Personality, 1,* 282–289.

Endler, N. S. (1961). Conformity analyzed and related to personality. *Journal of Social Psychology, 53,* 271–283.

Endler, N. S. (1981). Persons, situations and their interactions. In A. M. Rabin, J. Aronoff, A. M. Barclay, & R. A. Zucker (Eds.), *Further explorations in personality* (pp. 114–151). New York: Wiley.

Endler, N. S., & Magnusson, D. (Eds.). (1976). *Interactional psychology and personality.* Washington, DC: Hemisphere.

Entin, E. E., & Raynor, J. O. (1973). Effects of contingent future orientation and achievement motivation on performance in two kinds of tasks. *Journal of Experimental Research in Personality, 6,* 314–320.

Epstein, G. F. (1969). Machiavelli and the devil's advocate. *Journal of Personality and Social Psychology, 11,* 38–41.

Epstein, R. (1965). Authoritarianism, displaced aggression and social status of the target. *Journal of Personality and Social Psychology, 2,* 585–589.

Epstein, R. (1966). Aggression toward outgroups as a function of authoritarianism and imitation of aggressive models. *Journal of Personality and Social Psychology, 3,* 574–579.

Epstein, S. (1961). Food related responses to ambiguous stimuli as a function of hunger and ego strength. *Journal of Consulting Psychology, 25,* 463–469.

Epstein, S. (1972). The nature of anxiety with emphasis upon its relationship to expectancy. In C. D. Spielberger (Ed.), *Anxiety: Current trends in theory and research* (Vol. II, pp. 292–339). New York: Academic Press.

Epstein, S., & Smith, R. (1956). Thematic apperception as a measure of the hunger drive. *Journal of Projective Techniques, 20,* 372–384.

Erdelyi, M. H. (1974). A new look at the new look: Perceptual defense and vigilance. *Psychological Review, 81,* 1–25.

Erdelyi, M. H., & Goldberg, B. (1979). Let's not sweep repression under the rug: Toward a cognition psychology of repression. In J. F. Kihlstrom & F. J. Evans (Eds.), *Functional disorders of memory* (pp. 355–402). Hillsdale, NJ: Lawrence Erlbaum Associates.

Eriksen, B. A., & Eriksen, C. W. (1972). *Perception and personality.* Morristown, N.J.: General Learning Press.

Eriksen, C. W., & Lazarus, R. S. (1952). Perceptual defense and projective tests. *Journal of Abnormal and Social Psychology, 47,* 302–308.

Erikson, E. (1950). *Childhood and society.* New York: Norton.

Erikson, E. (1963). *Childhood and society* (2nd ed.). New York: Norton.

Erikson, E. (1964). *Insight and responsibility.* New York: Norton.

Erikson, E. (1968). *Identity: Youth and crisis.* New York: Norton.

Erikson, E. (1982). *The life cycle completed.* New York: W. W. Norton.

Ettinger, R. F., Nowicki, S., & Nelson, D. A. (1970). Interpersonal attraction and the approval motive. *Journal of Experimental Research in Personality, 4,* 95–99.

Evans, G. W., & Howard, R. B. (1973). Personal space. *Psychological Bulletin, 80,* 334–344.

Evans, R. G. (1982). Skill versus chance tasks: Comparison of locus of control, defensive externality, and persistence. *Personality and Social Psychology Bulletin, 8,* 129–133.

Exline, R. V. (1963). Explorations in the process of person perception: Visual interaction in relation to competition, sex, and need for affiliation. *Journal of Personality, 31,* 1–20.

Exline, R., Gray, G., & Schuette, D. (1965). Visual behavior in a dyad as affected by interview content and sex of respondent. *Journal of Personality and Social Psychology, 1,* 201–209.

Exline, R., Thibaut, J., Brannon, C., & Gumpert, P. (1961). Visual interaction in relation to Machiavellianism and an unethical act. *American Psychologist, 16,* 396.

Falbo, T. (1977). Multidimensional scaling of power strategies. *Journal of Personality and Social Psychology, 35,* 537–547.

Faytinger, S. (1978). Internal–external control as a moderator of teaching style and student's satisfaction. *Psychological Reports, 43,* 1070.

Fenichel, O. (1945). *The psychoanalytic theory of neurosis.* New York: Norton.

Festinger, L. (1954). A theory of social comparison processes. *Human Relations, 7,* 117–140.

Festinger, L. (1957). *A theory of cognitive dissonance.* Stanford, CA: Stanford University Press.

Fincham, F., & Barling, J. (1978). Locus of control and generosity in learning disabled, normal achieving, and gifted children. *Child Development, 49,* 530–533.

Fineman, S. (1975). The influence of perceived job climate on the relationship between managerial achievement motivation and performance. *Journal of Occupational Psychology, 48,* 113–124.

Fishman, C. (1965). Need for approval and the expression of aggression under varying conditions of frustration. *Journal of Personality and Social Psychology, 2,* 809–816.

Fishman, D. B. (1966). Need and expectancy as determinants of affiliative behavior in small groups. *Journal of Personality and Social Psychology, 4,* 155–164.

Fiske, D. W., & Maddi, S. R. (Eds.). (1961). *Functions of varied experience.* Homewood, IL: Dorsey Press.

Fitzsimmons, S. J., & Marcuse, F. L. (1961). Adjustment in leaders and non-leaders as measured by the sentence completion projective technique. *Journal of Clinical Psychology, 17,* 380–381.

Fodor, E. M., & Farrow, D. L. (1979). The power motive as an influence on use of power. *Journal of Personality and Social Psychology, 37,* 2091–2097.

Foley, L. A., & Chamblin, M. H. (1982). The effect of race and personality on mock juror's decisions. *Journal of Psychology, 112,* 47–51.

Form, W. H., & Nosow, S. (1958). *Community in disaster.* New York: Harper & Row.

Foulkes, D., & Foulkes, S. H. (1965). Self-concept, dogmatism, and tolerance of trait inconsistency. *Journal of Personality and Social Psychology, 2,* 104–111.

Frankel, A. S., & Barrett, J. (1971). Variations in personal space as a function of authoritarianism, self-esteem, and racial characteristics of a stimulus situation. *Journal of Consulting and Clinical Psychology, 37,* 95–98.

Frankel, V. (1962). *Man's search for meaning.* Boston: Beacon.

Frede, M. C., Gautney, D. B., & Baxter, J. C. (1968). Relationships between body image boundary and interaction patterns on the MAPS test. *Journal of Consulting and Clinical Psychology, 32,* 575–578.

Freedman, M. B., Leary, T. F., Ossorio, A. G., & Coffey, H. S. (1951). The interpersonal dimension of personality. *Journal of Personality, 20,* 143–161.

French, E. G., & Chadwick, I. (1956). Some characteristics of affiliation motivation. *Journal of Abnormal and Social Psychology, 52,* 296–300.

French, J. R. P., & Raven, B. (1959). The bases of social power. In D. Cartwright (Ed.), *Studies in social power* (pp. 150–167). Ann Arbor: University of Michigan, Institute for Social Research.

Frenkel-Brunswik, E. (1949). Intolerance of ambiguity as an emotional and perceptual personality variable. *Journal of Personality, 18,* 108–143.

Friedell, M. F. (1968). A laboratory experiment in retaliation. *Journal of Conflict Resolution, 12,* 357–373.

Friedlander, F. (1971). Congruence in organization development. *Academy of Management Proceedings,* 153–161.

Friedrichs, R. W. (1960). Alter versus ego: An exploratory assessment of altruism. *American Sociological Review, 25,* 496–508.

Fromm, E. (1947). *Man for himself.* New York: Holt, Rinehart & Winston.

Fromm, E. (1955). *The sane society.* New York: Holt, Rinehart & Winston.

Fromm, E. (1956). *The art of loving.* New York: Harper & Row.

Fromme, D. K., & Beam, D. C. (1974). Dominance and sex differences in nonverbal responses to differential eye contact. *Journal of Research in Personality, 8,* 76–87.

Fry, P. S. (1975). Effects of male and female endorsement of beliefs on the problem solving choices of high and low dogmatic women. *Journal of Social Psychology, 96,* 65–77.

Frye, R. L., & Bass, B. M. (1963). Behavior in a group related to tested social acquiescence. *Journal of Social Psychology, 61,* 263–266.

Frye, R. L., Vidulich, R. N., Meierhoefer, B., & Joure, S. (1972). Differential T-group behaviors of high and low dogmatic participants. *Journal of Psychology, 81,* 301–309.

Gabennesch, H., & Hunt, L. L. (1971). The relative accuracy of interpersonal perception of high and low authoritarians. *Journal of Experimental Research in Personality, 5,* 43–48.

Gage, N. L., & Cronbach, L. (1955). Conceptual and methodological problems in interpersonal perception. *Psychological Review, 62,* 411–422.

Gagné, E. E., & Parshall, H. (1975). The effects of locus of control and goal setting on persistence at a learning task. *Child Study Journal, 5,* 193–199.

Garber, J., & Seligman, M. E. P. (Eds.). (1980). *Human helplessness.* New York: Academic Press.

Garcia, L. T., & Griffitt, W. (1978a). Authoritarianism-situation interaction in the determination of punitiveness: Engaging authoritarian ideology. *Journal of Research on Personality, 12,* 469–478.

Garcia, L. T., & Griffitt, W. (1978b). Evaluation and recall of evidence: Authoritarianism and the Patty Hearst case. *Journal of Research on Personality, 12,* 57–67.

Gardner, R. W., Jackson, D. N., & Messick, S. J. (1960). Personality organization in cognitive controls and intellectual abilities. *Psycholgical Issues, 2*(4, Whole No. 8).

Gavin, J. F. (1973). Self-esteem as a moderator of the relationship between expectancies and job performance. *Journal of Applied Psychology, 58,* 83–88.

Geen, R. G. (1980). Test anxiety and cue utilization. In I. G. Sarason (Ed.), *Test anxiety: Theory, research and applications* (pp. 43–61). Hillsdale, NJ: Lawrence Erlbaum Associates.

Geis, F. (1978). Machiavellianism. In H. London & J. E. Exner, Jr. (Eds.), *Dimensions of personality* (pp. 305–365). New York: Wiley.

Geis, F. L., Christie, R., & Nelson, C. (1970). In search of the Machiavel. In R. Christie & F. L. Geis (Eds.), *Studies in Machiavellianism* (pp. 76–95). New York: Academic Press.

Geis, F. L., & Moon, T. H. (1981). Machiavellianism and deception. *Journal of Personality and Social Psychology, 41,* 766–775.

Gergen, K. J., & Bauer, R. A. (1967). Interaction effects of self-esteem and task difficulty on social conformity. *Journal of Personality and Social Psychology, 6,* 16–22.

Gergen, K. J., Gergen, M. M., & Meter, K. (1972). Individual orientations to prosocial behavior. *Journal of Social Issues, 28,* 105–130.

Ghiselli, E. E. (1963). The validity of management traits in relation to occupational level. *Personnel Psychology, 16,* 109–112.

Ghiselli, E. E., & Johnson, D. A. (1970). Need satisfaction, managerial success, and organizational structure. *Personnel Psychology, 23,* 569–576.

Gibb, C. A. (1947). The principles of traits of leadership. *Journal of Abnormal and Social Psychology, 42,* 267–284.

Gibb, C. A. (1969). Leadership. In G. Lindzey & E. Aronson (Eds.). *The handbook of social psychology* (2nd. ed., Vol. 4, pp. 205–282). Reading, MA: Addison-Wesley.

Gifford, R. (1982). Projected interpersonal distances and orientation choices: Personality, sex, and social situation. *Social Psychology Quarterly, 45,* 145–152.

Gold, J. A., Ryckman, R. M., & Rodda, W. C. (1973). Differential responsiveness to dissonance manipulations by open and closed-minded subjects in a forced compliance situation. *Journal of Social Psychology, 90,* 73–83.

Goldman, K. (1975). Need achievement as a motivational basis for the risky shift. *Journal of Personality, 43,* 346–356.

Goldstein, J. W., & Rosenfeld, H. M. (1969). Insecurity and preference for persons similar to oneself. *Journal of Personality, 37,* 253–268.

Goldstein, K. M., & Blackman, S. (1978). *Cognitive style.* New York: Wiley.

Goodstadt, B. E., & Hjelle, L. A. (1973). Power to the powerless: Locus of control and the use of power. *Journal of Personality and Social Psychology, 27,* 190–196.

Gordon, C. M., & Spence, D. P. (1966). The facilitating effects of food set and food deprivation on responses to a subliminal food stimulus. *Journal of Personality, 34,* 406–415.

Gordon, L. V., & Medland, F. F. (1965). Leadership aspiration and leadership ability. *Psychological Reports, 17,* 388–390.

Gore, P. M., & Rotter, J. B. (1963). A personality correlate of social action. *Journal of Personality, 31,* 58–64.

Gorfein, D. (1961). Conformity behavior and the authoritarian personality. *Journal of Social Psychology, 53,* 121–125.

Gormly, A. V., & Clore, C. L. (1969). Attraction, dogmatism, and attitude similarity-dissimilarity. *Journcl of Experimental Research in Personality, 4,* 9–13.

Gough, H. G. (1964). *The CPI manual.* Palo Alto, CA: Consulting Psychologists' Press.

Granberg, D. (1972). Authoritarianism and the assumption of similarity to self. *Journal of Experimental Research in Personality, 6,* 1–4.

Grant, D. L., & Bray, D. W. (1969). Contributions of the interview to assessment of management potential. *Journal of Applied Psychology, 53,* 24–34.

Green, L., & Haymes, M. (1977). Motivational antecedents of maturity of moral judgment. *Motivation and Emotion, 1,* 165–179.

Greenbaum, C. W. (1966). Effect of situational and personality variables on improvisation and attitude change. *Journal of Personality and Social Psychology, 4,* 260-269.

Griffitt, W. B. (1966). Interpersonal attraction as a function of self-concept and personality similarity–dissimilarity. *Journal of Personality and Social Psychology, 4,* 581-584.

Griffitt, W. B. (1969). Personality similarity and self-concept as determinants of interpersonal attraction. *Journal of Social Psychology, 78,* 137-146.

Griffitt, W. (1970). Environmental effects on interpersonal affective behavior: Ambient effective temperature and attraction. *Journal of Personality and Social Psychology, 15,* 240-244.

Griffitt, W., & Veitch, R. (1971). Hot and crowded: Influences of population density and temperature on interpersonal affective behavior. *Journal of Personality and Social Psychology, 17,* 92-98.

Grimes, J. W., & Allinsmith, W. (1961). Compulsivity, anxiety and school achievement. *Merrill-Palmer Quarterly, 7,* 247-271.

Guilford, J. P. (1959). *Personality.* New York: McGraw-Hill.

Guilford, J. S. (1952). Temperament traits of executives and supervisors measured by the Guilford personality inventories. *Journal of Applied Psychology, 36,* 228-233.

Hackman, J. R., & Lawler, E. E., III. (1971). Employee reactions to job characteristics. *Journal of Applied Psychology, 55,* 259-286.

Hackman, J. R., & Morris, C. G. (1975). Group tasks, group interaction process, and group performance effectiveness: A review and proposed integration. In L. Berkowitz (Ed.), *Advances in experimental social psychology* (Vol. 8, pp. 45-99). New York: Academic Press.

Hackman, J. R., & Oldham, G. R. (1976). Motivation through the design of work: Test of a theory. *Organizational Behavior and Human Performance, 16,* 250-279.

Haigh, G. V., & Fiske, D. W. (1952). Corroboration of personal values as selective factors in perception. *Journal of Abnormal and Social Psychology, 47,* 394-398.

Hammes, J. A. (1961). Manifest anxiety and perception of environmental threat. *Journal of Clinical Psychology, 17,* 25-26.

Hammes, J. A. (1964). The personal distance effect as a function of esthetic stimulus, anxiety and sex. *Journal of Clinical Psychology, 20,* 353-354.

Hanawalt, N. G., & Richardson, H. M. (1944). Leadership as related to the Bernreuter personality measures: IV. On item analysis of responses of adult leaders and non-leaders. *Journal of Applied Psychology, 28,* 397-411.

Hanawalt, N. G., Richardson, H. M., & Hamilton, R. J. (1943). Leadership as related to Bernreuter personality measures: II. On item analysis of responses of college leaders and non-leaders. *Journal of Social Psychology, 17,* 251-267.

Hancock, J. G., & Teevan, R. C. (1964). Fear of failure and risk-taking behavior. *Journal of Personality, 32,* 200-209.

Hardy, K. R. (1957). Determinants of conformity and attitude change. *Journal of Abnormal and Social Psychology, 54,* 289-294.

Hare, A. P., & Bales, R. F. (1963). Seating position and small group interaction. *Sociometry, 26,* 480-486.

Harnett, D. L., Cummings, L. L., & Hammer, W. C. (1973). Personality, bargaining style and payoff in bilateral monopoly bargaining among European managers. *Sociometry, 36,* 325-345.

Harrell, T. W. (1969). The personality of high earning M.B.A.'s in big business. Personnel Psychology, 22, 457-463.

Harrell, W. A., & Hartnagel, T. (1976). The impact of Machiavellianism and the trustfulness of the victim on laboratory theft. *Sociometry, 39,* 157-167.

Harvey, O. J. (1965). Some situational and cognitive determinants of dissonance resolution. *Journal of Personality and Social Psychology, 1,* 349-355.

Harvey, O. J., & Beverly, G. D. (1961). Some personality correlates of concept change through role playing. *Journal of Abnormal and Social Psychology, 63,* 125-130.

Harvey, O. J., Hunt, D. E., & Schroder, H. M. (1961). *Conceptual systems and personality organization.* New York: Wiley.

Haymes, M., & Green, L. (1977). Motivational maturity and helping behavior. *Journal of Youth and Adolescence, 6,* 371–391.

Haythorn, W. (1953). The influence of individual members on the characteristics of small groups. *Journal of Abnormal and Social Psychology, 48,* 276–284.

Haythorn, W., Couch, A. S., Haefner, D., Langham, P., & Carter, L. F. (1956a). The behavior of authoritarian and equalitarian personalities in groups. *Human Relations, 9,* 57–74.

Haythorn, W., Couch, A. S., Haefner, D., Langham, P., & Carter, L. F. (1956b). The effects of varying combinations of authoritarian and equalitarian leaders and followers. *Journal of Abnormal and Social Psychology, 53,* 210–219.

Hearn, C. B., & Seeman, J. (1971). Personality integration and perception of interpersonal relationships. *Journal of Personality and Social Psychology, 18,* 138–143.

Hechler, P. D., & Weiner, Y. (1974). Chronic self-esteem as a moderator of performance consequences of expected pay. *Organizational Behavior and Human Performance, 11,* 97–105.

Heckhausen, H. (1967). *The anatomy of achievement motivation.* New York: Academic Press.

Hekmat, H., & Theiss, M. (1971). Self-actualization and modification of affective disclosures during a social conditioning interview. *Journal of Counseling Psychology, 18,* 101–105.

Helmreich, R., Aronson, E., & LeFan, J. (1970). To err is humanizing sometimes. *Journal of Personality and Social Psychology, 16,* 259–264.

Helson, H., Blake, R. R., Mouton, J. S., & Olmstead, J. A. (1956). Attitudes as adjustments to stimulus, background, and residual factors. *Journal of Abnormal and Social Psychology, 52,* 314–322.

Hendrick, C., & Page, A. A. (1970). Self-esteem, attitude similarity, and attraction. *Journal of Personality, 38,* 588–601.

Hewitt, J., & Goldman, M. (1974). Self-esteem, need for approval, and reactions to personal evaluations. *Journal of Experimental Social Psychology, 10,* 201–210.

Hicks, J. A., & Stone, J. B. (1962). The identification of traits related to managerial success. *Journal of Applied Psychology, 46,* 428–432.

Hiers, J. M., & Heckel, R. V. (1977). Seating choice, leadership, and locus of control. *The Journal of Social Psychology, 103,* 313–314.

Higgs, W. J., & McGrath, J. E. (1965). *Social motives and decision-making behavior in interpersonal situations* (Tech. Rep. No. 4). Air Force Office of Scientific Research Report AF 49(638)–1291. University of Illinois at Champaign-Urbana.

Hines, M., & Mehrabian, A. (1979). Approach–avoidance behaviors as a function of pleasantness and arousing quality of settings and individual differences in stimulus screening. *Social Behavior and Personality, 7,* 223–233.

Hjelle, L. A., & Clouser, R. (1970). Susceptibility to attitude change as a function of internal–external control. *Psychological Record, 20,* 305–310.

Hoffman, M. L. (1953). Some psychodynamic factors in compulsive conformity. *Journal of Abnormal and Social Psychology, 48,* 383–393.

Hogan, J. C. (1978). Personological dynamics of leadership. *Journal of Research in Personality, 12,* 390–395.

Hogan, R. (1975). Empathy: A conceptual and psychometric analysis. *Counseling Psychologist, 5,* 14–18.

Hogan, R. (1982). A socioanalytic theory of personality. In M. Page (Ed.), *Nebraska Symposium on Motivation* (Vol. 30, pp. 56–89). Lincoln: University of Nebraska Press.

Hollander, E. P. (1954). Authoritarianism and leadership choice in a military setting. *Journal of Abnormal and Social Psychology, 49,* 365–370.

Holstein, C. M., Goldstein, J. W., & Bem, D. J. (1971). The importance of expressive behavior, involvement, sex and need-approval in inducing liking. *Journal of Experimental Social Psychology, 7,* 534–544.

Holtzman, W. H. (1952). Adjustment and leadership: A study of the Rorschach test. *Journal of Social Psychology, 36,* 179–189.

Hornaday, J. A., & Bunker, C. S. (1970). The nature of the entrepreneur. *Personnel Psychology, 23,* 47–54.

House, W. C. (1978). Effects of temporal delay and achievement motivation on the choice of achievement-related alternatives. *Psychological Reports, 42,* 550.

Hovland, C. I., & Janis, I. L. (1959). Summary and implications for future research. In I. L. Janis & C. I. Hovland (Eds.), *Personality and persuasibility* (pp. 225–255). New Haven, CT: Yale University Press.

Hrycenko, I., & Minton, H. L. (1974). Internal–external control, power position, and satisfaction in task-oriented groups. *Journal of Personality and Social Psychology, 30,* 871–878.

Hunt, D. E. (1970). A conceptual level matching model for coordinating learner characteristics with educational approaches. *Interchange, 1,* 68–82.

Hunt, D. E., & Sullivan, E. V. (1974). *Between psychology and education.* Hinsdale, IL: Dryden Press.

Hunter, E. C., & Jordan, A. M. (1939). An analysis of qualities associated with leadership among college students. *Journal of Educational Psychology, 30,* 497–509.

Huston, T. L. (1974). *Perspectives on interpersonal attraction.* New York: Academic Press.

Ivancevich, J. M., & McMahon, J. T. (1977). A study of task-goal attributes, higher order need strength, and performance. *Academy of Management Journal, 20,* 552–563.

Izard, C. E. (1960). Personality similarity and friendship. *Journal of Abnormal and Social Psychology, 61,* 47–51.

Izzett, R. R. (1976). Effects of self-praise and self-esteem on interpersonal attraction. *Representative Research in Social Psychology, 7,* 1–5.

Jackson, D. N., Hourany, L., & Vidmar, N. J. (1972). A four-dimensional interpretation of risk-taking. *Journal of Personality, 40,* 483–501.

Jacoby, J. (1971). Interpersonal perceptual accuracy as a function of dogmatism. *Journal of Experimental Social Psychology, 7,* 221–236.

Jahoda, M. (1959). Conformity and independence. *Human Relations, 12,* 99–120.

Janis, I. L. (1954). Personality correlates of susceptibility to persuasion. *Journal of Personality, 22,* 504–518.

Janis, I. L. (1955). Anxiety indices related to susceptibility to persuasion. *Journal of Abnormal and Social Psychology, 51,* 663–667.

Janis, I. L. (1958). *Psychological stress.* New York: Wiley.

Janis, I. L., & Feshbach, S. (1954). Personality differences associated with responsiveness to fear-arousing communications. *Journal of Personality, 23,* 154–166.

Janis, I. L., & Hovland, C. I. (Eds.). (1959). *Personality and persuasibility.* New Haven, CT: Yale University Press.

Janis, I. L., & Rife, D. (1959). Persuasibility and emotional disorder. In I. L. Janis & C. I. Hovland (Eds.), *Personality and persuasibility* (pp. 121–141). New Haven, CT: Yale University Press.

Jenks, R. J. (1978). Effects of sex, locus of control, and issue on attitude change. *Journal of Social Psychology, 106,* 283–284.

Johnson, C. D., & Gormly, A. V. (1975). Personality, attraction and social ambiguity. *Journal of Social Psychology, 97,* 227–232.

Johnson, C. D., Gormly, J., & Gormly, A. (1973). Disagreements and self-esteem: Support for the competence-reinforcement model of attraction. *Journal of Research on Personality, 7,* 165–172.

Johnson, H. H., & Izzett, R. R. (1969). Relationship between authoritarianism and attitude change as a function of source credibility and type of communication. *Journal of Personality and Social Psychology, 13,* 317–321.

Johnson, H. H., & Steiner, I. D. (1967). Some effects of discrepancy level on relationships between authoritarianism and conformity. *Journal of Social Psychology, 73,* 199–204.

Johnson, H. H., Torcivia, J. M., & Poprick, M. A. (1968). Effects of source credibility on the relationship between authoritarianism and attitude change. *Journal of Personality and Social Psychology, 9,* 179–183.

Johnson, J. J., & Cerreto, M. C. (1975). Internal–external control and interpersonal attraction to a similar and dissimilar stranger. *Psychological Reports, 37,* 1122.

Jones, E. E. (1954). Authoritarianism as a determinant of first-impression formation. *Journal of Personality, 23,* 107–127.

Jones, E. E., & Daugherty, B. N. (1959). Political orientation and the perceptual effects of an anticipated interaction. *Journal of Abnormal and Social Psychology, 59,* 340–349.

Jones, M. B. (1955). Authoritarianism and intolerance of fluctuation. *Journal of Abnormal and Social Psychology, 50,* 125–126.

Jones, R. E., & Melcher, B. H. (1982). Personality and the preference for modes of conflict resolution. *Human Relations, 35,* 649–658.

Jones, S. C., Knurek, D. A., & Regan, D. T. (1973). Variables affecting reactions to social acceptance and rejection. *Journal of Social Psychology, 90,* 269–284.

Jones, S. C., & Shrauger, J. S. (1968). Locus of control and interpersonal evaluations. *Journal of Consulting and Clinical Psychology, 32,* 664–668.

Jones, S. C., & Tager, R. (1972). Exposure to others, need for social approval and reactions to agreement and disagreement from others. *The Journal of Social Psychology, 86,* 111–120.

Jones, W. H., Nickel, T. W., & Schmidt, A. (1979). Machiavellianism and self-disclosure. *Journal of Psychology, 102,* 33–41.

Jourard, S. M. (1958). *Personal adjustment: An approach through the study of healthy personality.* New York: Macmillan.

Jung, C. G. (1953). Two essays on analytical psychology. In H. Read, M. Fordham, & G. Adler (Eds.), *Collected works* (Vol. 7). Princeton, NJ: Princeton University Press.

Jung, C. G. (1959). The archetypes and the collective unconscious. In H. Read, M. Fordham, & G. Adler (Eds.), *Collected works* (Vol. 9). Princeton, NJ: Princeton University Press.

Jung, C. G. (1960). The structure and dynamics of the psyche. In H. Read, M. Fordham, & G. Adler (Eds.), *Collected works* (Vol. 8). Princeton, NJ: Princeton University Press.

Kaess, W. A., Witryol, S. L., & Nolan, R. E. (1961). Reliability, sex differences, and validity in the leadership discussion group. *Journal of Applied Psychology, 45,* 345–350.

Kagan, J. (1972). Motives and development. *Journal of Personality and Social Psychology, 22,* 51–66.

Kanfer, F. H., & Marston, A. R. (1964). Characteristics of interactional behavior in a psychotherapy analogue. *Journal of Consulting Psychology, 28,* 456–467.

Karabenick, S. A., & Youssef, Z. I. (1968). Performance as a function of achievement motive level and perceived difficulty. *Journal of Personality and Social Psychology, 10,* 414–419.

Kates, S. L. (1959). First-impression formation and authoritarianism. *Human Relations, 12,* 277–286.

Katz, D., & Kahn, R. L. (1966). *The social psychology of organizations.* New York: Wiley.

Kelley, H. H. (1950). The warm–cold variable in first impressions of persons. *Journal of Personality, 18,* 431–439.

Kelley, H. H. (1973). The process of causal attribution. *American Psychologist, 28,* 107–128.

Kelley, H. H., & Stahelski, A. J. (1970). Social interaction basis of cooperators' and competitors' beliefs about others. *Journal of Personality and Social Psychology, 16,* 66–91.

Kelley, H. H., & Thibaut, J. W. (1969). Group problem solving. In G. Lindzey & E. Aronson (Eds.), *The handbook of social psychology* (2nd ed., Vol. 4, pp. 1–101). Reading, MA: Addison-Wesley.

Kelly, G. A. (1955). *The psychology of personal constructs.* New York: Norton.

Kelman, H. C. (1950). Effect of success and failure on "suggestibility" in the autokinetic situation. *Journal of Abnormal and Social Psychology, 45,* 267–285.

Kendon, A., & Cook, M. (1969). The consistency of gaze patterns in social interaction. *British Journal of Psychology, 60,* 481–494.

Kenis, I. (1978). Leadership behavior, subordinate personality, and satisfaction with supervision. *Journal of Psychology, 98,* 99–107.

Kerckhoff, A. C., & Davis, K. E. (1962). Value consensus and need complementarity in mate selection. *American Sociological Review, 27,* 295–303.

Kerr-Inkson, J. H. (1978). Self-esteem as a moderator of the relationship between job performance and job satisfaction. *Journal of Applied Psychology, 63,* 243–247.

Kidd, A. H., & Kidd, R. M. (1972). Relation of F test scores to rigidity. *Perceptual and Motor Skills, 34,* 239–243.

Kiessling, R. J., & Kalish, R. A. (1961). Correlates of success in leaderless group discussion. *Journal of Social Psychology, 54,* 359–365.

Kilmann, P. R., & Sotile, W. M. (1976). The effects of structured and unstructured leader roles on internal and external group participants. *Journal of Clinical Psychology, 32,* 848–856.

Kilmann, R. H., & Thomas, K. W. (1975). Interpersonal conflict-handling behavior as reflections of Jungian personality dimensions. *Psychological Reports, 37,* 971–980.

Kimmons, G., & Greenhaus, J. H. (1976). Relationship between locus of control and reactions of employees to work characteristics. *Psychological Reports, 39,* 815–820.

Kinder, B. N., & Kilmann, P. R. (1976). The impact of differential shifts in leader structure on the outcome of internal and external groups of participants. *Journal of Clinical Psychology, 32,* 857–863.

Kipnis, D., & Lane, W. P. (1962). Self confidence and leadership. *Journal of Applied Psychology, 46,* 291–295.

Kipnis, D., & Wagner, C. (1967). Character structure and response to leadership power. *Journal of Experimental Research in Personality, 2,* 16–24.

Kleck, R. E., Ono, H., & Hastorf, A. (1966). The effects of deviance upon face-to-face interaction. *Human Relations, 19,* 425–436.

Kleck, R. E., & Wheaton, J. (1967). Dogmatism and responses to opinion-consistent information. *Journal of Personality and Social Psychology, 5,* 249–252.

Klein, G. S. (1954). Need and regulation. In M. R. Jones (Ed.), *Nebraska Symposium on Motivation* (Vol. 2, pp. 224–274). Lincoln: University of Nebraska Press.

Klein, G. S. (1970). *Perception, motives, and personality.* New York: Knopf.

Klein, M. H. (1967). Compliance, consistent conformity, and persuasion. *Journal of Personality and Social Psychology, 5,* 239–245.

Kogan, N., & Wallach, M. A. (1964). *Risk-taking.* New York: Holt, Rinehart & Winston.

Kogan, N., & Wallach, M. A. (1967). Group risk taking as a function of member's anxiety and defensiveness. *Journal of Personality, 35,* 50–63.

Kohlberg, L. (1969). Stage and sequence: The cognitive-developmental approach to socialization. In D. A. Goslin (Ed.), *Handbook of socialization theory and research* (pp. 347–480). Chicago: Rand McNally.

Kohlberg, L. (1971). From is to ought: How to commit naturalistic fallacy and get away with it. In T. Mischel (Ed.), *Cognitive development and epistemology* (pp. 151–235). New York: Academic Press.

Kohlberg, L. (1973). *Collected papers on moral development and moral education.* Cambridge, MA: Moral Education Research Foundation.

Kolb, D. A., & Boyatzis, R. E. (1970). On the dynamics of the helping relationship. *Journal of Applied Behavioral Science, 6,* 267–289.

Kopfstein, J. H., & Kopfstein, D. (1973). Correlates of self-disclosure in college students. *Journal of Consulting and Clinical Psychology, 41,* 163.

Korman, A. K. (1967a). Relevance of personal need satisfaction for overall satisfaction as a function of self-esteem. *Journal of Applied Psychology, 51,* 533–538.

Korman, A. (1967b). Self-esteem as a moderator of the relationship between self-perceived abilities and vocational choice. *Journal of Applied Psychology, 51,* 65–67.

Korte, J. R., & Kimble, C. E., & Cole, J. R. (1978). Does locus of control similarity increase attraction? *Psychological Reports, 43,* 1183–1188.

Krebs, A. M. (1958). Two determinants of conformity: Age of independence training and n achievement. *Journal of Abnormal and Social Psychology, 56,* 130–131.

Krebs, D. L. (1970). Altruism — An examination of the concept and a review of the literature. *Psychological Bulletin, 73,* 258–302.

Kuhlman, D. M., & Marshello, A. (1975). Individual differences in the game motives of own, relative and joint gain. *Journal of Research on Personality, 9,* 240–251.

Kuhlman, E. (1976). Dogmatism and deference: The relationship between bureaucratic orientation and personality type. *The Alberta Journal of Educational Research, 22,* 179–186.

Kukla, A. (1974). Performance as a function of resultant achievement motivation (perceived ability) and perceived difficulty. *Journal of Personality and Social Psychology, 7,* 374–383.

LaFollette, W., & Belohular, J. (1982). The effect of motivational homogeneity on risk in decision making. *Journal of Psychology, 112,* 53–61.

Lamb, D. H. (1978). Anxiety. In H. London & J. E. Exner, Jr. (Eds.), *Dimensions of personality* (pp. 37–85). New York: Wiley.

Lamm, H., & Meyers, D. (1976). Machiavellianism, discussion time and group shift. *Social Behavior and Personality, 4,* 41–48.

Lamm, H., Schaude, E., & Trommsdorf, G. (1971). Risky-shift as a function of group member value of risk and need for approval. *Journal of Personality and Social Psychology, 20,* 430–435.

Larsen, K. S., Lancaster, L., Lesh, W., Redding, J., White, C., & Larsen, K. S. (1976). Approval seeking, situational pressures, and the willingness to administer shock to a victim. *Journal of Social Psychology, 99,* 87–95.

Larsen, K. S., Martin, A. J., Ettinger, R. H., & Nelson, J. (1976). Approval seeking, social cost and aggression: A scale and some dynamics. *Journal of Psychology, 94,* 3–11.

Latané, B., & Darley, J. M. (1970). *The unresponsive bystander: Why doesn't he help?* New York: Appleton-Century-Crofts.

Lazarus, R. S. (1966). *Psychological stress and the coping process.* New York: McGraw-Hill.

Lazarus, R. S., Eriksen, C. W., & Fonda, C. P. (1951). Personality dynamics and auditory perceptual recognition. *Journal of Personality, 19,* 471–482.

Lazarus, R. S., Yousem, H., & Arenberg, D. (1953). Hunger and perception. *Journal of Personality, 21,* 312–328.

Leary, T. (1957). *Interpersonal diagnosis of personality.* New York: Ronald Press.

Lecky, P. (1945). *Self consistency: A theory of personality.* New York: Island Press.

LeCompte, W. F., & Rosenfeld, H. M. (1971). Effects of minimal eye contact in the instruction period on impressions of the experimenter. *Journal of Experimental Social Psychology, 7,* 211–220.

Lefcourt, H. M. (1967). Effects of cue explication upon persons maintaining external control expectancies. *Journal of Personality and Social Psychology, 5,* 372–378.

Lefcourt, H. M. (1969). Need for approval and threatened negative evaluation on determinants of expressiveness in a projective test. *Journal of Consulting and Clinical Psychology, 33,* 96–102.

Lefcourt, H. M. (1976a). *Locus of control: Current trends in theory and research.* Hillsdale, NJ: Lawrence Erlbaum Associates.

Lefcourt, H. M. (1976b). Locus of control and the response to aversive events. *Canadian Psychological Review, 17,* 202–209.

Lefcourt, H. M., Gronnerud, P., & McDonald, P. (1973). Cognitive activity and hypothesis formation during a double entendre word association test as a function of locus of control and field dependence. *Canadian Journal of Behavioral Science, 5,* 161–173.

Lefcourt, H. M., Lewis, L., & Silverman, I. (1968). Internal versus external control of reinforcement and attention in decision-making tasks. *Journal of Personality, 36,* 663–682.

Lefcourt, H. M., Sordoni, C., & Sordoni, C. (1974). Locus of control, field dependence, and the expression of humor. *Journal of Personality, 42,* 130–143.

Lefcourt, H. M., & Wine, J. (1969). Internal versus external control of reinforcement and the deployment of attention in experimental situations. *Canadian Journal of Behavioral Science, 1,* 167–181.

Lehmann, S. (1970). Personality and compliance: A study of anxiety and self-esteem in opinion and behavior change. *Journal of Personality and Social Psychology, 15,* 76–86.

Leonard, R. L. (1975). Self-concept and attraction for similar and dissimilar others. *Journal of Personality and Social Psychology, 31,* 926–929.

Leventhal, H., & Perloe, S. I. (1962). A relationship between self-esteem and persuasibility. *Journal of Abnormal and Social Psychology, 64,* 385–388.

Levine, R., Chein, I., & Murphy, G. (1942). The relation of the intensity of a need to the amount of perceptual distortion: A preliminary report. *Journal of Psychology, 13,* 283–293.

Levinger, G. (1974). A three-level approach to attraction: Toward an understanding of pair relatedness. In T. L. Huston (Ed.), *Foundations of interpersonal attraction* (pp. 100–119). New York: Academic Press.

Libby, W. L., Jr., & Yaklevich, D. (1973). Personality determinants of eye contact and direction of gaze aversion. *Journal of Personality and Social Psychology, 27,* 197–206.

Liebhart, E. H. (1972). Empathy and emergency helping: The effects of personality, self-concern, and acquaintance. *Journal of Experimental Social Psychology, 8,* 404–411.

Linton, H. B. (1955). Dependence on external influence: Correlates in perception, attitudes, and judgement. *Journal of Abnormal and Social Psychology, 51,* 502–507.

Linton, H., & Graham, E. (1959). Personality correlates of persuasibility. In I. L. Janis & C. I. Hovland (Eds.), *Personality and persuasibility* (pp. 69–102). New Haven, CT: Yale University Press.

Lipetz, M. E. (1960). The effects of information on the assessment of attitudes by authoritarians and nonauthoritarians. *Journal of Abnormal and Social Psychology, 60,* 95–99.

Lipetz, M. E., & Ossorio, P. G. (1967). Authoritarianism, aggression, and status. *Journal of Personality and Social Psychology, 5,* 468–472.

Littig, L. W. (1963). Effects of motivation on probability preferences. *Journal of Personality, 31,* 417–427.

Liverant, S., & Scodel, A. (1960). Internal and external control as determinants of decision making under conditions of risk. *Psychological Reports, 7,* 59–67.

Lombardo, J. P., & Fantasia, S. C. (1976). The relationship of self-disclosure to personality, adjustment and self-actualization. *Journal of Clinical Psychology, 32,* 765–769.

Long, B. H., & Ziller, R. C. (1965). Dogmatism and predecisional information search. *Journal of Applied Psychology, 49,* 376–378.

Luchins, A. S. (1949). Rigidity and ethnocentrism: A critique. *Journal of Personality, 17,* 449–466.

Lutzker, D. R. (1960). Internationalism as a predictor of cooperative behavior. *Conflict Resolution, 4,* 426–430.

Mabel, S., & Rosenfeld, H. M. (1966). Relationship of self-concept to the experiences of imbalance in p-o-x situations. *Human Relations, 19,* 381–389.

Maddi, S. R. (1976). *Personality theories: A comparative analysis* (3rd ed.). Homewood, IL: Dorsey Press.

Magnusson, D., & Endler, N. S. (Eds.). (1977). *Personality at the crossroads: Current issues in interactional psychology.* Hillsdale, NJ: Lawrence Erlbaum Associates.

Maile, C. A. (1977). The apparent lack of self-esteem and persuasibility relationships. *The Journal of Psychology, 96,* 123–130.

Malof, M., & Lott, A. J. (1962). Ethnocentrism and the acceptance of Negro support in a group pressure situation. *Journal of Abnormal and Social Psychology, 65,* 254–258.

Mandler, G., & Sarason, S. B. (1952). A study of anxiety and learning. *Journal of Abnormal and Social Psychology, 47,* 166–173.

Mangan, G. L., Quartermain, D., & Vaughan, G. M. (1960). Taylor MAS and group conformity pressure. *Journal of Abnormal and Social Psychology, 61,* 146–147.

Marks, E. L., Penner, L. A., & Stone, A. V. W. (1982). Helping as a function of empathic responses and sociopathy. *Journal of Research in Personality, 16,* 1–20.

Marlowe, D. (1963). Psychological needs and cooperation: Competition in a two-person game. *Psychological Reports, 13,* 364.

Marquis, P. C. (1973). Experimenter–subject interaction as a function of authoritarianism and response set. *Journal of Personality and Social Psychology, 25,* 289–296.

Martin, H. J., & Greenstein, T. N. (1983). Individual differences in status generalization: Effects of need for social approval, anticipated interpersonal contact, and instrumental task abilities. *Journal of Personality and Social Psychology, 45,* 641–662.

Martin, W. E., Gross, N., & Darley, J. G. (1952). Studies of group behavior: Leaders, followers, and isolates in small organized groups. *Journal of Abnormal and Social Psychology, 47,* 838–842.

Masling, J. M., Greer, F. L., & Gilmore, R. (1955). Status, authoritarianism, and sociometric choice. *Journal of Social Psychology, 41,* 297–310.

Maslow, A. H. (1963). The need to know and the fear of knowing. *Journal of General Psychology, 68,* 111–124.

Maslow, A. (1965). Criteria for judging needs to be instinctoid. In M. Jones (Ed.), *Human motivation: A symposium,* pp. 33–47. Lincoln: University of Nebraska Press.

Maslow, A. H. (1968). *Toward a psychology of being.* New York: Van Nostrand Reinhold.

Maslow, A. H. (1970). *Motivation and personality* (2nd ed.). New York: Harper & Row.

Mathews, K. A., Batson, C. D., Horn, J., & Rosenman, R. H. (1981). "Principles in his nature which interest him in the fortune of others...": The heritability of empathic concern for others. *Journal of Personality, 49,* 237–247.

Matloff, J. L., & Doster, J. A. (1976). Need approval, modeling and perception of models' adjustment in behavior during an interview. *Psychological Reports, 39,* 531–534.

McArthur, L. Z., & Post, D. L. (1977). Figural emphasis and person perception. *Journal of Experimental Social Psychology, 13,* 520–536.

McClelland, D. C. (1958). The importance of early learning in the formation of motives. In J. W. Atkinson (Ed.), *Motives in fantasy, action, and society* (pp. 437–452). Princeton, NJ: Van Nostrand.

McClelland, D. C. (1961). *The achieving society.* Princeton, NJ: Van Nostrand.

McClelland, D. C. (1975). *Power: The inner experience.* New York: Irvington.

McClelland, D. C. (1981). Is personality consistent? In A. I. Rabin, J. Aronoff, A. M. Barclay, & R. A. Zucker (Eds.), *Further explorations in personality* (pp. 81–113). New York: Wiley.

McClelland, D. C., & Atkinson, J. W. (1948). The projective expression of needs, I. The effect of different intensities of the hunger drive on perception. *Journal of Psychology, 25,* 205–232.

McClelland, D. C., Atkinson, J. W., Clark, R. A., & Lowell, E. L. (1953). *The achievement motive.* New York: Appleton-Century-Crofts.

McClelland, D. C., & Boyatzis, R. E. (1982). Leadership motive pattern and long-term success in management. *Journal of Applied Psychology, 67,* 737–743.

McClelland, D. C., & Liberman, A. M. (1949). The effect of need for achievement on recognition of need-related words. *Journal of Personality, 18,* 236–251.

McClelland, D. C., & Teague, G. (1975). Predicting risk preferences among power related tasks. *Journal of Personality, 43,* 266–285.

McClelland, D. C., & Watson, R. I. (1973). Power motivation and risk-taking behavior. *Journal of Personality, 41,* 121–139.

McClelland, D. C., & Winter, D. G. (1969). *Motivating economic achievement.* New York: Free Press.

McClintock, C. G., Gallo, P., & Harrison, A. A. (1965). Some effects of variations in other strategy upon game behavior. *Journal of Personality and Social Psychology, 1,* 319–325.

McClintock, C. G., Harrison, A. A., Strand, S., & Gallo, P. (1963). Internationalism-isolationism, strategy of the other player and two-person game behavior. *Journal of Abnormal and Social Psychology, 67,* 631–636.

McCurdy, H. G., & Eber, H. W. (1953). Democratic versus authoritarian: A further investigation of group problem-solving. *Journal of Personality, 22,* 258–269.

McDavid, J. W., & Sistrunk, F. (1964). Personality correlates of two kinds of conforming behavior. *Journal of Personality, 32,* 420–435.

McGaffey, T. N. (1976). Motivational determinants of decision-making in a triadic coalition game. *Journal of General Psychology, 94,* 167–185.

McGhee, P. E., & Teevan, R. C. (1967). Conformity behavior and need for affiliation. *Journal of Social Psychology, 72,* 117–121.

McGovern, L. P. (1976). Dispositional social anxiety and helping behavior under three conditions of threat. *Journal of Personality, 44,* 84–97.

McGrath, J. E. (1964). *Social psychology: A brief introduction.* New York: Holt, Rinehart & Winston.

McGregor, D. (1960). *The human side of enterprise.* New York: McGraw-Hill.

McGuire, W. J. (1968). Personality and susceptibility to social influence. In E. F. Borgatta & W. W. Lambert (Eds.), *Handbook of personality theory and research* (pp. 1130–1187). Chicago: Rand McNally.

McKeown, C. D., Gahagan, J. P., & Tedeschi, J. T. (1967). The effect of prior power strategy on behavior after a shift of power. *Journal of Experimental Research in Personality, 2,* 226–233.

McLaughlin, B. (1970). Incidental learning and Machiavellianism. *Journal of Social Psychology, 82,* 109–116.

McLaughlin, D., & Hewitt, J. (1972). Need for approval and perceived openness. *Journal of Experimental Research in Personality, 6,* 255–258.

Meadows, I. S. G. (1980). Organic structure, satisfaction, and personality. *Human Relations, 33,* 383–392.

Medalia, N. Z. (1955). Authoritarianism, leader acceptance, and group cohesion. *Journal of Abnormal and Social Psychology, 51,* 207–213.

Megargee, E. I. (1969). Influence of sex roles on the manifestation of leadership. *Journal of Applied Psychology, 53,* 377–382.

Megargee, E. I., Bogart, P., & Anderson, B. J. (1966). Prediction of leadership in a simulated industrial task. *Journal of Applied Psychology, 50,* 292–295.

Mehrabian, A. (1968). Relationship of attitude to seated posture, orientation, and distance. *Journal of Personality and Social Psychology, 10,* 26–30.

Mehrabian, A., & Diamond, S. G. (1971a). Effects of furniture arrangement, props, and personality on social interaction. *Journal of Personality and Social Psychology, 20,* 18–30.

Mehrabian, A., & Diamond, S. G. (1971b). Seating arrangement and conversation. *Sociometry, 34,* 281–289.

Mehrabian, A., & Epstein, N. (1972). A measure of emotional empathy. *Journal of Personality, 40,* 525–543.

Mehrabian, A., & Ksionzky, S. (1972). Some determinants of social interaction. *Sociometry, 35,* 588–609.

Messé, L. A., Aronoff, J., & Wilson, J. P. (1972). Motivation as a mediator of the mechanisms underlying role assignments in small groups. *Journal of Personality and Social Psychology, 24,* 84–90.

Messick, S. (1970). The criterion problem in the evaluation of instruction: Assessing possible, not just intended outcomes. In M. C. Wittrock & D. Wiley (Eds.), *The evaluation of instruc-*

tion: Issues and problems (pp. 183–220). New York: Holt, Rinehart & Winston.

Messick, S. (1976). Personality consistencies in cognition and creativity. In S. Messick and Associates (Eds.), *Individuality in learning* (pp. 4–22). San Francisco: Jossey-Bass.

Meunier, C., & Rule, B. G. (1967). Anxiety, confidence, and conformity. *Journal of Personality, 35,* 498–504.

Meyers, D., & Lamm, H. (1976). The group polarization phenomenon. *Psychological Bulletin, 83,* 602–607.

Michelini, R., Wilson, J. P., & Messé, L. A. (1975). The influence of psychological needs on helping behavior. *Journal of Psychology, 91,* 253–258.

Midlarsky, E. (1971). Aiding under stress: The effects of competence, dependency, visibility, and fatalism. *Journal of Personality, 39,* 132–149.

Midlarsky, E., & Midlarsky, M. (1973). Some determinants of aiding under experimentally-induced stress. *Journal of Personality, 41,* 305–327.

Milham, J. (1974). Two components of approval score and their relationship to cheating following success and failure. *Journal of Research in Personality, 8,* 378–392.

Milham, J., & Kellogg, R. W. (1980). Need for social approval: Impression management or self-deception. *Journal of Research in Personality, 14,* 445–457.

Miller, G. R., & Rokeach, M. (1968). Individual differences and tolerance for inconsistency. In R. P. Abelson, E. Aronson, W. J. McGuire, T. W. Newcomb, M. J. Rosenberg, & P. H. Tannenbaum (Eds.), *Theories of cognitive consistency: A sourcebook* (pp. 624–633). Chicago: Rand McNally.

Miller, N. (1965). Involvement and dogmatism as inhibitors of attitude change. *Journal of Experimental Social Psychology, 1,* 121–132.

Miller, N., Doob, A. N., Butler, D. C., & Marlowe, D. (1965). The tendency to agree: Situational determinants and social desirability. *Journal of Experimental Research in Personality, 1,* 78–83.

Millman, S. (1968). Anxiety, comprehension, and susceptibility to social influences. *Journal of Personality and Social Psychology, 9,* 251–256.

Millon, T. (1957). Authoritarianism, intolerance of ambiguity, and rigidity under ego- and task-involving conditions. *Journal of Abnormal and Social Psychology, 55,* 29–33.

Mills, C. J., & Bohannon, W. E. (1980). Character structure and jury behavior: Conceptual and applied implications. *Journal of Personality and Social Psychology, 38,* 662–667.

Miner, J. B., Rizzo, J. R., Harlow, D. N., & Hill, J. W. (1974). Role motivation theory of managerial effectiveness in simulated organizations of varying degrees of structure. *Journal of Applied Psychology, 59,* 31–37.

Mischel, W. (1973). Toward a cognitive social learning reconceptualization of personality. *Psychological Review, 80,* 252–283.

Mischel, W. (1979). On the interface of cognition and personality: Beyond the person-situation debate. *American Psychologist, 34,* 740–754.

Mischel, W. (1984). On the predictability of behavior and the structure of personality. In R. A. Zucker, J. Aronoff, A. I. Rabin (Eds.), *Personality and the prediction of behavior* (pp. 269–305). New York: Academic Press.

Mischel, W., & Schopler, J. (1959). Authoritarianism and reactions to "sputnicks." *Journal of Abnormal and Social Psychology, 59,* 142–145.

Mitchell, H. E., & Byrne, D. (1973). The defendant's dilemma: Effects of juror's attitudes and authoritarianism on judicial decisions. *Journal of Personality and Social Psychology, 25,* 123–129.

Mitchell, T. R., Smyser, C. M., & Weed, S. E. (1975). Locus of control: Supervision and work satisfaction. *Academy of Management Journal, 18,* 623–631.

Mobbs, N. A. (1968). Eye-contact in relation to social introversion/extraversion. *British Journal of Social and Clinical Psychology, 7,* 305–306.

Moeller, G., & Applezweig, M. H. (1957). A motivational factor in conformity. *Journal of Ab-*

normal and Social Psychology, 55, 114–120.

Moore, J. C., Jr., & Krupat, E. (1971). Relationships between source status, authoritarianism, and conformity in a social influence setting. *Sociometry, 34,* 122–134.

Moore, L. H. (1935). Leadership traits of college women. *Sociology and Social Research, 20,* 136–139.

Moos, R. H., & Speisman, J. C. (1962). Group compatibility and productivity. *Journal of Abnormal and Social Psychology, 65,* 190–196.

Moran, G., & Comfort, J. C. (1982). Scientific juror selection: Sex as a moderator of demographic and personality predictors of impaneled felony juror behavior. *Journal of Personality and Social Psychology, 43,* 1052–1063.

Morgan, C. D., & Murray, H. A. (1935). A method for investigating fantasies. *Archives of Neurology and Psychiatry, 34,* 289–306.

Morrison, T. L., & Morrison, R. L. (1978). Self-esteem, need for approval and self-estimates of academic performance. *Psychological Reports, 43,* 503–507.

Morse, J. J. (1975). Person–job congruence and individual adjustment and development. *Human Relations, 28,* 841–861.

Morse, J. J., & Caldwell, D. F. (1979). Effects of personality and perception of the environment on satisfaction with task group. *Journal of Psychology, 103,* 183–192.

Morse, N. C., & Reimer, E. (1956). The experimental change of a major organizational variable. *Journal of Abnormal and Social Psychology, 52,* 120–129.

Mossholder, K. W., Bedeian, A. G., & Armenakis, A. A. (1981). Role perceptions, satisfaction, and performance: Moderating effects of self-esteem and organizational level. *Organizational Behavior and Human Performance, 28,* 224–234.

Moulton, R. W., Raphelson, A. C., Kristofferson, A. B., & Atkinson, J. W. (1958). The achievement motive and perceptual sensitivity under two conditions of motive-arousal. In J. W. Atkinson (Ed.), *Motives in fantasy, action and society* (pp. 350–359). Princeton, NJ: Van Nostrand.

Mueller, J. H. (1979). Anxiety and encoding processes in memory. *Personality and Social Psychology Bulletin, 5,* 288–294.

Mueller, J. H. (1980). Test anxiety and the encoding and retrieval of information. In I. G. Sarason (Ed.), *Test anxiety: Theory, research and applications* (pp. 63–86). Hillsdale, NJ: Lawrence Erlbaum Associates.

Mueller, W. J. (1966). Need structure and the projection of traits onto parents. *Journal of Personality and Social Psychology, 3,* 63–72.

Murphy, L. B., & Moriarity, A. E. (1976). *Vulnerability, coping and growth.* New Haven, CT: Yale University Press.

Murray, H. A. (1938). *Explorations in personality.* New York: Oxford University Press.

Murstein, B. I. (1976). *Who will marry whom? Theories and research in marital choice.* New York: Springer.

Murstein, B. I., & Pryer, R. S. (1959). The concept of projection: A review. *Psychological Bulletin, 56,* 353–357.

Mussen, P. H., & Porter, L. W. (1959). Personal motivations and self-conceptions associated with effectiveness and ineffectiveness in emergent groups. *Journal of Abnormal and Social Psychology, 59,* 23–27.

Nachtscheim, N., & Hoy, W. K. (1976). Authoritarian personality and control ideologies of teachers. *The Alberta Journal of Educational Research, 22,* 173–178.

Nadler, E. B. (1959). Yielding, authoritarianism, and authoritarian ideology regarding groups. *Journal of Abnormal and Social Psychology, 58,* 408–410.

Nielsen, S. L., & Sarason, I. G. (1981). Emotion, personality, and selective attention. *Journal of Personality and Social Psychology, 41,* 945–960.

Nisbett, R. E., & Gordon, A. (1967). Self-esteem and susceptibility to social influence. *Journal of Personality and Social Psychology, 5,* 268–276.

Noland, S. J., & Catron, D. W. (1969). Cooperative behavior among high school students on the prisoner's dilemma game. *Psychological Reports, 24,* 711-718.

Norem-Hebeisen, A. A., & Johnson, D. W. (1981). The relationship between cooperative competitive, and individualistic attitudes and differentiated aspects of self-esteem. *Journal of Personality, 49,* 415-426.

Nowicki, S., Jr., & Blumberg, N. (1975). The role of locus of control of reinforcement in interpersonal attraction. *Journal of Research in Personality, 9,* 48-56.

Offer, D., & Sabshin, M. (1974). *Normality.* New York: Basic Books.

Olczak, P. V., & Goldman, J. A. (1975). Self-actualization as a moderator of the relationship between attitude similiarity and attraction. *Journal of Psychology, 89,* 195-202.

Oldham, G. R. (1976). Job characteristics and internal motivation: The moderating effect of interpersonal and individual variables. *Human Relations, 29,* 559-569.

Oldham, G. R., Hackham, J. R., & Pearce, J. L. (1976). Conditions under which employees respond positively to enriched work. *Journal of Applied Psychology, 61,* 395-403.

O'Reilly, C. A., III. (1977). Personality-job fit: Implications for individual attitudes and performance. *Organizational Behavior and Human Performance, 18,* 36-46.

Organ, D. W., & Greene, C. N. (1974). Role ambiguity, locus of control, and work satisfaction. *Journal of Applied Psychology, 59,* 101-102.

Paivio, A., & Steeves, R. (1963). Personal values and selective perception of speech. *Perceptual and Motor Skills, 13,* 459-464.

Palmer, J., & Altrocchi, J. (1967). Attribution of hostile interest as unconscious. *Journal of Personality, 35,* 164-177.

Palmer, J., & Byrne, D. (1970). Attraction toward dominant and submissive strangers: Similarity versus complementarity. *Journal of Experimental Research in Personality, 4,* 108-115.

Pandey, J., & Griffitt, W. (1977). Benefactor's sex and nurturance need, recipient's dependency, and the effect of number of potential helpers on helping behavior. *Journal of Personality, 45,* 79-99.

Pandey, J., & Rastogi, R. (1979). Machiavellianism and ingratiation. *Journal of Social Psychology, 108,* 221-225.

Patterson, M. L. (1973). Stability and nonverbal immediacy behaviors. *Journal of Experimental Social Psychology, 9,* 97-109.

Patterson, M. L. (1976). An arousal model of interpersonal intimacy. *Psychological Review, 83,* 235-245.

Patterson, M. L., & Sechrest, L. B. (1970). Interpersonal distance and impression formation. *Journal of Personality, 38,* 161-166.

Pedersen, D. M. 1973). Personality and demographic correlates of simulated personal space. *Journal of Psychology, 85,* 101-108.

Pervin, L. A. (1968). Performance and satisfaction as a function of individual-environment fit. *Psychological Bulletin, 69,* 56-68.

Phares, E. J. (1965). Internal-external control as a determinant of amount of social influence exerted. *Journal of Personality and Social Psychology, 2,* 642-647.

Phares, E. J. (1968). Differential utilization of information as a function of internal-external control. *Journal of Personality, 36,* 649-662.

Phares, E. J. (1976). *Locus of control in personality.* Morristown, NJ: General Learning Press.

Phares, E. J., Ritchie, D. E., & Davis, W. L. (1968). Internal-external control and reaction to threat. *Journal of Personality and Social Psychology, 10,* 402-405.

Phares, E. J., & Wilson, K. G. (1971). Internal-external control, interpersonal attraction, and empathy. *Psychological Reports, 28,* 543-549.

Phillips, J. L., Aronoff, J., & Messé, L. (1971). Sex and psychological need in triadic bargaining. *Psychonomic Science, 22,* 329-331.

Pilkonis, P. A. (1977a). The behavioral consequences of shyness. *Journal of Personality, 45,* 596-611.

Pilkonis, P. A. (1977b). Shyness, public and private, and its relationship to other measures of social behavior. *Journal of Personality, 45,* 585–595.

Pines, H. A., & Julian, J. W. (1972). Effects of task and social demands on locus of control differences in information processing. *Journal of Personality, 40,* 407–416.

Porter, L. W., Lawler, E. E., II, & Hackman, J. R. (1975). *Behavior in organizations.* New York: McGraw-Hill.

Posavac, E. J. (1971). Need for approval as a moderator of interpersonal attraction based on attitude similarity. *Journal of Social Psychology, 85,* 141–142.

Posavac, E., & Pasko, S. J. (1971). Interpersonal attraction and confidence of attraction ratings as a function of number of attitudes and attitude similarity. *Psychonomic Science, 23,* 433–435.

Post, A. L., Wittmaier, B. C., & Radin, M. E. (1978). Self-disclosure as a function of state and trait anxiety. *Journal of Consulting and Clinical Psychology, 46,* 12–19.

Postman, L., Bruner, J. S., & McGinnies, E. (1948). Personal values as selective factors in perception. *Journal of Abnormal and Social Psychology, 43,* 142–154.

Postman, L., & Crutchfield, R. S. (1952). The interaction of need, set, and stimulus-structure in cognitive task. *American Journal of Psychology, 65,* 196–217.

Powell, F. A. (1962). Open- and closed-mindedness and the ability to differentiate message from source. *Journal of Abnormal and Social Psychology, 65,* 61–64.

Prociuk, T. J., & Breen, L. J. (1977). Internal–external locus of control and information-seeking in a college academic situation. *Journal of Social Psychology, 101,* 309–310.

Purcell, K. (1952). Memory and psychological security. *Journal of Abnormal and Social Psychology, 47,* 433–440.

Rabinowitz, S., Hall, D. T., & Goodale, J. G. (1977). Job scope and individual differences as predictors of job involvement: Independent or interactive? *Academy of Management Journal, 20,* 273–281.

Rabinowitz, W. (1956). A note on the social perceptions of authoritarians and non-authoritarians. *Journal of Abnormal and Social Psychology, 53,* 384–386.

Raden, D. (1980). Authoritarianism and overt aggression. *Psychological Reports, 47,* 452–454.

Raynor, J. O., & Smith, C. P. (1966). Achievement-related motives and risk-taking in games of skill and chance. *Journal of Personality, 34,* 176–198.

Reagor, P. A., & Clore, G. L. (1970). Attraction, test anxiety, and similarity–dissimilarity. *Psychonomic Science, 18,* 219–220.

Restle, F., Andrews, M., & Rokeach, M. (1964). Differences between open- and closed-minded subjects on learning-set and oddity problems. *Journal of Abnormal and Social Psychology, 68,* 648–654.

Reznikoff, M., Bridges, C., & Hirsch, T. (1972). Internal–external control orientation, self-description, and bridge playing expertise. *Psychological Reports, 31,* 683–689.

Rohde, K. J. (1952). The relation of authoritarianism of the aircrew member to his acceptance by the airplane commander. *American Psychologist, 7,* 310–311.

Richardson, H. M., & Hanawalt, N. G. (1943). Leadership as related to Bernreuter personality measures: I. College leadership in extracurricular activities. *Journal of Social Psychology, 17,* 237–249.

Richardson, H. M., & Hanawalt, N. G. (1944). Leadership as related to Bernreuter personality measures: III. Leadership among adult men in vocational and social activities. *Journal of Applied Psychology, 28,* 308–317.

Richardson, H. M., & Hanawalt, N. G. (1952). Leadership as related to Bernreuter personality measures: V. Leadership aamong adult females in social activities. *Journal of Social Psychology, 36,* 141–153.

Riley, J., & Armlin, N. J. (1965). The dogmatism scale and flexibility in maze performance. *Perceptual and Motor Skills, 21,* 914.

Rim, Y. (1963). Risk-taking and need for achievement. *Acta Psychologica, 21,* 108–115.

Rim, Y. (1966). Machiavellianism and decisions in violating risk. *British Journal of Social and Clinical Psychology, 5,* 30–36.

Rim, Y. (1979). Personality and means of influence in marriage. *Human Relations, 32,* 871–875.

Ritchie, E., & Phares, E. J. (1969). Attitude change as a function of internal–external control and communicator status. *Journal of Personality, 37,* 429–443.

Robbins, G. E. (1975). Dogmatism and information gathering in personality impression formation. *Journal of Research in Personality, 9,* 74–84.

Roberts, A. H, & Jessor, R. (1958). Authoritarianism, punitiveness, and perceived social status. *Journal of Abnormal and Social Psychology, 56,* 311–314.

Rokeach, M. (1948). Generalized mental rigidity as a factor in ethnocentrism. *Journal of Abnormal and Social Psychology, 43,* 259–278.

Rokeach, M. (1960). *The open and closed mind.* New York: Basic Books.

Rokeach, M. (1968). *Beliefs, attitudes, and values.* San Francisco: Jossey-Bass.

Rokeach, M. (1973). *The nature of human values.* New York: Macmillan.

Rosenbaum, M. E., Horne, W. C., & Chalmers, D. K. (1962). Level of self-esteem and the learning of imitation and nonimitation. *Journal of Personality, 30,* 147–156.

Rosenfeld, H. M. (1965). Effect of an approval-seeking induction on interpersonal proximity. *Psychological Reports, 17,* 120–122.

Rosenfeld, H. M. (1966). Instrumental affiliative functions of facial and gestural expressions. *Journal of Personality and Social Psychology, 4,* 65–72.

Rosenfeld, L. B., & Plax, T. G. (1976). Personality determinants of reticence. *Western Speech Communication, 35,* 22–31.

Rotter, J. B. (1966). Generalized expectancies for internal versus external control of reinforcement. *Psychological Monographs, 80* (Whole No. 609).

Rotter, J. B., & Mulry, R. C. (1965). Internal versus external control of reinforcements and decision time. *Journal of Personality and Social Psychology, 2,* 598–604.

Rotton, J., Blake, B. F., & Heslin, R. (1977). Dogmatism, trust and message acceptance. *Journal of Psychology, 96,* 81–88.

Rubin, J. Z., & Brown, B. R. (1975). *The social psychology of bargaining and negotiation.* New York: Academic Press.

Rubin, Z. (1970). Measurement of romantic love. *Journal of Personality and Social Psychology, 16,* 265–273.

Runyon, K. E. (1973). Some interactions between personality variables and management styles. *Journal of Applied Psychology, 57,* 288–294.

Rutter, D. R., Morley, I. E., & Graham, J. C. (1972). Visual interaction in a group of introverts and extraverts. *European Journal of Social Psychology, 2,* 371–384.

Rutter, D. R., & Stephenson, G. M. (1972). Visual interaction in a group of schizophrenic and depressive patients. *British Journal of Social and Clinical Psychology, 11,* 57–65.

Rychlak, J. F. (1963). Personality correlates of leadership among first level managers. *Psychological Reports, 12,* 43–52.

Samelson, F. (1958). The relation of achievement and affiliation motives to conforming behavior in two conditions of conflict with a majority. In J. W. Atkinson (Ed.), *Motives in fantasy, action, and society* (pp. 421–433). Princeton, NJ: Van Nostrand.

Sanders, J. L. (1976). Relationship of personal space to body image boundary definiteness. *Journal of Research in Personality, 10,* 478–481.

Sanders, J. L. (1977). The relationship of dogmatism to the non-recognition of perceptual ambiguity. *Journal of Psychology, 95,* 179–183.

Sanford, F. H. (1950). *Authoritarianism and leadership.* Philadelphia: Stephenson. (Copyright by Institute for Research on Human Relations, 2224 Locust St., Philadelphia, Pa.)

Sanford, R. N. (1936). The effect of abstinence from food upon imaginal processes: A preliminary experiment. *Journal of Psychology, 2,* 129–136.

Sanford, R. N. (1937). The effect of abstinence from food upon imaginal processes: A further experiment. *Journal of Psychology, 3,* 145–159.

Sarason, I. G. (1961). The effects of anxiety and threat on the solution of a difficult task. *Journal of Abnormal and Social Psychology, 62,* 165–168.

Sarason, I. G. (1972). Experimental approaches to test anxiety: Attention and the uses of information. In C. D. Speilberger (Ed.), *Anxiety: Current trends in theory and research* (Vol. 2, pp. 383–409). New York: Academic Press.

Sarason, I. G. (1973). Test anxiety and social influence. *Journal of Personality, 41,* 261–271.

Sarason, I. G. (Ed.) (1980). *Test anxiety: Theory, research and applications.* Hillsdale, NJ: Lawrence Erlbaum Associates.

Sarason, I. G. (1981). Test anxiety, stress, and social support. *Journal of Personality, 49,* 101–114.

Sarason, I. G., & Harmatz, M. G. (1965). Test anxiety and experimental conditions. *Journal of Personality and Social Psychology, 1,* 499–505.

Sarason, I. G., Pederson, A. M., & Nyman, B. (1968). Test anxiety and the observation of models. *Journal of Personality, 36,* 493–511.

Satow, K. L. (1975). Social approval and helping. *Journal of Experimental Social Psychology, 11,* 501–509.

Schachter, S. (1959). *The psychology of affiliation: Experimental studies of the sources of gregariousness.* Stanford, CA: Stanford University Press.

Schalon, C. L. (1968). Effect of self-esteem upon performance following failure stress. *Journal of Consulting and Clinical Psychology, 32,* 497.

Schiller, M. (1961). A new approach to leadership assessment. *Personnel Psychology, 14,* 75–86.

Schlenker, B. R., Helm, B., & Tedeschi, J. T. (1973). The effects of personality and situational variables on behavioral trust. *Journal of Personality and Social Psychology, 25,* 419–427.

Schneider, D. J. (1973). Implicit personality theory: A review. *Psychological Bulletin, 79,* 294–309.

Schneider, F. W., & Dalenay, J. G. (1972). Effect of individual achievement motivation on group problem-solving efficiency. *Journal of Social Psychology, 86,* 291–298.

Schneider, K. S. (1977). Personality correlates of altruistic behavior under four experimental conditions. *Journal of Social Psychology, 102,* 113–116.

Schroder, H. M., Driver, M. J., & Streufert, S. (1967). *Human information processing.* New York: Holt, Rinehart & Winston.

Schroder, H. M., & Suedfeld, P. (Eds.). (1971). *Personality theory and information processing.* New York: Ronald Press.

Schutz, W. C. (1967). *The FIRO scales.* Palo Alto: Consulting Psychologists Press.

Schwartz, S. H. (1974). Awareness of interpersonal consequences, responsibility denial, and volunteering. *Journal of Personality and Social Psychology, 30,* 57–63.

Schwartz, S. H. (1975). The justice of need and the activation of humanitarian norms. *Journal of Social Issues, 31,* 111–116.

Schwartz, S. H. (1977). Normative influences on helping. In L. Berkowitz (Ed.), *Advances in experimental social psychology* (Vol. 10, pp. 221–279). New York: Academic Press.

Schwartz, S. H., & Ben David, A. (1976). Responsibility and helping in an emergency: Effects of blame, ability and denial of responsibility. *Sociometry, 39,* 406–415.

Schwartz, S. H., & Clausen, G. T. (1970). Responsibility, norms, and helping in an emergency. *Journal of Personality and Social Psychology, 16,* 299–310.

Schwartz, S. H., Feldman, K. A., Brown, M. E., & Heingartner, A. (1969). Some personality correlates of conduct in two situations of moral conflict. *Journal of Personality, 37,* 41–57.

Schwartz, S. H., & Howard, J. A. (1981). A normative decision-making model of altruism. In J. P. Rushton & R. M. Sorrentino (Eds.), *Altruism and helping behavior* (pp. 189–211). Hillsdale, NJ: Lawrence Erlbaum Associates.

Scioli, F. P., Jr., Dyson, J. W., & Fleitas, D. W. (1974). The relationship of personality and decisional structure to leadership. *Small Group Behavior, 5,* 3–22.

Scodel, A., & Freedman, M. L. (1956). Additional observations on the social perceptions of authoritarians and non-authoritarians. *Journal of Abnormal and Social Psychology, 52,* 92–95.

Scodel, A., & Mussen, P. (1953). Social perceptions of authoritarians and non-authoritarians. *Journal of Abnormal and Social Psychology, 48,* 181–184.

Scodel, A., Ratoosh, P., & Minas, J. S. (1959). Some personality correlates of decision making under conditions of risk. *Behavioral Science, 4,* 19–28.

Scott, W. A., Osgood, D. W., & Peterson, C. (1979). *Cognitive structure.* Washington, DC: Winston.

Secord, P. F., & Backman, C. W. (1964). *Social psychology.* New York: McGraw-Hill.

Seeman, D. C. (1982). Leader style and anxiety level: Their relation to autonomic response. *Small Group Behavior, 13,* 192–203.

Seeman, M. (1963). Alienation and social learning in a reformatory. *American Journal of Sociology, 69,* 270–284.

Seeman, M., & Evans, J. W. (1962). Alienation and learning in a hospital setting. *American Sociological Review, 27,* 772–783.

Seligman, M. E. P. (1975). *Helplessness: On depression, development, and death.* San Francisco: Freeman.

Sermat, V. (1968). Dominance–submissiveness and competition in a mixed-motive game. *British Journal of Social and Clinical Psychology, 7,* 35–44.

Seyfried, B. A., & Hendrick, C. (1973). Need similarity and complementarity in interpersonal attraction. *Sociometry, 36,* 207–220.

Shapiro, D. (1965). *Neurotic styles.* New York: Basic Books.

Shaw, M. E. (1959). Acceptance of authority, group structure, and the effectiveness of small groups. *Journal of Personality, 27,* 196–210.

Shaw, M. E. (1981). *Group dynamics* (3rd ed.). New York: McGraw-Hill.

Shaw, M. E., & Harkey, B. (1976). Some effects of congruency of member characteristics and group structure upon group behavior. *Journal of Personality and Social Psychology, 34,* 412–418.

Sheffield, J., & Byrne, D. (1967). Attitude similarity–dissimilarity, authoritarianism, and interpersonal attraction. *Journal of Social Psychology, 71,* 117–123.

Sherif, M. (1936). *The psychology of social norms.* New York: Harper & Row.

Shostrom, E. L. (1963). *Personal orientation inventory.* San Diego: Educational and Industrial Testing Service.

Shrauger, S., & Altrocchi, J. (1964). The personality of the perceiver as a factor in person perception. *Psychological Bulletin, 62,* 289–308.

Silverman, A. F., Pressman, M. E., & Bartel, H. W. (1973). Self-esteem and tactile communication. *Journal of Humanistic Psychology, 13,* 73–77.

Silverman, I. (1964). Differential effects of ego threat upon persuasibility for high and low self-esteem subjects. *Journal of Abnormal and Social Psychology, 69,* 567–572.

Silverman, I., Ford, L. H., Jr., & Morganti, J. B. (1966). Inter-related effects of social desirability, sex, self-esteem, and complexity of argument on persuasibility. *Journal of Personality, 34,* 555–568.

Simas, K., & McCarry, M. (1979). Impact of recruiter authoritarianism and applicant sex on evaluation and selection decisions in a recruitment interview analogue study. *Journal of Applied Psychology, 64,* 483–491.

Simons, H. W. (1966). Authoritarianism and social perceptiveness. *Journal of Social Psychology, 68,* 291–297.

Sims, H. P., Jr., & Szilagyi, A. D. (1976). Job characteristic relationships: Individual and structural moderators. *Organizational Behavior and Human Performance, 17,* 211–230.

Singer, J. E. (1964). The use of manipulative strategies: Machiavellianism and attractiveness. *Sociometry, 27,* 128–149.

Sistrunk, F., & McDavid, J. W. (1965). Achievement motivation, affiliation motivation, and task difficulty as determinants of social conformity. *Journal of Social Psychology, 66,* 41–50.

Skolnick, P., & Heslin, R. (1971). Approval dependence and reactions to bad arguments and low credibility sources. *Journal of Experimental Research in Personality, 5,* 199–207.

Slater, P. E. (1955). Role differentiation in small groups. *American Sociological Review, 20,* 300–310.

Slotnick, R. S., & Bleiberg, J. (1974). Authoritarianism, occupational sex typing and attitudes toward work. *Psychological Reports, 35,* 763–770.

Smelser, W. T. (1961). Dominance as a factor in achievement and perception in cooperative problem solving interactions. *Journal of Abnormal and Social Psychology, 62,* 535–542.

Smith, C. P. (1963). Achievement-related motives and goal setting under different conditions. *Journal of Personality, 31,* 124–140.

Smith, G. H. (1954). Personality scores and the personal distance effect. *Journal of Social Psychology, 39,* 57–62.

Smith, M. B. (1969). *Social psychology and human values.* Chicago: Aldine.

Smith, R. E. (1972). Social anxiety as a moderator variable in the attitude similarity-attraction relationship. *Journal of Experimental Research in Personality, 6,* 22–28.

Smith, R. E., & Campbell, A. L. (1973). Social anxiety and strain toward symmetry in dyadic attraction. *Journal of Personality and Social Psychology, 28,* 101–107.

Smith, R. E., & Flenning, F. (1971). Need for approval and susceptibility to unintended social influence. *Journal of Consulting and Clinical Psychology, 36,* 383–385.

Smith, R. J., & Cook, P. E. (1973). Leadership in dyadic groups as a function of dominance and incentives. *Sociometry, 36,* 561–568.

Smith, S., Murphy, D. B., & Wheeler, L. S. (1964). Relation of intelligence and authoritarianism to behavioral contagion and conformity. *Psychological Reports, 14,* 248.

Smith, W. P. (1967). Power structure and authoritarianism in the use of power in the triad. *Journal of Personality, 35,* 64–90.

Snyder, M., Tanke, E. D., & Berscheid, E. (1977). Social perception and interpersonal behavior: On the self-fulfilling nature of social stereotypes. *Journal of Personality and Social Psychology, 35,* 656–666.

Solar, D., & Mehrabian, A. (1973). Impressions based on contradictory information as a function of affiliative tendency and cognitive style. *Journal of Experimental Research in Personality, 6,* 339–346.

Sommer, R. (1969). *Personal space: The behavioral basis of design.* Englewood Cliffs, NJ: Prentice-Hall.

Sorem, A. M., & Ketola, K. (1977). Machiavellianism and evaluation of cognitively balanced/ unbalanced situations. *Psychological Reports, 40,* 663–665.

Sorrentino, R. M. (1973). An extension of theory of achievement motivation to the study of emergent leadership. *Journal of Personality and Social Psychology, 26,* 356–368.

Spence, D. D., & Ehrenberg, B. (1964). Effects of oral deprivation on responses to subliminal and supraliminal verbal food stimuli. *Journal of Abnormal and Social Psychology, 69,* 10–18.

Spielberger, C. D. (1972). *Anxiety: Current trends in theory and research.* New York: Academic Press.

Staub, E. (1974). Helping a distressed person: Social, personality, and stimulus determinants. In L. Berkowitz (Ed.), *Advances in experimental social psychology* (Vol. 7, pp. 293–341). New York: Academic Press.

Staub, E. (1978). *Positive social behavior and morality* (Vol. 1). New York: Academic Press.

Staub, E., & Sherk, L. (1970). Need for approval, children's sharing behavior, and reciprocity in sharing. *Child Development, 41,* 243–252.

Steers, R. M. (1975a). Effects of need for achievement on the job performance–job attitude relationship. *Journal of Applied Psychology, 60,* 678–682.

Steers, R. M. (1975b). Task-goal attributes, n achievement, and supervisory performance. *Organizational Behavior and Human Performance, 13,* 392–403.

Steers, R. M., & Braunstein, D. N. (1976). A behaviorally-based measure of manifest needs in work settings. *Journal of Vocational Behavior, 9,* 251–266.

Steers, R. M., & Porter, L. W. (1979). *Motivation and work behavior* (2nd ed.). New York: McGraw-Hill.

Steers, R. M., & Spencer, D. G. (1977). The role of achievement motivation in job design. *Journal of Applied Psychology, 62,* 472–479.

Stein, M. L., & Stone, G. L. (1978). Effects of conceptual level and structure on initial interview behavior. *Journal of Counseling Psychology, 25,* 96–102.

Steiner, I. D. (1954). Ethnocentrism, and tolerance of trait inconsistency. *Journal of Abnormal and Social Psychology, 49,* 349–354.

Steiner, I. D. (1972). *Group process and productivity.* New York: Academic Press.

Steiner, I. D., & Johnson, H. H. (1963). Authoritarianism and "tolerance for trait inconsistency." *Journal of Abnormal and Social Psychology, 67,* 388–391.

Steiner, I. D., & Rogers, E. D. (1963). Alternative responses to dissonance. *Journal of Abnormal and Social Psychology, 66,* 128–136.

Steiner, I. D., & Vannoy, J. S. (1966). Personality correlates of two types of conformity behavior. *Journal of Personality and Social Psychology, 4,* 307–315.

Stogdill, R. M. (1974). *Handbook of leadership.* New York: Free Press.

Stollak, G. E. (1978). *Until we are six: Toward the actualization of our children's human potential.* New York: Krieger.

Stratton, L. O., Tekippe, D. J., & Flick, G. L. (1973). Personal space and self-concept. *Sociometry, 36,* 424–429.

Strickland, B. R. (1965). The prediction of social action from a dimension of internal–external control. *Journal of Social Psychology, 66,* 353–358.

Strickland, B. R. (1977). Approval motivation. In T. Blass (Ed.), *Personality variables in social behavior* (pp. 315–356). Hillsdale, NJ: Lawrence Erlbaum Associates.

Strickland, B. R., & Crowne, D. P. (1962). Conformity under conditions of simulated group pressure as a function of the need for social approval. *The Journal of Social Psychology, 58,* 171–181.

Strickland, B. R., & Crowne, D. P. (1963). Need for approval and the premature termination of psychotherapy. *Journal of Consulting Psychology, 27,* 95–101.

Strodtbeck, F. L., & Hook, L. H. (1961). The social dimensions of a twelve man jury team. *Sociometry, 24,* 397–415.

Sundstrom, E., & Altman, I. (1976). Interpersonal relationships and personal space: Research review and theoretical model. *Human Ecology, 4,* 47–67.

Tagiuri, R. (1969). Person perception. In G. Lindzey, & E. Aronson (Eds.), *Handbook of social psychology* (2nd ed., Vol. 3, pp. 395–449). Reading, MA: Addison-Wesley.

Talley, W. M., & Vamos, P. (1972). An exploratory study of dogmatism and its relation to group response. *Canadian Counsellor, 6,* 278–282.

Tannenbaum, A. S., & Allport, F. H. (1956). Personality structure and group structure: An interpretative study of their relationship through an event-structure hypothesis. *Journal of Abnormal and Social Psychology, 53,* 272–280.

Taylor, D. A., & Oberlander, L. (1969). Person perception and self-disclosure: Motivational mechanisms in interpersonal processes. *Journal of Experimental Research in Personality, 4,* 14–28.

Taylor, R. N., & Dunnette, M. D. (1974). Influence of dogmatism, risk-taking propensity, and intelligence on decision-making strategies for a sample of industrial managers. *Journal of Applied Psychology, 59,* 420–423.

Tedeschi, J., Burrill, D., & Gahagan, J. (1969). Social desirability, manifest anxiety, and social power. *Journal of Social Psychology, 77,* 231–239.

Tedeschi, J. T., Hiester, D. S., & Gahagan, J. P. (1969). Trust and the prisoner's dilemma game. *Journal of Social Psychology, 79,* 43–50.

Terborg, J. R., Richardson, P., & Pritchard, R. D. (1980). Person–situation effects on the prediction of performance: An investigation of ability, self-esteem, and reward contingencies. *Journal of Applied Psychology, 65,* 574–583.

Terhune, K. W. (1968). Motives, situation, and interpersonal conflict within prisoner's dilemma. *Journal of Personality and Social Psychology,* Monograph Supplement, *8*(3, Pt. 2), 1–24.

Terhune, K. W. (1970). The effects of personality on cooperation and conflict. In P. Swingle (Ed.), *The structure of conflict* (pp. 193–234). New York: Academic Press.

Tharenou, P. (1979). Employee self-esteem: A review of the literature. *Journal of Vocational Behavior, 15,* 316–346.

Thaw, J., & Efran, J. S. (1967). The relationships of the need for approval to defensiveness and goal setting behavior: A partial replication. *Journal of Psychology, 65,* 41.

Thibaut, J. W., & Riecken, H. W. (1955). Authoritarianism, status, and the communication of aggression. *Human Relations, 8,* 95–120.

Touhey, J. C. (1976). Personality correlates of attraction in response to attitude similiarity. *European Journal of Social Psychology, 7,* 117–119.

Touhey, J. C., & Villamez, W. J. (1980). Ability attribution as a result of variable effort and achievement motivation. *Journal of Personality and Social Psychology, 38,* 211–216.

Trapp, E. P., & Kausler, D. H. (1958). Test anxiety level and goal-setting behavior. *Journal of Consulting Psychology, 22,* 31–34.

Tripathi, R. R., & Agrawal, A. (1978). The achievement motive in leaders and non leaders: A role analysis. *Psychologia, 21,* 97–103.

Tuckman, B. W. (1964). Personality structure, group composition, and group functioning. *Sociometry, 27,* 469–487.

Tuckman, B. W. (1965). Development sequence in small groups. *Psychological Bulletin, 63,* 384–399.

Tuckman, B. W. (1966). Interpersonal probing and revealing and systems of integrative complexity. *Journal of Personality and Social Psychology, 3,* 655–664.

Tuckman, B. W. (1967). Group composition and group performance of structured and unstructured tasks. *Journal of Experimental Social Psychology, 3,* 25–40.

Tuckman, B. W., & Orefice, D. S. (1973). Personality structure, instructional outcomes, and instructional preferences. *Interchange, 4,* 43–48.

Tuddenham, R. D. (1959). Correlates of yielding to a distorted group norm. *Journal of Personality Assessment, 27,* 272–284.

Turner, W. D. (1948). Altruism and its measurement in children. *Journal of Abnormal and Social Psychology, 43,* 502–516.

Uejio, C. K., & Wrightsman, L. S. (1967). Ethnic-group differences in the relationship of trusting attitudes to cooperative behavior. *Psychological Reports, 20,* 563–571.

Uleman, J. S. (1971). Dyadic influence in an "ESP Study" and TAT measures of the needs for influence and power. *Journal of Personality Assessment, 35,* 248–251.

Uleman, J. S. (1972). The need for influence: Development and validation of a measure and comparison with the need for power. *Genetic Psychology Monographs, 85,* 157–214.

Vacchiano, R. B. (1977). Dogmatism. In T. Blass (Ed.), *Personality variables in social behavior* (pp. 281–314). Hillsdale, NJ: Lawrence Erlbaum Associates.

Vacchiano, R. B., Strauss, P. S., & Hochman, L. (1969). The open and closed mind: A review of dogmatism. *Psychological Bulletin, 71,* 261–273.

Vanderplas, J. M., & Blake, R. R. (1949). Selective sensitization in auditory perception. *Journal of Personality, 18,* 252–266.

Vaughan, G. M. (1964). The trans-situational aspect of conforming behavior. *Journal of Personality, 32,* 335–354.

Vaughan, G. M., & White, K. D. (1966). Conformity and authoritarianism revisited. *Journal of Personality and Social Psychology, 3,* 363–366.

Veroff, J. (1957). Development and validation of a projective measure of power motivation. *Journal of Abnormal and Social Psychology, 54,* 1-8.

Vidulich, R. N., & Kaiman, I. P. (1961). The effects of information source status and dogmatism upon conformity behavior. *Journal of Abnormal and Social Psychology, 63,* 639-642.

Vroom, V. H. (1960). *Some personality determinants of the effects of participation.* Englewood Cliffs, NJ: Prentice-Hall.

Wagman, M. (1955). Attitude change and the authoritarian personality. *Journal of Psychology, 67,* 3-24.

Wagner, C., Manning, S., & Wheeler, L. (1971). Character structure and helping behavior. *Journal of Experimental Research in Personality, 5,* 37-42.

Walster, E., Aronson, E., Abrahams, D., & Rottmann, L. (1966). Importance of physical attractiveness in dating behavior. *Journal of Personality and Social Psychology, 4,* 508-516.

Walters, R. H., & Parke, R. D. (1964). Social motivation, dependency, and susceptibility to social influence. In L. Berkowitz (Ed.), *Advances in experimental social psychoology* (Vol. I, pp. 231-276). New York: Academic Press.

Wanous, J. P. (1974). Individual differences and reactions to job characteristics. *Journal of Applied Psychology, 59,* 616-622.

Ward, L., & Wilson, J. P. (1980). Motivation and moral judgement as determinants of behavioral acquiescence and moral reasoning. *The Journal of Social Psychology, 112,* 271-286.

Warr, P. B., & Knapper, C. (1968). *The perception of people and events.* New York: Wiley.

Watson, D. (1971). Reinforcement theory of personality and social systems: Dominance and position in a group power structure. *Journal of Personality and Social Psychology, 20,* 180-185.

Watts, B. L., Messé, L. A., & Vallacher, R. R. (1982). Toward understanding sex differences in pay allocation: Agency, communion, and reward distribution behavior. *Sex Roles, 8,* 1175-1187.

Weed, S. E., & Mitchell, T. R. (1974). *Leadership style, subordinate personality and task type as predictors of performance and satisfaction with supervision.* (Tech. Rep. No. 74-60). University of Washington, Seattle.

Weiner, B., & Kukla, A. (1970). An attributional analysis of achievement motivation. *Journal of Personality and Social Psychology, 15,* 1-20.

Weiner, H., & McGinnies, E. (1961). Authoritarianism, conformity, and confidence in a perceptual judgement situation. *Journal of Social Psychology, 55,* 77-84.

Weiss, H. M., & Knight, P. A. (1980). The utility of humility: Self-esteem, information search and problem-solving efficiency. *Organizational Behavior and Human Performance, 25,* 216-223.

Wells, W. D., Weinert, G., & Rubel, M. (1956). Conformity pressure and authoritarian's personality. *Journal of Psychology, 42,* 133-136.

Wheeless, L. R., & Grotz, J. (1977). The measurement of trust and its relationship to self-disclosure. *Human Communication Research, 3,* 250-257.

White, B. J., & Alter, R. D. (1965). Dogmatism, authoritarianism and contrast effects in judgment. *Perceptual and Motor Skills, 20,* 99-101.

White, B. J., Alter, R. J., & Rardin, M. (1965). Authoritarianism, dogmatism, and usage of conceptual categories. *Journal of Personality and Social Psychology, 2,* 293-295.

White, B. L., & Watts, J. C. (1973). *Experience and environment: Major influences on the development of the young child.* Englewood Cliffs, NJ: Prentice-Hall.

White, R. W. (1959). Motivation reconsidered: The concept of competence. *Psychological Review, 66,* 297-333.

White, R. W. (1963). Ego and reality in psychoanalytic theory. *Psychological Issues, 3,* 1-210.

Whiteley, R. H., & Watts, W. A. (1969). Information cost, decision consequence, and selected personality variables as factors in predecision information seeking. *Journal of Personality, 37,* 325-341.

Wiener, B. (1978). Achievement strivings. In H. London & J. E. Exner, Jr. (Eds.), *Dimensions of personality* (pp. 1-57). New York: Wiley.

Wiggins, J. S. (1973). *Personality and prediction: Principles of personality assessment.* Reading, MA: Addison-Wesley.

Wiggins, J. S. (1980). Circumplex models of interpersonal behavior. In L. Wheeler (Ed.), *Review of personality and social psychology* (Vol. 1, pp. 265-294). Beverly Hills, CA: Sage Publications.

Wilkens, E. J., & deCharms, R. (1962). Authoritarianism and response to power areas. *Journal of Personality, 30,* 439-457.

Williams, C. D., Steele, M. W., & Tedeschi, J. T. (1969). Motivational correlates of strategy choices in the prisoner's dilemma game. *Journal of Social Psychology, 79,* 211-217.

Williams, E. (1974). An analysis of gaze in schizophrenics. *British Journal of Social and Clinical Psychology, 13,* 1-8.

Williams, J. L. (1971). Personal space and its relation to extraversion-introversion, *Canadian Journal of Behavioral Science, 3,* 156-160.

Williams, R. M. (1968). Values. In E. P. Sills (Ed.), *International encyclopedia of the social sciences.* New York: Crowell, Collier, & Macmillan.

Wilson, J. P. (1976). Motivation, modeling and altruism: A person × situation analysis. *Journal of Personality and Social Psychology, 6,* 1078-1086.

Wilson, J. P., & Aronoff, J. *Clustering among peripheral personality variables.* Unpublished manuscript.

Wilson, J. P., Aronoff, J., & Messé, L. A. (1975). Social structure, member motivation and group productivity. *Journal of Personality and Social Psychology, 32,* 1094-1098.

Wilson, J. P., & Petruska, R. (1984). Motivation, model attributes and prosocial behavior. *Personality and Social Psychology, 46,* 458-468.

Wilson, W., & Robinson, C. (1968). Selective intergroup bias in both authoritarians and non-authoritarians after playing a modified prisoner's dilemma game. *Perceptual and Motor Skills, 27,* 1051-1058.

Winch, R. F. (1955). The theory of complementary needs in mate selection: Final results on the test of the general hypothesis. *American Sociological Review, 20,* 552-554.

Winch, R. F. (1958). *Mate-selection.* New York: Harper & Row.

Wine, J. (1971). Test anxiety and direction of attention. *Psychological Bulletin, 76,* 92-105.

Wine, J. D. (1980). Cognitive-attention theory of test anxiety. In I. G. Sarason (Ed.), *Test anxiety: Theory, research and applications* (pp. 349-385). Hillsdale, NJ: Lawrence Erlbaum Associates.

Winter, D. G. (1973). *The power motive.* New York: Free Press.

Wispé, L. G. (1954). Psychological need, verbal frequency, and word association. *Journal of Abnormal and Social Psychology, 49,* 229-234.

Wispé, L. G., & Lloyd, K. E. (1955). Some situational and psychological determinants of the desire for structured interpersonal relations. *Journal of Abnormal and Social Psychology, 51,* 57-60.

Wolk, S., & Bloom, D. (1978). The interactive effects of locus of control and situational stress upon performance accuracy and time. *Journal of Personality, 46,* 279-298.

Wolk, S., & DuCette, J. (1974). Intentional performance and incidental learning as a function of personality and task directions. *Journal of Personality and Social Psychology, 29,* 90-101.

Wood, D., Pilisuk, M., & Uren, E. (1973). The martyr's personality: An experimental investigation. *Journal of Personality and Social Psychology, 25,* 117-186.

Worthy, M., Gary, A. L., & Kahn, G. M. (1969). Self-disclosure as an exchange process. *Journal of Personality and Social Psychology, 13,* 59-63.

Wright, J. M., & Harvey, O. J. (1965). Attitude change as a function of authoritarianism and punitiveness. *Journal of Personal and Social Psychology, 1,* 177-181.

Wrightsman, L. S., Jr. (1966). Personality and attitudinal correlates of trusting and trusthworthy behaviors in a two-person game. *Journal of Personality and Social Psychology, 4,* 328–332.

Wyer, R. S., & Carlson, D. E. (1979). *Social cognition, inference, and attribution.* Hillsdale, NJ: Lawrence Erlbaum Associates.

Yakimovich, D., & Saltz, E. (1971). Helping behavior: The cry for help. *Psychonomic Science, 23,* 427–428.

Yarrow, L. J., Rubenstein, J. L., & Pedersen, F. A. (1975). *Infant and environment: Early cognitive and motivational development.* Washington, DC: Hemisphere.

Zagona, S. V., & Zurcher, L. A., Jr. (1964). Participation, interaction and role behavior in groups selected from the extremes of the open–closed cognitive continuum. *Journal of Psychology, 58,* 255–264.

Zaidel, S. F., & Mehrabian, A. (1969). The ability to communicate and infer positive and negative attitudes facially and vocally. *Journal of Experimental Research in Personality, 3,* 233–241.

Zajonc, R. B., & Wahi, N. K. (1961). Conformity and need-achievement under cross-cultural norm conflict. *Human Relations, 14,* 241–250.

Zander, A. (1971). *Motives and goals in groups.* New York: Academic Press.

Zander, A., & Wulff, D. (1966). Members' anxiety and competence: Determinants of a group's aspirations. *Journal of Personality, 34,* 55–70.

Zeleny, L. D. (1939). Characteristics of group leaders. *Sociology and Social Research, 24,* 140–149.

Zellner, M. (1970). Self-esteem, reception, and influenceability. *Journal of Personality and Social Psychology, 15,* 87–93.

Author Index

A

Abdel-Halim, A. A., 319, 327, 343
Abelson, R. P., 346, 364
Abrahams, D., 182, 373
Abramovitz, C. V., 326, 343
Abramovitz, S. I., 326, 343
Adler, A., 52, 58-9, 343
Adler, G., 358
Adorno, T. W., 16, 52, 54, 63, 136, 163, 227, 239, 343
Agrawal, A., 215, 373
Ainsworth, L. H., 168, 343
Ainsworth, M. D., 57, 343
Akamatsu, T. J., 238, 343
Aldag, R. J., 319, 347
Allen, A., 340, 344
Allinsmith, W., 323-4, 355
Allport, F. H., 296, 330, 372
Allport, G. W., 15, 58-9, 132, 343
Altman, I., 181, 200, 297, 343, 372
Altrocchi, J., 128, 141, 143, 288, 343, 366, 370
Amidjaja, I. R., 291, 343
Anderson, B. J., 214, 218, 363
Andrews, J. D. W., 214, 343, 367
Andrews, M., 324, 367
Appley, M. H., 26, 29, 135, 228, 343, 349
Applezweig, M. H., 229, 364
Arenberg, D., 135, 360
Argyle, M., 200, 203, 344

Aries, E. J., 214, 343
Arlin, M., 327, 344
Armenakis, A. A., 327, 365
Armilla, J., 214-5, 344
Armlin, N. J., 168, 367
Aronoff, J., 12, 16, 49, 143, 145, 147-8, 182, 190, 197, 214, 217, 263-5, 291, 298-9, 301, 329-32, 344-5, 351, 362-4, 366, 375
Aronson, E., 182, 199, 346, 354, 356, 358, 364, 372, 374
Asch, S. E., 224, 226-7, 231, 344
Ashour, A. S., 297, 344
Assor, A., 143, 145, 148, 182, 190, 197, 276, 291, 344
Atkinson, J. W., 48, 130, 134, 139, 140, 171-2, 176, 218-9, 259, 320, 344, 362, 365, 368

B

Back, K. W., 229-30, 344
Backman, C. W., 181, 186, 370
Baker, J. M., 288, 348
Baldwin, M. V., 134, 347
Bales, R. F., 52-54, 70, 76-7, 81, 185, 208-9, 214-7, 220, 259, 308, 328, 344-6, 355
Barclay, A. M., 351, 362
Barling, J., 261, 352
Barnett, M. A., 256, 344
Barrett, J., 202, 353
Bartel, H. W., 204, 370

Bass, B. M., 214–5, 222, 240, 345, 353
Bastian, J. R., 176, 344
Batson, C. D., 256, 362
Battistich, V. A., 77, 147–8, 197, 345
Bauer, R. A., 231, 236, 354
Baxter, J. C., 201, 353
Beam, D. C., 202, 204, 353
Beckworth, J., 175, 345
Bedeian, A. G., 327, 365
Beer, M., 214–5, 343, 345
Bell, S. M., 343
Beloff, H., 228, 345
Belohular, J., 177, 360
Bem, D. J., 7, 194, 225, 340, 345, 356
Ben David, A., 258, 369
Benjamin, L. S., 77, 242, 345
Bennet, R. P., 290, 345
Bennis, W. G., 208, 345
Benson, P. L., 253, 345
Berg, K. S., 167, 251, 345
Berger, S. E., 288, 345
Berkowitz, L., 232, 343, 348, 369, 371, 374
Berkowitz, N. H., 282, 343
Berscheid, E., 144, 371
Bettinghouse, E., 167, 345
Beverly, G. D., 233, 355
Bibring, E., 24, 345
Bieri, J., 163, 233, 345–6
Bigoness, W., 291, 346
Biondo, J., 235, 346
Bixenstine, V. E., 282, 346
Blackman, S., 151, 155, 158–9, 166–9, 354
Blake, B. F., 233, 368
Blake, R. R., 134, 214, 230, 346, 356, 373
Blasi, A., 257, 346
Blass, T., 349, 372–3
Bleiberg, J., 138, 371
Blick, K. A., 282, 346
Block, J., 57, 159, 161, 346
Block, J., 159, 346
Bloom, D., 316, 375
Bloomfield, D. R., 282, 346
Blumberg, N., 198, 366
Blumstein, P. W., 283, 346
Bogart, K., 284, 346
Bogart, P., 214, 218, 363
Bohannon, W. E., 256, 364
Borg, W. R., 214–5, 346
Borgatta, E. F., 15, 76–9, 81, 209, 217, 220, 242–4, 287, 299, 301, 346, 349, 363
Boyatzis, R. E., 214, 259, 261–2, 276, 359, 362
Boylin, E. R., 175, 287, 351

Braginsky, D. D., 283, 346
Brannigan, G. G., 158, 238, 347
Brannon, C., 204, 284, 352
Braunstein, D. N., 321, 372
Bray, D. W., 214, 354
Bray, R. M., 214, 347
Breen, L. J., 162, 367
Brice, D. J., 177, 347
Bridges, C., 291, 367
Brief, A. P., 320, 347
Brody, N., 176, 347
Broughton, A., 203, 351
Brown, B. R., 272–4, 218, 284, 290, 347, 368
Brown, M. E., 260, 369
Brown, R. W., 168, 347
Brownell, P., 335, 347
Brozek, J., 134, 347
Brundage, L. E., 195, 287, 347
Bruner, J. S., 128, 182, 343, 367
Bryant, B. K., 138, 347
Buckhout, R., 214–5, 234, 345, 347
Buckley, N., 256, 347
Buhrenne, D., 287, 347
Bunker, C. S., 215, 357
Burch, S., 237, 347
Burdick, H. A., 235, 347
Burgoon, M., 237, 347
Burke, P. J., 137, 347
Burke, R. J., 261, 347
Burke, W. W., 215, 347
Burnes, A. J., 235, 347
Burnstein, E., 175, 347
Burrill, D., 288, 372
Butler, D. C., 234, 364
Byrne, D., 167, 179–80, 182–3, 188, 190–4, 197–9, 200–1, 251, 347–9, 364, 366, 370

C

Caldwell, D. F., 327, 365
Cameron, B., 177, 348
Campbell, A., 203, 348
Campbell, A. L., 192, 200, 371
Canning, R. R., 228, 348
Cantor, N., 17, 50, 348
Capage, J., 291, 348
Carbonari, J. P., 343
Carducci, B. J., 201, 348
Carlson, D. E., 103, 133, 376
Carlson, E. R., 140, 348
Carp, A., 214, 346
Carroll, S. J., 321, 348

Carter, L. F., 6, 214, 241–2, 252, 297, 302, 348, 356
Cartwright, D., 6, 70, 79, 83, 85–6, 114, 117, 172, 174, 176–7, 243, 348, 353
Cash, T. F., 195, 287, 347
Catron, D. W., 29, 366
Cattell, R. B., 15, 49, 52–4, 179, 208, 214–5, 249, 262, 348–9
Cavellin, B. A., 201, 349
Centers, R., 44, 179, 181, 184, 233–4, 349
Cerreto, M. C., 198, 358
Chadwick, I., 140, 353
Chalmers, D. K., 231, 368
Chambers, N., 282, 346
Chamblin, M. H., 252, 261, 353
Chaney, M. V., 291, 349
Chein, I., 135, 361
Chelune, G. J., 274, 349
Cherry, F., 167, 348
Chowdhry, K., 215, 349
Christie, R., 54, 63, 158, 163, 237, 279, 283, 349, 354
Clair, D. J., 214, 345
Clark, R. A., 48, 130, 171, 218, 231, 320, 362
Cleveland, S. E., 214–5, 349
Clausen, G. T., 258, 261, 369
Clore, C. L., 169, 191, 193, 354, 367
Clouser, R., 235, 356
Cofer, C., 26, 29, 135, 349
Coffey, H. S., 77, 353
Cohen, P. A., 177, 349
Cohen, R. J., 239, 349
Cole, J. R., 198, 360
Comfort, J. C., 252, 365
Conn, L., 288, 349
Connolly, K. J., 343
Cook, M., 203, 359
Cook, P., 158, 163, 349
Cook, P. E., 214, 216, 371
Cooper, S., 283, 349
Coopersmith, H. S., 57, 349
Corson, R. L., 204, 357
Costanzo, P. R., 228, 349
Cottrell, L. S., 242, 346
Couch, A. S., 81, 220, 241, 252, 297, 302, 346, 356
Cox, L., 226, 231, 350
Cozby, P. C., 202, 349
Craik, F. I. M., 166–7, 349
Crano, W. D., 169, 226, 299, 349
Cravens, R., 287–8, 349
Crockett, W. H., 137, 349

Cronbach, L. J., 130, 132, 318–9, 324, 350, 353
Crowne, D. P., 64, 229, 287–8, 349–50, 372
Crowther, B., 77–8, 209, 299, 346
Crutchfield, R. S., 135, 224, 226, 228, 230, 350, 367
Cummings, L. L., 291, 355

D

Dabbs, J. M., 236, 350
Daly, S., 203, 350
Darley, J. M., 70, 214, 244–5, 250, 258, 261, 360, 362
Daugherty, B. N., 142–3, 182, 358
Davids, A., 134, 350
Davis, H. P., 250, 302, 351
Davis, K. E., 181, 186, 229–30, 344, 359
Davis, M. H., 256, 350
Davis, W. L., 138, 162, 170, 350, 366
Dean, J., 200, 344
DeBolt, J. W., 214, 350
deCharms, R., 50, 138, 230, 350, 375
Deci, E. L., 93, 350
DeJulio, S., 201, 350
Delenay, J. G., 321, 369
Derlega, V. J., 195, 287, 347
Deutsch, M., 282, 292, 350
Diamond, S. G., 202, 363
Dies, R. R., 288, 350
Dietch, J. T., 283, 350
Dion, K. K., 195, 350
Dion, K. L., 195, 350
Dittes, J., 161, 350
DiVesta, F. J., 226, 231, 350
Doherty, W. J., 291, 350
Doll, P. A., 214, 345
Domelsmith, D. E., 283, 345, 350
Domino, G., 324, 350
Doob, A. N., 234, 364
Dosey, M. A., 201, 350
Doster, J. A., 287, 362
Douglas, J., 282, 346
Dovidio, J. F., 204, 351
Dowaliby, F. J., 324, 350
Driver, M. J., 163, 369
Druckman, D., 282, 350
DuCette, J., 163, 375
Duchnowski, A. J., 158, 238, 347
Duck, S. W., 186, 351
Duffy, K., 202, 350
Duke, M. P., 201, 351

Duncan, S., Jr., 200, 351
Dunnette, M. D., 159-60, 372
Dustin, D. S., 250, 302, 351
Dyson, J. W., 214, 217, 369

E

Eagly, A. H., 236, 351
Earl, R. W., 176, 344
Eber, H. W., 333, 363
Edwards, A. L., 143, 351
Efran, J. S., 175, 203, 287, 351, 373
Ehrenberg, B., 135, 371
Ehrlich, H. J., 158, 167, 233, 351
Eisenberg-Berg, N., 256, 351
Ellison, C. W., 292, 351
Ellyson, S. L., 204, 351
Elms, A. C., 224, 239, 351
Endler, N. S., 3, 6, 65, 229, 351, 361
England, G., 297, 344
Entin, E. E., 321, 351
Epstein, G. F., 237, 351
Epstein, N., 256, 363
Epstein, R., 250-1, 302, 351
Epstein, S., 135, 314, 351-2
Erdelyi, M. H., 130, 145, 352
Eriksen, B. A., 130, 352
Eriksen, C. W., 130, 134, 352, 360
Erikson, E., 19, 21, 26-28, 32-37, 38, 44, 50, 52-54, 56-61, 63, 352
Ervin, C. R., 200, 348
Ettinger, R. F., 194, 287, 352, 360
Evans, F. J., 352
Evans, G. W., 201, 352
Evans, J. W., 170, 370
Evans, R. G., 171, 352
Exline, R. V., 203-4, 284, 352
Exner, J. E., Jr., 354, 360, 375

F

Falbo, T., 283, 352
Fantasia, S. C., 292, 361
Farrow, D. L., 352
Faytinger, S., 335, 352
Feather, N. T., 171, 344
Feldman, K. A., 260, 370
Fenichel, O., 130, 352
Feshbach, S., 232, 357
Festinger, L., 19, 31, 179, 352
Fincham, F., 261, 352
Fineman, S., 335, 352

Firestone, I. J., 292, 351
Fisher, S., 214, 349
Fishman, C., 288, 352
Fishman, D. B., 259, 352
Fiske, D. W., 26, 128, 134, 352, 355
Fitzsimmons, S. J., 215, 352
Fleitas, D. W., 214, 217, 369
Flenning, F., 234, 371
Flick, G. L., 202, 372
Fodor, E. M., 302, 352
Foley, L. A., 252, 261, 353
Ford, L. H., Jr., 234, 370
Fordham, M., 358
Form, W. H., 262, 353
Fonda, C. P., 134, 360
Foulkes, D., 169, 352
Foulkes, S. H., 169, 353
Frankel, A. S., 202, 353
Frankel, V., 26, 353
Frede, M. C., 201, 353
Freedman, M. B., 77, 353
Freedman, M. L., 137, 370
French, E. G., 140, 353
French, J. R. P., 85, 353
Frenkel-Brunswik, E., 16, 52, 54, 136, 163, 165, 167, 227, 343, 353
Freud, S., 19, 23-4, 27, 29, 52, 54, 58-9
Friedell, M. F., 250, 282, 352
Friedlander, F., 308, 353
Friedrichs, R. W., 250, 353
Fromm, E., 19, 24-6, 52-4, 58-9, 353
Fromme, D. K., 202, 204, 353
Fry, P. S., 138, 324, 353
Frye, R. L., 240, 296, 324, 353

G

Gabennesch, H., 137, 353
Gage, N. L., 132, 353
Gagné, E. E., 171, 353
Gahagan, J. P., 282, 288, 363, 372
Gallo, P., 282, 362
Garber, J., 315, 353
Garcia, L. T., 252, 353
Gardner, R. W., 150, 353
Gary, A. L., 282, 375
Gautney, D. B., 201, 353
Gavin, J. F., 321, 354
Gebel, A. S., 214-5, 222, 345
Geen, R. G., 158, 354
Geis, F. L., 54, 63, 237, 260, 271, 279, 281, 283-5, 349, 354

Gergen, K. J., 231, 236, 249, 263, 354
Gergen, M. M., 249, 354
Ghisselli, E. E., 214, 334
Gibb, C. A., 212, 214-5, 222, 354
Gifford, R., 202, 354
Gilmore, R., 215, 362
Gold, C., 214, 344
Gold, J. A., 233, 354
Goldberg, B., 130, 352
Goldman, K., 176-7, 354
Goldman, M., 196, 199, 356
Goldstein, J. W., 192, 194-5, 354, 356
Goldstein, K. M., 151, 155, 158-9, 166-7, 354
Goodale, J. G., 319, 367
Goodstadt, B. E., 302, 354
Gordon, A., 228, 236, 365
Gordon, C. M., 135, 354
Gordon, L. V., 214, 354
Gore, P. M., 261, 354
Gorfein, D., 228, 354
Gormly, A. V., 157, 169, 192-3, 195, 199, 354, 357
Gormly, J., 199, 357
Goslin, D. A., 359
Gough, H. G., 49, 52-4, 141, 143, 337, 354
Graham, E., 234, 361
Graham, J. C., 203, 368
Granberg, D., 137, 354
Grant, D. L., 214, 354
Gray, G., 203, 352
Green, L., 51, 265, 354, 356
Greenbaum, C. W., 234, 236, 355
Greene, C. N., 327
Greenhaus, J. H., 327, 359
Greenstein, T. N., 234, 362
Greer, F. L., 215, 362
Griffitt, W. B., 183, 198, 252, 262-3, 353, 355, 366
Grimes, J. W., 323-4, 355
Gronnerud, P., 169, 360
Gross, N., 214, 362
Grotz, J., 281, 374
Guetzkow, H., 134, 347-8
Guilford, J. P., 15, 214, 355
Gumpert, P., 204, 284, 352

H

Hackman, J. R., 6, 307-8, 318-19, 355, 366-7
Haefner, D., 241, 252, 297, 302, 356
Haigh, G. V., 128, 134, 355
Hall, D. T., 319, 367

Hall, H. E., 215, 345, 367
Hammer, W. C., 291, 355
Hammes, J. A., 139, 202, 355
Hamilton, R. J., 214, 355
Hanawalt, N. G., 214-5, 355, 367
Hancock, J. G., 175, 355
Hardy, K. R., 228-30, 355
Hare, A. P., 214-5, 355
Harkey, B., 336, 370
Harlow, D. N., 214, 364
Harmatz, M. G., 238, 369
Harnett, D. L., 291, 355
Harrell, T. W., 214, 355
Harrell, W. A., 260, 283, 355
Harrison, A. A., 282, 362
Hartnagel, T., 260, 283, 355
Harvey, O. J., 49, 163, 233, 239, 325, 345, 355-6, 375
Hastorf, A., 144, 359
Hawkins, W. C., 214-5, 222, 345
Haymes, M., 51, 265, 354, 356
Haythorn, W., 241-2, 252, 292, 297, 302, 348, 356
Hearn, C. B., 170, 356
Hechler, P. D., 321, 356
Heckel, R. V., 214, 356
Heckhausen, H., 171-2, 219, 356
Heingartner, A., 260, 369
Hekmat, H., 292, 369
Helm, B., 282, 369
Helmreich, R., 199, 356
Helson, H., 230, 356
Hendrick, C., 197, 199, 356, 370
Heslin, R., 233-4, 368, 371
Hewitt, J., 196, 199, 239, 356, 363
Hicks, J. A., 215, 356
Hiers, J. M., 214, 356
Hiester, D. S., 282, 372
Higgs, W. J., 278, 356
Hill, J. W., 214, 364
Hillix, W. A., 177, 349
Hines, M., 183, 356
Hirsch, T., 291, 367
Hjelle, L. A., 235, 302, 354, 356
Hochman, L., 158, 373
Hoffman, M. L., 228, 356
Hogan, J. C., 214, 356
Hogan, R., 4, 51, 53, 207, 255-6, 356
Hollander, E. P., 215, 356
Holstein, C. M., 194-5, 356
Holtzman, W. H., 215, 356
Hook, L. H., 67, 372

Horn, J., 256, 362
Hornaday, J. A., 215, 357
Horne, W. C., 231, 368
Horowitz, J., 249, 262, 348
Horowitz, M., 234, 349
Horowtiz, M. W., 214-5, 345
Hourany, L., 176, 357
House, W. C., 176, 357
Houston, B. K., 201, 348
Hovland, C. I., 224-5, 231, 236, 357, 361
Howard, J. A., 256, 258, 345, 369
Howard, R. B., 201, 352
Hoy, W. K., 302, 365
Hrycenko, I., 335, 357
Hunt, D. E., 48, 163, 357, 325-6, 356-7
Hunt, L. L., 137, 353
Hunter, E. C., 214, 357
Huston, T. L., 178-9, 357

I

Ingham, R., 203, 344
Ivancevich, J. M., 319, 357
Iverson, M. A., 175, 345
Izard, C. E., 230, 357
Izzett, R. R., 199, 233, 357

J

Jackson, C., 326, 343
Jackson, D. N., 150, 176, 353, 357
Jacobson, L. I., 288, 345
Jacoby, J., 137, 357
Jahoda, M., 357
Janis, I. L. 224-5, 231-2, 236, 314, 357, 361
Jenks, R. J., 235, 357
Jessor, R., 251, 368
Johnson, C. D., 157, 192, 194, 199, 357
Johnson, D. A., 334, 354
Johnson, D. W., 292, 366
Johnson, H. H., 169, 228, 233, 357-8, 372
Johnson, J. J., 198, 358
Jones, E. E., 137-8, 142-3, 182, 358
Jones, M. B., 160, 358
Jones, M. R., 359, 362
Jones, R. E., 288, 358
Jones, S. C., 158, 199, 240, 358
Jones, W. H., 283, 358
Jordan, A. M., 214, 357
Jourard, S. M., 274, 292, 358
Joure, S., 296, 324, 353
Jung, C. G., 18-9, 26, 28-33, 58-9, 358

K

Kaess, W. A., 214-5, 358
Kagan, J., 39-40, 358
Kahn, G. M., 281, 307
Kahn, R. L., 307, 358, 375
Kaiman, I. E., 167, 228, 374
Kalish, R. A., 214, 359
Kanfer, F. H., 175, 358
Karabenick, S. A., 321, 358
Kates, S. L., 138, 358
Katz, D., 307, 358
Kausler, D. H., 175, 373
Kelley, H. H., 70, 133, 138, 144, 179, 194, 282, 358
Kellogg, R. W., 288, 364
Kelly, G. A., 19, 31, 163, 358
Kelman, H. C., 231, 359
Kendon, A., 203, 359
Kenis, I., 325, 359
Kerckhoff, A. C., 181, 186, 359
Kerr-Inkson, J. H., 321, 359
Ketola, K., 170, 371
Kidd, A. H., 168, 359
Kidd, R. M., 168, 359
Kiessling, R. J., 214, 359
Kihlstrom, J., 17, 50, 348, 352
Kilmann, P. R., 290, 326, 335, 359
Kimble, C. E., 198, 360
Kimmons, G., 327, 359
Kinder, B. N., 326, 359
Kipnis, D., 302, 334, 359
Kleck, R. E., 144, 169, 359
Klein, G. S., 24, 130-1, 150, 155, 359
Klein, M. H., 233-4, 359
Knapper, C., 127-8, 374
Knight, P. A., 171, 374
Knurek, D. A., 199, 358
Kogan, N., 173, 175, 177, 359
Kohlberg, L., 51, 56, 58-9, 61, 240, 257, 359
Kolb, D. A., 259, 261-2, 276, 359
Kopfstein, D., 287, 359
Kopfstein, J. H., 287, 359
Korman, A. K., 177, 321, 359-60
Korte, J. R., 198, 360
Krebs, A. M., 231, 360
Krebs, D. L., 250, 360
Kristofferson, A. B., 140, 365
Krupat, E., 228, 230, 364
Ksionsky, S., 192, 199, 259, 363
Kuhlman, D. M., 282, 292, 360

Kuhlman, E., 296, 360
Kukla, A., 176, 320, 360, 374

L

LaFolette, W., 177, 360
Lamb, D. H., 315, 360
Lambert, W. W., 346, 349, 363
Lamberth, J., 200, 348
Lamm, H., 173, 175, 177, 360, 365
Lancaster, L., 239, 360
Lane, W. P., 302, 359-60
Langham, P., 241, 252, 297, 302, 356
Lanzetta, J. T., 242, 348
Larsen, K. S., 239, 287-8, 360
Larsen, K. S., 239, 360
Latané, B., 70, 244-5, 250, 258, 261, 360
Lawler, E. E., III., 307, 319, 355, 367
Lazarus, R. S., 130, 134-5, 314, 352, 360
Leary, T., 77-9, 141, 197, 208-9, 353, 360
Lecky, P., 19, 31, 360
LeCompte, W. F., 131, 200, 360
Lee, D., 158, 167, 233, 351
LeFan, J., 199, 356
Lefcourt, H. M., 50, 158, 167, 169, 170-2,
    176, 204, 292, 316, 360-1
Lehmann, S., 232, 236, 361
Leonard, R. L., 199, 361
Lesh, W., 239, 360
Leventhal, H., 236, 361
Levin, P., 288, 343
Levine, R., 135, 361
Levinger, G., 181, 361
Levinson, D. J., 16, 52, 54, 136, 163, 227, 343
Levitt, C. A., 282, 243
Levy, S., 214-5, 345
Lewis, L., 171, 361
Libby, W. L., Jr., 203, 361
Liberman, A. M., 140, 362
Liebhart, E. H., 255, 361
Lindskvold, S., 291, 348
Lindzey, G., 342, 349, 353, 367
Linton, H. B., 229, 234, 361
Lipetz, M. E., 137, 250, 302, 361
Liska, A. E., 214, 350
Littig, L. W., 176, 361
Litwin, G. H., 176, 344
Liverant, S., 176-7, 361
Lloyd, K. E., 296, 375
Lockhard, R. S., 166-7, 349
Lombardi, D., 237, 347

Lombardo, J. P., 292, 361
London, H., 354, 360, 375
Long, B. H., 160, 361
Lott, A. J., 228, 362
Love, W., 214, 350
Lowell, E. L., 48, 130, 171, 218, 320, 362
Luchins, A. S., 167, 361
Lundy, R. M., 232, 345
Lutzker, D. R., 282, 361

M

Mabel, S., 170, 361
MacDonald, A. P., Jr., 235, 346
Maddi, S. R., 10, 11, 26, 33, 55, 352, 361
Magnusson, D., 6, 65, 351, 361
Maile, C. A., 236, 361
Malof, M., 228, 362
Mandler, G., 314, 362
Mangan, G. L., 227, 362
Mann, J. H., 242, 346
Marcuse, F. L., 215, 352
Marks, E. L., 255, 362
Marlowe, D., 64, 229, 234, 278, 288, 350, 362,
    364
Marquis, P. C., 215, 362
Marshello, A., 282, 292, 360
Marston, A. R., 175, 358
Martin, A. J., 234, 287, 257, 359
Martin, W. E., 214, 362
Masling, J. M., 215, 362
Maslow, A. H., 19-27, 33, 36-8, 43-4, 48, 50,
    56-9, 61, 132, 308, 319, 362
Mathews, K. A., 256, 345, 362
Matloff, J. L., 287, 359
McArthur, L. Z., 133, 362
McCarry, M., 138, 370
McClelland, D. C., 19, 31, 130, 134, 140,
    171-2, 176-7, 214, 218-9, 231, 259, 320,
    362, 363
McClintock, C. G., 282, 363
McCurdy, H. G., 333, 363
McDavid, J. W., 229-31, 363, 370
McDonald, P., 169, 360
McGaffey, T. N., 297, 363
McGehee, C. R., 214-5, 222, 345
McGhee, P. E., 229, 363
McGinnies, E., 128, 182, 228, 297, 343, 367,
    374
McGovern, L. P., 249, 363
McGrath, J. E., 6, 278, 356, 363

McGregor, D., 318, 363
McGuire, W. J., 11, 132, 150, 224-8, 231-4, 236, 346, 363-4
McKeown, C. D., 282, 364
McLaughlin, B., 260, 283, 363
McLaughlin, D., 239, 363
McMahon, J. T., 319, 357
Meadows, I. S. G., 334-5, 363
Medalia, S. G., 296, 363
Medland, F. F., 354
Megargee, E. I., 214, 218, 363
Mehrabian, A., 140, 157, 183, 192, 195, 199, 200, 202, 256, 259, 356, 363, 371, 376
Meidlinger, T., 138, 349
Meierhofer, B., 296, 324, 353
Meirowitz, B., 242, 348
Meisels, M., 201, 350
Melcher, B. H., 288, 358
Messé, L. A., 143, 145, 182, 190, 214, 217, 264-5, 291, 299, 301, 330-2, 344, 363-4, 366, 374-5
Messick, S., 150, 155, 353, 363-4
Meter, K., 249, 354
Meunier, C., 227, 364
Meyers, D., 173, 177, 365
Meyers, J. L., 348, 360
Michelini, R., 264, 364
Midlarsky, E., 253, 261, 363
Midlarsky, M., 253, 261, 363
Milgram, S., 224, 239, 351
Milham, J., 345, 364
Miller, G. R., 167, 233, 237, 345, 347, 364
Miller, N., 233-4, 364
Millman, S., 232, 364
Millon, T., 159, 364
Mills, C. J., 256, 364
Minas, J. S., 176, 370
Miner, J. B., 214, 364
Minton, H. L., 335, 357
Mirels, H., 287, 347
Mischel, T., 359
Mischel, W., 7, 16-7, 225, 233, 364
Mitchell, H. E., 194, 251, 364
Mitchell, T. R., 296, 324, 327, 364, 374
Mobbs, N. A., 203, 364
Moeller, G., 228-9, 343, 364
Moon, T. H., 282, 354
Moore, J. C., Jr., 228, 230, 364
Moore, L. H., 214, 365
Moos, R. R., 336, 364
Moran, G., 252, 365
Morgan, C. D., 129, 365

Morganti, J. B., 234, 370
Moriarity, A. E., 57, 365
Morley, I. E., 203, 368
Morris, C. G., 6, 355
Morrison, R. L., 175, 177, 365
Morrison, T. L., 175-6, 365
Morse, J. J., 325-7, 365
Morse, N. C., 330, 365
Morton, R. B., 214-5, 349
Mossholder, K. W., 327, 365
Moulton, R. W., 140, 214, 365
Mouton, J. S., 230, 345, 355
Mueller, J. H., 166, 365
Mueller, W. J., 143, 365
Mullens, M. C., 201, 351
Mulry, R. C., 170-2, 368
Murphy, D. B., 228, 371
Murphy, G., 135, 361
Murphy, L. B., 57, 365
Murray, H. A., 12, 19, 26-8, 41, 43, 47, 62-4, 129, 308, 323, 365
Murstein, B. I., 130, 179, 181, 184, 186, 365
Mussen, P. H., 136-7, 215, 256, 351, 365, 370

N

Nachtscheim, N., 302, 365
Nadler, E. B., 228, 365
Nelson, C., 194, 284, 354
Nelson, D. A., 352
Nelson, J., 287, 360
Ness, S., 256, 347
Newcomb, T. W., 215, 346, 349, 364
Nickel, T. W., 283, 358
Nielsen, S. L., 130, 365
Nisbett, R. E., 228, 236, 365
Nixon, M., 214, 348
Noble, A. M., 252, 347
Nolan, R. E., 214-5, 255
Noland, S. J., 290, 358-366
Norem-Hebeisen, A. A., 292, 366
Nosow, S., 262, 353
Nowicki, S., Jr., 194, 198, 352, 366
Nyce, P. A., 158, 347
Nyman, B., 238, 315, 369

O

Oberlander, L., 140, 372
Offer, D., 55, 366
Olczak, P. V., 199, 366
Oldham, G. R., 308, 318-19, 355, 366

Olmstead, J. A., 230, 356
Ono, H., 144, 359
O'Quin, K., 276, 291, 344
Orefice, D. S., 325, 373
O'Reilly, C. A., III, 282, 327, 366
O'Reilly, E. F., Jr., 346
Organ, D. W., 327, 366
Osgood, D. W., 150, 370
Ossorio, A. G., 77, 353
Ossorio, P. G., 250, 302, 361

P

Page, A. A., 199, 356
Page, M., 358
Paivio, A., 134, 366
Palmer, J., 182, 197, 288, 366
Pandey, J., 262-3, 282, 366
Parke, R. D., 17, 373
Parshall, H., 171, 353
Pasko, S. J., 182, 367
Patterson, M. L., 131, 200, 202, 366
Pearce, J. L., 319, 366
Pedersen, D. M., 202, 366
Pedersen, F. A., 57, 376
Pederson, A. M., 238, 315, 369
Penner, L. A., 255, 362
Pervin, L. A., 308, 366
Petersen, P., 161, 346
Peterson, C., 150, 283, 349, 370
Petrullo, L., 350
Petruska, R., 239, 266, 316, 375
Phares, E. J., 138, 162, 170, 198, 214, 235, 350, 366, 368
Phillips, J. L., 291, 366
Pilisuk, M., 282, 375
Pilkonis, P. A., 281, 366-7
Pines, H. A., 162, 171, 367
Plax, T. G., 277, 287, 290, 368
Poprick, M. A., 233, 358
Porter, L. W., 93, 215, 307, 365, 367, 372
Posavac, E. J., 182, 194, 367
Post, A. L., 282, 367
Post, D. L., 133, 362
Postman, L., 128, 134-5, 142, 182, 367
Potash, H. M., 282, 346
Powell, F. A., 167, 367
Pressman, M. E., 204, 370
Pritchard, R. D., 321, 373
Prociuk, T. J., 162, 367
Pryer, R. S., 130, 365
Purcell, K., 139, 367

Q

Quartermain, D., 227, 362

R

Rabin, A. I., 345, 351, 362, 364
Rabinowitz, S., 319, 367
Rabinowitz, W., 137, 367
Raden, D., 250, 367
Radin, M. E., 281, 367
Raphelson, A. C., 140, 365
Rardin, M., 165, 168, 374
Rastogi, R., 283, 366
Ratoosh, P., 176, 370
Raven, B., 85, 353
Raynor, J. O., 171, 176, 219, 321, 344, 351, 367
Read, H., 358
Reagor, P. A., 191, 367
Redding, J., 239, 360
Regan, D. T., 199, 358
Reimer, E., 330, 365
Reuder, M. A., 175, 345
Restle, F., 324, 367
Reznikoff, M., 291, 367
Richardson, H. M., 214-5, 321, 355, 367
Richardson, P., 321, 373
Riecken, H. W., 251, 302, 373
Rife, D., 232, 357
Riley, J., 168, 367
Rim, Y., 175-7, 282, 367-8
Riordan, C., 253, 345
Ritchie, D. E., 138, 366
Ritchie, E., 235, 368
Rizzo, J. R., 214, 364
Roback, H. B., 326, 343
Robbins, G. E., 160, 368
Roberts, A. H., 251, 368
Robinson, C., 282, 375
Rodda, W. C., 233, 354
Rodrigues, A., 233, 349
Rogers, E. D., 226, 372
Rohde, K. J., 215, 367
Rokeach, M., 49-54, 167-8, 233, 257, 324-5, 364, 367-8
Rosenbaum, M. E., 230-1, 350, 368
Rosenberg, M. J., 346, 364
Rosenfeld, H. M., 131, 170, 192, 195, 200, 202, 204, 354, 360-1, 368
Rosenfeld, L. B., 277, 287, 290, 367
Rosenman, R. H., 256, 362

Rotter, J. B., 50, 51-2, 54, 170-2, 261, 354, 368
Rottmann, L., 182, 374
Rotton, J., 233, 368
Rubel, M., 228, 374
Rubin, J. Z., 272-4, 278, 284, 290, 368
Rubin, Z., 200, 368
Rubinstein, J. L., 57, 376
Rule, B. G., 227, 364
Runyon, K. E., 327, 335, 368
Rushton, J. P., 203, 348, 369
Rutter, D. R., 203, 368
Rychlak, J. F., 214-5, 368
Ryckman, R. M., 233, 354
Ryder, R. G., 291, 350

S

Sabshin, M., 55, 366
Saltz, E., 261, 376
Samelson, F., 230-1, 368
Sanders, J. L., 160, 202, 368
Sanford, F. H., 295, 368
Sanford, R. N., 16, 52, 54, 135-6, 163, 227, 368
Sarason, I. G., 130, 159, 163, 166, 168, 215, 238, 248, 314-5, 323, 343, 354, 362, 365, 369, 375
Sarason, S. B., 314, 362
Sassenrath, J. M., 177, 347
Satow, K. L., 253, 369
Schachter, S., 21, 369
Schalon, C. L., 316, 369
Schaude, E., 175, 360
Schiller, M., 215, 369
Schlenker, B. R., 282, 369
Schmidt, A., 283, 358
Schneider, D. J., 128, 369
Schneider, F. W., 321, 369
Schneider, K. S., 261-2, 369
Schopler, J., 233, 364
Schroder, H. M., 49, 150, 163, 325, 356, 369
Schuette, D., 203, 352
Schumer, H., 324, 350
Schutz, W. C., 52, 53, 369
Schwartz, S. H., 70, 75, 244-6, 258, 260-1, 369
Scioli, F. P., Jr., 214, 217-8, 369
Scodel, A., 136-7, 176-7, 361, 370
Scott, W. A., 150, 370
Sechrest, L. B., 131, 200, 366
Secord, P. F., 181, 186, 370

Seeman, D. C., 332, 370
Seeman, J., 170, 356
Seeman, M., 170, 370
Seligman, M. E. P., 14, 20, 39, 40, 43, 51, 61, 315, 353, 370
Sermat, V., 277-78, 370
Seyfried, B. A., 197, 370
Shapiro, D., 156, 370
Shaw, M. E., 222, 333, 336, 370
Sheffield, J., 193, 370
Shelby, J., 237, 347
Shepard, H., 208, 345
Sheposh, J. P., 177, 349
Sherif, M., 159, 224, 370
Sherk, L., 253, 371
Shomer, R. W., 233, 349
Shostrom, E. L., 52, 54, 370
Shrauger, S., 128, 240, 358, 370
Shriver, B., 242, 348
Siegel, L. S., 256, 347
Sigal, J. A., 169, 349
Silverman, A. F., 204, 370
Silverman, I., 171, 234, 236, 361, 370
Sills, E. P., 375
Simas, K., 138, 370
Simons, H. W., 137, 370
Sims, H. P., Jr., 319, 370
Singer, J. E., 283, 370
Sistrunk, F., 229-31, 363, 370
Skolnick, P., 234, 371
Slater, P. E., 297, 371
Slotnick, R. S., 138, 371
Smelser, W. T., 336-7, 371
Smith, C. P., 176, 367, 371
Smith, G. H., 201, 371
Smith, M. B., 56, 61, 371
Smith, R., 135, 352
Smith, R. E., 191-2, 200, 234, 371
Smith, R. J., 214, 216, 371
Smith, S., 228, 371
Smith, W. P., 302, 371
Smyser, C. M., 327, 364
Snow, R. E., 318-9, 324, 350
Snyder, M., 144, 371
Solar, D., 140, 371
Sommer, R., 67, 371
Sordoni, C., 292, 361
Sorem, A. M., 170, 371
Sorrentino, R. M., 215, 218-9, 369, 371
Sotile, W. M., 326, 359
Speisman, J. C.., 336, 365
Spence, D. D., 135, 354, 371

Spencer, D. G., 321, 372
Spielberger, C. D., 314, 348, 352, 369, 372
Stahelski, A. J., 138, 179, 194, 282, 358
Stahlman, R. W., 214, 350
Staub, E., 11, 243-6, 253-5, 257, 261-2, 371
Steele, M. W., 278, 375
Steers, R. M., 93, 308, 321, 371-2
Steeves, R., 134, 366
Stein, M. L., 325, 372
Steiner, I. D., 68, 74, 123, 169, 226-8, 233, 308, 357, 372
Steinfatt, T., 167, 345
Stephenson, G. M., 203, 368
Stice, G. F., 214-5, 349
Stogdill, R. M., 210-13, 216-7, 219-20, 222, 307, 372
Stollak, G. E., 57, 372
Stone, A. V. W., 255, 362
Stone, G. L., 325, 372
Stone, J. B., 215, 356
Strand, S., 282, 363
Stratton, L. O., 202, 372
Strauss, P. S., 158, 373
Streufert, S., 163, 369
Strickland, B. R., 175, 229, 253, 261, 287, 372
Strodtbeck, F. L., 67, 372
Suedfeld, P., 150, 369
Sullivan, E. V., 325, 357
Sundstrom, E., 200, 372
Swingle, P., 373
Szilagyi, A. D., 319, 370

T

Tager, R., 158, 358
Tagiuri, R., 128-30, 350, 372
Talley, W. M., 296, 324, 372
Tanke, E. D., 144, 371
Tannenbaum, A. S., 296, 330, 372
Tannenbaum, P. H., 346, 364
Taylor, D. A., 140, 181, 343, 372
Taylor, R. N., 159, 160, 372
Teague, G., 177, 362
Tedeschi, J. T., 278, 282, 288, 363, 369, 372, 375
Teevan, R. C., 175, 229, 239, 349, 355, 363
Tekippe, D. J., 202, 372
Terborg, J. R., 321, 373
Terhune, K. W., 278, 290, 292, 373
Tharenou, P., 316, 373
Thaw, J., 175, 373
Theiss, M., 292, 356

Thelen, M. H., 238, 343
Thibaut, J. W., 70, 204, 251, 284, 302, 352, 358, 373
Thomas, K. W., 290, 359
Torcivia, J. M., 233, 358
Tosi, H. L., 321, 348
Touhey, J. C., 191, 194, 321, 373
Trapp, E. P., 175, 373
Tripathi, R. R., 215, 373
Trommsdorf, G., 175, 360
Tubbs, S. L., 237, 347
Tuckman, B. W., 49, 70, 290, 299, 308, 325-6, 373
Tuddenham, R. D., 230, 373
Tupes, E. C., 214-5, 346
Turner, W. D., 249, 262, 373

U

Uejio, C. K., 284, 373
Uleman, J., 277, 373
Uren, E., 282, 375

V

Vacchiano, R. B., 158, 167, 324, 373
Vallacher, R. R., 291, 374
Vamos, P., 296, 324, 372
Vanderplas, J. M., 134, 373
Vannoy, J. S., 227-8, 372
Vaughan, G. M., 226-8, 230, 362, 373
Veitch, R., 183, 355
Vernon, P. E., 343
Veroff, J., 19, 31, 374
Vidmar, N., 167, 176, 251, 345, 357, 374
Vidulich, R. N., 167, 228, 296, 324, 353, 374
Villamez, W. J., 321, 373
Vinacke, W. E., 291, 343, 349
Vinicur, D. L., 204, 351
Vroom, V. H., 215, 296, 325, 333, 374

W

Wagman, M., 233, 374
Wagner, C., 249, 334, 359, 374
Wahi, N. K., 231, 376
Walker, E. L., 139, 344
Wallach, M. A., 173, 175, 177, 359
Walster, E., 182, 374
Walters, R. H., 17, 373
Wanous, J. P., 319, 374
Ward, L., 51, 240, 374

Warr, P. B., 127-8, 374
Watson, D., 302, 336, 374
Watson, R. I., 176-7, 362
Watts, B. L., 291, 374
Watts, J. C., 57, 374
Watts, W. A., 162, 172, 374
Webber, A. W., 201, 348
Weed, S. E., 296, 324, 327, 364, 374
Weigel, R. H., 214, 344
Weiner, B., 176, 374
Weiner, H., 228, 374
Weiner, Y., 321, 356
Weinert, G., 228, 374
Weiss, H. M., 171, 374
Wells, W. D., 228, 374
Weng, B. R., 214, 350
Wheaton, J., 169, 359
Wheeler, L. S., 228, 249, 371, 373, 375
Wheeless, L. R., 281, 374
White, B. J., 165, 168, 374
White, B. L., 57, 374
White, C., 239, 360
White, K. D., 228, 373
White, R. W., 19, 22, 26, 31, 43, 58-9, 179, 374
Whiteley, R. H., 162, 172, 374
Wiggins, J. S., 51, 77, 207, 242-3, 375
Wiley, D., 363
Wilkens, E. J., 138, 375
Williams, C. D., 278, 375
Williams, E., 203, 375
Williams, J. L., 202, 375
Williams, R. M., 50, 375
Wilson, K. G., 198, 366
Wilson, K. V., 282, 346
Wilson, J. P., 12, 16, 49, 51, 214, 217, 238-9, 240, 264-6, 299, 301, 316, 330, 363-4, 374-5
Wilson, W., 282, 375

Winch, R. F., 141, 179, 375
Wine, J. D., 158-9, 204, 314-5, 361, 375
Winter, D. G., 19, 31, 47, 171, 363, 375
Wispé, L. G., 135, 296, 375
Witryol, S. L., 214-5, 358
Wittmaier, B. C., 281, 367
Wittrock, M. C., 363
Wolk, S., 163, 316, 375
Wood, D., 282, 375
Worthy, M., 281, 374
Wright, A., 253, 345
Wright, J. M., 239, 345, 374
Wrightsman, L. S., 282, 284, 373, 375
Wulff, D., 174, 376
Wurster, C. R., 214, 345
Wyer, R. S., 130, 133, 376

Y

Yakimovich, D., 261, 376
Yaklevitch, D., 203, 361
Yarrow, L. J., 57, 376
Young, P. C., 214-5, 222, 345
Yousem, H., 135, 360
Youssef, Z. I., 321, 358

Z

Zagona, S. V., 296, 324, 376
Zaidel, S. F., 157, 195, 376
Zajonc, R. B., 231, 376
Zander, A., 6, 70, 79, 83, 85-6, 114, 117, 172-4, 176, 243, 348, 376
Zeleny, L. D., 214, 376
Zellner, M., 236, 376
Ziller, R. C., 160, 361
Zucker, R. A., 345, 351, 362, 364
Zurcher, L. A., Jr., 296, 324, 376

Subject Index

A

Abasement:
activity level in stages of group process and, 95–100
concurrence and, 228–229
congruent reward systems and, 116
definition, 41, 63
emergent leadership and, 117, 119
group performance and, 310–311
group structure and, 112, 114, 115–123
incentive value of task dimensions and, 93, 94
information processing and, 153, 154
interpersonal attraction and, 187
modes of interdependence and, 109–110, 280
negotiation orientation and, 108, 110, 270
performance styles and, 101–103, 107
situational variables and, 90, 91
Achievement:
activity level in stages of group process and, 95–100
affiliation behavior and, 261–262
definition, 48, 63
emergent leadership and, 117–121
group performance and, 310–311, 335–336
group structure and, 112–123
incentive value of task dimension and, 93–94

information processing and, 153–157, 171–174, 176
leadership and, 214–215, 218–219, 231
modes of interdependence and, 109–110, 288–292
negotiation orientation and, 108–109, 270
performance styles and, 101–103, 107
person perception and, 140–141
situational variables and, 90–91
Acquaintanceship process:
interpersonal attraction and, 184–186
Affiliation:
activity level in stages of group process, 95–100
affiliation behavior and, 259–260
concurrence and, 229–230
definition, 43–46, 63–64
emergent leadership and, 117–120
group performance and, 310–311
group structure and, 112–123
incentive value of task dimensions and, 93–94
information processing and, 153–157
interpersonal attraction and, 196–197, 203
modes of interdependence and, 109–110
negotiation orientation and, 108, 110, 270, 288–292
performance styles and, 101–103, 107
person perception and, 139–140
situational variables, 90–91

Affiliation-Disaffiliation dimension: 8,
    76–80, 243–248
  empathy and, 255–257
  esteem-related variables and, 260–263
  interactional studies of use of, 260–263
  need for affiliation and, 260
  personal norms and, 258
  the prosocial personality, 254–255
  safety-related variables and, 248–254
  values, moral level and, 257
Aggression; 23–24, 31, 250–252, 256
Allport-Vernon-Lindzey test of values, 142
Anxiety:
  affiliation and, 248–250
  concurrence behavior and, 226–227, 232
  group performance and, 314–315, 323
  group structure and, 296–297
  information processing and, 154, 158, 174
  interpersonal attraction and, 188, 190–193
  safety needs and, 20–21
Approval:
  activity level in stages of group process,
    95–100
  affiliation and, 253–254
  concurrence and, 229, 233–235
  congruent reward systems and, 121–122
  definition, 41–42, 63
  emergent leadership and, 117, 119
  group performance and, 310–311
  group structure and, 112–123
  incentive value of task dimensions and,
    93–94
  information processing and, 153–154,
    157–158, 163–165
  interpersonal attraction and, 187, 194–196
  modes of interdependence and, 109–110,
    285
  negotiation orientation and, 108–110, 270
  performance styles and, 101, 103–104, 107
  situational variables and, 90–91
Archetypes: 18–19, 28
  Anima and Animus, 31–32
  the Great Mother, 30
  Mana, 19, 31
  Persona, 31–32
  the Shadow, 30
  Unity, 31
  X, 30
Authoritarianism:
  activity level in stages of group process,
    95–100

affiliation and, 250–253
concurrence and, 227–229, 232–233, 239
congruent reward systems and, 121–122
definition, 16, 63
emergent leadership and, 117, 119
group performance and, 310–311, 333–334
group structure and, 112–123, 295–297
incentive value of task dimensions and,
    93–94
information processing and, 153, 154,
    158–160, 165–169
interpersonal attraction and, 193–194
leadership and, 215, 221–222
modes of interdependence and, 109–110,
    279–281
negotiation orientation and, 108–110, 270
performance styles and, 101–103, 107
person perception and, 135–138
situational variables, 90–91

B

Bargaining stance:
  definition of, 81–82
  in negotiation processes, 269–291
  personality and, 108

C

Choice Dilemma Questionnaire: 173–177
Circumplex models:
  nature of, 7–8, 76–78, 208–209, 243
  personality contributions to use of, 100–107
Conceptual differentiation:
  cognitive style and, 150–151
  empirical studies, 165–167, 169–170
  information processing and, 151, 163–164
  personality and, 153
Congruence:
  individual and social characteristics,
    308–313
  personality and group structure, 327–338
  personality and member attributes, 316–317
  personality and the physical setting,
    313–316
  personality and reward systems, 118–123
  principle of, 307–308
Cognitive complexity:
  cognitive structure and, 49
  as an element of social processes, 8
  group performance and, 325–326

information processing and, 151, 163–165
Cognitive structure:
  elements of, 16, 49–51
  strength of, 49
Conformity:
  personality and, 226–231
  social influence processes and, 224–226
Competence motivation: 22, 34–36
Core and peripheral variables:
  Maddi's analysis, 10

D

Dependency:
  activity level in stages of group processes, 95–100
  affiliation and, 249
  congruent reward systems and, 121–122
  definition, 41–42, 63
  emergent leadership, 119–120
  group performance, 310–311, 336–338
  group structure and, 112–123
  incentive value of task dimensions and, 93–94
  information processing and, 153, 154–157
  interpersonal attraction and, 188, 197–198
  modes of interdependence and, 109–110
  negotiation orientation and, 108–110
  performance styles and, 101–103, 107
  person perception and, 143–149
  situational variables and, 90–91
Dogmatism:
  cognitive structure and, 49
  concurrence behavior and, 232–233
  group performance and, 324–325
  group structure and, 296
  information processing and, 158–160
  as a safety needs trait, 52
Dominance:
  activity level in stages of group processes and, 95–100
  affiliation and, 262
  definition, 47, 63
  emergent leadership and, 117–121
  group performance and, 310–311
  group structure and, 112–123, 302, 336–337
  incentive value of task dimensions and, 93–94
  information processing and, 153–154
  interpersonal attraction and, 197–198
  leadership and, 213–218, 230

  modes of interdependence and, 109–110, 274–278
  negotiation orientation and, 108–109, 270
  performance styles and, 101–103, 107
  person perception and, 141–149
  situational variables and, 90–91
Dominance scale, 141, 143, 276–277, 337

E

Ego strength:
  Erikson's conception of health, 60
  social influence and, 220–221
  strength of cognitive control, 49
Emergent leadership (see initiation-concurrence):
  in heterogeneous groups, 117–120
  personality and, 212–223
  social influence and, 210–212
EPPS, 143, 230
Esteem needs:
  affiliation-disaffiliation and, 263–268
  definition, 22
  deprivation of, 22–23
  gratification and, 61–62
  group structure and, 298–303
  information processing and, 154, 160–163, 172
  initiation-concurrence and, 211–213
  interpersonal attraction and, 189
  negotiation processes and, 270–274
  performance in groups and, 310–311, 330
  peripheral motives derived from, 46–48
  peripheral traits derived from, 53–55

F

F scale, 136, 216
FIRO, 204, 216
French Test of Insight, 204

G

Goal setting:
  cognitive style and, 151–152
  empirical studies, 174–177
  information processing and, 172–174
  personality and, 153
Group process:
  elements of, 79–83
Group structure: 293–294
  elements of, 83–88

personality and group structure, 294–300
personality and power and reward, 302–303
personality and rank, 300–302
Growth need strength, 319
Guilford Opinion Inventory, 216
Guilford-Zimmerman, 230

I

Information processing:
cognitive style and, 150–152
conceptual differentiation, 163–164
empirical relationship to personality, 153–177
goal setting, 172–177
processing flexibility, 164–165
processing persistence, 165–166
search flexibility, 155–156
search persistence, 156–157
selective attention, 154–155
stages of, 151–152
Initiation-concurrence dimension: 8, 76–80, 209–212, 223–226
personality and concurrence, 227, 238
personality and initiation, 212–223
responses to active influence, 238–241
Interactionist perspective on personality (see person by situation model):
conceptions of, 4–10
elements of, 8–9
Lewin and, 3
models of, 74–79, 89–126
Interpersonal attraction:
the acquaintanceship process, 184–186
enduring attraction, 186–187
initial attraction, 44, 182–184
nonverbal indices of, 200–205
personality moderators of, 187–205
stages of, 182–187
theoretical perspectives on, 178–182
Interaction process scores (IPS):
activity levels and personality, 102–103
performance styles and, 106–107
as the social field, 77
task and socioemotional dimensions, 78, 102–103, 217–218, 299, 301
Intimacy:
the affiliation dimension of group process and, 243–244
in Erikson's theory, 36
interpersonal attraction and, 186

and the motive of inclusion, 22, 43–46
as a psychological need, 44

L

Learned helplessness:
safety needs and, 39–41
Leary Interpersonal Check List, 141, 197
Locus of Control:
affiliation and, 261
cognitive schemata and, 49–54
concurrence and, 235
esteem needs and, 54
group performance and, 326–327
information processing and, 162, 170, 171
interpersonal attraction and, 198
negotiation orientation and, 290
person perception and, 138
safety needs and, 52
Love and belongingness needs:
affiliation-disaffiliation and, 258, 259
definition, 21, 43–46
deprivation of, 22, 43–46
gratification and, 61
group structure, 294
information processing and, 154, 163, 172
initiation-concurrence and, 210–211
interpersonal attraction and, 188
negotiation processes, 270–274
performance in groups, 310–311
peripheral motives derived from, 43–46
traits derived from, 53

M

MMPI, 136
Machiavellianism:
activity level in stages of group processes, 95–100
affiliation and, 260–261
concurrence and, 237
definition, 63
emergent leadership and, 117–121
group performance and, 310–311
group structure and, 112–123
incentive value of task dimensions and, 93–94
information processing and, 153–157, 177
modes of interdependence and, 109–110, 278–285
negotiation orientation and, 108, 109, 270

performance styles and, 101–103, 107
person perception and, 141–143
situational variables and, 90–91
Machiavellianism scale, 142
Manifest Anxiety Scale, 227
Modes of interdependence:
  definition, 82–83
  negotiation processes and, 108–111,
    269–292
Moral judgement:
  affiliation behavior and, 257
  cognitive schemata and, 50–51
  psychological maturity and, 56, 58–59

N

Need for power:
  dominance motive and, 47
  information processing and, 177
  mana archetype, 19, 31
Negotiation processes: 269–274
  personality and the adversarial mode,
    274–278
  personality and the exploitative mode,
    278–285
  personality and the ingratiating mode,
    285–288
  personality and the integrative mode,
    288–292
Non-verbal behavior:
  distance, 201–202
  eye contact, 203–204
  risk-taking and, 200–201
  touch and smiles, 204–205
Norms:
  as cognitive schemata, 49–51
  as elements of social processes, 8
  personal, 258
Nurturance:
  activity level in stages of group process and,
    94–99
  affiliation behavior and, 262–263
  definition, 48, 63
  emergent leadership and, 117–121
  group performance and, 310–311
  group structure and, 112–123
  incentive value of task dimensions and,
    93–94
  information processing and, 153–157
  modes of interdependence and, 109–110,
    288–291

negotiation orientation and, 108, 270
performance styles and, 102–104, 107
situational variables and, 90–91

O

Order:
  activity level in stages of group process,
    95–100
  congruent reward systems and, 121
  definition, 41–43, 63
  emergent leadership, 119–120
  group performance and, 310–311, 323–324
  group structure and, 112–123
  incentive value of task dimensions, 93–94
  information processing and, 153–159
  modes of interdependence and, 109–110,
    285
  negotiation orientation and, 108–110
  performance styles and, 101–103, 107
  situational variables and, 90–91

P

Performance:
  principle of congruence, 307–313
  personality and group structure, 327–338
  personality and situational factors, 313–317
  personality and task ambiguity, 317–327
Peripheral motives: 39–41
  derived from the need for esteem, 46–46
  derived from the need for love and
    belongingness, 43–46
  derived from the need for safety, 41–42
Person perception: 127
  empirical studies with personality variables,
    134–143
  interactional studies of, 143–149
  methods of inquiry, 130–132
  the new look school and, 128
Person by situation model:
  behavioral response, 76–79
  elements of the person, 62–64
  elements of the social process, 8–9
  elements of group process, structure, and
    outcome, 79–88
  individual subjective response in, 75–76
  negotiation processes, 107–111
  outcome, 123, 307–313
  performance styles, 100–107
  personality and group structure variables,
    111–122

personality and situational variables, 90–92
personality and task variables, 92–99
Persuasibility:
    personality variables and, 232–237
    social influence process of, 231–232
Physiological needs: 23, 25, 27, 31
    deprivation of, 39
    social perception and, 135
Power:
    group structure and, 84–86, 305–306,
        327–330
    personality and, 114–117
Prediction and control, 14, 20, 33–34, 39–40,
    61
Primary needs:
    acquired motives and, 11–15, 38
    acquired traits and, 15–17, 48–49
    in theories of personality, 19–37
Processing flexibility:
    empirical studies, 167–170
    cognitive style and, 150–151
    information processing and, 151, 164–165
    personality and, 153
Processing persistence:
    empirical studies, 170–172
    cognitive style and, 152
    information processing and, 151, 165
    personality and, 153
Prosocial personality, 254–255
Psychosocial maturity, 55, 62, 78

R

Recognition:
    activity level in stages of group process and,
        94–99
    definition, 46, 63
    emergent leadership and, 117–121
    group performance and, 310–311
    group structure and, 112–114
    incentive values of task dimensions and,
        93–94
    information processing and, 153–157
    modes of interdependence and, 108–109
    negotiation orientation and, 108, 270
    performance styles and, 102–104, 107
    situational variables and, 90–91
Reinforcement:
    need for study in person perception, 4, 6–7,
        133
    in social situations, 13–15, 73
    in theories of attraction, 179–181

S

Safety needs:
    affiliation-disaffiliation and, 263–268
    gratification and, 57–61
    group performance and, 328, 330
    group structure and, 298–300
    information processing and, 154, 163, 172
    initiation-concurrence and, 211
    interpersonal attraction and, 187–188
    negotiation processes and, 270–273
    peripheral motives derived from, 39–43
    peripheral traits derived from, 51–52
Safety-signal hypothesis, 40
Self-actualization:
    consequence of need gratification, 57–62
    criticism of, 56
    in Maslow's theory, 23, 58
    relation to Erikson's theory, 56–57, 60
Self-disclosure, 274
Selective attention:
    cognitive style and, 150–151
    empirical studies, 157–163
    information processing and, 151–154
    personality and, 157–163
Search flexibility:
    cognitive style and, 150–151
    empirical studies, 157–163
    information processing and, 151, 155–156
    personality variables and, 153
Search persistence:
    cognitive style and, 150–151
    empirical studies, 157–163
    information processing and, 151, 156
    personality and, 153
Sexual drive, 23–25, 27, 29, 31
Situational variables:
    basis for classification, 65
    group structure, 72–73
    personal attributes, 67–68
    physical attributes, 66–67
    task variables, 68–72
Socialization:
    acquired characteristics and, 12–15
    following epigenetic order, 32–33
    peripheral motives and, 39–48
    peripheral traits and, 49–55
    psychosocial maturity and, 55–62

T

Task variables:
    task dimensions, 68–70

task stages, 70–72
TAT, 130, 140, 197, 230–231, 278
Test Anxiety Questionnaire, 314
Theories of personality:
    Erikson, 32–37
    Freud, 23–24
    Fromm, 24–26
    Jung, 28–32
    Maslow, 19–23
    Murray, 26–28
Traits;
    acquired, 15–16
    definition, 15–16, 48–55

derived from esteem needs, 54
derived from love and belongingness needs,
    53
derived from safety needs, 52
relationship among, 16

V

Values:
    affiliation behavior and, 257
    as associated with basic needs, 50–54
    as part of cognitive structure, 49–51
    as an element of the social process, 8